CAMBRIDGE UNIVERSITY LIBRARY
GENIZAH SERIES 1

The Cambridge Genizah Collections: Their Contents and Significance

Cambridge University Library
Genizah Series
Edited by S. C. Reif

1. The Cambridge Genizah Collections: Their Contents and Significance, edited by Stefan C. Reif (2002)

2. Hebrew Bible Manuscripts in the Cambridge Genizah Collections
   Volume 1 Taylor-Schechter Old Series and other Genizah Collections in Cambridge University Library, by M. C. Davis, incorporating material compiled by H. Knopf (1978)
   Volume 2 Taylor-Schechter New Series, and Westminster College Cambridge Collection, by M. C. Davis (1980)
   Volume 3 Taylor-Schechter Additional Series 1–31, by M. C. Davis, assisted by B. M. Outhwaite (ready for the press)
   Volume 4 Taylor-Schechter Additional Series 32–225, with addenda to previous volumes, by M. C. Davis, assisted by B. M. Outhwaite (ready for the press)

3. Miscellany of Literary Pieces from the Cambridge Genizah Collections, by Simon Hopkins (1978)

4. Vocalised Talmudic Manuscripts in the Cambridge Genizah Collections
   Volume 1 Taylor-Schechter Old Series, by Shelomo Morag (1988)

5. A Hand-list of Rabbinic Manuscripts in the Cambridge Genizah Collections
   Volume 1 Taylor-Schechter New Series, by Robert Brody (1998)

6. Published Material from the Cambridge Genizah Collections: A Bibliography 1896–1980, edited by Stefan C. Reif (1988)

7. Palestinian Vocalised Piyyuṭ Manuscripts in the Cambridge Genizah Collections, by J. Yahalom (1997)

8. Targumic Manuscripts in the Cambridge Genizah Collections, by Michael L. Klein (1992)

9. Karaite Bible Manuscripts from the Cairo Genizah, by Geoffrey Khan (1990)

10. Arabic Legal and Administrative Documents in the Cambridge Genizah Collections, by Geoffrey Khan (1993)

11. Medical and Para-medical Manuscripts in the Cambridge Genizah Collections, by Haskell D. Isaacs, with the assistance of Colin F. Baker (1994)

12. Arabic and Judaeo-Arabic Manuscripts in the Cambridge Genizah Collections, Arabic Old Series, by Colin F. Baker and Meira Polliack (2001)

13. Published Material from the Cambridge Genizah Collections: A Bibliography 1980–1995, edited by Stefan C. Reif, Geoffrey Khan and Erica Hunter (in preparation)

14. Arabic and Judaeo-Arabic Manuscripts in the Cambridge Genizah Collections, New Series, by Avihai Shivtiel and Friedrich Niessen (in preparation)

THE CAMBRIDGE GENIZAH COLLECTIONS: THEIR CONTENTS AND SIGNIFICANCE

Edited by
STEFAN C. REIF

with the assistance of
SHULAMIT REIF

CAMBRIDGE
UNIVERSITY PRESS

PUBLISHED BY THE PRESS SYNDICATE OF THE UNIVERSITY OF CAMBRIDGE
The Pitt Building, Trumpington Street, Cambridge, United Kingdom

CAMBRIDGE UNIVERSITY PRESS
The Edinburgh Building, Cambridge CB2 2RU, UK
40 West 20th Street, New York, NY 10011–4211, USA
477 Williamstown Road, Port Melbourne, VIC 3207, Australia
Ruiz de Alarcón 13, 28014 Madrid, Spain
Dock House, The Waterfront, Cape Town 8001, South Africa

http://www.cambridge.org

First published 2002

Printed in the United Kingdom at the University Press, Cambridge

Typeset in Times

British Library cataloguing in publication data applied for

Library of Congress cataloguing in publication data applied for

ISBN 0 521 81361 1

Dedicated to the memory of
Professor Michael L. Klein
(1940–2000)

fastidious researcher, inspired teacher
and affable colleague

דרש וחקר ושאל היטב
יהי זכרו ברוך

CONTENTS

PREFACE

In the Michaelmas Term of 1994, the Genizah Research Unit at Cambridge University Library took advantage of the presence in Cambridge of four distinguished scholars on sabbatical leave from the Hebrew University of Jerusalem. A series of lectures on the general theme "The Impact of Genizah Discoveries on Recent Scholarship" was arranged at the Library, and each of the specialists spoke on a topic of his choice. The lectures were well attended, particularly by members of the Faculties of Oriental Studies and of Divinity, and lively discussions followed each of the presentations.

In the opening lecture, which was chaired by Dr Gordon Johnson, President of Wolfson College, Dr (now Professor) Menahem Kister, of the Hebrew University's Talmud and Hebrew Literature Departments, dealt with the Hebrew fragments of the apocryphal book of Ben Sira, discovered in the Cairo Genizah one hundred years ago. He evaluated their historical importance and explained their significance for a better understanding of the history of the Hebrew language. He also suggested fresh interpretations of several verses, most of them having some bearing on theological concepts.

In the next lecture, chaired by Dr Robert Gordon, then recently pre-elected to the Regius Chair of Hebrew at Cambridge, Professor Menahem Kahana, of the Hebrew University's Talmud Department, spoke about the discovery of tannaitic midrashim in the Cairo Genizah. He pointed out how these medieval fragments had not only provided early, reliable texts for known works but had also restored to Hebrew literature a number of lost works. He paid particular attention to *Sifre Zuṭa* on Deuteronomy.

The newly appointed University Librarian, Mr Peter Fox, introduced the third lecture, given by Professor Joseph Yahalom, of the Hebrew University's Hebrew Literature Department, on the life and work of Judah Halevi, with the emphasis on the poet's last years in Egypt and the Holy Land. Professor Yahalom evaluated the many poems and letters discovered in the Genizah and demonstrated how they illuminated the medieval culture of Andalusia and Halevi's attempts to settle in the Jewish homeland.

Professor Haggai Ben-Shammai, of the Hebrew University's Arabic Department, concluded the series with a paper on medieval history and religious thought, with Dr Fred Ratcliffe, University Librarian Emeritus, presiding. In that fourth lecture, Professor Ben-Shammai assessed the monumental contribution of Shelomo Dov Goitein to the exploitation of Genizah material for the purpose of reconstructing the everyday lives of ordinary people in the Mediterranean area of the Middle Ages. He also drew attention to the manner in which the Genizah documents had highlighted the names of lost thinkers and exegetes and had restored to scholarship versions of their seminal works.

Following these lectures, it was suggested by a number of participants that it would be appropriate to arrange another set of lectures and to publish them all, in a suitable context, to mark the centenary of the formal presentation of the Genizah Collection, in October 1898, to Cambridge University Library by Charles Taylor and Solomon Schechter. Another five lectures, on 'The Contribution of the Genizah Collection to the Study of Medieval Jewish Culture', were consequently given, in the Michaelmas Term of 1998, in the Morison Room of the University Library's new Exhibition Centre.

The first meeting was chaired by Professor Robert Gordon and was treated to a study of Aramaic Bible translations and commentaries by Professor Michael Klein, of the Hebrew Union College in Jerusalem. He demonstrated how a detailed review of the oldest extant fragments helps to illuminate such subjects as the synagogal-liturgical setting of the targum. Several new targumic texts and text-types discovered in the Genizah were noted, such as 'shorthand' manuscripts; collections of expansive readings for festivals and special sabbaths; introductory Aramaic poems to the targum of the *haftarot*; a fragment-targum of Onqelos; and various compositions of masorah to Onqelos. The paper concluded with a reading of an unparalleled targumic *tosefta* to the story of Cain and Abel (Genesis 4).

Professor Joel Kraemer, of the University of Chicago, gave the second presentation, on Jewish female literacy, and the chair was taken by Rosamond McKitterick, Professor of Early Medieval European History. Professor Kraemer drew attention to the numerous letters between women and members of their families to be found among the vast treasures in the documentary portion of the Cairo Genizah. There are also appeals and petitions by women to the community and to communal officials, as well as declarations in last wills and testaments. These precious and unique documents let us hear the female voice directly, unmediated by men. The letters give us a fine *aperçu* into the socio-economic and cultural status of women and into the entire family structure.

I myself introduced the third speaker, Professor Mordechai Friedman, of Tel Aviv University's Talmud Department, who spoke on three major aspects of medieval Jewish marriage and the family. He began with a re-examination of the question of child brides, on the basis of published and unedited fragments. The evidence confirmed that such marriages were irregular as far as legal minors were concerned and almost exclusively restricted to orphan girls. One case of homicide within the family, the murder of a wife and mother-in-law, is documented. Jewish marriage contracts of both the Palestinian and Karaite traditions include 'mutual obligations', whereby the groom's undertaking to honour and serve his wife are balanced by her undertaking to honour and serve him.

At the fourth session, chaired by the Sir Thomas Adams's Professor of Arabic, Tarif Khalidi, Professor Paul Fenton, of the Sorbonne, devoted his paper to Jewish-Muslim relations. He used Genizah texts to demonstrate that 'the principles of seclusion and discrimination inculcated by religious bigotry were often countered by the kind of economic and social realities that nurtured more tolerant attitudes'. Professor Fenton gave details of Genizah letters that reveal Jewish-Muslim partnerships unrestricted by social or religious dictates and personal contacts that were often quite intimate, despite official segregation.

The fifth and final session, as well attended as all its predecessors, was devoted to the talmudic and rabbinic fields and was chaired by the Reverend William Horbury, Professor of Early Christian and Jewish Studies. Professor Neil Danzig, of the Jewish Theological Seminary of America in New York, presented a detailed analysis of a well-known Genizah fragment containing a prayer on behalf of the Babylonian Geonim and the Exilarch, one part of which is in New York and the other in Cambridge. The combined text comprises a ninth-century liturgical handbook from a Babylonian synagogue, the contents of which include guidelines for the formulaic conclusion of a homily delivered on the sabbath and festivals.

The Reverend Dr Andrew Macintosh, who was at that time President of St John's College, and who attended all the Genizah centenary lectures, brought the proceedings to a close and referred to the Genizah's close connection with the College, especially with its Master in Schechter's day, Charles Taylor. He noted that Taylor had been enthusiastic about the study of talmudic Hebrew, and had published in 1877 an edition of *Pirqey Avot* which is still much used and appreciated. It had also been his financial support of Schechter that had facilitated the whole Genizah enterprise. Dr Macintosh reported that Professor Klein had been a popular Visiting Scholar at St John's College and expressed his pleasure that the College had appointed me to a fellowship.

Given that these nine lectures covered many of the major fields of Genizah research, it seemed to me that, with the addition of an appropriate essay of my own, a volume could be produced that would serve as the introductory volume in the 'Genizah Series' that has long been planned. I therefore brought such a proposal to the Steering Committee of the Taylor-Schechter Genizah Research Unit, under the chairmanship of Professor Malcolm Schofield, and it was heartily endorsed. The lecturers were asked to update and adjust the texts of their lectures as they saw fit and the articles that now appear in this volume represent these later versions of their papers. Assisted by my wife, Shulie, who undertook the technical preparation and the sub-editing, and did most of the indexing, I edited the scholarly content of the papers and added my own essay.

In that essay, which serves as an introduction to the others, I have tried to demonstrate that Genizah research is not simply the technical treatment of certain narrow topics in medieval Jewish literature and history, with limited relevance to the broader academic discipline, but has, in a little over a century, had a profound effect on almost every area of Jewish studies. I have done this by summarizing the contributions made by Genizah texts to various fields of study and by citing a few examples of the kind of manuscripts that have been deciphered and analysed. To this end, I have touched on the biblical Hebrew text, talmudic and halakhic matters and the evolution of Jewish liturgy. The history of the Holy Land and some leading personalities have received attention but the mundane activities of more ordinary folk have not been forgotten.

It is a source of considerable sadness to all those involved in these series of lectures and their publication that Professor Michael Klein is no longer with us. His death, a few months ago, at the early age of sixty, robbed Genizah research of one of its most important and industrious scholars. In the course of twenty years, Michael published some fourteen important articles on Genizah themes, and the second of his two seminal volumes on targumic material from the Genizah was published in the same series as the current volume and was indeed the first volume to be made available in electronic form on the Unit's web site. He was a visiting scholar in the University of Cambridge on a number of occasions and was most popular with all who came into contact with him. It is singularly appropriate that the University Library has agreed to dedicate this volume to his memory.

I am most grateful to the contributors for their kindness in agreeing to give the lectures and their co-operation in the editorial process; to all my colleagues in the Genizah Research Unit for their generous assistance in many matters relating to the lectures and their publication; to the University Librarian and the Library Syndicate for supporting the series and the creation of the volume; to the Faculty of Oriental Studies and to the Sidney and Elizabeth Corob Charitable Trust for contributing to the costs of the series; and to Cambridge University Press for seeing it efficiently through the publication process. I hope that it may be seen as a fitting tribute to the outstanding scholarship and prescience of Charles Taylor and Solomon Schechter, whose efforts of over one hundred years ago are still bearing sumptuous, scholarly fruit.

Stefan C. Reif

1

A Centennial Assessment of Genizah Studies

STEFAN C. REIF

The object of this paper is to set the scene for the other, more detailed presentations in this volume by summarizing the contributions made by Genizah texts to various aspects of Jewish studies, and by citing a few examples of the kind of manuscripts that have been deciphered and analysed.[1] It should then become apparent what all this means for a century of past academic development, as well as for its equivalent over the next hundred years. What I hope to demonstrate is that there is undoubtedly an essential technical side to Genizah research and an aspect of it that deals with minute literary, linguistic and historical detail. At the same time, I am anxious to prove that the discoveries and their interpretation also reveal totally unexpected scenarios and permit the reconstruction, as with a giant jigsaw, of a broad picture, depicting much of Jewish life as it was lived about a thousand years ago. I have recently published a volume that sets out to explain how, where and why the Genizah archive was amassed; who transferred it to famous research libraries, particularly to Cambridge University Library; and the manner in which scholars have exploited its contents since the last decade of the nineteenth century.[2] What has incidentally emerged is a remarkable tale of communal piety and superstition, scholarly co-operation and rivalry, and institutional care and neglect. That tale is a topic for consideration elsewhere. What is important in this present context is the fact that I have, in the course of preparing that volume, recently assessed the degree to which a number of areas of Jewish studies have been affected by Genizah discoveries. I am consequently able to offer fresh and pertinent comments under the five headings of Bible, Rabbinics, History, Daily Life and Literacy.

Bible

There are some variants to be found in the Genizah remnants of scrolls and codices which are significant for the history of scribal techniques and have yet to be adequately exploited for text-critical purposes. Nevertheless, the consonantal text

---

[1] An earlier version of this paper was delivered at the Toledo conference of the European Association for Jewish Studies in 1998 and appeared in *Jewish Studies at the Turn of the Twentieth Century*, eds J. T. Borrás and A. Sáenz-Badillos, vol. 1 (Leiden, Boston and Köln, 1999), pp. 577–608. I am grateful to the publishers, Brill of Leiden, for their kind permission to reproduce much of that article here.

[2] S. C. Reif, *A Jewish Archive from Old Cairo: The History of Cambridge University's Genizah Collection* (Richmond, Surrey, 2000).

was substantially as it is today and it is rather in the area of vocalization that major discoveries have been made. There were three major systems, two emanating from the Holy Land and one from Babylon, that were in vogue a thousand years ago. The tenth-century Tiberian system of Ben Asher that later came to be regarded as standard took some two or three centuries to establish its dominance in the field. Whether inspired by the Syriac Christian example, by Muslim concern for the accuracy of the Qur'an, or by an internal feud with the Karaite Jews who preferred the biblical to the rabbinic tradition, such attention to the accurate recording of the vocalized text left its mark on exegesis. The schools of Masoretes (literally, 'transmitters' or, perhaps, 'counters'), who surrounded the text with vowel points, cantillation signs and explanatory notes, inevitably recorded *pari passu* their own understanding of its meaning, or the understanding that they had inherited from generations of readers.[3] Their methodical approach also encouraged the development of those Hebrew philological studies that provided the basis for the literal interpretation of the Hebrew Bible in later medieval and modern times.[4]

The interest in making sense of the Hebrew text was of course primarily inspired by its regular recitation before the congregation in the synagogue. The material from the Cairo Genizah confirms that there existed annual Babylonian and triennial Palestinian lectionaries for both pentateuchal and prophetic readings. They did, however, exist in such variety that it is impossible to identify any one order that may be traced back to the early Christian centuries. According to the latest research, the system was not a rigid one, allowed for local variations and took the form of a double cycle every seven years.[5] In addition to Hebrew lectionaries used by the Jews,

---

[3] A. Dotan, *Encyclopaedia Judaica* 16 (Jerusalem, 1971), cols 1401–82; I. Yeivin, *Introduction to the Tiberian Masorah* (English translation of a Hebrew original, Missoula, 1980); E. J. Revell, *Hebrew Texts with Palestinian Vocalization* (Toronto, 1970); and M. C. Davis, *Hebrew Bible Manuscripts in the Cambridge Genizah Collections*, (2 vols; Cambridge, 1978 and 1980; and another two being prepared for the printer). See also the papers published in early issues of *Textus* and read at recent meetings of the International Organization for Masoretic Studies. For further details of the relevance of the Genizah to biblical studies, see S. C. Reif, 'The Cairo Genizah and its Treasures, with Special Reference to Biblical Studies' in *The Aramaic Bible: Targums in their Historical Context,* eds D. R. G. Beattie and M. J. McNamara (Sheffield, 1994), pp. 30–50.

[4] See, for example, D. Becker, 'Traces of Judah Ibn Quraysh in Manuscript, particularly in Genizah Fragments' and I. Eldar 'Mukhtaṣar (an abridgement of) Hidāyat al-Qāri': A Grammatical Treatise discovered in the Genizah' in *Genizah Research after Ninety Years. The Case of Judaeo-Arabic*, eds J. Blau and S. C. Reif (Cambridge, 1992), pp. 14–21 and 67–73; and D. Téné, '*Hashva'at Ha-Leshonot Viydi'at Ha-Lashon*' in *Hebrew Language Studies presented to Professor Zeev Ben-Hayyim*, eds M. Bar-Asher, A. Dotan, G. B. Sarfati and D. Téné (Hebrew; Jerusalem, 1983), pp. 237–87. For the Karaite contribution, see the forthcoming volume by G. Khan, *Early Karaite Grammatical Texts*, scheduled for publication in 2001 in SBL's 'Masoretic Studies' series, and n. 9 below.

[5] J. J. Petuchowski (ed.), *Contributions to the Scientific Study of the Jewish Liturgy* (New York, 1970), pp. xvii–xxi; B. Z. Wacholder in the first prolegomenon to the reprint (New York, 1971) of J. Mann's *The Bible as Read and Preached in the Old Synagogue* (Cincinnati,

Palestinian Syriac versions of the Christian scriptures have also been discovered. The range of biblical translations to be found in the Genizah testifies to the wide variety of languages in use when that archive was first built up. In the pre-Islamic centuries, the dominant language of the diaspora Jews was Greek so that it is hardly surprising to find fragments dating from the sixth to seventh centuries that were part of translations first prepared for them by Aquila some 500 years earlier.[6] Was it Jews or Christians who were using such versions in the sixth century and how did they come to be consigned to the Genizah? Is their use related to that of Origen's *Hexapla*, fragments of which have also come to us from the same source? Whether or not the Aquila just mentioned is, as has sometimes been suggested, to be identified with Onqelos, the reputed author of the main and literal synagogal targum, is not clarified by the Genizah texts. They do, nevertheless, add considerably to our knowledge of the development of that popular genre of Aramaic translation. Various compilations of targumic material, some hitherto unknown, have been identified among the Genizah texts. They include lengthy elaborations of the text, poetic versions of the narratives, and halakhic interpretations of verses that run counter to what is found in the talmudic sources.[7]

Because of the ancient nature of the custom to translate the Hebrew Bible into Aramaic, it was not abandoned when Arabic replaced Aramaic and Greek as the Jewish vernacular. Rather, it was incorporated into a trilingual version in which Arabic appeared side-by-side with Hebrew and Aramaic. The Arabic rendering, written in Hebrew characters and recording the popular dialect of that Semitic language used in the Jewish communities, originally existed in a variety of forms, many of them closely following the rabbinic and targumic traditions. Although they continued to exist well into the Middle Ages, they did gradually cede precedence to the version created by the tenth-century rabbinic authority in Babylon, Sa'adya ben

---

1940 and 1966, with I. Sonne); E. Fleischer's Hebrew articles, 'Inquiries concerning the Triennial Reading of the Torah in Ancient Eretz-Israel', *Hebrew Union College Annual* 62 (1991), pp. 43–61 and 'Annual and Triennial Reading of the Bible in the Old Synagogue', *Tarbiz* 61 (1992), pp. 25–43; S. Naeh, 'The Torah Reading Cycle in Early Palestine: A Re-Examination', *Tarbiz* 67 (1998), pp. 167–87.

[6] A. S. Lewis and M. D. Gibson, *Palestinian Syriac Texts from Palimpsest Fragments in the Taylor-Schechter Collection* (London, 1900); M. Sokoloff and J. Yahalom, 'Christian Palimpsests from the Cairo Geniza', *Revue d'Histoire des Textes* 8 (1978), pp. 109–32; F. C. Burkitt, *Fragments of the Books of Kings according to the Translation of Aquila* (Cambridge, 1897), and C. Taylor, *Hebrew-Greek Genizah Palimpsests from the Taylor-Schechter Collection* (Cambridge, 1900); C. Müller-Kessler and M. Sokoloff, *The Christian Palestinian Aramaic Old Testament and Apocrypha Version from the Early Period* (Groningen, 1997); A. Salvesen (ed.), *Origen's Hexapla and Fragments: Papers Presented at the Rich Seminar on the Hexapla* (Tübingen, 1998).

[7] M. L. Klein, *Genizah Manuscripts of Palestinian Targum to the Pentateuch* (2 vols; Cincinnati, 1986) and *Targum Manuscripts in the Cambridge Genizah Collections* (Cambridge, 1992); see also his article 'Targumic Studies and the Cairo Genizah', on pp. 47–58 below.

Joseph, which, like the targum of Onqelos, became the standard one.[8] It was Sa'adya who championed the rabbinic traditions against the powerful challenge mounted by their Karaite opponents who were distinguishing themselves in biblical exegesis and philological studies. For their part, the Karaites also made a polemical point by means of a linguistic usage. At one point in their history, they demonstrated their independent religious identity by recording the text of the Hebrew Bible in Arabic and not Hebrew characters.[9]

Scholarly understanding of the development of midrashim, throughout the millennium following the destruction of the Second Temple, also owes much to Genizah research. Hitherto, the earliest manuscripts were from the initial period of Ashkenazi Jewry in the western Jewish communities. Now, there are hundreds of fragments written in their eastern counterparts at a much earlier date and representing older textual traditions. What is more, new midrashim, anthologies and commentaries have been discovered, both halakhic and aggadic in nature, and a new picture has been drawn of the colourful and heterogeneous Jewish exegesis of the Hebrew Bible in the early Middle Ages and of the manner in which various texts were transmitted.[10] Such a variegated approach gave way to the more linguistic and

---

[8] J. Blau, 'On a Fragment of the Oldest Judaeo-Arabic Bible Translation Extant' in *Ninety Years* (see n. 4 above), pp. 31–39; C. F. Baker and M. Polliack, *Arabic and Judaeo-Arabic Manuscripts in the Cambridge Genizah Collections* (Cambridge, 2001); *Heritage and Innovation in Medieval Judaeo-Arabic Culture*, eds J. Blau and D. Doron (Ramat Gan, 2000); M Polliack, 'Types of Arabic Bible Translation in the Cairo Geniza based on the Catalogue of T-S Arabic', *Te'uda 15: A Century of Geniza Research* (Hebrew; Tel Aviv, 1999), pp. 109–25.

[9] G. Khan, 'The Early Karaite Grammatical Tradition' in *Jewish Studies at the Turn of the Twentieth Century* (see n. 1 above), pp. 72–80 and *Karaite Bible Manuscripts from the Cairo Genizah* (Cambridge, 1990); M. Polliack, *The Karaite Tradition of Arabic Bible Translation* (Leiden, New York and Köln, 1997); and see n. 4 above.

[10] Two helpful and reliable English guides to the whole midrashic field, as background to the relevance of the Genizah texts, are R. Kasher's article 'Scripture in Rabbinic Literature' in *Mikra: Text, Translation, Reading and Interpretation of the Hebrew Bible in Ancient Judaism and Early Christianity*, eds J. Mulder and H. Sysling (Assen/Maastricht and Philadelphia), pp. 547–94 and G. Stemberger's *Introduction to the Talmud and Midrash* (Edinburgh, 1996), originally an updated version of Hermann Strack's classic, but now an important work in its own right, with the latest scholarly data. M. Gaster's midrashic pieces were reprinted in his three volumes *Studies and Texts in Folklore: Magic, Mediaeval Romance, Hebrew Apocrypha and Samaritan Archaeology* (London, 1925–28). For examples of the treatment of Genizah fragments of midrashim, see M. Sokoloff, *The Geniza Fragments of Bereshit Rabba* (Jerusalem, 1982), and S. C. Reif, 'A Midrashic Anthology from the Genizah' in *Interpreting the Hebrew Bible: Essays in Honour of E. I. J. Rosenthal*, eds J. A. Emerton and S. C. Reif (Cambridge, 1982), pp. 179–225; L. Teugels, 'New Perspectives on the Origins of *Aggadat Bereshit*: The Witness of a Genizah Fragment' in *Jewish Studies at the Turn of the Twentieth Century* (see n. 1 above), pp. 349–57. Hebrew volumes on the kind of unusual midrashim found in the Genizah include S. A. Wertheimer, *Batei Midrashot*, ed. A. J. Wertheimer (Jerusalem, 1954); J. Mann, *The Bible as Read and Preached* (see n. 5 above); L. Ginzberg, *Genizah Studies in Memory of Doctor Solomon Schechter. I. Midrash and*

philological commentaries of the tenth to the twelfth centuries, and the written evidence from the Genizah records is one of the factors that precipitated such a change.[11] It was effected by the centralized and centralizing powers of the Babylonian rabbinic authorities in an effort to thwart Karaite efforts to discredit rabbinic interpretation as lacking the serious and literal dimension.

There are also some intriguing questions concerning the link between the biblical and quasi-biblical texts that occur both among the literature of the Dead Sea sect and in the Genizah corpora. It is sometimes forgotten that the first and fullest text of one of the sect's major religious tracts, the Damascus Document (or Zadokite Fragments), came to light among the Genizah finds fifty years before the contents of the Qumran caves made their sensational impact on Jewish and Christian history.[12] Nor indeed would it have been possible for the long-lost Hebrew text of the Wisdom of Ben Sira, written in the second pre-Christian century, to have been reconstructed without extensive input from the fragments found in the Ben Ezra synagogue.[13] But in which context did these two works continue to circulate in the intervening centuries and who copied them, and for what purpose, in Fatimid Cairo?[14] It is not perhaps so

---

Haggadah (New York, 1928); Z. M. Rabinovitz, *Ginzé Midrash* (Tel Aviv, 1976); and M. Kahana, *Manuscripts of the Halakhic Midrashim: An Annotated Catalogue* (Jerusalem, 1995) and his article 'The Tannaitic Midrashim' on pp. 59–73 below.

[11] As far as rabbinic commentaries are concerned, M. Perez has, for example, published important fragments of the work of Judah ibn Bal'am and Moses ibn Gikatilla in *Proceedings of the American Academy for Jewish Research* 57 (1991), pp. 1–16; *Sinai* 108 (1991), pp. 7–17; *Leshonenu* 55 (1992), pp. 315–22; *Hebrew Union College Annual* 63 (1993), pp. 1–17; and *Sinai* 113 (1994), pp. 262–76. M. Zucker did important work on Sa'adya's biblical scholarship in his Hebrew volumes *Rav Saadya Gaon's Translation of the Torah* (New York, 1959) and *Saadya's Commentary on Genesis* (New York, 1984) and Y. Ratzaby has published many additional fragments of Sa'adya's commentaries, as in *Sinai* 109 (1992), pp. 97–117, 193–211; and *Sinai* 111 (1993), pp. 1–26; see his edition of *Sa'adya's Translation and Commentary on Isaiah* (Kiryat Ono, 1993). Another important edition is that of A. Greenbaum, *The Biblical Commentary of Rav Samuel ben Ḥofni Gaon according to Geniza Manuscripts* (Hebrew; Jerusalem, 1979).

[12] Schechter published the Zadokite or Damascus Document (CD) in the first volume of his *Documents of Jewish Sectaries* under the sub-title *Fragments of a Zadokite Work* (Cambridge, 1910). The literature relating to CD is helpfully summarized in the excellent bibliography provided by F. García Martínez in Magen Broshi's *The Damascus Document Reconsidered* (Jerusalem, 1992). See also *The Damascus Document: A Centennial of Discovery*, eds J. M. Baumgarten, E. G. Chazon and A. Pinnick (Leiden, Boston and Köln, 2000), including S. C. Reif, 'The Damascus Document from the Cairo Genizah: Its Discovery, Early Study and Historical Significance', pp. 109–31.

[13] The whole story of the Cambridge Genizah fragments of Ben Sira is told in S. C. Reif, 'The Discovery of the Cambridge Genizah fragments of Ben Sira: Scholars and Texts' in one of a number of recent overviews of the field, *The Book of Ben Sira in Modern Research: Proceedings of the First International Ben Sira Conference, 28–31 July 1996, Soesterberg, Netherlands*, ed. P. C. Beentjes (Berlin and New York, 1997), pp. 1–22.

[14] The issue of the relationship between the Dead Sea Scrolls and the Genizah texts is summarized in S. C. Reif's entry 'Cairo Genizah' in *Encyclopaedia of the Dead Sea Scrolls*, eds L. H. Schiffman and J. C. VanderKam (Oxford and New York, 2000), pp. 105–8. See

remarkable to find versions of *Toledot Yeshu*, recording early Jewish folklore about Jesus, among the fragments.[15] On the other hand, no wholly satisfactory reason can be offered for the existence in the Cairo Jewish community of parts of a Nestorian Syriac hymn-book.[16] Perhaps these thirteenth- or fourteenth-century texts belonging to a feast of the Virgin Mary were sold as scrap when the Nestorian community faded out of existence in Cairo at that time or shortly afterwards.

Rabbinics

The distinction between biblical and rabbinic literature became pronounced only when authors and scribes took to prescribing and describing the contents of their codices in more definitive ways in the later Middle Ages. One should not therefore be surprised to find mixtures of contents in early Genizah folios, as in the case of the scrap of a prophetic lectionary that also contains an early version of a synagogal benediction.[17] That having been said, one may move on to more specific rabbinic literature and assess how the Genizah has contributed to our understanding of its development in the geonic period and soon afterwards. It is not rare to find among Genizah fragments talmudic sections, from both the *Bavli* and the *Yerushalmi*, that were later lost or removed, or to discover that post-Genizah texts have attracted all manner of adhesions. Sometimes the Genizah text is early enough to shed light on the origins of an expression that puzzled later generations. An unusual linguistic usage, a word of Greek or Persian origin, the exchange of one letter for another, a forgotten place name, or an unexpected abbreviation – such phenomena often led to corruptions in the text and it is not unusual for Genizah versions to uncover authentic readings.[18] Fragments of incunables and early editions of talmudic texts, some of them on vellum, and many of them from Spain (e.g. Guadalaxara) and Portugal (e.g. Faro), are another feature, albeit a limited one, of Genizah collections.[19] Genizah

---

also the interesting exchange in Hebrew between Y. Erder and H. Ben-Shammai in a section entitled 'Discussion: Karaism and Apocryphic Literature', *Cathedra* 42 (1987), pp. 54–86.

[15] For a detailed bibliography see R. Di Segni's Italian monograph *Il Vangelo del Ghetto* (Rome, 1985).

[16] S. P. Brock has edited and published Syriac liturgies from the Genizah in his articles 'East Syrian Liturgical Fragments from the Cairo Genizah' and 'Some Further East Syrian Liturgical Fragments from the Cairo Genizah' in *Oriens Christianus* 68 (1984), pp. 58–79 and 74 (1990), pp. 44–61. My colleagues, Dr F. Niessen and Dr E. Hunter, are currently preparing for publication a fragment containing Syriac quotations from the Pauline Epistles.

[17] T-S A42.2; see Davis, *Hebrew Bible Manuscripts* (see n. 3 above), vol. 1, p. 221 and S. C. Reif, *Published Material from the Cambridge Genizah Collections: A Bibliography 1896–1980* (Cambridge, 1988), p. 42.

[18] For general guidance in English to scientific study of talmudic texts, see the revised English version of E. Schürer's *The History of the Jewish People in the Age of Jesus Christ (175 B. C. – A. D. 135)* by G. Vermes and F. Millar, vol. 1 (Edinburgh, 1973), pp. 68–118; the richly informative volume *The Literature of the Sages. First Part: Oral Tora, Halakha, Mishna, Tosefta, Talmud, External Tractates*, ed. S. Safrai (Assen/Maastricht and Philadelphia, 1987); and G. Stemberger, *Introduction* (see n. 10 above).

[19] H. Z. Dimitrovsky, *S'ride Bavli: Fragments from Spanish and Portuguese Incunabula and Sixteenth Century Printings of the Babylonian Talmud and Alfasi* (2 vols; New York, 1979).

versions also contribute to a better understanding of linguistic developments. A clearer distinction between the Western Aramaic of Palestinian texts and the Eastern Aramaic of their Babylonian counterparts has become possible, with the result that the relevant dictionaries and grammars have been improved or, indeed, created from scratch.[20] Glosses on the text, some of them in Judaeo-Arabic or Judaeo-Greek, have helped to restore long-lost meanings, while the use in some manuscripts of vowel-points, following a variety of systems, has enabled experts in Hebrew linguistics to explain how different communities pronounced the Hebrew of their rabbinic texts.[21]

Two other developments, that are certainly reflected in the Genizah evidence, were the creation of supplements to the talmudic text, in the form of brief, additional tractates in the earlier geonic period, and the compilation of commentaries at a later date. Themes that are briefly treated in the standard tractates of the talmudic and immediate post-talmudic periods, or are dealt with there in scattered statements attached to various contexts, are expanded upon in the so-called 'Minor Tractates'.[22] If these tractates constitute the first stage of the process of commentary, the second stage is to be located in the statements made by various geonic authorities about the meaning of individual talmudic passages and preserved in their responsa.[23] The third stage is that of the compilation of running commentaries, such as that which appears to have been undertaken in the Babylonian centre of Pumbedita by Hai Gaon in the tenth and eleventh centuries but most of which has been lost, and that of his later contemporary, Ḥananel ben Ḥushiel, in Qayrawan, one of the most important Jewish communities in North Africa.[24] While investigative Genizah scholarship has played a

---

[20] On the matter of the Aramaic used in the rabbinic tradition, ample literature is cited by M. Sokoloff in the collection of essays that he edited entitled *Arameans, Aramaic and the Aramaic Literary Tradition* (Ramat Gan, 1983) and in his *A Dictionary of Jewish Palestinian Aramaic of the Byzantine Period* (Ramat Gan, 1990).

[21] S. Morag, *Vocalised Talmudic Manuscripts in the Cambridge Genizah Collections* (Cambridge, 1988); R. Brody, *A Hand-list of Rabbinic Manuscripts in the Cambridge Genizah Collections* (Cambridge, 1998); N. Danzig, *A Catalogue of Fragments of Halakhah and Midrash from the Cairo Genizah in the Elkan Nathan Adler Collection of the Library of the Jewish Theological Seminary of America* (New York and Jerusalem, 1997). See also the essays included in *Meḥqere Talmud: Talmudic Studies*, edited by J. Sussmann and D. Rosenthal (Jerusalem, 1990–93).

[22] M. B. Lerner, 'The External Tractates' in *The Literature of the Sages* (see n. 18 above), pp. 367–409.

[23] See, for example, the monumental work of B. M. Lewin in his *Oṣar Ha-Geonim* published in 13 volumes between 1928 and 1962. Details of his publications are given in his *Festschrift, Sefer Ha-Yovel... B. M. Lewin*, ed. J. L. Fishman (Maimon) (Hebrew; Jerusalem, 1940), pp. 1–32.

[24] Brody has summarized such development in his essay on 'The Cairo Genizah' included in B. Richler's *Hebrew Manuscripts: A Treasured Legacy* (Cleveland and Jerusalem, 1990), pp. 112–37. See also his important monograph *The Geonim of Babylonia and the Shaping of Medieval Jewish Culture* (New Haven and London, 1998) and M. Ben-Sasson, *The Emergence of the Local Jewish Community in the Muslim World: Qayrawan, 800–1057* (Hebrew; Jerusalem, 1997).

role in the reconstruction of these earlier developments, it has made nothing short of a massive contribution to the recovery of the later work of Nissim ben Jacob ibn Shahin. For instance, in a work (*Kitāb Miftāḥ Magālīq al-Talmūd*) whose title might justifiably be translated 'A Key to the Talmudic Treasure-Chest', he assisted the student of the vast talmudic literature by providing sources and parallels for many statements, as well as explanations of many recurrent themes.[25]

Another topic documented by a century of Genizah study is the early expansion of halakhic guidance. The earlier distinctions between the Babylonian talmudic traditions and their equivalents in the Land of Israel also found later expression in the formulation of their respective laws and customs. As the Babylonian teachers and institutions between and around the Tigris and the Euphrates began to grow in stature and influence, so it became necessary for the Palestinian communities to put on record those instances (*ma'asim* in Hebrew) in which they differed. A body of literature thus came into being, perhaps early in the seventh century, the purpose of which was to clarify, recall and maintain these differences.[26] The Genizah has supplied additions and improvements to the questions and the homilies of the *She'iltot*,[27] as it has contributed better texts to later compilations of Jewish religious law from the geonic period, such as the *Halakhot Pesuqot* and the *Halakhot Gedolot*.[28] From many fragments preserved in the Genizah, it emerges that a certain Pirqoi ben Baboi, whose name is either of Persian origin or perhaps represents some sort of *nom de plume*, decided that the time had come to usher in a new halakhic era

[25] Among the Hebrew works of Shraga Abramson that are central to Genizah research are his *Essa Meshali* (Jerusalem, 1943); *Ba-Merkazim Uva-Tefuṣot* (Jerusalem, 1965); *R. Nissim Gaon Libelli Quinque* (Jerusalem, 1965); and *'Inyanot Be-Sifrut Ha-Ge'onim* (Jerusalem, 1974). See also the essays and bibliography in the memorial booklet produced by the Israel Academy, *Le-Zikhro shel Shraga Abramson* (Jerusalem, 1997).

[26] For the history of *halakhah* and of responsa literature, see L. Ginzberg, *Geonica* (2 vols; New York, 1909); S. B. Freehof, *Responsa Literature* (Philadelphia, 1955); J. Newman, *Halachic Sources from the Beginning to the Ninth Century* (Leiden, 1969); A. M. Schreiber, *Jewish Law and Decision-Making: A Study Through Time* (Philadelphia, 1979); E. E. Urbach, *The Halakhah: Its Sources and Development* (E. T., Jerusalem, 1986); M. Lewittes, *Principles and Development of Jewish Law* (New York, 1987); E. N. Dorff and A. Rosett, *A Living Tree: The Roots and Growth of Jewish Law* (Albany, 1988); and G. Libson, 'Halakhah and Law in the Period of the Geonim' in *An Introduction to the History and Sources of Jewish Law*, eds N. S. Hecht, B. S. Jackson, S. M. Passamaneck, D. Piattelli and A. M. Rabello (Oxford, 1996), pp. 197–250. On Samuel b. Ḥofni, see D. E. Sklare, *Samuel ben Ḥofni Gaon and his Cultural World: Texts and Studies* (Leiden, New York and Köln, 1996). See also M. Margaliot, *Hilkhot 'Ereṣ Yisra'el min Ha-Genizah*, ed. I. Ta-Shma (Jerusalem, 1973).

[27] R. Brody, *The Textual History of the She'iltot* (Hebrew; New York and Jerusalem, 1991); M. B. Lerner, 'The Geniza Fragments of *She'iltot De-Rav Aḥai* in the Munich Library' in *A Century of Geniza Research* (see n. 8 above), pp.161–88.

[28] E. Hildesheimer (ed.), *Sefer Halakhot Gedolot* (Hebrew; 3 vols; Jerusalem, 1971, 1980 and 1988); N. Danzig, *Introduction to Halakhot Pesuqot* (Hebrew; New York, 1993).

and to put an end to any influence that the talmudists of the Holy Land might still have.[29]

The later Genizah material includes hundreds of fragments of the halakhic digest of the Babylonian Talmud that Isaac Alfasi prepared in the eleventh century. The first fully comprehensive code of Jewish law, the *Mishneh Torah* of Maimonides, completed in Cairo in 1180 is also, not surprisingly, well represented among the medieval fragments from the Ben Ezra synagogue.[30] Equally unsurprising is the fact that many of these fragments cover such themes as ritual slaughter, laws of inheritance and marital matters, all of which were of major concern to the daily lives of the community. Genizah wills reveal that some fathers tried to cut their families out of any inheritance, that women could bequeath property of their own and that there was considerable doubt about intentions expressed on what was wrongly thought to be a death-bed.[31] In the case of marriage documents, there are important remnants of Palestinian religious practice which demonstrate that in matters of personal status the emigrés from the Holy Land succeeded in maintaining their halakhic individuality for some time. Work on Karaite *ketubbot* has indicated how they differ palaeographically, linguistically and legally from their rabbinic counterparts and how they compare to Babylonian and Palestinian *halakhah*.[32] Via the Genizah, hundreds or maybe even thousands of authentic and original halakhic responses have now been recovered. Groups of decisions sent by thc authority himself by way of guidance to a number of questioners have surfaced. They have retained the original formulation, with the prefaces and conclusions of the author, and they often provide us with his name. Many texts can now therefore be traced to their composers and many decisions that had been lost or forgotten have come to light. It should not be forgotten that there are also Genizah responsa that date from the twelfth and thirteenth centuries, many of them emanating from Moses Maimonides himself or his son Abraham, occasionally in their own hands.[33]

---

[29] See the useful summary and bibliographical details in *Encyclopaedia Judaica* 13, cols 560–61.

[30] The project of the Israel Academy of Sciences to describe all the fragments from the Genizah in the talmudic and midrashic fields (directed by Professor Jacob Sussmann of the Hebrew University) has produced a wealth of information in this connection; see also the volumes by Brody and Danzig cited in n. 21 above.

[31] See J. Rivlin, *Inheritance and Wills in Jewish Law* (Hebrew; Ramat Gan, 1999).

[32] Two comprehensive studies of marriage documents, customs and lawsuits are M. A. Friedman's *Jewish Marriage in Palestine: A Cairo Geniza Study* (2 vols; Tel Aviv and New York, 1980), and his *Jewish Polygyny in the Middle Ages: New Documents from the Cairo Geniza* (Hebrew; Jerusalem, 1986). See also the discussion between Friedman and J. Olszowy-Schlanger in *A Century of Geniza Research* (see n. 8 above), pp. 127–57.

[33] See S. Assaf's Hebrew volumes *Gaonic Responsa* (Jerusalem, 1928); *Gaonica* (Jerusalem, 1933); *Responsa Geonica* (Jerusalem, 1942); *Texts and Studies* (Jerusalem, 1946); and *Tequfat Ha-Geo'nim Ve-Sifrutah* (Jerusalem, 1955). J. Blau's edition of *R. Moses b. Maimon: Responsa*, (4 vols; Jerusalem, 1957–61 and 1986) contains substantial Genizah material and other examples may be found in a number of articles by M. A. Friedman, as

It is now clear that monographs on halakhic themes were composed from at least as early as the tenth century. Sa'adya may have been one of the innovators in this field; he is certainly among those whose works on Jewish legal themes appear among the fragments. What has been recovered of his study of the laws of inheritance does not include any references to sources and may therefore be a remnant of an abbreviated format. As far as his practical guide to Jewish rules on testimonies and deeds (*Sefer Ha-Sheṭarot*) is concerned, fifty Genizah fragments (forty of them in Cambridge) have produced some 200 folios, amounting to over ninety per cent of the original work. Since the first scientific edition of Sa'adya's prayer-book was published, almost sixty years ago, many more fragments of the work have been located. Some of Sa'adya's successors in the Babylonian academies followed his example and produced their own halakhic monographs, Hai ben Sherira Gaon and Samuel ben Ḥofni of Sura demonstrating considerable creativity and exercising a major influence on subsequent halakhic developments.[34] Samuel ben Ḥofni, together with Sa'adya himself and the later scholar Tanḥum ben Joseph Yerushalmi, also wrote commentaries on the Hebrew Bible that demonstrated how one could remain faithful to the source, and at the same time provide rational and philosophical responses to the problems raised by the texts.[35]

In the field of rabbinic liturgy, what researchers have found particularly exciting has been the sheer novelty of so much of the material.[36] Firstly, there are novel or

---

listed in the various volumes of the *Index of Articles on Jewish Studies* published annually in Jerusalem, beginning in 1969.

[34] See Brody's work cited in n. 24 above, and details of the work of M. Ben-Sasson and R. Brody on Sa'adya's *Sefer Ha-Sheṭarot* as discussed in *Genizah Fragments* 19/2 (April, 1990), p. 2. See also G. Libson, 'The Structure, Scope and Development of the Halakhic monographs of Rav Shmeu'el ben Ḥofni Gaon' in *A Century of Genizah Research* (see n. 8 above) pp. 189–239. On Sa'adya's prayer-book, see N. Wieder, *The Formation of Jewish Liturgy in the East and the West* (2 vols; Hebrew; Jerusalem, 1998), vol. 2, pp. 559–658; and R. Brody, 'Note on the Conclusion of Se'adya Gaon's Prayerbook', *Tarbiz* 68 (1999), pp. 279–81.

[35] Some of the history of Jewish biblical exegesis is covered in S. C. Reif, 'Aspects of the Jewish Contribution to Biblical Interpretation' in *The Cambridge Companion to Biblical Interpretation*, ed. J. Barton (Cambridge, 1998), pp. 143–59, and there are important essays in this field in *Genizah Research*, eds Blau and Reif (see n. 8 above).

[36] For recent work on the contribution of the Genizah to the scientific study of Jewish liturgy, see Wieder, *Formation* (see n. 34 above); S. C. Reif, *Judaism and Hebrew Prayer* (Cambridge, 1993), especially pp. 122–52, and 'The Genizah and Jewish Liturgy: Past Achievements and a Current Project', *Medieval Encounters* 5 (1999), pp. 29–45, as well as a more detailed Hebrew version of part of the latter paper in *From Qumran to Cairo: Studies in the History of Prayer*, ed. J. Tabory (Jerusalem, 1999), pp. 121–30. The edition of Sa'adya's prayer-book currently available is that of I. Davidson, S. Assaf and B. I. Joel, *Siddur R. Saadja Gaon* (Jerusalem, 1941; Jerusalem^2, 1963) and the fullest study of the Palestinian rite to date is that of E. Fleischer, *Eretz-Israel Prayer and Prayer Rituals as Portrayed in the Geniza Documents* (Hebrew; Jerusalem, 1988). For a thorough guide to the bibliography on Jewish liturgical matters, see J. Tabory, *Jewish Prayer and the Yearly Cycle: A List of Articles*, supplement to *Kiryat Sefer* 64 (Jerusalem, 1992–93), and a substantial collection of *addenda* to that publication that appeared together with his facsimile edition of the Hanau

otherwise unknown benedictions that were subsequently forgotten or rejected for halakhic reasons, such as those used in connection with recitations of the *shema*ʻ, collections of Psalms, the Yom Kippur confession, and the second chapter of the mishnaic tractate *Shabbat*; and with the kindling of lights at the onset of the sabbath, and the washing of the hands (three versions) during the *seder* of the first eve of Passover. Scholarly research has been enriched by previously unknown texts of the *qaddish*; the *ʻamidah* for weekdays, sabbaths and festivals; the morning benedictions and the grace after meals (including the sections beginning *ha-raḥaman*); and the references to special days in the body of standard sabbath and festival prayers. There have also been indications of a more extensive usage of Psalms and other biblical verses; novel ceremonials associated with the use of the Torah scroll in the synagogue; a variety of pentateuchal and prophetic lectionaries; and the honorific mention of living personalities in the prayers.

Furthermore, the inclusion of the Ten Commandments and of the Song at the Sea as integral parts of the liturgy, and of mystical and messianic expansions to the *qedushah*, *shema*ʻ, *qiddush*, *havdalah*, and Passover Haggadah, have been newly identified. It has, in addition, been possible to trace the influence of what were clearly the two major rites, that is, those of the Land of Israel and Babylon, on the formation of all later prayer texts, as well as the success that each had in leaving traces of its customs on the traditions and preferences of the other. The use of Hebrew, Aramaic and Judaeo-Arabic has been noted not only in prayers and liturgical poems that had traditionally been expressed in one or other of these particular languages but also in other contexts where the expected language is somewhat surprisingly replaced by one of the others. A rich variety of texts testify to contemporary efforts to utilize Judaeo-Arabic for the transation and interpretation of some regular Hebrew prayers, a well as liturgical poetry.

As far as prayers for individuals are concerned, one appealed to God to bless the twelfth-century Imam, ʼal-Amīr bi-ʼaḥkām Allāh, and read as follows:[37]

> And we pray for the life of our distinguished sovereign lord and Muslim leader . . . commander of the faithful, and for the royal princes and for all the royal family, and for those who devotedly assist the king and for those who do battle for him against his foes.

---

prayer-book of 1628 (eds J. Tabory and M. Rapeld, Ramat Gan, 1994). See also J. Tobi, ʻThe Role of Arabic in Jewish Liturgy and Literature according to the Geniza Textsʼ in *A Century of Geniza Research* (see n. 8 above), pp. 47–70 and R. Langer, *To Worship God Properly: Tensions between Custom and Halakhah in Judaism* (Cincinnati, 1998).

[37] A detailed study of prayers for dignitaries, including T-S NS 110.26, here cited, has been produced by P. B. Fenton, *ʻTefillah Beʻad Ha-Rashut U-Reshut Beʻad Ha-Tefillahʼ*, *Mi-mizraḥ Umi-Maʻarav* 4 (1984), pp. 7–21 and N. Danzig's thorough analysis of the history of the *yequm purqan* prayer appears on pp. 74–122 below. See also M. A. Friedman, ʻR. Yeḥiel b. Elyakim's Responsum Permitting the Reshutʼ in *Mas'at Moshe: Studies in Jewish and Islamic Culture Presented to Moshe Gil*, eds E. Fleischer, M. A. Friedman and J. L. Kraemer (Hebrew; Jerusalem, 1998), pp. 328–67. On liturgical ceremonies around Jerusalem, see H. Ben-Shammai, ʻA Unique Lamentation on Jerusalemʼ and E. Fleischer, ʻPilgrimsʼ Prayer at the Gates of Jerusalemʼ in the Gil *Festschrift* just noted, pp. 93–102 and 298–327.

May Almighty God come to their assistance and to ours, subdue those who arise against us and against them, and inspire them to deal kindly with us and with all his people, the house of Israel, and let us say Amen.

The thousands of folios and hundreds of authors that the Genizah has restored to us have effectively created a whole new field of study. While they once had 40,000 compositions available to them, the enthusiasts for medieval Hebrew poetry now have 150% additional material to contend with. Earlier texts – some on papyrus, perhaps as early as the eighth century – are now available, authorship is better established, and whole new schools of poets have been added to the history of Hebrew verse. We have been made aware of the degree to which the entire literary genre blossomed in geonic Palestine and it has even been suggested that it represented the primary Jewish entertainment of the time. Its main characteristics have been identified and deep insights offered into its aesthetic value. Researchers have described its extensive and complicated rules, its utilization of earlier sources and its assumptions about the high level of literacy on the part of the Jewish community. It is possible to uncover the emergence of a Saadyanic school in Babylon and to identify the linguistic and structural innovations that it daringly made. Comparisons may be made between the style and content of such poems and those composed in places as far away as Byzantium, Italy, North Africa and Spain.[38] One of the most exciting of recent finds relates to an exchange of poetry between the famous tenth-century linguist and poet, Dunash ibn Labraṭ, and his wife.[39]

---

[38] The pioneering work was done by the late M. Zulay, A. M. Habermann, J. Schirmann, S. Spiegel and N. Allony. An excellent introduction to the whole subject, with an extensive bibliography, is Ezra Fleischer's *Hebrew Liturgical Poetry in the Middle Ages* (Hebrew; Jerusalem, 1975) and his own list of publications, prepared by T. Beeri and S. Ben-Ari, is to be found in the Hebrew *Festschrift* edited for him by S. Elizur, M. D. Herr, G. Shaked and A. Shinan entitled *Knesset Ezra: Literature and Life in the Synagogue: Studies Presented to Ezra Fleischer* (Hebrew; Jerusalem, 1994). See especially his Hebrew article 'The Cultural Profile of Eastern Jewry in the Early Middle Ages as reflected by the Payyetanic Texts of the Geniza' in *A Century of Geniza Research* (see n. 8 above), pp. 1–22. See also the work of S. Elizur, as exemplified in her *Poet at a Turning Point: Rabbi Yehoshua bar Khalfa and his Poetry* (Hebrew; Jerusalem, 1994). Outstanding Genizah research on poetry is also currently being done by J. Yahalom; see, for example, the Hebrew volumes *A Collection of Geniza Fragments of Piyyute Yannai* (Jerusalem, 1978); *Liturgical Poems of Shim'on Bar Megas* (Jerusalem, 1984); and *Maḥzor Eretz Israel: A Genizah Codex* (Jerusalem, 1987); and his English volume *Palestinian Vocalised Piyyut Manuscripts in the Cambridge Genizah Collections* (Cambridge, 1997). See also L. Weinberger, *Jewish Hymnography: A Literary History* (London, 1998). The English reader is best advised to consult, as an introductory volume, T. Carmi's *Penguin Book of Hebrew Verse* (Harmondsworth, 1981), at the beginning of which the editor rightly notes that 'scholars are still engaged in the arduous task of processing thousands of manuscripts from the hoard of the Cairo Genizah.'

[39] Fleischer's full treatment of the poem (T-S NS 143.46) was published in Hebrew in his article 'On Dunash Ben Labrat, his Wife and his Son: New Light on the Beginnings of the Hebrew-Spanish School', *Jerusalem Studies in Hebrew Literature* 5 (1984), pp. 189–203. An English summary appeared in *Genizah Fragments* 7 (April, 1984), p. 3.

There is also a whole range of mystical material in the Genizah, called *hekhalot* literature because it purports to describe the celestial palaces. The difficulty here is in dating the origins of these traditions, establishing the precise context in which they were used, and defining how they related to what are regarded as more standard rabbinic works. It is by no means clear whether what is found in the Genizah is a mere remnant of a religious expression once much more powerful and influential or is a move towards the more mystical and spiritual in reaction to the growing centrality of the halakhic voice. Some have argued that these texts represent the devotions of pious individuals and small mystical groups while others prefer to give them a greater communal relevance within the rabbinic practice of the early medieval period. What also remains to be clarified is whether what we are seeing is evidence of borrowings by one set of traditions from another or overlaps within a rabbinic Judaism that was broader than is sometimes credited.[40]

History

The next area to be considered is that of more general historical developments. As non-Muslims, Jews inevitably suffered disabilities at all times and severe persecution on occasion but the dominant theme of the Genizah period, as S. D. Goitein was fond of pointing out, was that of cultural symbiosis.[41] It is now clear that Muslims, Christians and Jews in the oriental countries did not live intellectually ghettoised lives. They were aware of each other's religious texts and traditions, sometimes recording these in their own languages and literatures, and at other times subjecting them to criticism and even derision. In a religious debate with Rabbanites and Karaites conducted at the end of the tenth century, the Fatimid vizier, Ya'qub ibn Killis, a convert from Judaism to Islam, cited the content of the prayer-book of

---

[40] P. Schäfer, *Geniza-fragmente zur Hekhalot Literatur* (Tübingen, 1984); P. B. Fenton, *The Treatise of the Pool* (London, 1981) and *Deux traités de mystique juive* (Lagrasse, 1987); M. Idel, *Kabbalah: New Perspectives* (New Haven and London, 1984); R. Goetschel (ed.), *Prière, Mystique et Judaïsme* (Paris, 1987), especially P. S. Alexander's 'Prayer in the Heikhalot Literature' on pp. 43–64 ; M. Bar-Ilan, *The Mysteries of Jewish Prayer and Hekhalot* (Hebrew; Ramat Gan, 1987); and M. D. Swartz, *Mystical Prayer in Ancient Judaism: An Analysis of Ma'aseh Merkavah* (Tübingen, 1992).

[41] S. D. Goitein, *Jews and Arabs: Their Contacts through the Ages* (London, Melbourne and Henley, 1955); E. I. J. Rosenthal, *Judaism and Islam* (London, 1961); B. Lewis, *The Jews of Islam* (Princeton, 1984); M. R. Cohen and A. L. Udovitch (eds), *Jews among Arabs: Contacts and Boundaries* (Princeton, 1989); N. A. Stillman, *The Jews of Arab Lands: a History and Source Book* (Philadelphia, 1979). For more detailed examination of the social and political status of Jews and Christians under Islam, see Bat Ye'or, *The Dhimmi: Jews and Christians under Islam* (E. T., London, 1985) and *The Decline of Eastern Christianity under Islam: From Jihad to Dhimmitude Seventh–Twentieth Century* (E. T., London, 1996), and P. B. Fenton, 'Interfaith Relations as Reflected in the Genizah Documents', *Bulletin of the Israeli Academic Center in Cairo* 21 (1997), pp. 26–30 and on pp. 152–59 below. For a number of important articles on the Genizah's contribution to more general historical developments, see *Mas'at Moshe* (see n. 37 above) and D. Frank (ed.), *The Jews of Medieval Islam: Community, Society and Identity* (Leiden and New York, 1995)

Sa'adya ben Joseph in order to heap ridicule on the Jewish liturgy.[42] Religious thinkers took account of what was being said and written by the theological opposition, so much so that it is at times possible to reconstruct that opposition by way of the views of such thinkers.[43] Although there was the occasional romantic tryst between a man and woman of different religious allegiance,[44] intermarriage was not a phenomenon of the time. Conversion, however, certainly was, especially on the part of those anxious to climb social and political ladders. Some such converts made life difficult for their former co-religionists while others retained a certain sympathy for them, even engaging them in religious dialogues. But the movement was not always in one direction and there are accounts of Muslim and Christian anger at conversions to Judaism.[45] The records of rabbinical courts make reference to approaches made by non-Jews, women as well as men, who wished to throw in their religious lot with the Jews.[46] The Genizah's most famous and detailed example of a Christian convert to Judaism is, of course, John Dreux of Oppido, Italy, who became Obadiah Ha-Ger.[47] There is also one remarkable Cambridge Genizah document, from the late eleventh century, in which reference is made to a Jewish husband and a Muslim wife. The daughter has been with her impoverished mother but is now offered a better standard of living by her affluent father:[48]

> Now, my daughter, I do not know with whom you are, with the Jews who are the stock of your father, or with the stock of your mother, the Muslims. But this I wish you to

[42] M. R. Cohen and S. Somekh, 'In the Court of Ya'qub ibn Killis: A Fragment from the Cairo Genizah', *Jewish Quarterly Review* 80 (1980), pp. 283–314.

[43] H. Ben-Shammai has, by way of the Genizah data, made interesting studies of the intellectual interchanges between Jews and Muslims, as in his article 'Mediaeval History and Religious Thought' on pp. 136–51 below. The theological tensions between Jews and Christians are well exemplified in the excellent edition of *The Polemic of Nestor the Priest* by D. J. Lasker and S. Stroumsa (Hebrew and English; 2 vols; Jerusalem, 1996).

[44] A remarkable account of a love affair between a Jew and a Christian is to be found in Or.1080 J93; see S. D. Goitein, *A Mediterranean Society*, 6 vols including the index completed by P. Sanders (Berkeley, Los Angeles and London, 1967–93), vol. 5, pp. 314–16 and Reif, *Published Material* (see n. 17 above), p. 406.

[45] On the matter of conversions, see N. Golb, 'Notes on the Conversion of European Christians to Judaism in the Eleventh Century', *Journal of Jewish Studies* 16 (1965), pp. 69–74, especially concerning T-S 12.732; Goitein, *A Mediterranean Society* (see n. 44 above), vol. 2, pp. 299–311; and S. Stroumsa, 'On Jewish Intellectual Converts to Islam in the Early Middle Ages', *Pe'amim* 42 (1990), pp. 61–75.

[46] M. A. Friedman, *Jewish Polygyny* (see n. 32 above), especially pp. 332–39, concerning converts, the subject of T-S G2.66 and T-S 12.232.

[47] Most of the relevant publications are cited by N. Golb in his important article 'The Music of Obadiah the Proselyte and his Conversion', *Journal of Jewish Studies* 18 (1967), pp. 43–63 and the Cambridge Genizah fragments central to the story are T-S K5.41, T-S Misc.35.31, T-S 10K21 and T-S 8.271.

[48] The document is Or.1080 J21 at Cambridge University Library, published in English translation by S. D. Goitein in his 'Parents and Children: A Geniza Study on the Medieval Jewish Family', *Gratz College Annual of Jewish Studies* 4 (1975), pp. 55–57.

know: even if they wanted to sell you to me, who are my own daughter, I would buy you and rescue you from their hands...

The Karaites, for their part, were by no means a minor sect that broke away from rabbinic Judaism and soon declined. Many Genizah texts testify to the considerable success of their religious philosophy, practice and communal life. Starting with Schechter's discovery of the law-book of Anan ben David, the earliest proponent of the movement,[49] a century of research has demonstrated the major role played by the Karaites in the social, economic, cultural and religious development of the Jewish communities of the Near East from the eighth to the twelfth centuries. It is clear that they had a number of doctrines, traditions and linguistic terms that are in tandem with those recorded in the literature uncovered in the Dead Sea scrolls. It therefore seems unlikely that their religious commitments were totally novel and revolutionary. Their identity in the first century or two of their documented activity was by way of smaller groups, sometimes at theological loggerheads and sometimes even within the broader rabbinic structure, but gradually these sects joined forces in an anti-talmudic alliance. This ultimately led to a blossoming of Karaite culture from the tenth to the twelfth centuries, precisely the period best represented in the Genizah texts. Such texts testify to close social relations and even intermarriage, as well as religious differences, between Karaites and Rabbanites. The rabbinic leadership was shamed by the Karaite example into demonstrating that they too had a love for Hebrew and for the Hebrew Bible and the quantity and quality of biblical exegesis became the beneficiaries. Even in the area of religious law, the Karaite concern for fixing their own calendar, for kosher food, for ritual purity, for avoiding marriages between relatives, and for maintaining a fire-free sabbath were strong enough to make a significant impact on rabbinic behaviour. At times, the talmudic Jews felt under pressure to intensify their own strictness while in other cases they positively flaunted their own interpretations.[50]

---

[49] S. Schechter, *Documents of Jewish Sectaries, vol. 2: Fragments of the Book of the Commandments of Anan* (Cambridge, 1910).

[50] J. Mann, *Texts and Studies in Jewish History and Literature* (2 vols; Cincinnati and Philadelphia, 1931–35; and the reprint of Philadelphia/New York, 1991, with G. Cohen's important essay on 'The Reconstruction of Gaonic History'); *Karaite Anthology: Excerpts from the Early Literature*, ed. L. Nemoy (New Haven and London, 1952); Z. Ankori, *Karaites in Byzantium: The Formative Years 970–1100* (New York and Jerusalem, 1959); N. Wieder, *The Judean Scrolls and Karaism* (London, 1962), with an updated reprint currently being planned by the Ben-Zvi Institute in Jerusalem; *Karaite Studies*, ed. P. Birnbaum (New York, 1971); M. Gil, *The Tustaris: Family and Sect* (Hebrew; Tel Aviv, 1981); *Studies in Judaica, Karaitica and Islamica presented to L. Nemoy*, ed. S. R. Brunswick (Ramat Gan, 1982); G. Khan, *Karaite Bible Manuscripts* and M. Polliack, *The Karaite Tradition* (see n. 9 above); J. Olszowy-Schlanger, *Karaite Marriage Documents from the Cairo Geniza: Legal Tradition and Community Life in Mediaeval Egypt and Palestine* (Leiden, 1998); M. Gil, 'Karaite Antiquities' in *A Century of Geniza Research* (see n. 8 above), pp. 71–107; see also nn. 4 and 9 above.

The evidence about the Khazars recovered from manuscripts found in the Genizah has given a jolt to scepticism about the authenticity of the traditions concerning this Jewish kingdom between the Black Sea and the Caspian that apparently flourished from the eighth to the eleventh centuries. There is an account of how Jews settled among the Khazars and influenced them to adopt such customs as circumcision and the sabbath. The Khazarian king is reported to have been influenced by his wife and his Jewish minister to convert to Judaism and to have been criticized by the Christian and Muslim rulers for contemplating such a move. In a text at least a century older than Judah Ha-Levi's *Kuzari*, the tale is told of how leading teachers of Judaism, Christianity and Islam were summoned by the Khazarian king to debate the relative merits of their religions and how the Jewish view was confirmed by sacred texts discovered in a cave. What is more, the correspondence between King Joseph and the diplomat Ḥisdai ibn Shapruṭ is no longer restricted to one letter from the Spanish Jewish nobleman enquiring about the origins of this strange Jewish kingdom, the nature of its religious practice and any information it has about the future of the world, and a reply from the Khazar ruler that covers the conversion, the nature of local Judaism, the royal family and what is to be expected in the coming age. There is now a set of correspondence that has recently been interpreted as relating to Ḥisdai and touching on the Khazars, as well as on aspects of Jewish life in Byzantium, Italy and eastern Europe.[51]

If the Genizah discoveries have illuminated obscure corners of Khazar and Karaite history, they have aimed brilliant flood-lights at what were once the dark expanses of Palestinian Jewish history. From knowing virtually nothing about how the Jews of the homeland conducted their personal, public and intellectual lives in the centuries immediately before and after the Crusader invasion that began in 1099, we now have access to a welter of data about people, places and events. It turns out that the Jews were encouraged to resettle Jerusalem after the Arab conquest of the seventh century and that, despite the difficult economic conditions and political upheavals brought about by competing Muslim claims to the territory, communities grew and flourished. Fragments relate to Ramla as the capital city and to the havoc wreaked there by the terrible earthquake of 1033, to Tyre and Acre as busy sea ports, to Tiberias as a centre of Torah and textiles, and to Ashkelon as a particularly strong fortress.[52] It was

---

[51] The first Cambridge Genizah document to be published in connection with the Khazarian correspondence was T-S Misc.35.38, treated by S. Schechter, 'An Unknown Khazar Document', *Jewish Quarterly Review*, N. S., 3 (1912–13), pp. 181–219. P. Kokovtsov made a major contribution to the field in his Russian publications but there are comprehensive studies in English of the various manuscripts, also including T-S 12.122 (on Kiev), T-S J2.71 and T-S Misc.35.45, by D. M. Dunlop, *The History of the Jewish Khazars* (Princeton, 1954) and by N. Golb and O. Pritsak, *Khazarian Hebrew Documents of the Tenth Century* (Ithaca and London, 1982). A more popular and controversial study of the subject is A. Koestler's *The Thirteenth Tribe* (London, 1976).

[52] For many years, Mann's *The Jews in Egypt and in Palestine under the Fāṭimid Caliphs* (reprinted edition with preface and reader's guide by S. D. Goitein; two volumes in one; New York, 1970) was the most informative guide in English to the history of Palestinian Jewry in

perhaps as a result of the earthquake that part of the synagogal premises of the Palestinian Jews in Ramla was still in a state of ruin in 1039. To obtain funding for repairs and maintenance, the leaders leased part of the property to a private individual, Ṣedaqah, son of Yefet, at an annual rental of half a gold piece.[53] There were of course even more miserable times. During the first half of the eleventh century, for instance, letters refer to the battles between Bedouin insurgents and the Fatimid rulers and provide gruesome details of the robbery, rape and crippling overtaxation suffered by the local Jews.[54]

Later, Jews fought alongside Muslims in a desperate effort to defend the Holy Land against the Crusader attacks and, when they failed, those unable to flee suffered massacres or capture. As some eye-witness accounts relate, major fund-raising efforts had to be made in other Jewish centres to pay the ransoms demanded by some Christians for the release of Jewish prisoners. Those who did escape made their way northwards to the cities of the Lebanese coast or southwards to Egypt and many documents testify to their resilience in maintaining their traditions and their identity for two or three centuries. Jews even survived in small groups in Crusader Palestine, returned with Saladin in 1187 in larger numbers, and were strengthened by *`aliyah* from western Europe.[55] The later history of Palestinian Jewry is also documented in the Genizah. There are details of places of pilgrimage and accounts of the major settlements in Jerusalem and Safed in the sixteenth century. It emerges that financial assistance and spiritual encouragement were provided by the leaders of Egyptian Jewry well into the sixteenth century and there is correspondence that refers to major rabbinic figures such as Joseph Karo and Isaac Luria.[56]

---

the Genizah period. It has now, however, been overtaken by the remarkably comprehensive treatment of the sources produced by M. Gil in *A History of Palestine 634–1099* (Cambridge, 1992; based on the original 3-volume Hebrew edition, *Palestine during the First Muslim Period (634–1099)*, Tel Aviv, 1983).

[53] Gil, *Palestine* (Hebrew edition), vol. 2, pp. 419–20 on Add. 3358 (see n. 52 above).

[54] *War and Society in the Eastern Mediterranean, 7th–15th Centuries*, ed. Y. Lev (Leiden, New York and Köln, 1997), especially Elinoar Bareket's contribution 'Personal Adversities of Jews during the Period of the Fatimid Wars in Eleventh Century Palestine', pp. 153–62.

[55] S. Assaf, *Texts and Studies* (Hebrew; Jerusalem, 1946); J. Braslavi, *Studies in our Country: Its Past and Remains* (Hebrew; Tel Aviv, 1954); J. Prawer, *The Latin Kingdom of Jerusalem* (London, 1972); S. D. Goitein, *Palestinian Jewry in Early Islamic and Crusader Times in the Light of the Geniza Documents* (Hebrew; Jerusalem, 1980); J. Prawer (ed.), *The History of Jerusalem: The Early Islamic Period 638–1099* (Hebrew; Jerusalem, 1987); J. Prawer and H. Ben-Shammai (eds), *The History of Jerusalem: Crusaders and Ayyubids (1099–1250)* (Hebrew; Jerusalem, 1991).

[56] Immigration and pilgrimage to the Holy Land during the classical Genizah period is again dealt with by Gil in his *History of Palestine* (see n. 52 above), pp. 609–31. There are numerous accounts of the general phenomenon during the late medieval and early modern periods; see, for example, on the Jewish side H. M. Adler, *The Itinerary of Benjamin of Tudela* (London, 1907) and on the Christian side H. F. M. Prescott, *Jerusalem Journey: Pilgrimage to the Holy Land in the Fifteenth Century* (London, 1954) and *Once to Sinai: The Further Pilgrimage of Friar Felix Fabri* (London, 1957). For details of a journey, see T-S Misc.22.277 and special prayers are included in T-S Ar.53.2. The redisovery of the village of Kefar Marus through the Genizah documentation is reported in *Genizah Fragments* 8

Interestingly, neither Babylon, which ultimately succeeded in imposing its halakhic authority on most of the Jewish world, nor the community of the Holy Land which long maintained a major influence in and around the eastern Mediterranean, could retain control over the expanding communities of Egypt, North Africa (including the 'bridging' Mediterranean island of Sicily) and Spain. They left indelible marks on the fabric of Jewish religious life and struggled competitively to maintain their authority in these centres but, after the political deterioration in Palestine and the decline of the Babylonian gaonate, the situation underwent considerable change. While allegiance had previously been owed to the Babylonian and Palestinian academies and no move had been made without reference to their spiritual mentors, the western or Maghrebi communities came of age during the classical Genizah period and developed enough confidence to make their own decisions. Documents relating to such centres as Qayrawan in Tunisia and Andalusian Spain, and making mention of their personalities and institutions, demonstrate without doubt their new powers not only in the social, economic and political fields but also, concomitantly, as Jewish religious trend-setters. This is not to say that these communities themselves were free from persecution and could enjoy unhampered development. The rising power of Muslim fanaticism in Spain and North Africa brought their golden ages to an end in due course but not before they had left a remarkable literary and documentary heritage.[57] Fortunately for lovers of

(October, 1984), p. 4 and the relevant fragments are T-S K21.69, T-S Ar.49.164 and T-S AS 74.25 and 227. Details of Jewish connections between later Egypt and Palestine are given by Abraham David in *Genizah Fragments* 15 (April,1988), p. 2, on the basis of Or.1080 J193 and T-S 13J24.21. For references to Joseph Karo, see *Genizah Fragments* 8 (October, 1984), p. 2 and the original Genizah manuscripts T-S Misc.10.80 and T-S 13J24.28, while Luria's business ventures are documented in T-S 12.589 which was published by E. J. Worman, 'Un Document concernant Isaac Louria', *Revue des Etudes Juives* 57 (1909), pp. 281–82. Hebrew publications include E. Reiner, 'Pilgrims and Pilgrimage to Eretz Yisrael 1099–1517' (doctoral dissertation, Hebrew University of Jerusalem, 1988); Z., Ilan and E. Damati, *Meroth: The Ancient Jewish Village* (Hebrew; Tel Aviv, 1987); M. E. Artom and A. David, *From Italy to Jerusalem: The Letters of Rabbi Obadiah of Bertinoro from the Land of Israel* (Ramat Gan, 1997); A. David's article on T-S Misc.22.277 in *Sefer Bar-Adon* (*Yisrael 'Am Va-'Areṣ* 7–8; Tel Aviv, 1994), pp. 223–30 and his 'The Involvement of the later Nagids of Egypt in the Affairs of the Jewish Community in Eretz-Israel' in *A Century of Geniza Research* (see n. 8 above), pp. 293–332; and his Hebrew volume *Immigration and Settlement in the Land of Israel in the 16th Century* (Jerusalem, 1993).

[57] On the competing claims to leadership by the Palestinian, Babylonian and Egyptian Jews, and the development of other centres, see the volumes by Mann and Gil earlier mentioned, as well as H. Malter, *Saadia Gaon: His Life and Works* (Philadelphia, 1921); M. R. Cohen, *Jewish Self-Government in Medieval Egypt: The Origins of the Office of Head of the Jews, ca. 1065–1126* (Princeton, 1980); A. Grossman, *The Babylonian Exilarchate in the Geonic Period* (Hebrew; Jerusalem, 1984); E. Bareket, *The Jewish Leadership in Fustat in the First Half of the Eleventh Century* (Hebrew; Tel Aviv, 1995), *The Jews of Egypt 1007–1055* (Hebrew; Jerusalem, 1995) and *Fustat on the Nile: The Jewish Elite in Medieval Egypt* (Leiden, Boston and Köln, 1999), as well as her supplementary article 'The Jewish Leadership in Fustat in the First Half of the Eleventh Century', *Michael* 14 (1997), pp. 77–88; M. Ben-Sasson, *The Jews of Sicily 825–1068: Documents and Sources* (Hebrew;

Jewish history, the movement of the relevant populations, in the case of both the Palestinian and the Maghrebi centres, was in the direction of Egypt, where Cairo was ready to become the new hub of Jewish political, socio-economic and religious activity and the Genizah depository was waiting to absorb their remarkable records.

These records include clearer and more personal accounts of the lives and literary activity of some of medieval Jewry's most outstanding figures. Although no Genizah fragment has been identified as containing the actual handwriting of Sa'adya, there are hundreds that record his work and clearly demonstrate that he was the pioneer in a number of fields. He offered new translations and commentaries of the Hebrew Bible and composed the first comprehensive anthology of Jewish prayer and poetry. He introduced a new type of halakhic literature that devoted single monographs to individual subjects and he was responsible for pioneering developments in the Jewish use of Hebrew and Judaeo-Arabic, the study of grammar, the presentation of Jewish religious thought, and the systematic chronicling of Jewish legal procedure. Above all, the few inaccurate pieces of information about Sa'adya's life that circulated among the learned in the nineteenth century have now been replaced by more reliable data from the Genizah. Sa`adya emerges as a powerful polemicist who engaged in controversies not only with the local Babylonian leadership but also with the Jews of the Land of Israel in the matter of the calendar, with the Karaites on the subject of Jewish theology, and with sceptical intellectuals regarding the validity of the Hebrew Bible. He broadened the intellectual horizons of the Babylonian gaonate and greatly extended its political influence. Given the rich texture of his life, and the prolific nature of his literary productivity, it is not surprising that hardly a month passes without the discovery of some new Genizah text relating to his personal and scholarly activities.[58]

Jerusalem, 1991) and *The Emergence of the Local Jewish Community in the Muslim World: Qayrawan 800–1057* (Hebrew; Jerusalem^2, 1997); M. Gil, *In the Kingdom of Ishmael* (Hebrew; 4 vols; Tel Aviv and Jerusalem, 1997); see also, more generally, M. Ben-Sasson, 'Cairo Genizah Treasures and their Contribution to Jewish Historiography', *Bulletin of the Israeli Academic Center in Cairo* 21 (1997), pp. 3–12 and J. S. Gerber, 'My Heart is in the East' in *The Illustrated History of the Jewish People*, ed. N. R. M. de Lange (Toronto, 1997), pp. 141–97. Much Genizah material is cited by E. Ashtor in his *The Jews of Moslem Spain* (3 vols; Philadelphia, 1973–84, based on the Hebrew edition of 1960–66) and the subject is well summarized by J. S. Gerber, *The Jews of Spain* (New York, 1992). On the medieval history of Maghrebi Jewry, see H. Z. Hirschberg, *History of the Jews in North Africa* (2 vols; Leiden, 1974–80, based on the Hebrew edition of Jerusalem, 1965).

[58] S. Schechter, *Saadyana: Geniza Fragments of Writings of R. Saadya Gaon and Others* (Cambridge, 1903); H. Malter, *Saadia Gaon: His Life and Works* (Philadelphia, 1921); S. Skoss, *Saadia Gaon: The Earliest Hebrew Grammarian* (Philadelphia, 1955); Brody, *The Geonim of Babylonia* (see n. 24 above). Among the most important Hebrew reconstructions of his works that make significant use of Genizah material are *Siddur R. Saadja Gaon* (see n. 36 above); the publications of M. Zucker and Y. Ratzaby noted in n. 11 above; and N. Allony, *Ha-'egron* (Jerusalem, 1969). Currently in the press is an edition of his systematic chronicling of Jewish legal procedure *Sefer Ha-Sheṭarot* (*Book of Testimonies and Decrees*) by M. Ben-Sasson and R. Brody (see n. 34 above). The 1995 conference of the Society for

Another distinguished medieval Jew whose life has been remarkably illuminated by the manuscripts from Cairo is the poet and philosopher from Muslim Spain, Judah Ha-Levi. More than a thousand Genizah fragments provide not only additional texts of his poetry but also details of his stay in Egypt towards the end of his life. It was always well known that he set out from his native Andalusia on a pilgrimage to the Holy Land, where he expected to spend his last days, but it has now become clear that he stopped off in Egypt for a few months early in 1141 and enjoyed a remarkable period of local acclaim and poetic productivity. He was the guest of honour at many soirées and he penned a number of lyrical compositions in honour of his patrons. Such patrons were among the most distinguished leaders of Cairene Jewry in the political, judical and commercial fields and their papers, preserved in the Genizah, provide the details of Ha-Levi's stay in Egypt. Contrary to what tradition tells us about his ultimate settlement in the Jewish homeland, might he perhaps have ended his days in Egypt in a dizzy spell of parties? Thanks to the eagle eye of Shelomo Dov Goitein, the story is now known to have a more romantic ending. In a small fragment of a few lines that he found in Cambridge in 1975, Goitein was able to decipher the name of the famous poet and the information that he set sail eastwards from Alexandria on 14 May, 1141, presumably arriving in Palestine within ten days. That would have given him a month to visit the holy sites before his death in July, a pilgrimage by him that is hinted at, if not clearly spelt out, in another Genizah text. Apparently, then, his 'Zionist' ambitions, so clearly expressed in his writings, were finally realized.[59]

Long before the Genizah discoveries were made, Maimonides was regarded as one of Jewish history's greatest figures. That such a reputation was well deserved has become clearer as some sixty fragments in his own handwriting and others closely relating to him have surfaced among the Cairo treasures. Folios from draft copies of his *Commentary on the Mishnah*, his *Mishneh Torah* and his *Guide for the Perplexed* show him at work and reveal some of his thought-patterns, particularly concerning the order in which he presented his material, the extent to which he justified his views by reference to earlier sources, and the terminology that he employed. That he found time not only for composing three of medieval Judaism's most famous text-books but also much else besides is convincingly demonstrated by the fragments from the Ben Ezra synagogue.[60] As a medical expert who ran clinics in the Islamic court of what

---

Judaeo-Arabic Studies held in Strasbourg was devoted to 'Saadiah Gaon: Pioneer of Judaeo-Arabic' and the proceedings are now being prepared for publication by P. B. Fenton.

[59] Goitein, *A Mediterranean Society* (see n. 44 above), vol. 5, pp. 448–50, 464–65 and his article 'The Biography of Rabbi Juda Ha-Levi in the Light of the Cairo Geniza Documents', *Proceedings of the American Academy for Jewish Research* 28 (1959), pp. 41–56; E. Fleischer, '"The Essence of our Land and its Meaning": Towards a Portrait of Judah Halevi on the basis of Geniza Documents', *Pe'amim* 68 (1996), pp. 4–15; J. Yahalom, on pp. 123–35 below. The fragment about Ha-Levi's voyage to Palestine, T-S AS 146.6, was published by Goitein, 'Did Yehuda Halevi Arrive in the Holy Land?', *Tarbiz* 46 (1977), pp. 245–50.

[60] Details of the Maimonides autographs are to be found in S. D. Sassoon's list in the introduction to *Maimonidis Commentarius in Mischnam*, ed. R. Edelmann (Hafniae, 1956),

was then New Cairo (while possibly finding occasional spiritual solitude in its impressive library), he was much in demand for specialist opinion, as well as consultations and prescriptions, and there are even a few survivors from his medical library. One lengthy letter contains many compliments about Rambam's skill as a physician and begs him to agree, regardless of the amount of fees involved, to take on as a student the writer's own son.[61] The majority of enquiries addressed to him were of course on matters of Jewish law. Rushed off his feet with professional, literary and communal commitments, Rambam could rarely do more than append a brief decision to the foot of the enquiry but the survival of hundreds of such responsa indicate that he dealt efficiently with many of the questions addressed to him.[62] It turns out that his rise to fame and power in Cairo was due at least in part to his marriage into a local family and his successful mounting of a fund-raising campaign that permitted the ransom of a large number of Jewish captives. We also now have texts that spell out his appointment as the official head of the Jewish community (*ra'is al-yahud*) and that testify to his brother David's last journey before he was drowned on a business trip in the Indian Ocean.[63] There is also the description of a meeting with the great

---

with facsimiles in plates XX–LXI, with addenda provided by S. A. Hopkins, 'A New Autograph Fragment of Maimonides' *Hilkhot Ha-Yerushalmi*', *Journal of Semitic Studies* 38 (1983), pp. 273–96, which deals with Genizah fragments T-S Ar.34.169 and T-S F17.7a. For a general bibliography of publications on Maimonides in the European languages, see D. R. Lachterman, 'Maimonidean Studies 1950–86', *Maimonidean Studies* 1 (1990), pp. 197–216.

[61] The appeal to Maimonides to accept the writer's son as a medical student is in T-S 16.291 and has been edited and translated by J. L. Kraemer in his 'Six Unpublished Maimonides Letters from the Cairo Genizah', *Maimonidean Studies* 2 (1991), pp. 73–80 while his text on sexual potency is to be found in T-S Ar.44.79, as described by H. D. Isaacs and C. F. Baker, *Medical and Para-Medical Manuscripts in the Cambridge Genizah Collections* (Cambridge, 1994), p. 47. On the matter of solitude, see S. Harvey, 'Maimonides in the Sultan's Palace' in *Perspectives on Maimonides: Philosophical and Historical Studies*, ed. J. L. Kraemer (Oxford, 1991), pp. 47–75.

[62] For some examples of letters and decisions by Maimonides, see Kraemer's article (see n. 61 above) and also his 'Maimonides' Letters Yield their Secrets' *Genizah Fragments* 16 (1988), pp. 3–4 and 'Two Letters of Maimonides from the Cairo Geniza', *Maimonidean Studies* 1 (1990), pp. 87–98; see also Goitein *A Mediterranean Society* (see n. 44 above), vol. 2, pp. 159–61 and M. A. Friedman, 'Social Realities in Egypt and Maimonides' Rulings on Family Law' in *Sobre la Vida y Obra de Maimonides: I Congresso Internacional (Cordoba, 1985)*, ed. J. P. del Rosal (Cordova, 1991), pp. 177–86. The famous fragment containing his recommendation for Isaac al-Dar'i is T-S 12.192, one of the two letters edited by Kraemer in 1990. Blau's edition of *R. Moses b. Maimon: Responsa* (see n. 33 above) is an essential reference tool.

[63] Details of the biography of Maimonides supplied by Genizah material are provided by S. D. Goitein, *Letters of Medieval Jewish Traders* (Princeton, 1973), pp. 207–12 and 'Moses Maimonides, Man of Action: A Revision of the Master's Biography in Light of the Geniza Documents', in *Hommage à Georges Vajda*, eds G. Nahon and C. Touati (Louvain, 1980), pp. 155–67; and M. Ben-Sasson, 'Maimonides in Egypt: The First Stage', *Maimonidean Studies* 2 (1991), pp. 3–30. The four fragments concerning his ransom, appointment, brother David and friendly meeting are T-S 16.9, T-S J2.78, Or.1081 J1 and T-S 8J14.18.

leader that was singularly friendly. The visitor was warmly received and entertained with lemon cakes while his little son was amused by the leader's son, Abraham.[64]

Daily Life

The Genizah texts are also uniquely qualified to provide insights into the lives of the average individuals of yesteryear and the topics covered range across a wide spectrum of mundane matters, often correcting widespread misapprehensions about the true nature of practical Jewish life a thousand years ago.[65] Marital arrangements, for instance, were by no means always controlled by the male to the detriment of the female. It seems that when Rabbanites married Karaites, it was possible to make an agreement whereby each side agreed not to offend the religious susceptibilities of the other. In one such marriage, between the Karaite woman, Nesi'ah, daughter of Moses, and the leading Rabbanite, David, son of Daniel, the *ketubbah*, dated 1082, stipulates precisely how she will behave in religious matters. She will not violate her Karaite customs by sitting with him and enjoying the sabbath lights, nor will she eat that part of the animal's tail that is permitted by Rabbanite law. As far as the calendar is concerned, she refuses to profane any day declared to be a festival by her sect, but she does agree to observe his religious holidays too.[66] The conditions set by the bride, Fa'iza, the daughter of Solomon, in Fustat in 1047, identify her and her family as people who knew what they wanted from the bridegroom, Ṭuvia, son of Eli, and were obviously very much concerned that he might not be able to meet their standards. The central part of his declaration makes interesting reading[67]:

> I shall behave towards her in the way that fine Jews behave towards their decent wives...I shall associate with good men and not corrupt ones. I shall not bring home licentious individuals, buffoons, frivolous men, and good-for-nothings. I shall not enter the home of anyone attracted to licentious behaviour, to corruption and to revolting activities. I shall not associate with them in eating, drinking or any other activity. I

---

[64] P. B. Fenton, 'A Meeting with Maimonides', *Bulletin of the School of Oriental and African Studies* 45 (1982), pp. 1–4, with two plates. For a general bibliography of publications on Maimonides in Hebrew, see B. Ben-Shammai, 'Twenty-Five years of Maimonides Research: a Bibliography 1965–80', *Maimonidean Studies* 2 (1991), Hebrew section, pp. 17–42.

[65] Except where otherwise indicated, much of the information given here about daily life is based on Goitein's classic set of volumes *A Mediterranean Society* (see n. 44 above).

[66] The topic of marriage is discussed in Goitein, *A Mediterranean Society* (see n. 44 above), vol. 1, pp. 48–49 and in vol. 3, pp. 47–159, especially pp. 55–61, and some important fragments are T-S 18J4.5, T-S 20.6, T-S 13J25.20 and T-S 12.175. The 'mixed' Karaite-Rabbanite marriage, T-S 24.1, was already dealt with by Schechter in *Jewish Quarterly Review* 13 (1901), pp. 218–21 and is noted by Goitein in *A Mediterranean Society* (see n. 44 above), vol. 3, p. 158. On marriage, see M. A. Friedman, *Jewish Marriage* (see n. 32 above), especially vol. 1, pp. 312–46 and 379–450, and vol. 2, pp. 1–88, and his *Jewish Polygyny* (see n. 32 above); as well as pp. 160–77 below.

[67] The conditions extracted from Ṭuvia, son of Eli, recorded in T-S 20.160, are fully discussed and translated by Friedman in his article 'Pre-Nuptial Agreements: A Geniza Study', *Diné Israel* 6 (1975), pp. cxi–cxiv, and noted by Goitein in *A Mediterranean Society* (see n. 44 above), vol. 3, p. 157.

> shall not purchase a slave-girl for myself, as long as this Fa'iza is my wife, unless she explicitly consents. I shall not leave Fustat, Egypt, to travel abroad, unless she specifically agrees.

Other, more unfortunate women, were delighted to have the opportunity to marry at all. In a case brought before the rabbinic court of David, son of Abraham and grandson of Maimonides, a woman agreed that her future husband should retain the right to have other wives. She felt obligated to him for having rescued her from her Arab captors by paying a ransom and was obviously aware that her bargaining position had been weakened by the fact that they had raped her, together with a number of other Jewish women, during captivity.[68] There was an even sadder ending to another story which began with the husband giving his very attractive wife a conditional divorce to be activated if he failed to return from a trip abroad. After his lengthy absence, she took advantage of his offer and married a man with more opportunity to stay at home. When the first husband heard of this, he returned home and, in the physical confrontation that followed, both men and the woman met their deaths.[69] It should not be imagined that all women functioned only as housewives. Some provided medical services for other women while others specialized in wholesale dealing, in the sale of flour, in the teaching of embroidery, in book sales, or in the making of perfumes.[70] One of the most remarkable was Karima ('dear one'), daughter of 'Ammar, popularly known as Wuḥsha ('Desirée'), who was independently minded enough to make her own way in the commercial world, to fight for her financial rights in business deals, and to build up a large fortune as a banker.[71]

Whatever financial backing they enjoyed, some marriages encountered problems that involved them in litigation, as is documented by many of the court records preserved in the Genizah. One woman complained to the authorities that in fifteen years of married life she had not only received neither gifts, jewellery nor clothes from her husband but that he distressed and beat her, and said that he would divorce her only if she renounced her rights to a settlement. Another unfortunate wife, in a bitter letter to her uncle, bewails the treatment she is receiving from her husband and her mother-in-law. Husbands too sometimes had cause for complaint and some

---

[68] Friedman deals with the court record relating to the rape victim, T-S 8K13.11, in *Jewish Polygyny* (see n. 32 above), pp. 95–106.

[69] Details of this *crime passionnel*, reported in T-S 8.111, are in Goitein, *A Mediterranean Society* (see n. 44 above), vol. 3, pp. 80–81.

[70] Goitein summarizes the broad activities of women in *A Mediterranean Society* (see n. 44 above), vol. 3, pp. 312–59 and interesting examples of the professions they pursued are to be found in T-S 24.76, T-S 16.22, T-S 12.493, T-S 20.175 and T-S NS 320.7.

[71] Goitein, 'A Jewish Business Woman of the Eleventh Century', *Seventy-Fifth Anniversary Volume of the Jewish Quarterly Review*, eds A. A. Neuman and S. Zeitlin (Philadelphia, 1967), pp. 225–47 and in *A Mediterranean Society* (see n. 44 above), vol. 3, pp. 346–52, the details derived from Add. 3420d, T-S 8J5.5, T-S Ar.4.5, T-S 10J7.10, T-S Misc.8.102 and T-S AS 145.3.

threatened to run off without divorcing their wives, leaving them in a state of marital limbo (*'agunah*), neither divorced nor living with a husband. One unhappy man made such a threat in the context of a demand to the head of his community for a judgement that would release him from some of the financial burden involved in making a settlement. He claimed that the marriage had been arranged against his will and that his wife's character and behaviour were so intolerable that three years with her had seemed to him like twenty. And now the final straw had been the arrival of his mother-in-law![72] One strong-minded woman was appalled by her husband's absence from home and the news that he might be contemplating a trip to Turkey. Writing on behalf of the whole family, both male and female, she lectured him in no uncertain terms about the damage that would be done to their reputation if he indulged in such foolish travel and how such behaviour would adversely affect the marriage prospects of their single daughter. A distinguished member of the community such as he should rejoin his family and if the reason for his reluctance to return was related to tax problems, she suggested the name of an expert who could offer him sound advice in this connection.[73]

In the fields of education and synagogal matters, some women exercised an influence on arrangements. One lady of the house, clearly something of a matriarch, and a shrewd one at that, took the trouble of sending a Ḥanukkah gift to her grandchild's private tutor. A mother and grandmother made a generous donation to the community on condition that their son/grandson would be invited to undertake the public reading of the Esther scroll on the feast of Purim and drew up a legal document to that effect, not only to protect their investment, as it were, but also to ensure that the arrangement could not be cancelled by the boy's father.[74] As far as boys were concerned, educational activity at home was soon complemented by attendance at school and the story there was apparently just as often one of naughtiness as of diligence. A scribbled note from a rather cross teacher informed the father of little Abu el-Ḥassan that his son had at first been most conscientious but that

---

[72] The wife/husband relationship receives Goitein's attention in *A Mediterranean Society* (see n. 44 above), vol. 3, pp. 160–223, with the two bitter complaints to be found in T-S 8J22.27 and T-S 10J9.13 noted by him on pp. 186 and 175–76. Fragments that shed light on cases of wives being abandoned include T-S 12.179, T-S 18J2.10 and Or.1080 J7, as discussed in *A Mediterranean Society*, vol. 1, p. 58, and the dissatisfied husband, whose appeal is recorded in T-S 8J14.2, occurs in *A Mediterranean Society,* vol. 3, p. 204. For a detailed study of women's letters from the Genizah, see J. L. Kraemer's article on pp. 178–216 below.

[73] F. Kobler included a translation of the angry wife's letter (T-S 13J21.10) in his *Letters of Jews Throughout the Ages* (London, 1953), vol. 1, pp. 233–34, based on Mann's text in *The Jews in Egypt* (see n. 52 above), vol. 1, p. 242, but this is supplemented by the comments of J. L. Kraemer, 'Spanish Ladies from the Cairo Geniza', *Mediterranean Historical Review* 6 (1991), pp. 247–48.

[74] One of the most important studies of educational material in the Genizah is Goitein's article 'Side Lights on Jewish Education from the Cairo Geniza', *Gratz College Anniversary Volume* (=*GCAV*), eds I. D. Passow and S. T. Lachs (Philadelphia, 1971), pp. 83–110. The Purim reference (T-S NS J2) is cited there on pp. 92–99 and the Ḥanukkah gift (T-S 12.425) is reported in Goitein, *A Mediterranean Society* (see n. 44 above), vol. 2, p. 188.

one of the class, egged on by the others, had soon put to a stop to this by breaking the newcomer's writing board. One teacher had to admit that he had smacked his pupil excessively, and that if he had been a more robust child he might even have punished him more, but all to no avail.[75] Some teachers had taken up the profession as impoverished immigrants and perhaps it was they who suffered most from the late payment of fees. There is certainly no lack of evidence for such tardy settlement of educational bills and Goitein's translation of one fragment exemplifies one such sad situation, as described in a letter from a teacher to the communal treasurer regarding the fees of the orphans in his school:[76]

> I now ask your excellency to kindly give an order to pay me their fees so that I should have something to spend for the holidays. I might perhaps like to taste a piece of meat, for I have not bought meat more than eight times from last Pentecost to this Pentecost. God knows that I would not have mentioned this to my lord, had I not known that my lord does not tolerate such a state of affairs.

Despite individual cases to the contrary, travel was the exception rather than the rule for scholars and for the many craftsmen and artisans – represented in as many as 250 different trades – then living in the Egyptian Jewish community.[77] Businessmen, on the other hand, had to travel the length and breadth of the Mediterranean, and also undertook voyages across the Indian Ocean, to make their livings. Such trips not only involved painful separations, sometimes even for a number of years; they also carried all the dangers associated with any form of travel in those turbulent times.[78] Wide varieties of goods, ranging from bales of cloth, through animal hides and articles of clothing, to items of food and drink, were imported and exported by the Jewish merchants of Cairo (sometimes women as well as men).[79] Their primary concern was not with particular commodities but with anything that could keep their capital working for them. As one entrepreneur put it, 'Do not leave a single penny idle...buy when God gives you the chance and export on the first ship to set sail.'[80]

---

[75] The report about the failure of excessive physical punishment to make any impact, in the text of T-S 8J28.7, is translated by Goitein in *GCAV* (see n. 77 above), p. 91, together with the story of poor Abu el-Ḥassan's broken board (T-S Ar.53.65) on p. 92.

[76] The complaint about non-payment of fees (British Library, Or.5542.23) is translated by Goitein on pp.96–97 of the article in *GCAV* (see n. 74 above).

[77] This estimate is offered by Ben-Sasson, 'Cairo Genizah Treasures' (see n. 57 above), p. 9.

[78] The whole subject is dealt with by Goitein in *A Mediterranean Society* (see n. 44 above), vol. 1, pp. 273–352 and among the most important fragments are: T-S 13J36.6, T-S 8J19.27, T-S NS J3, T-S 10J17.18, T-S 10J18.1, T-S 13J20.25, T-S 8J28.12, T-S 24.78 and T-S 20.113. The most vivid description of a shipwreck occurs in T-S 12.114, David Kaufmann Collection XI and T-S 16.54; see Goitein, *A Mediterranean Society,* vol. 1, p. 321.

[79] For a survey of the range of medieval Jewish trade in the Mediterranean as known from the Genizah source, see Goitein, *A Mediterranean Society* (see n. 44 above), vol. 1, pp. 75–147 and 148–272.

[80] Notes advising broad commercial activities and concerning a businessman's lack of ready cash are in T-S 8J41.2, T-S 20.180, David Kaufmann Collection XXVIII and Dropsie

Honesty and trust between partners was not untypical of business life since joint commercial ventures were sometimes a feature of relations between groups or families for a number of generations. There were even cases where Jews and Muslims who were partners arranged for profits made on the sabbath to be directed only to the latter.[81] When David ben Solomon wished to move a huge amount of capital (600 pieces of silver) from Cairo to Qayrawan in 1267, he asked his friend Isaac ben Abraham to take the money as a loan from him in Egypt and to repay it to him later in the Tunisian city.[82] Payment by cheque rather than by cash was also a procedure adopted in the Genizah period. The dealer deposited his cash with a banker or broker and made his payment by writing on a piece of paper the sum in Coptic numerals and Arabic words that the banker was to pay the specified bearer, together with the date, and a biblical verse intended to ward off any attempt at fraud![83] From some accounting records, it is clear that, in twelfth-century Egypt, one column was used for debits and another for credits, at least two centuries before this procedure was adopted in Italy and became generally standard.[84] A letter written from Alexandria to Qayrawan in 1052 reports that, in view of the unstable situation, the writer has just buried some cash in the earth. He knows that this will horrify his astute business associate, in this case his brother, who prefers to have his money working for him, but he claims that he would rather have criticism on this score than censure for losing the money.[85]

As far as tax is concerned, Jews were doubly unfortunate since every non-Muslim was required by Islamic law to pay the government an annual poll tax of two dinars (as much as a low monthly wage), simply for existing, and as an indication of his inferior status. Jews from other countries were also obliged to make this payment and there was even a special office to deal with those from the Land of Israel and its environs then resident in Egypt.[86] A young man wrote to his mother of an incident one Sunday morning. As he set out on a journey, a policeman challenged him: 'Do you intend to depart, still in possession of the government's unpaid poll tax? I shall

College (now Center for Judaic Studies at the University of Pennsylvania) 389; see Goitein, *A Mediterranean Society* (see n. 44 above), vol. 1, p. 200.

[81] Relations between partners is covered in Goitein, *A Mediterranean Society* (see n. 44 above), vol. 1, pp. 164–83 and it is P. B. Fenton who draws attention to the matter of sabbath profits in 'Interfaith Relations' (see n. 41 above), p. 26; see also his article on pp. 152–59 below.

[82] The movement of capital from Cairo to Qayrawan is reflected in the notarized document T-S 12.515, published by Mann, *Texts and Studies* (see n. 50 above), vol. 1, pp. 360–61.

[83] Remnants of medieval cheques are located in T-S Ar.30.184 and noted in Goitein, *A Mediterranean Society* (see n. 44 above), vol. 1, p. 241.

[84] The relevance of the Genizah to the history of accounting has been demonstrated by M. Scorgie in his comments on T-S NS 321.7a and similar fragments in *Genizah Fragments* 29 (April, 1995), p. 2, based on his articles in *Accounting Business and Financial History* and in *Accounting Historians' Journal*, both in 1994.

[85] On the matter of the burial of cash, see T-S 13J26.9 (Goitein, *A Mediterranean Society* (see n. 44 above), vol. 1, p. 265).

[86] Aspects of tax problems and related incidents are provided by Goitein in *A Mediterranean Society* (see n. 44 above), vol. 1, pp. 64 and 300, and vol. 2, pp. 95–96 and 380–94.

not leave you until you accompany me to the police station.'[87] Often the community made the payment on behalf of especially needy or worthy individuals as part of its general policy of social welfare, sometimes reserving anonymity for some recipients of charity in order to maintain their dignity.[88] Another, and even more urgent drain on communal resources was the cost of ransoming captives. These sad victims had not only to be ransomed but also clothed, maintained and sent home. Meanwhile, the Muslim government insisted on receiving the poll tax and port duty on behalf of each of them.[89]

As far as synagogal affairs are concerned, the manuscripts from medieval Egypt reveal that the Babylonian and Palestinian congregations in Fustat vied with each other for new members, the former boasting of the honours they gave to visitors and the fine cantors they engaged, while the latter parried with claims that they had more attractive Bibles and Torah scrolls (as well as beautiful carpets), that their services were shorter, and that young boys were permitted to take part in the services.[90] At times, the tensions about which liturgical rites were more authoritative grew so great that representations were made to the Muslim caliphate requesting a ruling.[91] There are reports of brawls, of disgust with lascivious behaviour, and of congregants being banned as persistent troublemakers. A letter from Ramla in 1052 reports a physical fight on Yom Kippur between Jews from Tyre and others from Tiberias, which had to be halted by the police.[92] A beadle is accused of conducting himself like a 'boss' and not as a servant of the congregation. Another is upbraided for permitting his whole family of fifteen souls to take up full board and residence on the synagogue premises, and for even allowing them to play with pigeons (breeding and racing them?) on the

---

[87] The account of the Sunday morning arrest is in T-S 13J16.10. Other relevant fragments are T-S 20.174, T-S 13J36.2, T-S 10J17.20, Or.1080 J87 and T-S 12.289.

[88] The general theme of charity is closely studied by M. Gil in his *Documents of the Jewish Pious Foundations from the Cairo Geniza* (Leiden, 1976) and Mark Cohen is currently preparing a volume on communal payments for charitable purposes that are recorded in the Genizah texts.

[89] The ransoming of captives is touched upon by Mann, *Texts and Studies* (see n. 50 above), vol. 2, pp. 344–45 and by Goitein in *A Mediterranean Society* (see n. 44 above), vol. 1, pp. 329–30, vol. 2, pp. 137–38, and vol. 5, pp. 373–76 and 462–64. The primary Genizah sources are T-S 13J34.3, T-S 10J24.9, T-S 12.238 and T-S 16.9.

[90] The particular tensions between Babylonian and Palestinian communities, such as those reflected in T-S 13J26.24, T-S 18J4.12, Alliance Israélite Universelle VII.A.17 and Dropsie College (now Center for Judaic Studies at the University of Pennsylvania) 354, are treated in Goitein, *A Mediterranean Society* (see n. 44 above), vol. 2, p. 52 and *Palestinian Jewry in Early Islamic and Crusader Times in the Light of the Geniza Documents* (Hebrew; Jerusalem, 1980), pp. 52–69; Gil, *A History of Palestine* (see n. 52 above), paras 762–72, pp. 527–39; Reif, *Hebrew Prayer* (see n. 36 above), pp. 154–64 and 181–91.

[91] Examples may be found in G. Khan, *Arabic Legal and Administrative Documents in the Cambridge Genizah Collections* (Cambridge, 1993), pp. 291–94.

[92] Reports of synagogal brawls, as summarized by Goitein in *A Mediterranean Society* (see n. 44 above), vol. 2, p. 168, are found in T-S 13J16.21, T-S Ar. 38.131 and Jewish Theological Seminary ENA 2736.20.

roof.[93] Sometimes, it was the official who did the complaining. A cantor asked Maimonides for permission to abandon the recitation of some liturgical poems introduced in a small Egyptian village where he officiated. Although he received a response that was sympathetic to his disapproval of the novel poetry, he was advised, for the sake of communal harmony, to continue to recite it.[94]

With regard to broader culture and its various aspects, it is hardly surprising to find that such areas as music, art and the physical sciences reflect the achievements and interests of the Islamic world of the day.[95] Illness and its treatment, for instance, were of major concern to the public and to the doctors, who consequently represented one of the most important professions. They functioned not only as medical practitioners but also as pharmacists, using many different kinds of plants, each with its own special effect. The most common complaints related to the eyes and they were fortunately able, even at that period, to perform operations to remove growths and obstructions. Headaches also troubled many patients and, in those cases, in addition to drugs, doctors were able to offer such external treatment as cold compresses. Large numbers in the community were troubled by sexually related matters. Men came to see physicians about impotence and fertility and were anxious to locate the best aphrodisiacs. Women asked about period pains and loss of blood, and about pregnancy and abortion. The medical experts did their best but there were often tragic aspects to these problems about which they could do little. They advised sensible diets, careful hygiene and the avoidance of excess in any human activity as the best ways of avoiding illness, particularly in connection with the digestive system, but not all patients took their advice.[96] A fair proportion of them preferred to spend

---

[93] For the religiously questionable interests of the beadle, see T-S 18J4.12, discussed in the broader context of the activities of such officials in Goitein, *A Mediterranean Society* (see n. 44 above), vol. 2, pp. 82–91.

[94] Fragments dealing with such correspondence with the Maimonidean family are Or.1080 J33, T-S 8J21.12 and T-S 12.608, as noted in Goitein, *A Mediterranean Society* (see n. 44 above), vol. 2, pp. 89, 160 and 219.

[95] The richest source for illustrated material in the Cambridge Genizah collections are the binders T-S K5 and T-S K10, many of which have already been researched by Professor Bezalel Narkiss and his team of Jewish art historians in Jerusalem and published in the *Journal of Jewish Art*. The lioness may be viewed in T-S Ar.51.60; the block-print in Or.1080 J50 (see *Genizah Fragments* 5 (April, 1983), p. 1, and 6 (October, 1983), p. 4); and the musical notes of Obadiah in T-S K5.41; see Reif, *A Jewish Archive* (see n. 2 above), pp. 152, 199 and 200.

[96] The medical data is derived from Isaacs and Baker, *Medical and Para-Medical Manuscripts* (see n. 61 above) which covers 1,616 Genizah fragments. The general information is owed to their introduction, pp. vii–xvii, and the details of particular diseases and treatments may be traced back to the relevant fragments by way of the excellent indexes. See also P. B. Fenton's brief but helpful summary 'The Importance of the Cairo Genizah for the History of Medicine', *Medical History* 24 (1980), pp. 347–48, and the more recent work of Z. Amar and E. Lev as in their volumes on the history of medicine in the medieval Holy Land, e.g. *Physicians and Medications in Jerusalem from the 10th Century to the 18th Century* (Hebrew; Tel Aviv, 2000).

their money on astrologers, magicians and diviners who gave them amulets to wear and formulas to recite, many of which were later preserved in the Genizah.[97] The trained professionals resented such people as 'quacks' but did acknowledge that there was a limit to what they themselves could do. Some admitted to their patients that true healing was in the hands of heaven.[98]

Literacy

If we may move from mundane matters to those of a more intellectual dimension, some comments are now in order on books, languages, literacy and education. Although the number of complete Hebrew codices that have survived from the ninth and tenth centuries is still only in single figures and their content predominantly biblical, and it is well recognized that orality played a major role in the rabbinic educational process, the evidence of the Genizah leaves little room for doubt that many of its fragments originally belonged to codices of various types of literature originating in the oriental communities of those centuries. The Hebrew codex apparently made its appearance in the eighth century, perhaps under the influence of Islam, which had borrowed the medium from the Christian and Classical worlds. Within three centuries, it became the standard medium for textual transmission. Quires were composed, catchwords included, sections numerated, lines justified, margins set, and the ruling-board (*masṭara*) was employed to facilitate the planning of the lines. Studies of Genizah fragments are gradually revealing how this whole process developed from a primitive state to a format that was more standardized and sophisticated but remained, as yet, fairly simple.[99]

---

[97] Some magical content occurs in the para-medical items described by Isaacs but more specific coverage is included in J. Naveh and S. Shaked, *Amulets and Magic Bowls: Aramaic Incantations of Late Antiquity* (Jerusalem and Leiden, 1985) and *Magic Spells and Formulae: Aramaic Incantations of Late Antiquity* (Jerusalem, 1993); L. Schiffman and M. D. Swartz, *Hebrew and Aramaic Incantation Texts from the Cairo Genizah: Selected Texts from the Taylor-Schechter Box K1* (Sheffield, 1992); and P. Schäfer and S. Shaked, *Magische Texte aus der Kairoer Geniza* (3 vols; Tübingen, 1994, 1997 and 1999). The theological background is provided in *Envisioning Magic: A Princeton Seminar and Symposium*, eds P. Schäfer and H. G. Kippenberg (Leiden, New York and Köln, 1997), especially in the articles 'Magic and Religion in Ancient Judaism' by Schäfer, pp. 19–43; 'Jewish Magic in the Greek Magical Papyri' by H. D. Betz, pp. 45–63; and 'On Judaism, Jewish Mysticism and Magic' by M. Idel, pp. 195–214.

[98] A delightful admission that healing is in God's hands is to be found in T-S AS 152.34, entry no. 1078 on p. 80 of the Isaacs/Baker volume (see n. 61 above), reproduced there in plates 16–17.

[99] Information about the Jewish adoption and use of the codex may be found in. S. Lieberman, *Hellenism in Jewish Palestine: Studies in the Literary Transmission, Beliefs and Manners of Palestine in the I Century B. C. E. – 4 Century C. E.* (New York[2], 1962), pp. 203–9; E. G. Turner, *The Typology of the Early Codex* (Philadelphia, 1977); C. M. Roberts and T. C. Skeat, *The Birth of the Codex* (London[2], 1983); R. H. Rouse and M. A. Rouse, 'Codicology, Western European' in *Dictionary of the Middle Ages* 3 (New York, 1983), pp. 475–78; M. Beit-Arié, 'How Hebrew Manuscripts are Made' in *A Sign and a Witness: 2,000*

Where there are sets of volumes, there is inevitably a need to store them together. In this connection, it has indeed recently been demonstrated that in the Jewish communities of North Africa in the ninth and tenth centuries texts were being widely copied and circulated and that extensive libraries, covering various languages, were being amassed and sold. Such libraries included not only the classical Jewish sources but also the newest commentaries on the one hand and more general learning on the other. They were actively built up by individuals, sometimes businessmen rather than specialized scholars, and by communities, through gifts, appeals and purchases, and they were made available for academic use by students and for ritual use by congregants. By creating, copying, lending and disseminating the contents of these libraries, the Maghrebi Jews belonging to the social and intellectual elite introduced a wide variety of literary works to other communities and thereby exercised a powerful influence on the levels of Jewish cultural achievement. The impressive contents of the Cairo Genizah are in no small degree due to the arrival there of many Jewish refugees from Tunisia and to the transfer of the bibliographical riches of the North African communities to the Egyptian centre.[100] Book-lists are also a common feature of the Genizah discoveries and demonstrate the existence of reference literature for educational activities by the community. Bibles, prayer-books, talmudic texts and commentaries, Jewish legal and theological tracts, as well as scientific, medical and philosophical works, are among the items that are regularly listed, sometimes in the

---

years of Hebrew Books and Illustrated Manuscripts, ed. L. S. Gold (New York and Oxford, 1988), pp. 35–46; I. M. Resnick, 'The Codex in Early Jewish and Christian Communities', *Journal of Religious History* 17 (1992), pp. 1–17; S. C. Reif, 'Codicological Aspects of Jewish Liturgical History', *Bulletin of the John Rylands University Library of Manchester* 75 (1993), pp. 117–31, and 'The Genizah and Jewish Liturgy' (see n. 36 above). Papyrus is still used for some of the older Genizah material (e.g. T-S 6H9–21) and there are also examples of cloth being used for the recording of texts (e.g. T-S 16.31). See C. Sirat, *Les papyrus en caractères hébraïques trouvés en Egypte* (Paris, 1985) and her brief note on T-S 6H9–21 in *Genizah Fragments* 5 (April, 1983), pp. 3–4. See also M. Haran, 'The Codex, the *Pinax* and the Wooden Slats', *Tarbiz* 57 (1988), pp. 151–64, with an additional note in *Tarbiz* 58 (1989), pp. 523–24; S. Z. Havlin, 'From Scroll to Codex', *Alei Sefer* 16 (1990), pp. 151–52 and 160–61; and M. Bar-Ilan, 'Ha-Ma'avar Mi-Megillah Le-Qodeqs', *Sinai* 107 (1991), pp. 242–54. The pentateuchal codex was known to the oriental Jews as *masḥaf torah*, as in e.g. T-S 12.791, or *masḥaf de-'orayta*, as in e.g. T-S A41.41.

[100] For details of books, scribes and orality, see *The Hebrew Book: An Historical Survey*, eds R. Posner and I. Ta-Shma (Jerusalem, 1975); M. Beit-Arié, *Hebrew Codicology* (Paris, 1976; Jerusalem^2, 1981); Goitein, *A Mediterranean Society* (see n. 44 above), vol. 2, pp. 228–40; S. C. Reif, 'Aspects of Mediaeval Jewish Literacy' in *The Uses of Literacy in Early Mediaeval Europe*, ed. R. McKitterick (Cambridge, 1989), pp.134–55; B. Gerhardsson, *Memory and Manuscript* (Lund and Copenhagen, 1961; republished with a new preface by the author and a foreword by J. Neusner, Grand Rapids, MI and Livonia, MI, 1998); M. J. Carruthers, *The Book of Memory: A Study in Medieval Culture* (Cambridge, 1990); W. A. Graham, *Beyond the Written Word: Oral Aspects of Scripture in the History of Religion* (Cambridge, 1987; paperback edition, 1993); *Transmitting Jewish Traditions: Orality, Textuality and Cultural Diffusion*, eds Y. Elman and I. Gershony (New Haven and London, 2000). For much information about libraries in the Genizah period, I am indebted to M. Ben-Sasson for providing a copy of his unpublished Hebrew paper '*Sifriyot Ha-Magreb Bi-Genizat Qahir*'.

context of a public sale. Those lists written by R. Joseph Rosh Ha-Seder also record his plans for his future work and demonstrate that he saw no problem with rewriting the scholarly tracts of his predecessors.[101]

While literacy may be defined as an acquaintance with literature, it may mean, and indeed more often today does mean, the ability to read and write a language or more than one language. Among the oriental Jews of the Genizah period, Hebrew, Aramaic and Arabic were used in a variety of contexts by different people for sundry reasons, with each of these languages exercising an influence on the others. Hebrew obviously continued to be the language of the formal cycles of biblical readings, was adopted for masoretic notes on the biblical text, and was retained as the language of midrashim. It was also used for the statutory prayers and for the composition of liturgical poetry, although in the latter case it must be stressed that it took on all manner of novel linguistic elements in order to allow the poets full rein for their lyrical originality. It remained the 'holy tongue' and left a particularly strong linguistic legacy with the communities that were closely influenced by the Palestinian centre, which had laid so much stress on the Hebrew Bible and studies of its linguistic structure. There was, however, constant tension about whether the biblical or the rabbinic variety of Hebrew was the authoritative form for post-biblical works, as well as persistent competition from its two sister languages. The script in which many Hebrew texts were written moved gradually away from the square towards the semi-cursive and the cursive from the middle of the eleventh century, with the greatest degree of movement taking place in the Babylonian and North African communities.[102] Aramaic was restricted to a more scholarly role, being used for the Talmud, both Babylonian and Palestinian, and for commentaries on it as well as codes and rulings extracted from it. It became the language most closely associated with the theory and practice of Jewish religious law. It was also employed for targumim and for some parts of the liturgy. Some of the earliest prayers survived in

---

[101] Goitein, *A Mediterranean Society* (see n. 44 above), vol. 2, pp. 206 and 248, vol. 5, pp. 3–4 and 425, and on the ransom of books (a Latin note is in T-S 12.722), see vol. 5, pp. 85, 376 and 529, and B. Kedar, *Jerusalem in the Middle Ages: Selected Papers* (Hebrew; Jerusalem, 1979), pp. 107–11. See also Goitein, 'Books Migrant and Stationary: A Geniza Study' in *Occident and Orient: A Tribute to the Memory of Alexander Scheiber*, ed. R. Dan (Budapest and Leiden, 1988), pp. 179–98, citing T-S Ar.5.1 and T-S NS J271. The sale of the library of Rabbi Abraham Ḥasid is documented in T-S 20.44; see E. J. Worman, 'Two Book Lists from the Cambridge Genizah Fragments', *Jewish Quarterly Review* 20 (1908), pp. 450–63. See also M. Frenkel, 'Book Lists from the Genizah as a Source for the Cultural and Social History of the Jews in Mediterranean Society' in *A Century of Genizah Research* (see n. 8 above), pp. 333–49.

[102] The development of Hebrew over the centuries and its varying form in different contexts is touched upon by W. Chomsky, *Hebrew the Eternal Language* (Philadelphia, 1964); E. Y. Kutscher, *A History of the Hebrew Language*, ed. R. Kutscher (Jerusalem, 1982); and A. Sáenz-Badillos, *A History of the Hebrew Language* (E. T., Cambridge, 1993). On the scripts, see E. Engel, 'Styles of Hebrew Script in the Tenth and Eleventh Centuries in the Light of Dated and Datable Geniza Documents' in *A Century of Genizah Research* (see n. 8 above), pp. 365–410.

Aramaic because they had been composed in what had been a popular language while some of the latest liturgical material was written in Aramaic because it thus acquired a high level of intellectual sophistication.[103]

Arabic was of course the dominant language of the huge Islamic empire of the Genizah period but the Jews preferred to read and write it in Hebrew and not in Arabic script. This Arabic, currently entitled Judaeo-Arabic, preserves more vernacular forms and later dialectical features than classical Muslim Arabic, and is also characterized by the occurrence of many Hebrew, as well as some Aramaic words and phrases. Arabic proper, if it may be described as such, was used only rarely by a minority of Jews, generally those in administrative, religious, medical and commercial professions that involved close contact with the Muslim world. Judaeo-Arabic, on the other hand, was so widespread that, according to one estimate, it is represented in almost half of the texts recovered from the Genizah. It was Judaeo-Arabic that was chosen for biblical commentary and translation; for studies of rabbinic literature and Jewish religious law; and to provide grammatical, liturgical and philosophical guidance. Folklore and belles-lettres are well represented and there are important works in the fields of science and medicine. Among the more mundane items are letters, accounts, lists and legal documents.[104] But the situation was never quite so clear-cut. Mundane letters were also written in Hebrew, poems were composed in Aramaic, rubrics for the Hebrew prayers were couched in Judaeo-Arabic and Hebrew vowel-points were attached to Judaeo-Arabic texts. Sometimes the same work was composed in both Hebrew and Judaeo-Arabic.[105]

---

[103] For a useful summary of the various Aramaic dialects, see K. Beyer, *The Aramaic Language: Its Distribution and Sub-Divisions* (E. T., Göttingen, 1986) and important work has also been done by M. Sokoloff (see n. 20 above).

[104] Basic work on Judaeo-Arabic as an independent Jewish language has been done by Joshua Blau, the world's expert in the field, in his *The Emergence and Linguistic Background of Judaeo-Arabic* (Oxford, 1965); *A Study of the Origins of Middle Arabic* (Jerusalem, 1981); and *Studies in Middle Arabic and its Judaeo-Arabic Variety* (Jerusalem, 1988). Colin Baker has produced a useful summary of the relevant Genizah genres in his 'Judaeo-Arabic Material in the Cambridge Genizah Collections', *Bulletin of the School of Oriental and African Studies* 58 (1995), pp. 445–54; see also the essays on a variety of Judaeo-Arabic topics in *Ninety Years*, eds Blau and Reif (see n. 4 above). The limited use of Arabic by Jews is explained by Geoffrey Khan in 'The Arabic Fragments in the Cambridge Genizah Collections', *Manuscripts of the Middle East* 1 (1986), pp. 54–60 and 'Arabic Documents in the Cairo Genizah', *Bulletin of the Israeli Academic Center in Cairo* 21 (1997), pp. 23–25. For the latest collection of essays on Judaeo-Arabic, see *Heritage and Innovation*, eds J. Blau and D. Doron (see n. 8 above).

[105] The unusual occurrence of particular Jewish languages in unexpected contexts is noted and documented in Reif, 'Aspects of Mediaeval Jewish Literacy' in R. McKitterick's volume (see n. 100 above), pp. 148–49, and Khan has dealt with the Arabic transcriptions of the Hebrew Bible in his *Karaite Bible Manuscripts* (see n. 9 above). The relationship between the different Jewish languages is discussed by R. Drory, *The Emergence of Hebrew-Arabic Literary Contacts at the Beginning of the Tenth Century* (Hebrew; Tel Aviv, 1986) and by David Téné in his article on comparative linguistics '*Hashva'at Ha-Leshonot*' (see n. 4

As is well know, Jewish use of languages other than Hebrew by way of Hebrew script and characteristic, Jewish vocabulary, was not restricted to the Arabic-speaking world. Elsewhere too, the Jews were anxious to have their linguistic cake and to eat it. While assimilating culturally by adopting the local language, they maintained their Jewish identity by hebraizing various aspects of its form. What is perhaps less widely appreciated is the degree to which such Jewish languages, defined by socio-linguists as 'ethnolects', are represented among the Genizah manuscripts.[106] In addition to Judaeo-Arabic, although in much more limited number, the Genizah researcher encounters texts in Judaeo-Greek, Judaeo-Spanish, Judaeo-German (Yiddish) and Judaeo-Persian. Although we are here more interested in the significance of such texts for the history of Jewish literacy and culture, it should not be forgotten that they provide essential evidence for those researching the earliest histories of the non-Semitic languages on which they are based. [107]

What may be said about the extent of Jewish literacy some eight centuries ago? The evidence from the Genizah convincingly demonstrates that written material of a great variety of content existed in the Jewish community in and around Cairo from the tenth to the thirteenth centuries. In the region of at least 210,000 manuscript fragments, yielding a total of at least three times that number of individual leaves, the majority of them dating from those centuries, have survived the ravages of time and the elements, to excite the interest of the modern researcher. One may therefore confidently assume that the original hoard deposited in the Ben Ezra synagogue was greatly in excess of that number and itself represented only a proportion of what was

---

above), pp. 237–87. See also J. Blau, 'Hebrew Written in Arabic characters: An Instance of a Radical Change in Tradition' in *Heritage and Innovation* (see n. 104 above), pp. 27–31.

[106] For some very helpful remarks and bibliography about 'ethnolects', see 'Adaptations of Hebrew Script', in two parts by Benjamin Hary and H. I. Aronson, in *The World's Writing Systems*, eds P. T. Daniels and W. Bright (New York and Oxford, 1996), pp. 727–42.

[107] Concerning the various 'Jewish' languages, see the Haifa periodical *Jewish Languages*; A. Bendavid, *Leshon Ha-Miqra U-leshon Ḥakhamim* (Tel Aviv, 1967); S. Federbush, *Ha-Lashon Ha'-Ivrit Be-Yisrael Uva-'Amim* (Jerusalem, 1967); J. Blau, *A Grammar of Mediaeval Judaeo-Arabic* (Hebrew; Jerusalem, 1961). The Judaeo-Greek texts have recently been edited by Nicholas de Lange in his *Greek Jewish Texts from the Cairo Genizah* (Tübingen, 1996); for some of the historical background, see S. B. Bowman, *The Jews of Byzantium* (Alabama, 1985). For a brief guide to the Judaeo-Spanish Genizah items, see E. Gutwirth and S. C. Reif, *Ten Centuries of Hispano-Jewish Culture* (Cambridge, 1992). In the matter of Yiddish in the Genizah, Simon Hopkins provides information about new discoveries and those that preceded them in his article 'A Fragment of *Pirqe Avot* in Old Yiddish', *Proceedings of the World Congress of Jewish Studies 1981* 8/3 (Jerusalem, 1982), pp. 153–57, and 'A Geniza Fragment of Pirqe Avot in Old Yiddish', *Tarbiz* 52 (1983), pp. 459–67. The Genizah fragments here referred to are T-S Misc.36.L.1, T-S E3.114 and T-S 10K22. S. Shaked is the leading authority in the field of Judaeo-Persian and has summarized the situation and published some texts in his 'Two Judaeo-Iranian Contributions: Fragments of Two Karaite Commentaries on Daniel in Judaeo-Persian' in *Irano-Judaica: Studies Relating to Jewish Contacts with Persian Culture throughout the Ages*, ed. S. Shaked (Jerusalem, 1982), pp. 304–22; see also Khan, *Grammatical Texts* (see n. 4 above).

actually produced in the communities in and around Cairo.[108] It is therefore in no way surprising to find evidence of a concern on the part of adults that their children, as indeed they themselves, should enjoy a reasonable level of literacy. One father was conscious of the fact that an opportunity to demonstrate his prowess in public was a necessary incentive for his son. He therefore instructed his son's teacher to prepare him for the recitation in the synagogue of passages from the Prophets and the Esther Scroll. If numeracy may be included under the general heading of literacy, it should be noted that references are also found to arithmetic, although less frequently than to Hebrew and Arabic. One mother had a contract drawn up according to which her son would be taught Arabic script and arithmetic at an agreed fee of two dinars. His language lessons were intended to train him to write a well-composed Arabic letter without spelling mistakes, while his education in arithmetic aimed at mastery in the abacus, decimals, and accounts. Being largely phonetic, Hebrew could be taught analytically letter by letter, although there is evidence of at least one pedagogical innovator who preferred the global method. That teacher, in a small provincial town in Egypt in the twelfth century, incurred the wrath of a rabbinic judge in Cairo who gave strict instructions for him to revert to the more traditional methods.[109]

Girls did not automatically receive such an education but occasionally there were parents who made special arrangements for them, usually for biblical studies.[110] One mother was so anxious that her daughter should receive a sound education that she made a death-bed request in a letter written in her own hand to her sister. She asked her to take on the responsibility for ensuring this, although she was aware that this

---

[108] See Goitein, *A Mediterranean Society* (see n. 44 above), vol. 2, p. 173; Beit-Arié, *Hebrew Codicology* (see n. 100 above), pp. 9–19; S. A Hopkins, 'The Oldest Dated Document in the Geniza?' in *Studies in Judaism and Islam Presented to S. D. Goitein*, eds S. Morag, I. Ben-Ami and N. A. Stillman (Jerusalem, 1981), pp. 83–98; and Reif, 'Aspects of Mediaeval Jewish Literacy' (see n. 100 above).

[109] Genizah and other medieval material relating to education is dealt with in the Hebrew volumes by S. Assaf, *Meqorot Le-Toledot Ha-Ḥinukh Be-Yisrael* (4 vols; Tel Aviv, 1925–43); Nathan Morris, *A History of Jewish Education* (3 vols; Jerusalem, 1960, 1964 and 1977); S. D. Goitein, *Jewish Education in Muslim Countries Based on Records from the Cairo Geniza* (Jerusalem, 1962); and J. Safran, *Studies in the History of Jewish Education* (Jerusalem, 1983). See also Goitein, *A Mediterranean Society* (see n. 44 above), vol. 2, pp. 173–83 and 185–90 and his 'Side Lights' in *GCAV* (see n. 74 above), pp. 83–110. The fragments relating to the preparations for synagogal reading, to the study of Arabic and arithmetic, and to the global method are T-S Ar.30.36, T-S NS J401 and T-S 13J23.20, which are edited, translated and discussed by Goitein in *GCAV*, pp. 89, 93–94, 97–99, 102, 106–7 and 109–10.

[110] On girls and women, see Goitein, *A Mediterranean Society* (see n. 44 above), vol. 2, pp. 183–85, and for women's letters see the article by J. L. Kraemer, pp. 00-00 below. The loss of a little girl who was a fine biblical scholar is recorded in Jewish Theological Seminary, ENA 2935.17, and dealt with by Goitein in *GCAV* (see n. 74 above), p. 87.

would strain the family resources. The text is at once moving and instructive, well worth citing, at least in part (in Goitein's translation)[111]:

> This is to inform you, my lady, dear sister – may God accept me as a ransom for you – that I have become seriously ill with little hope of recovery, and I have dreams indicating that my end is near. My lady, my most urgent request of you, if God, the exalted, indeed decrees my death, is that you take care of my little daughter and make efforts to give her an education, although I know well that I am asking you for something unreasonable, as there is not enough money – by my father – for support, let alone for formal instruction. However, she has a model in our saintly mother...my lady, only God knows how I wrote these lines!

The fact that there are a number of letters in which wives are directly addressed by their husbands, as against others in which a male colleague is requested to pass on written information by word of mouth to the writer's spouse, appears to demonstrate that women were not universally illiterate. Since there are specific letters and documents that appear to be written in female hands, it is clear that some women were acquainted not only with reading but also with writing. It should, however, be acknowledged that even these occurrences are in the legal, communal and personal spheres, rather than in the literary. Even if Cairo was better known among the communities of the Jewish world for its economic activity than for its academic prowess, there are still clear indications in the Genizah of a fairly high level of literacy. Scholarly notes, invitations to lectures, details of refresher courses – all point to an intense degree of educational activity, while the remainder of the evidence confirms that it was not an élitist or an exclusivist preoccupation.[112]

Having ranged over a wide area of the Genizah evidence, we are now in a position to summarize that material's impact on Jewish studies. It seems incontrovertible that these texts are not exclusively relevant to technical manuscript studies and to the close analysis of authoritative religious literature but have much to say about a great variety of Jewish and general activities in the Mediterranean area of the early medieval period. They shed light on many aspects of political, social and cultural history and are therefore deserving of the attention not only of scholars committed to deciphering and editing them but also of their colleagues throughout the field of Jewish studies who have broader intellectual interests. They will certainly repay close examination in their second century as they did in their first.

---

[111] The woman's death-bed request occurs in Genizah Misc. 6* in the Library of the Jewish Theological Seminary and receives the attention of Goitein in *GCAV* (see n. 74 above), pp. 85–87 and 100–1.

[112] See J. Mann, 'Listes des Livres provenant de la Gueniza', *Revue des Etudes Juives* 72 (1921), pp. 163–83 and *Texts and Studies* (see n. 50 above), pp. 643–84; and Goitein, *A Mediterranean Society* (see n. 44 above), vol. 2, pp. 191–211.

2

Genizah Manuscripts of Ben Sira

MENAHEM KISTER

Hidden wisdom and concealed treasure,
What is the use of either? (Ben Sira 41:14)

Introduction

Most of the post-biblical literature found in the Genizah reflects rabbinic or medieval Judaism. Ben Sira (otherwise known as Sirach or Ecclesiasticus, henceforth BS), together with the Damascus Document[1] and Aramaic Levi[2] are rather surprising exceptions since these three compositions are products of the Judaism of the Second Temple period. Many BS fragments, originally belonging to six[3] different manuscripts, have been identified to date, and cover about two-thirds of this wisdom book. Before the discovery of the Genizah, BS had been known throughout the centuries in two ancient versions, namely, the Greek and the Syriac (henceforth G and S respectively).

The discovery of a leaf from the most important manuscript of BS in the Genizah (which was later designated as MS B) proved to be the beginning of the Genizah era. The leaf was bought by Mrs Agnes Lewis, apparently in Egypt, and was given to Solomon Schechter for identification. Schechter was indeed the right man for the task, not only because of his erudition and critical acumen, but also because he had demonstrated his interest in the book several years earlier when he published a collection of all the quotations from it to be found in rabbinic literature.[4] This leaf of

[1] C. Rabin, *The Zadokite Documents* (Oxford², 1958); *The Damascus Document Reconsidered*, ed. M. Broshi (Jerusalem, 1992).

[2] H. L. Pass and J. Anderzen, 'Fragment of an Aramaic text of the Testament of Levi', *Jewish Quarterly Review* 12 (1900), pp. 651–61; R. H. Charles and A. Cowley, 'An early source of the Testaments of the Patriarchs', *Jewish Quarterly Review* 19 (1907), pp. 566–83; J. C. Greenfield and M. E. Stone, 'Remarks on the Aramaic Testament of Levi from the Geniza', *Revue Biblique* 86 (1979), pp. 214–30.

[3] The sixth MS has been published and identified only recently. See: A. Scheiber, 'A new leaf of the fourth manuscript of the Ben Sira from the Genizah', *Magyar Könyvszemle* 98 (1982), pp. 179–85 = 'An additional page of Ben Sira in Hebrew', *Jubilee Volume in Honor of... Joseph B. Soloveitchik*, eds S. Israeli, N. Lamm and Y. Raphael, vol. 2 (Hebrew; Jerusalem – New York, 1984), pp. 1179–85; A. Di Lella, 'The newly discovered sixth manuscript of Ben Sira from the Cairo Geniza', *Biblica* 69 (1988), pp. 226–38.

[4] S. Schechter, 'The quotations from Ecclesiasticus in rabbinic literature', *Jewish Quarterly Review* 3 (1891), pp. 682–706.

BS is housed at Cambridge University Library,[5] together with the excited letter of Schechter to Mrs. Lewis, which reads:

> Dear Mrs Lewis, I think we have reason to congratulate ourselves. For the fragment I took with me represents a piece of the original Hebrew of Ecclesiasticus. It is the first time that such a thing was discovered. Please do not speak yet about the matter till tomorrow. I will come to you tomorrow about 11 p.m. [sic!] and talk over the matter with you how to make the matter known. In haste and great excitement, Yours sincerely, S. Schechter.

Schechter immediately recognised the fact that the Genizah manuscript before him, written in the tenth century CE, represented the original Hebrew of BS, or, perhaps more precisely, a genuine Hebrew text of BS (second century BCE). Most scholars concurred with this premise, and the Genizah manuscripts excited the whole world of Semitic and biblical learning, even attracting the attention of such a prominent figure as Theodor Nöldeke. Some scholars, however, expressed their opposition. D. S. Margoliouth, Laudian Professor of Arabic at Oxford, rejected Schechter's thesis and attacked him vigorously and personally,[6] and those who came to share his doubts included E. Bickel[7] and, later, C. C. Torrey,[8] H. L. Ginsberg[9] and others.[10] The question is whether the Genizah manuscripts of BS contain a genuine Hebrew text of the book, or simply represent a medieval retranslation. The scholars who rejected the genuineness of the fragments were, to say the least, very decisive in their statements, Margoliouth referring to the Genizah fragments as 'this rubbish',[11] while H. L. Ginsberg claimed (as late as 1955) that they are 'composed in an idiom which is for the most part hideous'. Ginsberg goes on to say: 'It is reported that fragments of the Hebrew BS have been discovered in the Wilderness of Judah ... If they are at least pre-Arab it is probable that ... they will be found to be as unlike the Hebrew [i.e. the Genizah fragments] as imaginable'.[12] But the discovery of the BS scroll at Masada[13]

---

[5] CUL Or.1102.

[6] See his articles in the *Expository Times* 10–11 (1898–1900).

[7] G. Bickel, 'Der hebräische Sirachtext eine Rückübersetzung', *Vienna Oriental Journal* 13 (1899), pp. 251–56.

[8] C. C. Torrey, 'The Hebrew of the Geniza Sirach', *Alexander Marx Jubilee Volume*, ed. S. Lieberman, English section (New York, 1950), pp. 585–602.

[9] H. L. Ginsberg, 'The original Hebrew of Ben Sira 12:10–14', *Journal of Biblical Literature* 74 (1955), pp. 93–95.

[10] S. Lieberman, *Hayerushalmi Kiphshuto*: *A Commentary* (Hebrew; Jerusalem, 1934), p. 289, n. 1; see also G. Alon, *Studies in Jewish History*, vol. 2 (Hebrew; Jerusalem, 1958), p. 142.

[11] *Expository Times* 10 (1898–99), p. 434.

[12] *Expository Times* 10 (1898–99), p. 93.

[13] Y. Yadin, *The Ben Sira Scroll from Masada* (Jerusalem, 1965) = *Eretz Israel* 8 (1965), pp. 1–49 (English), 1–46 (Hebrew).

in 1964, as well as of some fragments of BS in Qumran,[14] put an end to the dispute by proving, by and large, precisely the opposite. It is now clear that the Genizah fragments do reflect, in their general essence and in most specific cases, a genuine Hebrew text of BS. Having these ancient textual witnesses at our disposal, we can evaluate with much more certainty the originality, as well as the many textual defects, of the Genizah fragments.

On the other hand, a hymn of BS preserved in the so-called Psalms Scroll from Qumran[15] proves that the version found in the Genizah (BS 51:13 ff.) is a retranslation of the Syriac that includes some of its grave textual errors, as already convincingly argued by Bickel in 1899.[16] In this very hymn, the Hebrew terms בית המדרש and ישיבה appear in the Genizah manuscript, in what would seem to be their first occurrences in Jewish literature. If, however, this text is a medieval retranslation from S, such a fact does, of course, make all the difference in using it as evidence for the history of these terms. In the case of verses that appear in the Genizah fragments (throughout the book), and in which doublets occur, the first or the second half of these doublets is frequently explained as owing its origin to a retranslation from the Syriac. It is unclear why, when and by whom these retranslations were appended to the original text, but the phenomenon of retranslations from Syriac in the Middle Ages is significant in itself for our understanding of cultural relations in that period.

In the case of BS, then, we are fortunate enough to be able to confront theories with facts and we learn that reality may often be more complex than monolithic theories. Another lesson may be learnt from the text reconstructions made with such certainty by Margoliouth,[17] Ginsberg[18] and others. All such reconstructions are hazardous, especially when one has no sample of the original text.[19] The textual history of the Hebrew BS thus seems to have some bearing on the methods of reconstructing a text on the basis of its ancient translations, and thus on 'lower criticism' of the Hebrew Bible, rather than on 'higher criticism', as proposed by Margoliouth.

The recent finds in the Judean Desert make it clear that Schechter's theory, in the revised form propounded by Israel Lévi,[20] was by and large correct and there can be little doubt now that the Genizah manuscripts essentially reflect the original Hebrew

---

[14] M. Baillet and J. T. Milik, *Discoveries in the Judean Desert*, vol. 3 (Oxford, 1962), pp. 75–77.

[15] J. A. Sanders, *Discoveries in the Judean Desert*, vol. 4 (Oxford, 1965), pp. 43, 79–85.

[16] See n. 7 above; I. Lévi, *L'Ecclésiastique*, vol. 2 (Paris, 1901), pp. xxi–xxvii and his commentary on pp. 224–33; M. Delcor, 'Le text hébreu du cantique de Siracide LI, 13 et ss. et les anciennes versions', *Textus* 6 (1968), pp. 27–47; P. W. Skehan, 'The acrostic poem in Sirach 51:13–30', *Harvard Theological Review* 64 (1971), pp. 387–400.

[17] See *Expository Times* 11 (1899–1900), p. 92.

[18] See n. 9 above, p. 93.

[19] Compare Bickel's restoration of BS 51:13–30 (see n. 7 above) with the text of the Psalms Scroll (see n. 15 above). Bickel had the ingenious idea that these verses constitute an acrostic psalm, and was proved right by the discovery at Qumran.

[20] I. Lévi (see n. 16 above), in his introduction.

of BS. With the assistance of G and S, a text close to the original of BS can often be proposed. It should be mentioned that there are even some cases in which the text of a Genizah fragment is superior in minor details to one in the Masada scroll.[21] The Hebrew texts of BS informs us of the Hebrew language used a few decades before the Hasmonean revolt, for which period we scarcely have any Hebrew texts (other than the last chapters of Daniel) that may be dated with any certainty. Thus the Hebrew text, mainly known from the Genizah, is a unique witness to an otherwise unknown stage in the development of the Hebrew language. The language of BS stands somewhere between biblical Hebrew on the one hand, and Aramaic and mishnaic Hebrew on the other. The influence of Aramaic is especially strong. In my opinion, the language of BS is a literary idiom, partly reflecting contemporary usage, for which we have virtually no other source. His work is full of rare words and *hapax legomena*,[22] and his love of puns leads to their extensive use. Some of these were already incomprehensible to readers two or three generations after his time.

Sometimes one finds in BS a word with a significant nuance. Thus, for instance, we read in 3:11 כבוד איש כבוד אביו // ומרבה חטא מקלל אמו , 'The honour of a man is the honour of his father // and he who dishonours his mother commits a grave sin'. מקלל (ἀδοξία in G, ܨܥܪܘ in S) is the antonym to מכבד, and it is clear from the context that, according to BS, 'honouring' one's parents means working for them and

[21] In 42:8 the Masada Scroll has על חשבון שותף ודרך, whereas MS B reads: על חשבון חובר ואדון. The margins of MS B have the alternative readings שותף instead of חובר and וארח instead of ואדון. חובר is a rare synonym for the common word שותף. אדון seems to be a graphical error for the word ארח (originally, 'fellow-traveller'; see Job 34:8), which was erroneously taken in the Masada Scroll to be the common word ארח = 'road' and replaced by the word דרך.

[22] Examples of such cases are: 1) איככה (10:31) 'how much so'; see M. Kister, 'Some Notes on Biblical Expressions and Allusions and the Lexicography of Ben Sira' in *Sirach, Scrolls and Sages: Proceedings of a Second International Symposium on the Hebrew of the Dead Sea Scrolls, Ben Sira and the Mishnah*, eds T. Muraoka and J. F. Elwolde (Leiden, 1999), pp. 161–62. 2) נשא פנים (2:22; 42:1) 'to be ashamed'; see M. Kister, 'Notes' (see above, in this note), pp. 168–71. 3) תמהות (42:4; read: תמחות; Masada Scroll: תמחי); see S. Naeh, 'Polishing measures and cleaning scales': a chapter from the Tractate of Weights and Measures', *Tarbiz* 59 (1990), pp. 379–95. 4) חלק , 'to create' (Arabic *ḫalaqa*; for further parallels see M. Kister, 'A contribution to the interpretation of Ben Sira', *Tarbiz* 59 (1990), p. 334). 5) עלה על (33:13) '[food] fit for [*sb*]' is found elsewhere only in *Avot de-Rabbi Nathan,* Version A, in a textually problematic passage; see S. Schechter and C. Taylor, *The Wisdom of Ben Sira* (Cambridge, 1899), p. 55; M. Kister, *Studies in Avot de-Rabbi Nathan: Text, Redaction and Interpretation* (Hebrew; Jerusalem, 1998), p. 47. 6) דאג (35:1; 50:4), 'to take care', also appears in the Bar Kochba letters; see E. Y. Kutscher, *Hebrew and Aramaic Studies* (Hebrew; Jerusalem, 1977), p. 56. 7) דין (14:1; 30:21, 23; 37:2; 38:18), 'grief'; see M. Kister and E. Qimron, 'Observations on 4QSecond Ezekiel (4Q385 2–3)', *Revue de Qumran* 15 (1992), pp. 599–600. 8) זיף (11:7), 'deem false'; see Z. Ben-Hayyim, 'The gleanings of Ephraim', *Hebrew and Arabic Studies in Honour of Joshua Blau*, ed. H. Ben-Shammai (Hebrew; Jerusalem, 1993), pp. 97–98 and n. 3. 9) קמע, 'to oppress' (Arabic *qama'a*); see M. Kister, 'Contribution' (see above, in this note), p. 34. 10) See also below, text 3 (ההם, כיוצא בו).

taking care of their needs.[23] This usage illuminates the words of Jesus in Mark 7:10, 'For Moses said: "Honour your father and your mother", and "he who speaks evil of his father or mother, let him surely die"... but you ... no longer permit him to do anything to his father and mother.' The verses quoted use the Hebrew words כבד and מקלל. Jesus did not mean 'evil speaking' (κακολογεῖν in the Gospel), but rather 'dishonour', i.e. neglect.

Textual Interpretations

I would now like to present new interpretations of some verses in BS (quite differently interpreted by previous scholars), which would not have been possible without the Genizah manuscripts. The complex textual and linguistic problems of BS will be illustrated by the examples I have chosen but I will refrain from dealing with delicate problems relating to the *Vorlage* of the ancient versions. The verses chosen are intelligible only through the Genizah manuscripts, and all of them except the first have some bearing on aspects of Second-Temple Judaism and early Christianity.

1. 25:17: רע אשה ישחיר מראה איש // ויקדיר פניו לדוב

This verse is often translated as **'The wickedness of a woman makes black a man's look, and darkens his countenance like that of a bear.'**

Such a translation of the final expression in the verse is highly problematic. G shares with the Genizah fragment the strange metaphor of the bear at the end of the verse. S may be corrupt in rendering this word. But once we have the Hebrew text, the 'bear' may be removed from the verse and the text allowed to make much more sense. דוב may easily be a noun derived from the root דאב, just as we find in the Masada scroll תור for תאר (43:9, 18). In fact, a biblical by-form of the root דאב is דוב, as in the expression מדיבות עינים in Leviticus 26:16. I therefore suggest rendering the end of the verse: **'and darkens his countenance in grief.'**

2. 7:14: אל תסוד בעדת שרים // ואל תישן דבר בתפלה

This verse is often translated as **'Prate not in the assembly of elders, and repeat not [your] words in your prayer.'**

G has: μὴ ἀδολέσχει ἐν πλήθει πρεσβυτέρων καὶ μὴ δευτερώσῃς λόγον ἐν προσευχῇ σου; S: ܠܐ ܬܬܝܬܪ ܢܦܫܟ ܒܟܢܘܫܬܐ ܕܩܫܝܫܐ. ܘܠܐ ܬܫܢܐ ܡܠܬܐ ܒܨܠܘܬܟ. The Hebrew original could not have been restored on the basis of these two versions. But with the Hebrew now before us, it is not difficult to perceive that the *Vorlage* of S was תסתיר, which is a slight misreading of תסתיד, a unique verb found elsewhere in the Hebrew fragments of BS from the Genizah (8:17, 9:3, 9:14, 42:12). This is a *hitpa'el* form of סוד, corresponding to the *qal* form that occurs in the Genizah fragment of 7:14. The two versions differ in rendering a verb derived from the root שני, either in the *qal* (meaning 'to repeat', G and H) or in the *pi'el* (meaning 'to change', S). Both translators, however, have 'your prayer'. This might have been

[23] See J. C. Greenfield, '*Adi baltu*: care for the elderly and its reward', *Archiv für Orientforschung* 19 (1982), p. 312.

a most significant piece of evidence for prayer in BS's times. It would have been most intriguing to know what it was that attracted BS's disapproval. Was it the repetition of the prayer, or the alteration of its formulas? The implications of any of these alternative renderings could have been far-reaching for the history of prayer in early Judaism.

But according to the Hebrew text another, quite different, interpretation may be offered. שנה דבר means 'to tell a secret', 'to spread gossip'. Thus we read in 42:1 [בוש...] משנות דבר תשמע // ומחסוף כל דבר עצה, 'be ashamed... to repeat the word you have heard, and to lay bare any council' [or, 'any secret']. The same Greek words μὴ δευτερώσῃς λόγον appear in 19:7 in the context of keeping a secret, and refraining from gossip. This is the meaning of the idiom שנה בדבר in Proverbs 17:9. The Hebrew text should be interpreted quite differently if the word בתפלה is vocalised *be-tiflah* (derived from the root תפל) rather than *bi-tefillah*. תפלה in Job 1:22 is rendered in the LXX ἀφροσύνη, 'foolishness'. The meaning of the stich would, then, be 'do not gossip foolishly'. This fits perfectly with the first stich, if it is noted that the verb תסוד is derived from סוד, 'secret'. This textual reconstruction is possible only on the basis of the reading that occurs in the Hebrew Genizah text. I therefore suggest rendering the second half of the verse: **'and do not foolishly repeat gossip.'**

3. 26:16: שמש זורחת במרומי מעל // יפה אשה בדביר בחור
'The sun shines in the heights [according to G: **'in God's heights'], and a wife is beauty** [or, according to G: **the beauty of a wife is] in ...'**
G reads at the end of the verse: ἐν κόσμῳ οἰκίας αὐτῆς; S: ܒܟܘܬܠܐ ܕܒܝܬܗ. Once we have the Genizah fragment, it is obvious that S is a paraphrase of the original Hebrew, whereas G mistakenly read רביד for דביר. On the other hand, we should in the Genizah fragment emend בחור ('a young man, a bachelor') to בתה [= ביתה]. The meaning of the Hebrew text is, then, that although the beauty of a good wife is comparable with the shining sun, a good woman, unlike the sun, should not be seen in public, but rather stay in her home. The meaning of the biblical Hebrew דביר is the 'Holy of Holies', the part of the Temple that only the high priest was allowed to enter just once a year and it seems rather strange to use this particular word, even as a metaphor. The possibility of such a bold and strange figure cannot be totally excluded; it would, however, be preferable to interpret the word here quite differently. As long ago appreciated, the word דביר is derived from the root דבר meaning the 'back' (as the equivalent root in Arabic; see ידבר עמים תחתנו in Psalms 47:4, literally 'He makes peoples submit their backs to our [feet]'). It seems more likely, then, that דביר ביתה in this verse means the inner [literally in Hebrew: back] part of any house. This was considered to be the appropriate place for a modest wife; see Psalms 128:3: אשתך כגפן פריה בירכתי ביתך, 'your wife will be like a fruitful vine in the inner part of your house'. I suggest that the Hebrew word דביר, meaning the inner part of a house in general, became a *terminus technicus* for the Holy of Holies but continued to exist in its broader sense in living Hebrew usage, as attested by BS. It is worth mentioning that Ben-Yehuda defined the word דביר in his dictionary as 'the inner part of any

house, and especially of the Temple of Jerusalem'.[24] This definition was made on the basis of mere etymological considerations, without any textual documentation. I think that our verse supplies the documentation. The verse should consequently be rendered: **'The sun shines in the heights, and a wife's beauty in the inner parts of her house.'**[25]

4. 38:17: המר בכי והחם מספד // ושית אבלו כיוצא בו
יום ושנים בעבור דמעה// והנחם בעבור עון
'Make bitter weeping and lamentation, and make mourning such as befits him. A day, two days for crying, and be consoled on account of transgression.'
והחם is the reading in the margin of MS B, whereas the actual text of the manuscript has והתם. G has πίκρανον κλαυθμὸν καὶ θέρμανον καπετόν. The *Vorlage* of G must have been the Hebrew word החם. D. Talshir has recently noted that the verb הום is found in the Nirab inscription (בכוני והום אתהמו);[26] that Targum Onqelos renders תתגודדו by תתחממון or תתחממו;[27] and that the Babylonian Talmud uses the expression אחים (ב)הספדא (*Shabbat* 153b).[28] It is clear that the form of this root with a *ḥet* rather than a *he* is a bye-form. G seems to testify to the existence of this bye-form at a very early date (unless it is considered a misreading by the Greek translator of his *Vorlage*).[29] But could it not be that BS himself meant it to be a pun, the root מרר having the meanings both of 'flow' and 'bitter', and the root חמם having the meanings both of 'lament' (the *hiph'il* is causative) and 'warm'? At any rate, from the linguistic point of view, the form החם in the margin of MS B is more accurate. It should also be noted that כיוצא ב in mishnaic Hebrew means 'similar to', whereas in this verse it has the meaning, evidently unique in Hebrew literature, of 'befit' (see also 10:28). Z. Ben-Hayyim has successfully demonstrated the semantic relation of these two meanings.[30]

These two verses in BS have a parallel in BT, *Mo'ed Qaṭan* 27b: '*Weep not for the dead* in excess, *neither mourn him* beyond the appropriate measure[31] ... Three days for weeping, and seven for lamenting... hereafter, the Holy One, blessed be He, says: You are not more compassionate towards him [i.e., the departed] than I.' The reading בעבור עון in the Genizah fragment would appear to convey the idea that too much

[24] E. Ben-Yehuda, *Thesaurus Totius Hebraitatis*, vol. 2 (Jerusalem – Tel Aviv, 1948), p. 868.
[25] In the discussion that followed the presentation of this paper at Cambridge University Library, Professor H. Ben-Shammai suggested that דביר might be compared to Syriac *dūvārā* and Arabic *tadbīr*, both meaning 'management', 'order'. The Greek κόσμος should be interpreted, according to this suggestion, in the sense of 'order' (rather than as a translation of the inferior reading רביד).
[26] G. A. Cooke, *A Text-book of North-Semitic Inscriptions* (Oxford, 1903), p. 189–90.
[27] See J. N. Epstein, *Mavo le-Nusaḥ ha-Mishnah* (Jerusalem, 1948), pp. 1303–04.
[28] D. Talshir, 'תתערדון in the Peshitta', *Tarbiz* 49 (1980), p. 86.
[29] See 43:4: MS reads מהם instead of מחם.
[30] Z. Ben-Hayyim, ''*Erkhey millim*', *Sefer Shemu'el Yeivin*, eds S. Abramski, Y. Aharoni, H. M. Gevaryahu and B. Z. Luria (Hebrew; Jerusalem, 1970), pp. 435–39.
[31] Compare 'such as befits him' in BS.

weeping and lamentation are a religious transgression. But how can we account for the fact that such theological opposition to excessive lamentation is never mentioned by BS, and that this verse occurs in a personal rather than a religious context? I therefore find it preferable to read in our verse יום ושנים בעבור דמעה// והנחם בעבור עין. Reading עין for עון involves only a slight orthographic alteration; in fact, in many ancient manuscripts *waw* and *yod* are indistinguishable. The verse would then have the sense that one should cry for two days, but no more, since one has to spare one's eyes. This precise idea appears in a story in BT, *Shabbat* 151b: 'R. Ḥanina's daughter died, [but] he did not weep for her. Said his wife: Have you sent away a fowl from your house? [i.e., isn't she important enough for you to weep for her?]. [Shall I suffer] two [evils], – he retorted –bereavement and blindness?'. If the original reading in BS is עין, then the *baraita* in *Mo'ed Qaṭan* seems to be based on BS, reading there עון. It should be emphasised that the ancient versions differ markedly in this verse from the Genizah Hebrew manuscript. By and large, I tend to prefer the Genizah text of this verse, but the reconstruction of the *Vorlage* of each version and of the original wording of the verse is especially complicated. Be that as it may, the reading עון (or עין) certainly cannot be dismissed as 'nonsense', as indeed it is in the most recent edition of BS by Di Lella.[32]

5. 39:16-18: [מעשי] אל כלם טובים // וכל צורך בעתו יספיק
ב[ד]ברו יעריך נר // ומוצא פיו אוצרו
ת--- רצונו יצליח // ואין מעצור לתשועתו

This is the reading in the Genizah fragment, which was, in fact, the first leaf to be discovered. In my view, it should be translated:

'The works of God are all good, and He supplies every need in its (proper) time.
By His word He arranged a pile, and the utterance of His mouth is His store-house [or, treasure].
His will makes successful(?) [----] , and there is no restraint in His deliverance.'

The second verse is rendered by G as ἐν λόγῳ αὐτοῦ ἔστη ὡς θημονιὰ ὕδωρ ('by his word, water stood as a heap'), interpreting נד as נד מים ('a heap of water'; see Joshua 3:13, 16 and Psalms 33:7, 78:13, and see below), while S read in his *Vorlage* יערוך נר, meaning 'to kindle a light' (see Psalms 132:17). S took the verse to mean sunrise and sunset, מוצא having apparently reminded the translator of מוצא שמש, while אוצרו was understood as the place where the sun hides after sunset.[33] Thus S paraphrased the verse: ܒܡܕܢܚܘܗܝ ܕܢܚ ܫܡܫܐ ܘܒܡܥܪܒܘܗܝ ܡܛܫ ܢܘܗܪܗ ܠܗ. The interpretation of S seems untenable, and the interpretation of G rather forced. What is really being stated in the original Hebrew text (emending נר with G to נד) is that God created all his works at the beginning, as if he arranged for himself a great pile (the root ערך fits this sense very well), or a store-house (אוצר), from which he supplies from time to time the needs of the world. As BS puts it in verse 30: 'All these [i.e., snakes etc.] are created for their uses (לצורכם), and are in the store-house

[32] A. A. Di Lella, *The Wisdom of Ben Sira* (*The Anchor Bible*; New York, 1987), p. 440.
[33] See the Manual of Discipline, 1QS 10:2.

to be requisitioned in due time', i.e. the cosmic 'store-house', or treasure, of God. We have here, according to this interpretation, a peculiar theological concept of BS concerning the creation of the world and its management by God.

A most interesting parallel to this concept is found in a passage of the Syriac poet Narsai (fifth century CE) , who writes: ܘܟܕ܆ ܨܒܝܢܗ ܐܝܬܘܗܝ ܣܝܡܬܗ ܘܥܘܬܪܐ ܡܠܬܗ ܗܝ܆ ܐܘܚܪ ܠܥܒܕ̈ܘܗܝ܆ ... ܠܥܠܬܐ ܘܦܫܛ ܒܫܬܐ ܬܘܩܢ̈ܘܗܝ܆. 'And although His will is His treasure and His word is richness, He delayed His works... extended His work of creation to six days').[34] The word and the will of God are his treasure (Syriac ܣܝܡܬܗ = Hebrew אוצר). God could have created all the world at once, but he instead preferred to have his word as his treasure, and make use of it in due time. The similarity between this passage and BS 39:16-18, 30 is striking. Narsai could not have borrowed it directly or indirectly from Ben Sira, since both S and G translate the verse quite differently. The question regarding the link between Ben Sira and Narsai therefore remains open.

It should be noted that the parallelism נד // אוצר is to be found in Psalms 33:7 (כונס כנד מי הים נותן באוצרות תהומות). The Masoretic text is vocalised *ned* and understood to mean 'a pile', but LXX, Vulgate, Peshitta, Targum and some rabbinic midrashim read the word as *nod*, meaning 'a waterskin' (the RSV, for instance, translating 'He gathered the water of the sea as in a bottle'). Our BS verse is the earliest evidence for the Masoretic pronunciation of the word in this verse as נד (*ned*) = 'a pile'.

Unfortunately, the first word in the next verse has faded. Variations of this sentence occur elsewhere in BS. At the beginning of a poetic unit (42:15), BS states באמר ה׳ מעשיו ופעל רצונו לקחו, which I would translate 'By the word of God His works [were formed], and His saying is the agent of His will'. At the end of this poetic unit (43:26), we read למענו יצלח מלאך ובדבריו יפעל רצון, which I would translate 'For His sake He [i.e., God] makes an angel successful(?), and by His words He accomplishes His will'. It is clear that the wording of 43:26 is very close to our verse, 39:17–18. It has not been recognised that 43:26 is clearly based on Isaiah 55:11 כן יהיה דברי אשר יצא מפי לא ישוב אלי ריקם כי אם עשה את אשר חפצתי והצליח אשר שלחתיו, which was understood by BS to mean 'So shall my word be when it goes forth from my mouth; it shall not return to me empty, but I shall accomplish that which I will, and make successful (?) the one whom I sent'. אשר שלחתיו was interpreted as מלאך; רצון is BS's equivalent to the biblical אשר חפצתי; יפעל is used in BS instead of עשה in Isaiah. This is an illuminating example of BS's stylistic preferences (פעל, an ancient poetic, biblical form, alongside the late biblical רצון meaning 'will'). The wording of our verse (39:18) is evidently also based on Isaiah 55:11. It could have been important for reconstructing BS's conceptions of Divine will, word, and deed, and the role of angels. Unfortunately, however, it remains unsolved, because the crucial word is not legible in the Genizah fragment.

---

[34] Ph. Gignoux, *Homélies de Narsaï sur la Création* (*Patrologia Orientalis* 34/3–4, Turnhout, 1968), p. 552.

6. 42:21: גבורת חכמתו תכן // אחד הוא מעולם
ל[א נוסף] ולא נאצל // ולא צריך לכל מבין
(a) 'He established (תכן) the might of His wisdom,
(b) from eternity He is one;
(c) Nothing has been added (to Him) and nothing taken away (from Him),
(d) and he needs no one to teach him.'
The chiastic parallelism in BS is clear: a // d; b // c. This verse is based on Isaiah 40:13–14, 'Who has plumbed (תכן) the spirit of the Lord, and as his counsellor has instructed Him? Whom did He consult and who taught Him (ויבינהו)...?' BS thus identifies the 'might of His wisdom', apparently an epithet of God's *sophia* (see Wisdom 7:25), with God's spirit. It seems that the main thrust of this verse is that God has not been changed by the creation of his wisdom. His wisdom is appointed by him and known to him, not instructing him; it is created by Him, and is not a separate divine being. If this interpretation of BS's words is correct, then we have here a polemic against some bold theological speculations concerning the nature of σοφία and its divine substance (Is God's wisdom created? Is God's wisdom distinct from himself? How can the relation between God and his wisdom be defined?) that anticipate, to a certain extent, Christian doctrines concerning the Logos. The text can be established with certainty only on the basis of the Genizah manuscripts.

7. 30[33]:31, MS E: [--------אחד עבדך כאח חשב[הו // וא[ל תקנא ב, 'If you have only one slave, treat him as your brother, do not enslave [yourself] for the sake of [his price] [or, **blood].'**
The verse stands in sharp contrast to the preceding verses. It constitutes an exception to BS's cruel recommendations for the severe treatment of slaves: If you have only one slave, you have to treat him very gently, otherwise you may lose him, together with his services.[35] The second stich is translated by G: ὅτι ἐν αἵματι ἐκτήσω αὐτόν. S has: ܘܠܐ ܬܬܠܒܫ ܒܕܡܐ ܕܢܦܫܟ. The Hebrew may be restored ואל תקנא ב[דם נפשך]. It has been suggested that the verse originally had דמים, in plural, meaning 'money', 'price' (as in Aramaic and mishnaic Hebrew), rather than 'blood'.[36] A slightly different restoration could be, accordingly, [וא]ל תקנא ב[דָמָו/בדמי נפשך]. This vague verse should be compared to 9:2 אל תקנא לאשה נפשך // להדריכה על במותיך, 'Do not give possession over yourself to a woman, that she should set a foot upon your strength'. Noting the structure common to both verses also helps to confirm the Genizah text of 9:2, which has been disregarded by many editors of BS. Both in 9:2 and in our verse the idiom אל תקנא נפשך (תקנא read as *taqne, hiph'il* of קנה) has the meaning 'Do not give possession over yourself'. Hence my translation 'If you have only one slave, treat him as your brother, do not enslave yourself for the sake of his price [or, blood].' BS is saying that by reducing expenditure on one's only slave (or

[35] The next verse is: כי אם עניתו יצא ואבד // באיזה ד[רך תבקשו], 'If you mistreat him, he will .... //; in which direction will you look for him?'. The words יצא ואבד may mean either 'run away' or 'die'.
[36] See R. Smend, *Die Weisheit des Jesus Sirach*, vol. 2 (Berlin 1906), p. 303.

by torturing him)[37], one may need (in the absence of this slave) to do all the slave's work, thus 'enslaving himself'. S understood the Hebrew word תקנא to mean 'fight',[38] and the last words were conceived as a construction (ܒܕܡܐ ܕܢܦܫܟ, literally, 'with the blood of your soul [or, of yourself]').

An obscure passage in the *Odes of Solomon* (an early Christian work, probably of the second century CE) reads: ܠܐ ܬܩܢܐ ܢܘܟܪܝܐ ܒܕܡܐ ܕܢܦܫܟ ܘܐܦܠܐ ܬܒܥܐ ܠܡܟܠܘ ܠܩܪܝܒܟ, 'Do not buy a stranger with the blood of your soul [or, of yourself], and do not wish to deceive your neighbour'. It has recently been noted that the first stich is borrowed from BS 30[33]:39[31].[39] The verse was transferred in the *Odes of Solomon* from the context of utilitarian morality (in this chapter cruel and cynical) to a spiritual context of sublime religious ethics.

The original language of the *Odes of Solomon* is still disputed: is the Syriac text a translation of a Greek original or was this work originally written in Syriac? In this verse, it is clear that the author of the Odes of Solomon did not use the Greek translation, nor did he use the Syriac translation of BS as we have it. The text he had before him was תקנא rather than תתכתש, which he understood differently from S.[40] This datum is significant for a better understanding of the world of its author, and may argue for a Semitic rather than a Greek original.

In conclusion

The new interpretations given to the verses just discussed demonstrate the importance of further study of the text of BS. Such study cannot be undertaken without taking into account all the textual witnesses that are extant, namely, the Genizah fragments, the Masada scroll, and the two versions (G and S). The Hebrew text of BS, most of which has been preserved only in the Genizah, is indispensable for any endeavour to elucidate the original text of BS. It is through these medieval leaves from the Genizah that we have a knowledge and a better understanding of an otherwise obscure stage in the development of the Hebrew language. It is thanks to such fragments that we have become acquainted with the original form of an ancient Hebrew masterpiece.

---

[37] See n. 35 above.

[38] See Z. Ben-Hayyim, '*Sefer Asatir*', *Tarbiz* 14 (1943), p. 189.

[39] R. Köbert, 'Ode Salomons 20, 6 und Sir 33, 31', *Biblica* 58 (1977), pp. 529–30. This important note has had no effect on recent editions; see J. H. Charlesworth's introduction to the Odes of Solomon in *The Old Testament Pseudepigrapha*, vol. 2 (Garden City, New York, 1985), p. 732 and M. Frazmann (*The Odes of Solomon: An Analysis of the Poetical Structure and Form*, Göttingen, 1991, p. 155) who erroneously cites Köbert as emending קנא to קנט, and fails to see the implications of this striking parallel for the Odes of Solomon and establishing its text.

[40] Note that the word נוכריא ('stranger') in the Odes of Solomon 20:6 is an antonym of אח ('brother') in BS 30[33]:39[31] (and of קריבא, 'neighbour', in Ode 20:6?). Could the word have been added to the verse in BS before it was borrowed by the Odes of Solomon? Contrast Köbert's suggestion about considering נוכריא as a vocative.

3

Targumic Studies and the Cairo Genizah

MICHAEL L. KLEIN

The rabbis of the midrash declared: כל מי שמתחיל במצוה ואינו גומרה ובא אחר וגומרה נקראת על שם שלשני [שגומרה] ‘A worthy deed begun by one person and completed by another is attributed to the latter one [who completes it].’[1] In the present instance, no single person could have possibly completed the deed single-handedly. It therefore behoves us to celebrate the centenary of the Taylor-Schechter Genizah Collection by mentioning Solomon Schechter, who brought the veritable treasure from Cairo to the University of Cambridge one hundred years ago, and its current curator, Stefan Reif, who has completed the ‘mitzvah’ of sorting and conserving the collection and who continues indefatigably to describe and make accessible all of its 140,000 fragments to scholars and researchers of every discipline in Judaic and cognate studies.

The subject of this paper is the contribution of the Cairo Genizah manuscripts to the field of targumic studies. The targums, it will be recalled, are the early Aramaic translations of the Hebrew Bible, and the Cambridge Genizah Collections contain some 1,600 examples of such texts. I should like to begin with a close analysis of one of the oldest manuscripts from the Cairo Genizah – and indeed the oldest extant fragment of targum to the Pentateuch, except for a very small remnant of Leviticus in Aramaic from Qumran. This manuscript, as we shall see, sheds light not only on a passage from the book of Exodus which it translates, but, more importantly, on the purpose of the Aramaic targum, its status and sanctity amongst the sacred literature of ancient Judaism, and on the place of the targum in the liturgy of the ancient synagogue. I shall then describe several other unique fragments of targum discovered in the Cairo Genizah, which contribute valuable new information to our field of studies. I plan to conclude with the reading and translation of one of the most fascinating interpretative targumic texts to the Cain and Abel story – also from the Cairo Genizah, but (may I be forgiven for mentioning it in this context!), from the Bodleian Collection in Oxford.

I. Targumic Fundamentals and MS A

The first manuscript to be considered is T-S (Old Series) 20.155, otherwise known as MS A, that was first identified and published by Paul Kahle in 1930,[2] and eleven

---

[1] *Bereschit Rabba*, eds J. Theodor and Ch. Albeck (Jerusalem, 1965²), §85, pp. 1034–35; see *Devarim Rabbah* 8:5 and *Tanḥumah*, ‘*Eqev* 6.

[2] P. Kahle, *Masoreten des Westens* (=*MdW*) (2 vols; Stuttgart, 1927–30; reprinted Hildesheim, 1967).

smaller fragments of the same manuscript from the Cambridge New and Additional Series, that I was privileged to discover half a century later.[3]

Manuscript A is a vellum scroll written in relatively wide columns, similar to those of a Hebrew Torah scroll. The vellum was ruled with a stylus, both vertically to mark the limits of the columns and horizontally to delineate the lines from which the letters of script were to be suspended. The original targumic text was written only on the *recto* of the scroll. The writing on the *verso* of the manuscript is by a later hand, containing a lectionary of the triennial cycle – probably added after the original scroll was damaged and could no longer be used for recitation of the targum in the synagogal ritual.

The script of the text has been conservatively dated by the paleographer Malachi Beit Arié 'to the eighth/ninth century, or even earlier.'[4] Paul Kahle had more boldly dated it to the seventh or beginning of the eighth century.[5] S. A. Birnbaum went even further in his compendium *The Hebrew Scripts*, dating it to the middle of the seventh century, and pointing to eleven scribal features that are much earlier.[6] The text is vocalized in a sparse early Palestinian supralinear system, to which standard Tiberian sublinear vowels and accents were later added sporadically. Also, the ciphers יה(=15) and יו(=16), encased in small linear frames, were inserted in the blank lines at the beginning of the fifteenth and sixteenth triennial weekly readings in the book of Exodus, at 21:1 and 22:24, respectively. As is well known, these ciphers were later replaced by טו (9+6=15) and טז (9+7=16), in order to avoid the use of יה and יו, which also represent abbreviated forms of the divine name, for the profane purpose of numeration.

The surviving fragments of MS A are all from the book of Exodus – three from chapter 4, and all the others from chapters 20–23. We may therefore assume that the original manuscript encompassed at least that entire book and, very likely, contained the whole Pentateuch. The text is basically unilingual, in Aramaic, with only lemmata, or brief headings of two or three Hebrew words, at the beginning of each verse. The divine name in the Aramaic text is written as a full tetragrammaton, *yod-*

[3] M. L. Klein, 'Nine Fragments of Palestinian Targum to the Pentateuch from the Cairo Genizah (Additions to MS A)', *Hebrew Union College Annual* 50 (1979), pp. 149–64; and *Genizah Manuscripts of Palestinian Targum to the Pentateuch* (=*GMPT*) (2 vols; Cincinnati, 1986).

[4] Communicated privately and recorded in M. L. Klein, *GMPT* (see n. 3 above), vol. 1, p. XXXVII.

[5] *MdW* (see n. 2 above), vol. 2, pp. 2*–3*.

[6] S. A. Birnbaum, *The Hebrew Scripts: their Development over a Period of 3,000 Years* (2 vols; Leiden, 1954–1971), vol. 1, cols 164–167, item 91A. Some reservations have, however, been expressed regarding Birnbaum's methodology; see Klein, 'Nine Fragments' (see n. 3 above), p. 152, n. 17. In a recent, oral communication, and after a fresh comparative study of the script, Edna Engel of the Palaeographical Project at the Jewish National and University Library, Jerusalem, favoured a dating to the eighth century, and possibly earlier. Regarding the early dating of this manuscript, see also J. L. Teicher, 'A Sixth Century Fragment of the Palestinian Targum?', *Vetus Testamentum* 1 (1951), pp. 125–29.

hé-waw-hé, rather than the common abbreviations of two *yod*s, three *yod*s, *yod-waw-yod*, and similar devices, or the substitution of some other less explicit divine appellation, such as are found in almost all later targumic manuscripts. We may also note in this context that the translation/transcription of the divine name is not preserved in the small targum fragment of Leviticus from Qumran, and the Hebrew tetragrammaton is consistently replaced by the generic אלה 'God' in the Targum to Job from Qumran.

The reason that I am citing all these technical details is for the light that they shed upon the much broader and fundamental question regarding the *raison d'être* of the targumim and their status in the ancient and early-medieval synagogue. This question was revisited most recently by Abraham Tal of Tel Aviv University, at a meeting of the International Organization for Targumic Studies in July, 1998. Tal suggested that the purpose of the official Jewish targumim, Onqelos to the Pentateuch and Jonathan to the Prophets, was to prevent the alteration and modernization of the language and orthography of the original Hebrew version of these biblical books, such as was occurring in the Dead Sea Scrolls, as well as in the Hebrew Bible of the Samaritans. In contrast to the prevailing view of the nineteenth and early twentieth centuries, which held that Mishnaic Hebrew was an artificial scholastic dialect, in which the rabbis of the first centuries composed their religious teachings (after the model of Latin for Christian clerics in medieval Europe), there is today a virtual consensus amongst scholars that Mishnaic Hebrew represents the living dialect, spoken and written, of the Jews of Palestine during that period. For the ancient rabbis, who preached the divine origin of every word and every spelling in the Hebrew Bible, and who based many legal and moral teachings on the archaic orthography or ancient and curious vocabulary of the Hebrew Bible, modernization of the text into contemporary usage posed a double threat: the violation and potential loss of the *ipsissima verba dei*, and the undermining of the textual basis for early rabbinic exegesis and law. Tal argued that by commissioning the Aramaic translations for a bilingual society that was conversant with both Hebrew and Aramaic, the rabbis protected what they considered to be the original Hebrew version from any alteration or corruption. All modernization and explication would henceforth be carried out in the Aramaic targum and in other rabbinic literature, while the integrity of the God-given Hebrew would be fully guaranteed.

Another view of the origins of the targumim, expressed by the medieval French commentator Rashi (R. Solomon b. Isaac of the eleventh century) among others, is that they were produced for women and other unlettered folk, who could not understand the original Hebrew Bible.[7] Neither this, nor Tal's theory, attributes an intrinsically laudable purpose to the origin of the targum, but rather views it as a begrudged accommodation to the ignorance of the masses, or as a protective shield for the truly sacred text. As such, one would hardly expect the targum to be accorded

[7] Commentary to BT, *Megillah* 21b: ובנביא אפי' אחד קורא ושנים מתרגמין שהתרגום אינו אלא להשמיע לנשים ועמי הארץ שאינן מכירין בלשון הקודש והתרגום הוא לעז הבבליים ובתרגום של תורה צריכין אנו לחזור שיהו מבינין את המצות אבל בשל נביאים לא קפדי עלייהו כולי האי.

particularly high status in the hierarchy of ancient Jewish literature. It seems to me that MS A, the earliest and most important targum manuscript from the Cambridge Genizah Collection, undermines these and similarly denigratory theories, at least at a somewhat later period.

Let us return to some of the details mentioned earlier. MS A is written in the mode of an actual Hebrew Torah scroll. The full writing of the divine name indicates that the manuscript was accorded the highest level of sanctity. The addition of vowels – a departure from the Torah scroll tradition, according to which not even a single dot may be added – implies concern for the accurate pronunciation of the Aramaic, just as the further addition of cantillation signs indicates that the text is likely to have been chanted in a traditional tune, as was the Hebrew Torah. It is precisely this type of targum manuscript that would have justified the rabbinic law of salvaging targum texts together with Hebrew Scripture from a fire on the sabbath: כל כתבי הקודש מצילין אותן מפני הדליקה... ואף על פי שכתובין בכל לשון טעונין גניזה 'All Holy Scriptures are to be rescued from the conflagration... and, regardless of the language in which they are written, they require consignment to a *genizah*.'[8] Thus, as early as the second century, the targumim are categorized as 'Holy Scripture' and, as such, certain sabbath restrictions may be violated in order to save them from a fire. The second half of this mishnah would seem to address a situation in which the scrolls had actually been damaged by the fire, and had been disqualified from use in the synagogue. Here too, regardless of their language, they are to be respectfully confined to a *genizah*, and not simply discarded as waste.

The Tosefta, another second-century rabbinic source, indicates that the targum was part of the curriculum of study in the schools of the period. As is well known, there are certain biblical passages, mostly involving embarrassing sins committed by the major ancestral figures, such as the worship of the golden calf or sexual offences, that the rabbis forbade to be translated into Aramaic in the synagogue during the reading of the Torah or the Prophets. Moreover, the Tosefta states that the story of David and Bathsheba must not be read in public, neither in Hebrew nor in Aramaic translation, לא נקראין ולא מתרגמין. But the Tosefta continues: והסופר מלמד כדרכו 'the school-teacher, however, teaches these passages in his usual manner.'[9]

Genizah manuscripts from the Cambridge collections confirm that the Aramaic targumim, in this case probably Onqelos to the Pentateuch and Jonathan to the *hafṭarot* from the Prophets, were taught to Jewish children in Iraq, as late as the twelfth century. In his monumental work, *A Mediterranean Society*, S. D. Goitein cites several letters that mention the preparation of young boys for recitation of the targum during synagogue services. Goitein writes: 'A long business letter sent from Cairo to a merchant on a trip to India contains also this remark: "Your boy Faraj now reads the Targūm accompanying the lections – as I guaranteed you he would."'[10]

---

[8] Mishnah, *Shabbat* 16.1.
[9] Tosefta, *Megillah* 4(3).38.
[10] S. D. Goitein, *A Mediterranean Society* (5 vols; Berkeley, Los Angeles and London, 1967–88), vol. 2, p. 175.

Another Genizah fragment preserves the yet-unfulfilled hopes of a father that his son might ascend the *anbol*, or elevated platform, in the centre of the synagogue together with him at the next sabbath service, 'where the boy would chant the section of the weekly lection apportioned to his father, or the Targūm..."so that my heart should be happy."'[11]

I suggest that the status of the Aramaic targum in mishnaic and talmudic times was so elevated that some rabbis were concerned about its usurping the primal position of the Hebrew Bible itself. They, therefore, promulgated restraining rules, such as those stipulating that 'the *meturgeman* (who also stood on the *bimah* or platform) must not raise his voice above that of the Torah reader',[12] and 'that the reader of the Hebrew Bible must not assist the *meturgeman*, lest the congregation get the mistaken impression that the targum is contained in the original Torah scroll.'[13] It is, however, perfectly clear that these rules are not meant to diminish the sanctity of the targum itself. This is further evident from the rabbinic attribution of the original authorship of the targumim to Ezra the Scribe (fifth century BCE), and their later reconstruction to Onqelos the proselyte, under the tutelage of the school of Rabbi Aqiva, and to the great tannaitic sage and disciple of Hillel, Jonathan ben Uzziel.[14] The authority and esteem reflected in these attributions of source served to enhance the status enjoyed by the targumim in rabbinic times, regardless of the degree of historicity that we might grant these statements. Consider, also, a story recorded in the Palestinian Talmud: 'Rabbi Samuel bar Isaac (late third century CE) entered the synagogue and saw a man reciting the targum, while leaning [slouched?] on a column. He admonished him: "It is forbidden; just as the Torah was given [at Sinai] in fear and awe, so must we treat it with fear and awe."'[15] Note that the sage makes no allowance for the fact that only an Aramaic translation was being read in this lax manner and not the Hebrew Torah itself!

Returning, then, to MS A and to the earlier Targum manuscripts of Leviticus and Job from Qumran, it is evident that the rabbinic statements requiring the oral recitation of the targum in the synagogal service, were no longer fully heeded – if they ever had been. As previously mentioned, these manuscripts are identical in format to their contemporary Hebrew Bible counterparts. Moreover, by the time of the redaction of the Mishnah, the rule דברים שנאמרו בפה בפה ודברים שנאמרו בכתב בכתב 'teachings originally transmitted orally (such as mishnah, midrash and targum) must continue to be recited orally; and those given in writing (i.e. Hebrew Scripture) may be recited only from a written text'[16] had lost all practical validity. It is clear from the

---

[11] Goitein (see n. 10 above), p. 177.

[12] BT, *Berakhot* 45a: .אין המתרגם רשאי להגביה קולו יותר מן הקורא

[13] BT, *Megillah* 32a: .הקורא בתורה לא יסייע למתורגמן כדי שלא יאמרו תרגום כתוב בתורה

[14] BT, *Megillah* 3a, where the word מפרש 'explicated' in Nehemiah 8:8 is taken to mean that Ezra provided a targumic translation alongside the reading of the Torah (מפרש זה תרגום). This 'original' targum was eventually forgotten and had to be reconstructed: אלא שכחום .וחזרו ויסדום

[15] PT, *Megillah* 74d.

[16] PT, *Megillah* 74d.

exquisite MS A, as well as from the many other early vellum codices of targum, and especially the collections of festival readings according to the early rite of the land of Israel, that the restrictions against chanting the targum from a written scroll or codex were no longer heeded. I shall return to this point shortly, when I have to reconsider an earlier interpretation of the *serugin* or 'shorthand' targum manuscripts from the Cambridge Genizah collections.

Before leaving MS A, I should like to mention briefly two more of its invaluable contributions to Judaic studies. Several translations and interpretations of legal passages in this manuscript contradict either the halakhic exegesis of the prevailing traditions deriving from the schools of Hillel and Aqiva, or the undisputed anonymous mishnah of Rabbi Meir and Rabbi Judah the Patriarch. An example, discussed at length by Joseph Heinemann,[17] is the translation of the Hebrew verb בער in Exodus 22:4 with יקד 'devour by fire' rather than with אכל or פקר 'devour by the grazing of animals'. This rendition undermines the scriptural basis for one of the four major categories of torts, or civil damages, listed in the opening passage of the mishnaic tractate *Bava Qamma*. Targumic translations of this sort have in turn generated questions about the dating of the Palestinian targumim, such as whether translations that are not in accordance with mishnaic traditions imply a pre-mishnaic date of composition. Other non-normative halakhic interpretations contained in the Palestinian targumim seem to indicate that they originate in the rival school of Shammai and Rabbi Ishmael rather than in that of Hillel and Aqiva, which later became predominant and normative in Judaism.

Lastly, though not exhaustively, it should be noted that the Genizah manuscripts of Palestinian targum made a vast contribution to the reconstruction of Jewish Palestinian Aramaic. Two short quotations from Eduard Kutscher's *Studies in Galilean Aramaic*[18] will suffice to illustrate that estimation. The situation prior to the discovery and study of the Genizah manuscripts and the potential contribution of the Genizah texts were best described at the beginning of his English summary. There he noted that the current formulation 'of Galilean Aramaic Grammar is distorted by the fact that it is based upon corrupt texts, since European Jewry, who chiefly studied the Babylonian Talmud, both consciously and unconsciously grafted many of it dialectal forms – which are Eastern Aramaic – upon that of the Galilean. This situation may be rectified, first of all by making use of the fragments of the Palestinian Talmud, those of the Midrashim and of the Palestinian Targum which were found in the Cairo Geniza, and of inscriptions of the period in question.'[19] Referring specifically to the

---

[17] 'Early Halakhah in the Palestinian Targumim', *Journal of Jewish Studies* 25 (1974), pp. 116–24. See also G. Schelbert, 'Exodus XXII 4 im Palästinischen Targum', *Vetus Testamentum* 8 (1958), pp. 253–63; and M. L. Klein, *GMPT* (see n. 3 above), vol. 2, pp. 78–79.

[18] *Tarbiz* 21 (1950), pp. 192–205; 22 (1951), pp. 53–63, 185–92; 23 (1952), pp. 36–60; reprinted in a Hebrew booklet (Jerusalem, 1952); translated into English by M. Sokoloff, (Ramat Gan, 1976).

[19] Hebrew booklet (see n. 18 above), p. 66.

Genizah targum manuscripts in the body of the essay, Kutscher writes: 'In my opinion, these are the most reliable texts. Except for ordinary scribal errors, they have no faults.'[20] Indeed, four decades later, S. E. Fassberg published *A Grammar of the Palestinian Targum Fragments from the Cairo Genizah*,[21] based entirely upon these texts, that were so highly assessed for their linguistic purity by Kutscher.

II. New Texts and Text-types

As noted above, there are new targumic texts and text-types that have emerged from the Cairo Genizah. Within the present framework, it will be possible to do no more than briefly describe several of these significant finds.

1. One recent discovery in the Genizah collections consists of four miniature manuscripts of Targum Onqelos written in the *serugin*, or shorthand, system, in which only the first few letters of each Aramaic word, or the first few words of each verse, are recorded. Three manuscripts are from the Cambridge collections and the fourth is from the Library of the Jewish Theological Seminary of America in New York. When they were first published, I suggested that they were 'crib-notes' of the *meturgeman*, who was required to declaim the targum by heart during public worship in the synagogue.[22] This suggestion presupposed that the note-maker was conforming to the rabbinic rule quoted above that oral law must be transmitted orally and written law must be read from a written text. It was further supported by a story about the same Rabbi Samuel bar Isaac cited above, who entered a synagogue and saw a school-teacher teaching targum from a written scroll (חמא חד ספר מושט תרגומא מן גו סיפרא). He admonished him: 'It is forbidden; words received orally must be transmitted orally; those received in writing, in writing (אסיר לך דברים שנאמרו בפה בפה ודברים שנאמרו בכתב בכתב).[23] This early amora, or sage of the Talmud, who is known to have spent a significant portion of his career in Babylonia, may have imported this attitude to Palestine of the late third century. This would seem to explain the apparent contradiction between the meticulously written scroll and codices of targum originating in Palestine, and the much later Eastern crib-notes that helped the poor *meturgeman*, with a failing memory, conceal his weakness from his congregation – or encouraged him in his belief that he was not in violation of the rule of orality, since he was reading from shorthand and not from a fully written text.

There is, however, another explanation that suggests itself. The four independent manuscripts of shorthand Onqelos are all of special texts. The three Cambridge pieces contain Exodus 19 and 20, the reading for the Shavu'ot festival, which includes the Ten Commandments. The fourth, from New York, contains the Song of Moses from Deuteronomy 32. These were especially well-known texts that were

[20] Sokoloff (see n. 18 above), p. 3.

[21] *A Grammar of the Palestinian Targum Fragments from the Cairo Genizah* (Atlanta, 1991).

[22] '*Serugin* (Shorthand) of Onqelos from the Cairo Genizah', in *Let Your Colleagues Praise You: Studies in Memory of Stanley Gevirtz* [= *Maarav* 8 (1992)], pp. 275–87; and briefly, in 'Targumic Texts as Mnemonic Device', *Genizah Fragments* (October, 1995), p. 2.

[23] PT, *Megillah* 74d.

traditionally memorized. In fact, the custom regarding the latter was based on Deuteronomy 31:19: 'record this song and teach it to the Israelites; place it in their mouths (כתבו לכם את השירה הזאת ולמדה את בני ישראל שימה בפיהם). It may, therefore, very well be that by the period covering the twelfth to the fifteenth century, to which these fragments are dated, there was no general custom of reciting all targum from memory, even in the Eastern tradition such as that of Iraq. I am also told by Ezra Fleischer that manuscripts of medieval liturgical poetry have been found in the Genizah collections, written in shorthand. Now surely, the rules of 'oral Torah' would not have applied to such late compositions. Rather, Fleischer argues, these were the 'crib-notes' of vain cantors, preferring to give the impression that they knew the famous poems by heart.[24]

2. The Cairo Genizah has yielded beautiful vellum collections of Palestinian Targum readings for special sabbaths and festivals. This comports with the Palestinian liturgical rite, described in the Mishnah,[25] as interrupting the regular order of the triennial Torah readings and replacing them with the special readings for the occasion at hand. This is also in contrast to the Babylonian custom, prevailing to this day, according to which the regular weekly lections continue as usual, supplemented by a special, final reading (מפטיר) for the occasion. Eight to ten such fascicles have been identified amongst the various Genizah collections.[26] Although the finest and most extensive of these is from the T-S Old Series (MS AA),[27] I should like to cite the Oxford manuscript (MS F)[28] on account of its rhymed colophon, in which the medieval scribe, in a move of some rarity, states his purpose, and describes this targumic genre:

> This is the booklet of Jacob, son of Joseph, son of Ṣemaḥ. May God open his heart to the study of His Torah, and may He enlighten his eyes through His salvation and show him the building of His Temple and His chamber. Amen! Amen! with His speed, and may all Israel be included in His blessing. It contains the targum for the additional prayer of all the festivals and the targum for Ḥanukkah.
> Eleven by the count [= 5011 *anno mundi* = 1251 CE] [29]

זה הדפתר ליעקב בן יוסף בן צמח יי׳ יפתח לבו לתלמד
תורתו ויאיר עיניו בישועתו ויראהו בנין היכלו ולשכתו
אמן אמן במהרתו וכל ישראל בכלל ברכתו:
יש בו תרגום מוספים שלכל המועדים ותרגום לחנוכה
יא׳ למני

[24] I am grateful to Professor Fleischer for this private communication.
[25] Mishnah, *Megillah* 3.4: חוזרין לכסדרן ; לכל מפסיקין.
[26] See M. L. Klein, *GMPT* (see n. 3 above), vol. 1, pp. xxiii–xxvi.
[27] Cambridge University Library, T-S B13.4, ff. 1–2; Or.1080 B18.1, ff. 1–6; and T-S NS 218.61.
[28] Bodleian Library, Oxford, MS Heb.c.43, ff. 57–65.
[29] P. Kahle, *MdW* (see n. 2 above), vol. 2, p. 49; and M. L. Klein, *GMPT* (see n. 3 above), vol. 1, pp. 306–7; see also p. 306, n. 4, in that volume, for an alternate interpretation of the date cipher.

3. Also related to the readings of special sabbaths and festivals are Aramaic introductory poems that were composed for these occasions. These are primarily for the *hafṭarot*, the supplementary readings from the Prophets, that were accompanied by Targum Jonathan. Many of the poems are formal *reshuyot*, the request by the *meturgeman* for the permission of the congregation and its leaders to proceed with the translation of the *hafṭarah*. As we mentioned above, tradition attributed the authorship of the Targum to the Prophets to Jonathan ben Uzziel. Many of the poems, therefore, contain paeans of legendary praise to this ancient sage. Although this genre had been known to scholars since the nineteenth century,[30] three new fragments were recently identified among the Cambridge Genizah manuscripts. One (T-S H15.27), contains a reference by name to a prominent eleventh-century Spanish rabbi: 'With the permission of our master and teacher, prince of princes, and with the permission of our master and teacher Samuel, head of all scholars' ומרשות מרינו ורבינו נגיד נגידיא ומרשות מר[ינו] ור[בינו] שמואל ראש כל חכימיא. This seems to be a reference to Samuel Ha-Nagid of Granada (993–1055 CE). Another (T-S AS 71.64, folio 2v), relates the mystical legend of how birds that flew above Rabbi Jonathan were devoured by the flame [halo?] of the divine Glory that descended upon him as he sat studying the Torah in intense devotion, ופריש יהו[נ]תן בר עוזיאל...דבשעתא דהוה לעי באוריתא כל ציפר גפא ד[הו]ה פרח עלוהי באויר רקיע שמיא הוה מתוקד משלהובית יקרא דשרי עלוהי.[31]

4. Another new text-type that appeared in the Cambridge Genizah collections was a single page of Fragment-Targum of Onqelos to Numbers 16–18. Whereas this selective anthological genre had been well known for the Palestinian targumim – though not fully understood in terms of its *raison d'être* – it was totally unattested for Onqelos. A careful comparison of the Onqelos passage with its counterparts in the Palestinian Fragment-Targums revealed no textual or redactional relationship between the two. The selections of targumic words and phrases are totally independent of one another and the rationale for each set of choices remains a mystery.[32]

5. Similar to the Fragment-Targum are extracts of Onqelos that we have identified as 'proto-masorah' to this official targum. The masorah to Onqelos has been known for centuries in its several formats, as marginal notes to Onqelos texts, as separate collections of these notes, as alphabetical lists, and as topical lists. In fact, nineteen fragments belonging to fifteen distinct manuscripts of masorah to Onqelos were identified in Cambridge, during preparation of the catalogue of targumic manuscripts.[33] The main purpose of the targumic masorah was to indicate and list rare

[30] L. Zunz, *Literaturgeschichte der Synagogalen Poesie* (Berlin, 1865), pp. 79–80.

[31] M. L. Klein, 'Introductory Poems (*R'shuyot*) to the Targum of the Hafṭarah in Praise of Jonathan ben Uzziel' in *Bits of Honey: Essays for Samson H. Levey*, eds S. F. Chyet and D. H. Ellenson, (Atlanta, 1993), pp. 43–56.

[32] M. L. Klein, 'A Fragment-Targum of *Onqelos* from the Cairo Genizah' in *Solving Riddles and Untying Knots: Biblical, Epigraphic and Semitic Studies in Honor of Jonas C. Greenfield*, eds Z. Zevit, S. Gitin and M. Sokoloff (Winona Lake, 1995), pp. 101–5.

[33] M. L. Klein, *Targumic Manuscripts in the Cambridge Genizah Collections* (Cambridge, 1992).

translations, in order to prevent their disappearance by hyper-correction at the hands of later well-meaning copyists. A typical example is the note to Genesis 1:5:... יום דמתרג' יממא ו...באורי.. וסימ 'the common noun יום is translated יממא six times throughout the Pentateuch, and the citations are...'[34] Scholars have long wondered how the medieval masoretes composed these lists, before the computer era, or even, as far as we know, before the use of index cards.

The discovery of several 'reduced' texts of Onqelos, preserving only masoretically significant words and phrases, seems to have provided the answer. These extracts of Onqelos are about one-third the length of the complete targum, and would have served as a convenient intermediate form, from which the masoretic counting and lists would be composed. Hence our name 'proto-masorah' to Onqelos.[35]

Other targumic texts and text-types from the Cairo Genizah that deserve at least a brief mention are such items as Aramaic acrostic poems on Nisan, the first of the months, and omens based on the position and hue of the new moon (Exodus 12); poems on the Song of the Sea (Exodus 15) and the Death of Moses (Deuteronomy 34).[36] Likewise, the collections of targumic *toseftot* from the Genizah that contain expansive aggadic interpretations of biblical narratives written in targumic style. In some texts, these *toseftot* are spliced into the running targum, while in a number of Genizah manuscripts they are reproduced as separate collections. These, too, have been described elsewhere,[37] and what must suffice in the present context is the presentation of what may be the single most fascinating and fanciful of targumic *toseftot* to the entire book of Genesis. To this is devoted our final section.

III. And Cain Said to Abel... (Genesis 4:8)

The lacuna in the Hebrew Bible at Genesis 4:8 is well known, and has elicited rabbinic explanation and exegesis for almost two thousand years. The text reads ויאמר קין אל הבל אחיו ויהי בהיותם בשדה ויקם קין אל הבל אחיו ויהרגהו, 'And Cain said to Abel, his brother... and when they were in the field, Cain set upon his brother Abel and killed him.' What did Cain say to Abel? The Samaritan Hebrew Pentateuch preserves the

---

[34] See, e.g., A. Berliner, *Die Massorah zum Targum Onkelos* (Leipzig, 1887), p. 1. For a recent introduction, see M. L. Klein, 'The Masorah to Onqelos: A Neglected Targumic Work', *Dutch Studies on Near Eastern Languages and Literatures* 2 (1996), pp. 81–100.

[35] M. L. Klein, 'Manuscripts of Proto-Massorah to Onqelos', in *Estudios Masoréticos* [*X Congreso de la IOMS; En memoria de Harry M. Orlinsky*], eds E. Fernández Tejero and M. T. Ortega Monasterio (Madrid, 1993), pp. 73–88.

[36] E. Fleischer, 'The Great New Moon', *Tarbiz* 37 (1967–68), pp. 265–78; M. L. Klein, *GMPT* (see n. 3 above); and J. C. Greenfield and M. Sokoloff, 'Astrological and Related Omen Texts in Jewish Palestinian Aramaic', *Journal of Near Eastern Studies* 48 (1989), pp. 201–14.

[37] M. L. Klein, 'Targumic Toseftot from the Cairo Genizah', in *Salvacion en la Palabra: Targum–Derash–Berith: En Memoria del Professor Alejandro Diez Macho*, ed. D. Muñoz Leon (Madrid, 1986), pp. 409–18. See also R. Kasher, *Targumic Toseftot to the Prophets* (Jerusalem, 1996), which includes many texts from the Cairo Genizah.

logically missing phrase נלכה השדה 'Let us go to the field'[38] and the Septuagint and the Palestinian targums reflect this phrase in their translations. Nevertheless, the exegetical temptation of a lacuna in the Masoretic Text, especially in a passage fraught with primordial questions, could hardly be resisted by the rabbis of the midrash and the *meturgeman* of the *toseftot*.

The perennial questions of the Cain and Abel story barely require rehearsing. If they are the only recorded children of Adam and Eve, whom did they marry and how did the population of the world propagate? If they alone possessed all the wealth of the earth, one as a shepherd and the other as a farmer, did they barter their products in order to survive? If each offered up a voluntary thanksgiving sacrifice from his first yield, why did God accept one and reject the other? Was this sufficient ground to provoke the first case of fratricide – or were there perhaps deeper psychological undercurrents that merely surfaced at a moment of unrelated provocation?

The author of the targumic *tosefta* to Genesis 4:8 exploits the opportunity represented by the textual lacuna, as if it were infinite. First, he deals with the immediate question of God's discrimination between the two offerings. He does this by retrojecting a contemporary philosophical debate on the subject of divine justice into the primeval mouths of Cain and Abel. He then moves on to analyse the underlying motives of this sibling rivalry that culminated in murder.
The following is a translation of the text in Oxford Bodleian MS Heb.c.74r:[39]

> Then Cain said to Abel his brother: There is neither justice nor judge, nor is there any world beside this one (לית דינא ולית דיינא ולית עלמא בר מן דין). Abel answered: There is justice and there is a judge, and there is another world for requiting evil and good. [NB: a possible reflection of the dispute between the Sadducees and Pharisees on whether justice and retribution, if not evident in this world, are eventually executed in the world to come.][40] At that moment Cain considered what he might do to him, but found nothing suitable. Afterwards, his wrath subsided, [NB: the eventual act is not done in the heat of the initial argument] and he said to Abel: Now let there not be a quarrel between me and you; separate from me and take the flock as your lot. [NB: the borrowing of the theme of the peaceful and anachronistic separation of Abraham from Lot, after Gen. 13:8–9.] Said Abel to him: All that I desire is a fair division. After Abel had gone to his sheep and departed from Cain, Cain had second thoughts and said: What have I done? The summer months will pass, and I shall have no milk to drink and no wool to wear. He pursued him and, upon reaching him, said: This is not a fair division. You take half the flock and half the land; and I shall take half the flock and half the land. To which Abel said: As you please. And they made the division at that

[38] A. Tal, *The Samaritan Pentateuch* (Tel Aviv, 1994), p. 4.
[39] According to M. L. Klein, *GMPT* (see n. 3 above), vol. 1, pp. 10–13; first published by M. Ginsburger, *Das Fragmententhargum* (Berlin, 1899; reprinted, Jerusalem, 1969), pp. 71–72.
[40] See S. Eisenberg, 'An Anti-Sadducee Polemic in the Palestinian Targum Tradition', *Harvard Theological Review* 63 (1970), pp. 433–44, and earlier discussions by G. Vermes and P. Grelot, to which he refers there on p. 434, n. 4.

> moment. Abel added: This is an equal division, done in fairness; and, with that, departed. Cain then tried to graze his portion of the sheep, but found he was unable to graze sheep, without neglecting the tilling of his land. He returned to Abel once again: There is a fairer division than this; you take the flock as your lot and I shall take the land as mine. Abel acceded to Cain's request. [NB: Cain is portrayed as being by nature quarrelsome; Abel is, by contrast, highly accommodating.]

And now the *tosefta* gets to the bottom of it all, namely, Cain and Abel as the paradigm of all human conflict:

> Now Cain had been bearing a grudge against Abel prior to this event, for Abel's [twin] sister was Cain's wife; and she was not as good-looking as Cain's [twin] sister, who was Abel's wife. [NB: the marriage of each to the other's twin minimized the inevitable incest.] When Cain recalled what was in his heart, he said [to himself]: Now I have found an opportunity to vent my hatred. He ran after him and said: Get off my land, which I have taken as my lot! And Abel had nowhere to go. [NB: the perennial competition between farmer and herdsman.] And he [Cain] did not know where to strike him. [NB: How would he have known how to commit the first murder, never having witnessed even an accidental death?] He looked about here and there, and saw two birds fighting, whereupon one rose up against the other and struck it on its mouth, causing its blood to spurt forth, until it died. [NB; a further phraseological influence from the early Moses narratives in Exodus 2:12–13.] Cain then learnt the lesson from it and did the same to Abel his brother. Upon seeing that he was dead, he feared that his father [Adam] would challenge him to produce him [Abel]. Not knowing what to do, he looked up and noticed the bird that had killed its fellow putting its beak into the ground, in order to dig [a hole] and bury its dead fellow and cover it with earth. At that moment, Cain did the same to Abel, so that [his father] might not find him. [NB: a possible source of how to dispose of a dead body.]

In conclusion, the Cairo Genizah has deepened our understanding of almost every aspect of targumic studies. It firmly establishes the status of the targumim in the synagogue as well as in the schoolhouse. New texts and text-types have broadened our appreciation of the scope of targumic creativity from late antiquity and through the medieval period. The Genizah texts have provided undiluted sources for the study of Jewish Palestinian Aramaic. And last, but certainly not of least interest, they have preserved some of the most fascinating exegetical interpretations of biblical narrative. For all of this and much more, we commemorate with these published studies the insightful scholars who salvaged the Genizah and transferred its precious contents to European libraries during the nineteenth century.

4

The Tannaitic Midrashim

MENAHEM KAHANA

A History of Finds

I would like to commence this paper with a moving citation from Solomon Schechter, the great discoverer of the Genizah of Cairo. At the end of his article 'A Hoard of Hebrew Manuscripts', Schechter expressed some of his personal feelings in the following sentences:

> Looking over this enormous mass of fragments about me, in the sifting and examination of which I am now occupied, I cannot overcome a sad feeling stealing over me, that I shall hardly be worthy to see all the results which the Genizah will add to our knowledge of Jews and Judaism. The work is not for one man and not for one generation. It will occupy many a specialist, and much longer than a lifetime. However, to use an old adage, 'It is not thy duty to complete the work, but neither art thou free to desist from it.'[1]

There is no doubt that Schechter's assessment was correct and that scholars will continue to identify with his sentiments even in future generations. We do, however, now know considerably more about the Genizah than a hundred years ago, and this paper will attempt to exemplify our knowledge in the field of the tannaitic midrashim.

The discovery of the Cairo Genizah has opened up new horizons in many areas of talmud-related study. The field of the halakhic midrashim produced by the tannaitic sages in the early centuries of the Common Era is no exception. Research on the tannaitic midrashim involves integrative and interdisciplinary work that includes philological analysis, literary criticism, biblical interpretation, halakhic history and aggadic development. But we first of all need texts and here the main contribution of the Genizah is in two areas: 1) the provision of early, reliable texts for the midrashim already known; 2) the discovery of fragments of lost midrashim.[2]

The well-known halakhic midrashim that have been the subject of commentaries since the Middle Ages, and that were published by the early Christian printers of

---

[1] S. Schechter, *Studies in Judaism*, vol. 2 (Philadelphia, 1908), pp. 29–30.

[2] See Schechter's own general estimate of the Genizah's expected contribution to the field of the midrashim: 'They are of the utmost importance to the student of Jewish tradition, giving not only quite a new class of manuscripts unknown to the author of the *Variae Lectiones*, but also restoring to us parts of old Rabbinic works long ago given up as lost forever' (*Studies* (see n. 1 above), p. 10).

Hebrew books in the sixteenth century, consist of four titles: 1) The *Mekhilta of Rabbi Ishmael* on Exodus; 2) The *Sifra* on Leviticus; 3) The *Sifre* on Numbers; and 4) The *Sifre* on Deuteronomy. Critical editions of these midrashim were published, for the most part, during the first third of the twentieth century. They were based mainly on complete manuscripts preserved in European libraries in Oxford, London, Berlin, Munich and Rome. Several of them did not take account of Genizah sources,[3] while others made only marginal use of them.[4]

The early printed editions and most of the complete manuscript codices represent Western textual traditions of the midrashim. They are full of copyists' errors and 'scribal emendations', some of them purposely made in order to elucidate difficult passages. Other such emendations were made with a view to harmonising the halakhic midrashim with the normative halakhah, or with corresponding sections in the Mishnah and the Babylonian Talmud. This process was influenced by the great authority of these two works in comparison with the halakhic midrashim. On the other hand, the Eastern textual tradition that was preserved in the Genizah fragments is, in many instances, of older vintage and reflects the original text of the midrash, before it was 'corrected' in the medieval Jewish academies of Europe. The Genizah fragments therefore provide us with a key to a better understanding of the tannaitic midrashim.

In addition to Genizah discoveries, the methods of philological-historical scholarship have been improved by outstanding modern talmudic scholars such as J. N. Epstein, C. Albeck, S. Lieberman and E. S. Rosenthal. We are today, therefore, much better placed to explain midrashic passages that presented commentators and earlier editors with so many difficulties.

The contribution of the Genizah fragments to a new understanding of the halakhic midrashim is particularly obvious in the following areas: 1) The matter of new and original readings; 2) Awareness of the special characteristics of rabbinic Hebrew; 3) Recognition of the arrangement and division of the midrashim; 4) Recognition of the technical language of the midrash; 5) Sharper articulation of the differences between the main tannaitic schools; 6) Reconstruction of the biblical text that was used by the Tannaim and that occasionally differs from the Masoretic Text; 7) Analysis of the activity of the redactors of the midrash, in the matters of the transfer of passages from one place to another and the reworking of the text; 8) Distinguishing between different levels of redaction; 9) Isolation of old glosses and later additions that infiltrated the midrashic text after its redaction. It may be stated in general that with the help of the Genizah we can now attempt to uncover the full meaning of these complex works by investigating their texts, their literal meaning, and their literary and ideological content.

---

[3] *Siphre D'Be Rab* (on Numbers), ed. H. S. Horovitz (Leipzig, 1917); *Mechilta D'Rabbi Ismael*, eds H. S. Horovitz and I. A. Rabin (Frankfurt am Main, 1931).

[4] *Mekilta de-Rabbi Ishmael*, ed. J. Z. Lauterbach (Philadelphia, 1933–35); *Siphre ad Deuteronomium*, ed. L. Finkelstein (Berlin, 1939).

Up to this point, we have been dealing with the well-known midrashim. But, in addition to these four midrashim, some of the sages of the Middle Ages had in their libraries at least three other such halakhic midrashim, also composed in the tannaitic period: 1) The *Mekhilta of Rabbi Shim'on bar Yoḥai* on Exodus; 2) The *Sifre Zuṭa* on Numbers; and 3) The *Mekhilta* on Deuteronomy. Scholars of talmudic literature, especially I. Lewy, D. Hoffmann and H. S. Horovitz, tried to reconstruct these works from the indirect quotations they found in two compositions of the thirteenth century: the *Midrash Ha-Gadol* of Rabbi David ha-'Adeni from Yemen and the *Yalquṭ Shim'oni* of Rabbi Simeon of Frankfurt.[5]

With the discovery of the Cairo Genizah, a number of fragments of these three lost midrashim have been found. Schechter himself succeeded, with his excellent insight, in identifying three fragments of the *Mekhilta of Rabbi Shim'on* on Exodus.[6] He also published two pages of the *Sifre Zuṭa*,[7] and six pages of the *Mekhilta* on Deuteronomy.[8] Other researchers have succeeded in discovering additional fragments of the lost midrashim. Some of these fragments have also been included in recent editions of the lost tannaitic midrashim. Particularly noteworthy is the new edition of the *Mekhilta of Rabbi Shim'on* on Exodus, edited by J. N. Epstein and E. Z. Melamed in Jerusalem in 1955. This edition is based substantially on Genizah fragments, which cover approximately forty per cent of the midrash.

The recovery of these lost midrashim is clearly of great importance for talmudic research in both its halakhic and aggadic aspects. This partial reconstruction, with the utilisation of the Genizah, enables us to improve our knowledge in many such areas as: 1) The literary characteristics of the different midrashim and their connection with more ancient compositions; 2) The authority of the Bible and its text in the halakhic midrashim; 3) The development of midrashic methods; 4) The schools of R. Aqiva and R. Ishmael and the division of the midrashim according to these schools; 5) The names of the sages in the different midrashim; 6) The tendentious redaction of the midrashim; 7) The archaic halakhah and polemics against 'heretics' in the halakhic midrashim; 8) The relationship of the midrashim to the Mishnah, the Tosefta, and the Talmuds; 9) The time and place of the redaction of the midrashim.

The main problems with Genizah material stem from its wide dispersal in different libraries and from the absence of comprehensive catalogues of the fragments according to specific fields. In order to overcome this obstacle, two professors at the Hebrew University of Jerusalem, E. E. Urbach and J. Sussmann, established the 'Mishnah Project' about forty years ago. The purpose of this project was and is to prepare comprehensive catalogues of all the Genizah fragments and other manuscript

---

[5] See I. Lewy, 'Ein Wort über die "Mechilta des R. Simon"', *Jahresbericht des jüdisch-theologischen Seminars* (Breslau, 1889), pp. 1–40; D. Hoffmann, *Mechilta de-Rabbi Simon b. Jochai* (Frankfurt am Main, 1905) and *Midrasch Tannaim zum Deuteronomium* (Berlin, 1909); H. S. Horovitz, *Der Sifre Suṭṭa* (Breslau, 1910).

[6] See Hoffmann, *Mechilta* (see n. 5 above), p. IX.

[7] *JQR* 6 (1894), pp. 656–63.

[8] *JQR* 16 (1904), pp. 446–52, 695–99; *Festschrift zum siebzigsten Geburstag Israel Lewy's*, eds M. Brann and I. Elbogen (Breslau, 1911), Hebrew Section, pp. 187–92.

sources that include the Mishnah, the Tosefta, the two Talmuds and the halakhic digest of R. Isaac Alfasi.

Inspired and assisted by this project, I decided twenty-five years ago to concentrate on the field of tannaitic midrashim. Since then, I have searched for additional manuscripts of the halakhic midrashim in the world's libraries, especially in those that house material from the Cairo Genizah. At the same time, I have systematically examined the holdings of the Institute of Microfilmed Hebrew Manuscripts in the Jewish National Library in Jerusalem. Since the fall of the Iron Curtain, I have thrice visited the libraries in St. Petersburg and Moscow, where I have succeeded in identifying new textual witnesses, both direct and indirect, to the tannaitic midrashim.

The sum of my efforts in this area is represented by an annotated catalogue of the manuscripts of the halakhic midrashim.[9] In this volume, I describe the complete and fragmentary manuscripts of the seven halakhic midrashim, and most importantly, approximately six hundred leaves from the Genizah. The folios from the Genizah and other manuscript sources are sorted according to their original codices. For example, the large codex of the lost *Mekhilta of Rabbi Shim'on* is a combination of fifty almost complete pages from the Firkovich collection in St. Petersburg, and thirty-four smaller fragments, preserved in the Alliance Israélite Universelle collection in Paris, the Gaster collection in the John Rylands University Library of Manchester, the Adler collection in the Jewish Theological Seminary in New York, and the Taylor-Schechter collection in Cambridge.

In the past, hardly any of the researchers who published midrashic fragments or analysed them paid attention to the codices to which they originally belonged. For instance, E. Y. Kutscher wrote a brilliant article about the excellent rabbinic Hebrew of the Genizah fragments of the *Mekhilta of Rabbi Ishmael* and characterised them as 'proto-texts'.[10] But he based his thesis on only one fragment of two folios in Oxford. Now, with the help of the new catalogue, it becomes clear that this fragment belongs to a codex of which forty-two folios have been preserved. They are to be found, in twenty-four separate fragments in Oxford, Cambridge, the British Library, the University of Pennsylvania, and the Antonin Collection in St. Petersburg. The catalogue includes detailed descriptions of 110 codices. The internal division of the codices is interesting and it is perhaps possible to conclude from the data something about the relative popularity of the various midrashim. The *Sifra* on Leviticus takes first place with forty-nine codices. The remainder follow at a meaningful distance, with the *Sifre* on Deuteronomy represented in twenty-one codices, the *Mekhilta of Rabbi Ishmael* in sixteen, the *Sifre* on Numbers in ten, the *Mekhilta of Rabbi Shim'on* in eight, and the *Mekhilta* on Deuteronomy in four. The last one in the line-up is the rare midrash, *Sifre Zuṭa* on Numbers, represented in two codices, which altogether amount to only seven folios.

---

[9] M. Kahana, *Manuscripts of the Halakhic Midrashim: An Annotated Catalogue* (Jerusalem, 1995).

[10] E. Y. Kutscher, 'Geniza Fragments of the *Mekilta of Rabbi Yishma'el*', *Leshonenu* 32 (1968), pp. 103–16.

I hope that this catalogue will provide a basis for the editing of new scientific editions of all the halakhic midrashim. It may also be helpful to scholars in various fields of Jewish studies who are interested in examining the texts of particular midrashic passages. There can be no doubt that it is incomplete and that additional manuscripts and fragments will ultimately be discovered. But, as is well known, the perfect is the dangerous enemy of the good, or, in the words of the Mishnah in *'Avot* 5.16 already cited by Schechter: 'It is not thy duty to complete the work, but neither art thou free to desist from it.'

A Recent Find

I would now like to report a new discovery concerning the halakhic midrashim that I made during my visits to Russia. In the Russian National Library in St. Petersburg there are two collections of Hebrew manuscripts. The first is the one that belonged to the Archimandrite of the Russian Orthodox Church in Jerusalem over a century ago, Antonin Kapustin, and is composed almost entirely of material from the Cairo Genizah. The second, enormous collection is that of the Karaite Jew, Abraham Firkovich. Firkovich acquired his manuscripts in different places in the Orient. He was in Egypt thirty years before Schechter and purchased many manuscripts there. It is not yet clear whether Firkovich ever visited the Ben Ezra synagogue, where the Genizah was amassed. It is, however, interesting that parts of the same codices are sometimes to be found in Firkovich's collection and in the Genizah collections at Cambridge and in other libraries. I have already mentioned one such example from the large codex of the *Mekhilta of Rabbi Shim'on*. It is possible that these codices were acquired in other synagogues in Cairo and did not originate in the Genizah of the Ben Ezra synagogue. That issue requires separate study[11] but the fascinating nature of the material in the Firkovich collection has impelled me to include it in this discussion.

The main purpose of my trips to Russia was to try to find hitherto unknown manuscripts of the halakhic midrashim, especially of the three lost midrashim. I was able to identify much new material from the well known midrashim,[12] but my expectations concerning the lost midrashim were destined to be frustrated. Try as I might, I was unable to locate any new manuscript material of these works. I did, however, derive some small satisfaction from one manuscript of the first Arabic-Hebrew collection of Firkovich, no. 3949. This manuscript contains a commentary on Deuteronomy in Judaeo-Arabic, and includes quotations from talmudic sources. After close examination, I was able to conclude that the author was the Karaite scholar, Yeshu'ah ben Judah, known in Arabic as Abū al-Faraj Furqān. This scholar was active in Jerusalem in the eleventh century. Poznanski and Mann have already

---

[11] See M. Ben-Sasson, 'Firkovich's Second Collection: remarks on historical and halakhic material', *Jewish Studies* 31 (Hebrew; 1991), pp. 47–60.

[12] See M. Kahana, 'Midrashic fragments in the libraries of Leningrad and Moscow', *Asufot* 6 (1992), pp. 41–50.

shown how he tended to incorporate in his works talmudic and rabbinic quotations.[13] My colleague, Haggai Ben-Shammai, has recently devoted an article to this scholar.[14] It was he who encouraged me to embark on a study of Yeshu'ah in the days when it was possible to catch only a glimpse of the riches of the Russian National (then the Saltykov-Shchedrin) Library with the aid of a few microfilms that had been sent to Oxford.

I found in this manuscript some twenty unknown quotations from tannaitic midrashim on verses from Deuteronomy. It was clear that these had been taken from a midrashic source. This is evident from the way that some of the quotations are introduced by the author, such as קאלו אלאולון פי 'the first sages said on the verse...', followed by the commentary, or, explicitly קאלת אלמכלה, 'the *Mekhilta* said', where אלמכלה is the terminology generally used by the Karaites when quoting from a halakhic midrash. In my primary description of this manuscript, I proposed that the source of some but not all of these quotations was the lost *Mekhilta* to Deuteronomy. The reason for my qualification was the occurrence, in some of the quotations, of characteristic terminology from the school of R. Aqiva, a fact that does not fit well with the *Mekhilta* to Deuteronomy, which belongs to the school of R. Ishmael. At the end of the article, I expressed the hope that the matter would be clarified with the discovery of more new material.[15]

My hopes were not dashed. On another visit to St. Petersburg, I concentrated on examining some thirty manuscripts of Yeshu'ah ben Judah. I was overjoyed to find in them more than one hundred additional quotations of tannaitic teachings on Deuteronomy, unknown from any other talmudic sources. What is more, any suggestion that these may be Karaitic forgeries or liberal paraphrasing does not stand up to close examination, primarily because of the established reliability of Yeshu'ah, as supported by his many other quotations from known sources.[16] Moreover, the linguistic terminology of the quotations themselves includes rare and original rabbinic usages, which could not have been invented by a medieval scholar.

On checking the new quotations, I was surprised to discover a strong connection between these and the *Sifre Zuṭa* on Numbers. The *Sifre Zuṭa* is a very special midrash with regard to its terminology, language, names of the rabbis, and particular halakhic teachings. Some of the great scholars of the past already noted this and,

---

[13] See S. Poznanski, *The Karaite Literary Opponents of Saadiah Gaon* (London, 1908), pp. 48–53; J. Mann, *Texts and Studies in Jewish History and Literature*, vol. 2 (Philadelphia, 1935), pp. 36–39.

[14] H. Ben-Shammai, 'Yeshuah ben Yehudah: a characterisation of a Karaite scholar of Jerusalem in the eleventh century', *Pe`amim* 32 (1987), pp. 3–20.

[15] See Kahana (see n. 12 above), pp. 54–56.

[16] See Kahana (see n. 12 above), pp. 52–54; O. Tirosh-Becker, 'Preliminary studies in rabbinic quotations embedded in the Pentateuch commentaries of the Karaite scholar Yeshu'a Ben Yehuda' *Massorot* 5–6 (1991), pp. 313–40 and 'A linguistic study of mishnaic quotations embedded in Yeshu'a ben Yehuda's commentary on Leviticus', *Massorot* 7 (1993), pp. 145–86.

more recently, our late, revered teacher, Saul Lieberman, devoted a book to it.[17] In the works of Yeshu'ah, I found the same elements that make the *Sifre Zuṭa* so special. This is evident from a whole variety of midrashic expressions that appear only in that work and in no other talmudic sources, for example, אמר לא אמרתי אלא, הא מה הדבר, הא צרכתה לומר, והלא אומר וכי דין הוא. The close links between the quotations of Yeshu'ah and the *Sifre Zuṭa* are also exemplified in the names of the Tannaim, various linguistic combinations and some contextual parallels.[18]

From all these data, one conclusion is clear. The source of the new midrashic quotations is not the *Sifre* on Deuteronomy, nor the lost *Mekhilta* on Deuteronomy that I was hoping to find, but a third midrash on Deuteronomy. It seems indisputable that this midrash, whose existence was until now totally unknown, is a continuation of the *Sifre Zuṭa* on Numbers. In the light of this conclusion, it is certainly appropriate to refer to the new midrash as the *Sifre Zuṭa* on Deuteronomy. It is ironic that it is only because of the Karaites, who were generally opposed to the Oral Law, that we are able to reconstruct a hitherto unknown layer of the Oral Law literature. This midrash was obviously part of Yeshu'ah ben Judah's library and was subsequently lost. To date, I have identified the use of the *Sifre Zuṭa* on Deuteronomy in only one or two rabbinic compositions. The Persian midrash *Pitron Torah* published by my late teacher, E. E. Urbach, in Jerusalem in 1978, and maybe also *Midrash Ḥadash* published by J. Mann and I. Sonne in *The Bible as Read and Preached in the Old Synagogue*, vol. 2 (Cincinnati, 1966).

In addition to providing us with a new source of tannaitic teachings, the discovery of the *Sifre Zuṭa* on Deuteronomy may help to free scholars of the halakhic midrashim of some misconceptions. At the end of the last century, in an impressive study of the tannaitic midrashim, D. Hoffmann set out the clear differences between the midrashic schools of R. Aqiva and R. Ishmael in their methods of teaching, in the names of the central rabbis they cite, and in their midrashic terminology.[19] In addition, he demonstrated that the double sets of halakhic midrashim that have come down to us represent the traditions of these two schools, and that for each of the books of the Pentateuch, except for Genesis, there was one midrash from the school of R. Aqiva, and another from that of R. Ishmael. To the school of R. Aqiva belong the *Mekhilta of Rabbi Shim'on* on Exodus, the main part of the *Sifra* on Leviticus, the *Sifre Zuṭa* on Numbers, and the *Sifre* on Deuteronomy, while the school of R. Ishmael has bequeathed us the *Mekhilta of Rabbi Ishmael* on Exodus, a number of additions to the *Sifra* on Leviticus (such as the Thirteen Hermeneutic Rules of R. Ishmael and the teachings on the sections about forbidden marriages, the public exposition of which was forbidden by R. Aqiva), the *Sifre* on Numbers and the *Mekhilta* on Deuteronomy.

---

[17] S. Lieberman, *Siphre Zuṭṭa (The Midrash of Lydda)*, (New York, 1968).

[18] For more details, see M. Kahana, 'Citations from a new tannaitic midrash on Deuteronomy and their relationship to *Sifre Zuta*', *Proceedings of the Eleventh World Congress of Jewish Studies*, Division C, vol. 1 (Hebrew; Jerusalem, 1994), pp. 23–30.

[19] D. Hoffmann, 'Zur Einleitung in die halachischen Midraschim', *Jahresbericht des Rabbiner-Seminars* (Berlin, 1886–87), pp. 1–92.

Following Hoffmann, other scholars subsequently developed and further documented this theory, which permitted not only a differentiation between the two schools but also an identification of the unique qualities of each of the tannaitic midrashim.[20]

At the same time, it has to be said that the acceptance of some conventional views about these midrashim has prevented scholars, including myself, from reaching some simple and important conclusions that should have emerged from both general and detailed studies. In the first place, it is clear that all the midrashim from the school of R. Ishmael are exemplary in their comparative unity. In contrast, the four midrashim of the school of R. Aqiva are not homogeneous and should be divided into three distinct groups: 1) The *Sifra* on Leviticus and the *Sifre* on Deuteronomy; 2) The *Mekhilta of Rabbi Shim'on* on Exodus; 3) The *Sifre Zuṭa* on Numbers.

This division in itself points to the probability that the three groups in the school of R. Aqiva are simply fortuitous representatives of the literary output of three different schools. It is possible that such an output originally included three parallel midrashic commentaries on each of the books from Exodus to Deuteronomy. Indeed, the discovery of a third tannaitic midrash on Deuteronomy that is a continuation of the *Sifre Zuṭa* on Numbers provides additional support for such a theory. It is obvious that the question regarding the extent of the compositions of the school of R. Aqiva must remain open since, in addition to the midrashim mentioned, there are also in the Tosefta and the Talmuds many *baraitot* of the schools of R. Aqiva and R. Ishmael that originated in tannaitic compilations that are lost. This discussion about such possibilities will at least make it easier for future discoveries to be slotted into the literary-historical schema being proposed.

I would like to emphasise two general points that arise out of the discussion just concluded: 1) We have to be aware of the limited nature of our knowledge regarding tannaitic literary creativity. It is beyond any doubt that this creativity was richer and more extensive than that reflected in the extant material. We should therefore be doubly careful before arriving at any definitive conclusions based on the limited sources available to us. On the other hand, the paucity of such material should not deter us from assessing and analysing the information we do have. 2) In this connection, I wish to make one tentative remark. As already mentioned, we have in our possession representative texts of three different midrashic trends from the school of R. Aqiva. In contrast, the texts from the school of R. Ishmael are more homogeneous and probably represent the literary creation of just one group. This fact surely testifies to the dominance of the school of R. Aqiva at the end of the tannaitic period. Such a dominance is also indicated by two further pieces of information, namely, that the Mishnah was edited according to the school of R. Aqiva, and that the teachings of R. Aqiva were highly respected among the Amoraim. This subject is certainly worthy of further study and discussion.

---

[20] See especially J. N. Epstein, *Prolegomena ad Litteras Tannaiticas* (Hebrew; Jerusalem, 1957), pp. 499–741.

An Example

We will now offer two specific examples that do not have far-reaching implications but clearly illustrate how the Genizah material makes possible a more precise understanding of the halakhic midrashim. Both examples are taken from the portion of 'Amalek' in the *Mekhilta of Rabbi Ishmael* on Exodus, on which I am currently working. There are two critical editions of this *Mekhilta*. The first, by Horovitz, did not make use of any Genizah material. The second, by Lauterbach, utilises a few folios from the Genizah, but ignores most of them in the list of variant readings.[21]

Let us start with a comment on the verse from Exodus 17:13 that briefly describes Joshua's victory over Amalek: 'And Joshua discomfited Amalek and his people with the edge of the sword.' The phrase 'with the edge of the sword' (לפי חרב) was given two explanations in the *Mekhilta*:[22]

לפי חרב - ר׳ יהושע אומר לא נוולם אלא דנם ברחמים

ר׳ אליעזר אומר לפי חרב למה נאמר - למדנו שהמלחמה הזאת לא היתה אלא על פי הגבורה

> With the edge of the sword – R. Joshua says:
> He did not disfigure them but treated them with some degree of mercy.
> R. Eliezer says: With the edge of the sword – Why is this said?
> We can learn from this that this war was only by order of the Almighty.

The commentators were unable to explain how R. Joshua derived this interpretation from our verse. In the *Sifre* on Deuteronomy, we find another interpretation of the phrase לפי חרב in Deuteronomy 13:16 that sheds light on the teaching of R. Joshua in the *Mekhilta* passages:[23] לפי חרב - לתוך פיה של חרב שלא ינוולם, 'By the edge of the sword – with the end of the sword, so as not to disfigure them.'

In other words, one should kill by using the sharp end of the sword, not its other parts, so that death is caused with a minimum of suffering and disfigurement. A close parallel to this is found in a Genizah fragment of the lost *Mekhilta* on Deuteronomy, published by Schechter:[24] לפי חרב – לא בחצים ולא ברמחים ולא בראשו של סייף אלא בפיו 'With the edge of the sword – not with arrows or spears, or the tip of the lance, but with the sharp end'. We also find in the Mishnah, *Sanhedrin* 7.3, that the Tannaim, when dealing with execution by the sword, discuss how it should be performed with the least disfigurement of the body.

Having explained R. Joshua's comment, we must now attempt to identify the Tanna who is disagreeing with him. Lauterbach and Horovitz, basing themselves on the printed version, the Munich manuscript and *Midrash Ḥakhamim*, offered the text ר׳ אליעזר, R. Eliezer. In the Oxford manuscript and the *Yalquṭ Shim'oni*, we find ר׳ אלעזר, R. Eleazar. But in a Genizah fragment in Westminster College Library,

[21] See his introduction to the *Mekhilta*, vol. 1 (see n. 4 above), pp. XXXVIII–XLII.
[22] The quotation and English translation are from ed. Lauterbach (see n. 4 above), p. 147.
[23] *Sifre on Deuteronomy*, *Pisqa* 94, ed. Finkelstein (see n. 4 above), p. 155.
[24] See *Midrasch Tannaim* (see n. 5 above), p. 70.

Cambridge (Talmudica I.112), as well as in the *Mekhilta of Rabbi Shim'on*, p. 123, we find ר׳ לעזר המודעי, R. Eleazar of Modi'im.

It is clear that the reading in the Genizah fragment is superior because R. Eleazar of Modi'im is normally R. Joshua's opponent in a number of cases, including the issue of Amalek. Moreover, this controversy between them matches their respective viewpoints concerning the whole issue of Amalek as well as in other places in the *Mekhilta*. R. Joshua generally comments on the verses in a more literal fashion, while R. Eleazar of Modi'im tends to focus on the religious aspects of Moses's actions, such as praying, fasting, invoking the names of the forefathers and the fear of sin.[25]

In our example, R. Joshua comments in a more literal way by explaining that they were killed by the sharp end of the sword, in order not to disfigure them, while R. Eleazar of Modi'im emphasises the religious aspect by stressing that the war was on the orders of God. As has been indicated, it was only the Genizah fragment that correctly identified the rabbi who took issue with R. Joshua. In the other versions, the epithet המודעי 'of Modi'im' has been dropped from the text. Some of the versions have retained the shortened ר׳ אלעזר, R. Eleazar, while other textual witnesses attempted to 'correct the error' by adding the letter *yod*, thereby reading ר׳ אליעזר , R. Eliezer.

Having identified the second Tanna as R. Eleazar of Modi'im, we are left puzzled by his teaching. It seems that he wanted to emphasise that, although the verses suggest that the war against Amalek was directed by Moses, without divine consultation, the whole episode was in fact divinely inspired. How does he reach this conclusion on the basis of the phrase לפי חרב, 'by the edge of the sword'? Scholars have had great difficulty in trying to reconcile this teaching with the biblical text. Some commentators have suggested that לפי is equivalent to על פי ה׳, 'by the order of God', but the word ה׳ does not appear in the text. Horovitz suggested that לפי חרב is equivalent to לפי הרב, 'by the mouth of the teacher', but even if we accept this exchange of guttural letters, the teacher would still be Moses, not God.

In the Genizah fragment , however, we find a complete sentence that is missing in the other versions:

ר׳ לעזר המודעי אומר לפי חרב למה נאמר
לפי שלמדנו על מלחמה זו שלא היתה אלא על פי הגבורה
ומנין למלחמה זו שהיתה על פי הגבורה
ת״ל לפי חרב - מלמד על מלחמה זו שלא היתה אלא על פי הגבורה

R. Eleazar of Modi'im says: With the edge of the sword – Why is this said?
Because we have learned that this war was only by order of the Almighty.
And from whence do we know that this war was according to the will of the Almighty?
As it is said, 'by the edge of the sword' –

---

[25] See W. Bacher, *Die Agada der Tannaiten* (Strasbourg, 1903), pp. 196–211. See also D. Boyarin, *Intertextuality and the Reading of Midrash* (Bloomington and Indianapolis, 1990), pp. 71–79; M. Kahana, *The Two Mekhiltot on the Amalek Portion* (Hebrew; Jerusalem, 1999), pp. 288–320.

This teaches us that the war was commanded only by the Almighty.

At first glance, all we seem to have here is a repetition of the same idea. The repetition does, however, also appear in a good manuscript of the second *Mekhilta*, the *Mekhilta of Rabbi Shim'on*,[26] and is worthy of further consideration.[27] In my opinion, what we have here is a reference to somewhere else in the Torah where the expression לפי חרב is used. Perhaps the relevant verse is Deuteronomy 20:13, which discusses the divine command about the occupation of a city and states that the inhabitants should be smitten לפי חרב. The use of the same term in our verse is explained by R. Eleazar of Modi'im as inferring that, in our case too, it was by the command of God.[28] What is clear is that only the Genizah fragment incorporates the original flavour of the teaching, which includes R. Eleazar of Modi'im's justification of his explanation. It is possible that the other versions dropped this sentence through the process of homoioteleuton, or because the copyists did not understand that the reference here is to another biblical verse.

Another Example

The last verse of the Amalek episode provides us with another example. The verse states: ויאמר כי יד על כס יה מלחמה ליי בעמלק מדר דר, 'And he said the hand upon the throne of the Lord, the Lord will have war against Amalek from generation to generation.' The midrash according to the Lauterbach edition, p. 160, comments:

ויאמר כי יד על כס יה מלחמה ליי וגו' -
רבי יהושע אומר לכשישב הקב"ה על כסא מלכותו ותהי הממשלה שלו באותה שעה מלחמה ליי בעמלק.
רבי אלעזר המודעי אומר נשבע הקב"ה בכסא הכבוד שלו אם אניח נין ונכד של עמלק תחת כל השמים
שלא יהו אומרים גמל זה של עמלק רחילה זו של עמלק
רבי אליעזר אומר נשבע המקום בכסא הכבוד שלו שאם יבא אחד מכל אומות העולם להתגייר
שיקבלו אותו ישראל ומביתו של עמלק לא יקבלו אותו
שנאמר ויאמר דוד אל הנער המגיד לו אי מזה אתה ויאמר בן איש גר עמלקי אנכי
נזכר דוד באותה שעה מה שנאמר למשה רבינו

---

[26] MSS JTS, ENA 349 (Mic. 4954) and EMC 827 (Mic. 4930). See M. Kahana, *The Two Mekhiltot* (see n. 25 above), pp. 123–40.

[27] About the term לפי שלמדנו in the Genizah fragment, see also *Mekhilta*, tractate Amalek, ed. Lauterbach (see n. 4 above), vol. 2, p. 146, in all the witnesses: 'Until the Going Down of the Sun. Because we have learned (לפי שלמדנו) about all other kingdoms that they engage in battle only during the first six hours of the day. This wicked kingdom, however, engaged in battle from morning to evening.' Hence, the meaning of לפי שלמדנו is that we have learned this elsewhere; but this rare term requires further research.

[28] It is interesting that in Genesis 34:26 the same expression לפי חרב is used to describe Simeon and Levi's murder of the men of Shechem. Ancient sources, such as the Testament of Levi 5:3, reveal that the sword was received from heaven. See J. Kugel, 'The story of Dinah in the Testament of Levi', *Harvard Theological Review* 85:1 (1992), pp. 25–28. It is not beyond the bounds of possibility that there is an indirect connection between these apocryphal works on Genesis and the tannaitic explanation of the words לפי חרב as meaning 'according to the will of God'.

אם יבא אחד מכל אומות העולם להתגייר שיקבלו אותו ומביתו של עמלק אל יקבלו אותו
מיד ויאמר אליו דוד דמך על ראשך כי פיך ענה בך
לכך נאמר מדר דר. דבר אחר מדר דר
רבי יהושע אומר מדר אלו חיי העולם הזה; דור - אלו חיי העולם הבא
רבי אלעזר המודעי אומר מדורו של משה ומדורו של שמואל
רבי אליעזר אומר מדורו של משיח שהם שלושה דורות שנאמר ייראוך עם שמש ולפני ירח דור דורים.

And He Said: 'The hand Upon the Throne of the Lord, the Lord Will Have War,' etc.
R. Joshua says: When the Holy One, blessed be He, will sit upon the throne of His kingdom
and His reign will prevail, at that time 'the Lord will have war with Amalek.'
R. Eleazar of Modi'im says: The Holy one, blessed be He, swore by the throne of His glory:
I will not leave any offspring or progeny of Amalek under the entire heaven,
so that people will not be able to say:
This camel belongs to Amalek, this ewe lamb belongs to Amalek.
R. Eliezer says: God swore by the throne of His glory
that if a person of any of the nations should come desiring to be converted to Judaism,
Israel shall receive him,
but a person from the house of Amalek they shall not receive.
For it is said: 'And David said unto the young man that told him: Whence art thou?
And he answered: I am the son of an Amalekite stranger' (2 Samuel 1:13).
At that moment David recalled what had been told to Moses our teacher –
that if a person of any of the nations should come desiring to be converted to Judaism,
Israel should receive him,
but a person from the house of Amalek they should not receive.
Immediately: 'And David said unto him: Thy blood be upon thy head;
for thy mouth hath testified against thee' (2 Samuel 1:16).
In this sense it is said: 'From generation to generation'.
Another interpretation: *From generation to generation*
R. Joshua says: 'From generation,' – that is, from the life of this world;
'to generation,' - that is, from the life of the world to come.
R. Eleazar of Modi'im says: From the generation of Moses and from the generation of Samuel.
R. Eliezer says: From the generation of the Messiah which really consists of three generations.
And whence do we know that the generation of the Messiah consists of three generations?
It is said: 'They shall fear Thee while the sun endureth
and so long as the moon, a generation and two generations.' (Psalms 72:5).

Let us now examine more closely the first sentence of R. Joshua. All the commentators[29] understand that R. Joshua is explaining this verse in connection with the end of the days, when God will again be king of all the earth. This is in contrast to R. Eleazar of Modi'im, who suggests that the war will be fought by a king of flesh and blood. Some scholars have gone so far as to suggest that this debate between R.

---

[29] See G. J. Blidstein, 'The monarchic imperative in rabbinic perspective', *AJS Review* 7–8 (1982–83), pp. 20–21.

Joshua and R. Eleazar of Modi'im reflects their differing opinions concerning the Bar Kochba revolt and related messianic claims.[30]

Even the simple meaning of R. Joshua's teaching is puzzling. Is God not sitting on His divine throne at this moment too? And does He not have the reigns of power in His hand? In a Genizah fragment at Columbia University Library (X 893 IN Z 65), we find the following:

> רבי יהושע אומר לכשישב המלך על כסא שליה באותה שעה מלחמה ליי בעמלק – 'R. Joshua says, when the king will sit on the throne of God, at the same time the Lord will have war with Amalek.'

The variant reading על כסא שליה, 'on the throne of the Lord', is to be found only in the Genizah fragment, while the variant המלך instead of הקב״ה is also attested in an Oxford manuscript, in *Yalquṭ Shim'oni*, in *Midrash Ḥakhamim*, and in the commentary to the *Mekhilta* in MS Mantua 56. Only the printed version and the Munich manuscript have הקב״ה or הקדוש. It is clear that the term המלך refers not to the divine but to a human king upon whom the obligation to obliterate the seed of Amalek becomes imperative when he ascends the throne. This is to be found in the *Sifre* on Deuteronomy *Pisqa* 67, p. 132.

> R. Judah says: Israel were given three commands on entering the (holy) land:
> to appoint a king, to build the temple, and to obliterate the seed of Amalek.
> I do not know which precedes the other... as it says
> 'and he said, the hand upon the throne of the Lord, the Lord will have war against Amalek'(Exodus 17:16).
> When the king will sit on the throne of God (משישב המלך על כסא יי)
> you will destroy the seed of Amalek.
> And from whence do we know that the throne of God refers to the king (ומנין שכסא יי זה המלך)?
> From the verse 'And Solomon sat on the throne of God as king' (1 Chronicles 29:23).

The last sentence of the *Sifre* is remarkably like the Genizah version of the *Mekhilta*: לכשישב המלך על כסא שליה, 'When the king will sit on the throne of God'. But the copyists and students of the *Mekhilta* did not understand this sentence, which rightly explains our verse כי יד על כס יה. They therefore 'corrected' it by adding לכשישב המלך על כסא <מלכותו ותהי הממשלה שלו>, 'When the king will sit upon the throne <of his kingdom and his reign will prevail>.' The printed version and the Munich manuscript went one stage further, changing המלך, 'the king', to הקב״ה, 'The Holy One Blessed be He'. But it is clear that in the original version R. Joshua held that the commandment was for a king of flesh and blood and interpreted the phrase 'The hand upon the throne of the Lord' as a temporal clause. In contrast, R. Eleazar of Modi'im and R. Eliezer understood it as an oath. And so the explanations of the commentators and the theses of the scholars become redundant.

---

[30] See J. Elbaum, 'R. Eleazar Hamodai and R. Joshua on the Amalek Pericope', *Studies in Aggada and Jewish Folklore*, eds I. Ben-Ami and J. Dan (Hebrew section; Jerusalem, 1983), pp. 106–7.

In the framework of this article, it is impossible to explain the whole teaching and the many variants in the Genizah fragment. We will look at one aspect only. It seems that what we have here are two separate arguments between three tannaitic sages, R. Joshua, R. Eleazar of Modi'im and R. Eliezer. The first is based on the beginning of the verse: 'And he said: the hand upon the throne of the Lord', and the second on the end of the verse: 'From generation to generation'. This seems clear from the opening comments of each section as well as from the content.

But this simple and clear distinction between the two crumbles away when we look at the additional sentence between the two sections: '<In this sense it is said: "From generation to generation". Another interpretation>: From generation to generation': <לכך נאמר מדר דור.דבר אחר> מדור דוד. This problematic sentence is documented in all the western witnesses: MSS Oxford and Munich, the printed edition, *Yalquṭ Shim'oni*, *Midrash Ḥakhamim* and *Leqaḥ Ṭov*. But 1) This is a surprising conclusion to the first section, which does not deal at all with the words 'From generation to generation'; and 2) It seems strange to find the next section starting with 'Another interpretation' when it is in fact the first interpretation of the words 'From generation to generation'.

A Genizah text is yet again revealing. One Cambridge Genizah fragment (T-S AS 82.17) has the same version as the western textual witnesses. The excellent fragment in Columbia University Library does not, however, have the ending 'In this sense it is said: "From generation to generation"', and, instead of ד"א (=דבר אחר), it has נ"א. The letters נ"א are in fact the number of the paragraph, 51, according to the division of the Amalek tractate to be found in all the good textual witnesses of the *Mekhilta* in the Genizah. Paragraph 51 (נ"א) comes in the Genizah text after paragraph 47 (מ"ז) at the beginning of the first section; paragraph 48 (מ"ח) before R. Eleazar of Modi'im; paragraph 49 (מ"ט) in the middle of his commentary; and paragraph 50 (נ) before R. Eliezer. Another proof that paragraph 51 is the last paragraph in the second portion of the tractate Amalek is to be found in another Genizah fragment (Westminster College, Talmudica I.112), which appends to the title of the second section the number of paragraphs: פרשה ב הלכי נ"א, 'Section B, 51 paragraphs'.

As may be expected, what we have here are two separate tannaitic arguments on the two different parts of the verse, as they indeed also appear in the second *Mekhilta of Rabbi Shim'on*. In addition, it is possible that this Genizah fragment can explain how the other textual witnesses came about. In these witnesses, as well as in Cambridge fragment T-S AS 82.17, the original division into paragraphs of the *Mekhilta* has not been preserved. At some point, a copyist erroneously changed the נ"א to ד"א and these letters were later understood as the abbreviation for דבר אחר, introducing another interpretation. But because what follows is the first explanation of the words 'From generation to generation', they tried artificially to correct this by adding at the end of the previous section: 'In this sense it is said "From generation to generation"' (לכך נאמר מדר דר).

If what I have suggested is correct, the original version of the *Mekhilta* is to be found only in the Genizah fragment at Columbia University Library. All the other textual witnesses are 'corrected' versions. It is difficult to imagine that this complicated 'correction' was carried out in isolation in each textual witness. Rather, the correction was probably made in one archetype, from which all the European versions (in Germany, France and Italy), the Byzantine *Leqaḥ Ṭov* and the Eastern Cambridge Genizah fragment are derived. This proposed stemma of the manuscripts of the *Mekhilta* is corroborated by other evidence.[31]

In conclusion, the examples that I have presented here demonstrate the importance of the Cairo Genizah in reconstructing the original versions of the halakhic midrashim and their commentaries. The main task that faces us today is the preparation of new editions of all the talmudic literature that should include critical and literary commentaries. Only after this has been accomplished will we be able to assess definitively the contribution of the Genizah to the field of rabbinic studies. In the meantime, the Genizah encourages us to undertake this important task. I hope that we will be worthy of it.

[31] See the discussion both in this example and in the others cited in my article, 'The critical editions of *Mekhilta De-Rabbi Ishmael* in the light of the Genizah fragments', *Tarbiz* 55 (1986), pp. 489–524, and in my book (see n. 25 above), pp. 66–114. See also D. Boyarin, 'From the hidden light of the Geniza: towards the original text of the *Mekhilta d'Rabbi Ishmael*', *Sidra* 2 (1986), pp. 5–13.

5

Two Insights from a Ninth-Century Liturgical Handbook: The Origins of Yequm Purqan *and* Qaddish de-Ḥadata

NEIL DANZIG

This year we are celebrating the centenary of the Genizah, one hundred years having passed since Solomon Schechter made his fortuitous trip to Cairo in the winter of 1896–97. Although much has been published from the Genizah in the past hundred years that has revolutionized Jewish scholarship in so many areas, in no area has the Genizah contributed more than in the field of geonic literature. As the heads of the Jewish academies in Iraq during the early medieval period (approximately the seventh to the eleventh centuries), the Babylonian Geonim flourished in a geographic area allied to the Genizah in Cairo, and during much of the period in which the majority of material entered the Genizah, that is, from the second half of the tenth until the end of the twelfth century. For this reason, a significant amount of information relating to the Geonim was uncovered among the riches of the Genizah.[1]

While many writings by the Geonim, mostly in the form of legal texts and responsa, were known prior to the discovery of the Genizah, the *history* of the geonic era was shrouded in relative darkness, and the degree of literary creativity in areas other than halakhah on the part of the Geonim and other authors of that time, was all but unknown. This cloud of ignorance was mostly due to the linguistic and cultural boundaries that hindered access by European rabbis, already in the medieval period, to texts written in Judaeo-Arabic, the language in which many of these geonic texts were composed. In the mid-nineteenth century, several modern scholars attempted to sort out issues of literature, history and biography bearing on that period, beginning with S. J. Rapaport (SHI'R) who published pioneering studies on two of the Geonim, Sa'adya and Hai, in addition to other related studies on oriental rabbis.[2] But they were

[1] The ENA and T-S leaves mentioned below combine to make up the text under discussion. In order to minimize confusion, I will quote sections of the combined text without identifying the leaf on which it occurs. I hope to publish a complete and annotated text of these leaves in another context. A detailed overview of the acquisition of material from the Cairo Genizah, and of the first published discoveries from that source, may be found in the introduction to N. Danzig, *A Catalogue of Fragments of Halakhah and Midrash from the Elkan Nathan Adler Collection of the Library of the Jewish Theological Seminary of America* (Hebrew; New York and Jerusalem, 1997).

[2] See I. E. Barzilay, *Shlomo Yehuda Rapaport [Shir] (1790–1867) and his Contemporaries* (Tel Aviv, 1969), especially pp. 36–41. For an overview of the Geonim and their works, see R. Brody, *The Geonim of Babylonia and the Shaping of Medieval Jewish Culture* (New Haven and London, 1998). For an examination of the period more oriented to history than to literature, see M. Gil, *In the Kingdom of Ishmael,* vol. 1 (Hebrew; Jerusalem, 1997).

also handicapped for the same reason, in that much of the significant information never found its way north to Christian Europe. Moreover, there existed few, if any, authentic historical data, such as letters and documents, by which one could flesh out the real history of the period. The situation totally changed with the discovery of the Genizah. Suddenly, there was an avalanche of hundreds of important documents and letters, as well as texts of other types, penned by the Geonim and their contemporaries. Some of these were quickly published within the decade that followed the discovery, acquisition and sorting of the Genizah material, with the lion's share (at least at first) appearing in periodicals and other volumes printed in England. This flurry of scholarship came in two parts, from the late 1890s until the First World War, and then again from the 1920s until the Second World War, and most of these publications were devoted to material housed at Cambridge University Library.[3]

The general interest in the literature of the Babylonian Geonim on the part of scholars of *Wissenschaft des Judentums* was part of two developing interests on the part of European scholars in general during the late eighteenth century. Firstly, an air of fascination with things 'Oriental' wafted through the major universities and museums, and expeditions to the Near East were dispatched to uncover the riches of the ancient world and to bring them back to Europe whenever possible. Searching out the Genizah in Cairo was but a small part of this 'Oriental fever' but one that produced the greatest rewards for Jewish scholars.[4] Actually, among the first publications of Genizah material were biblical palimpsests of the Greek and Syriac translations of the Bible – items that remain to this day some of the oldest and most important specimens found in the Genizah – and these were published by Christian scholars, but their publication fanned the flames of interest on the part of Jewish scholars in this material that, at first, trickled to Europe from Cairo.[5] Secondly, as a product of the Emancipation, Jewish scholars began to take an interest in Spanish Jewry of the medieval period, with figures such as Samuel ibn Nagrela and other poets, grammarians and authors becoming role models of an 'enlightened' Jewish elite, different from the Eastern European model that had come to be regarded as a symbol of backwardness and of intellectual and social immobility.[6] It was from these roots that there developed an interest in the Genizah in Cairo, a source in which there lay details of the history and literature of a Jewry removed for the most part from Europe, and certainly from Eastern Europe. Although this agenda was left unstated by the early Genizah scholars at the turn of the century, I believe that many of them

[3] See my essay 'Geonic jurisprudence from the Cairo Genizah: an appreciation of early scholarship', *Proceedings of the American Academy for Jewish Research* (forthcoming). That lecture was delivered in Boston in December 1997 at the AAJR sessions devoted to the centenary of the Genizah.

[4] L. Deuel, *Testaments of Time* (New York, 1965), pp. 351–81.

[5] For a listing of these palimpsests, see M. Sokoloff and J. Yahalom, 'Christian palimpsests from the Cairo Genizah', *Révue d'Histoire des Textes* 8 (1978), pp. 109–32; see also Danzig, *Catalogue* (see n. 1 above), p. 5, n. 5, and p. 14, n. 32.

[6] I. Schorsch, *From Text to Context* (Hanover and London, 1994), pp. 82, 86–87, 186.

hoped the Genizah would reveal to the world a richer and broader Jewish past, one that would be the envy of other cultures and meet the West on its own terms. In fact, the Genizah surpassed all such expectations.

It was in order to preside at the Jewish Theological Seminary in New York that Solomon Schechter, the so-called 'discoverer' of the Genizah, left Cambridge in 1902, just a few brief years after his Cairo expedition.[7] In view of this Seminary link with Cambridge, it is appropriate that this paper comes as a result of joining together two parts of one manuscript that fell into the Cairo Genizah. One part (consisting of two complete leaves: ENA 4053.1+2, and one small fragment: ENA 3564.2), once owned by Elkan Nathan Adler of London, is now in his manuscript collection at the Jewish Theological Seminary (hereafter JTS) in New York, and the other, containing three connected leaves, is found in the Taylor-Schechter Genizah Collection in Cambridge (T-S Misc.24.1). The Adler fragment is well known and much of it has been published several times, while the Cambridge piece has never been published, nor even mentioned in any publication, as far as I have been able to verify. Certainly, the relationship between the two pieces has not been noted.[8] The item was written in the last quarter of the ninth century, as attested by the names of the Babylonian Geonim appearing in one of the Adler leaves, and is thus among the oldest datable items in the entire Genizah.[9] The leaves are of vellum and are sewn together vertically, in the form of a long strap (not as a codex). The scribe wrote the text in very small square characters in one direction on the *recto* before inverting the strap and continuing the text in the opposite direction on the *verso*. The Adler leaves are consecutive and the text connects directly with the Cambridge leaf.

In the catalogue of Adler's manuscript collection, published in Cambridge in 1921, the pair of leaves, Adler 4053, is described as follows: 'Fragment of an early Siddur (the Geonim Zemaḥ ben Paltoi and Zemaḥ ben Ḥayyim being mentioned as alive), 2 pp.' Reference is also made to a smaller joining piece in volume 3564, folio 2, and a fascimile of one side of one of the longer leaves is reproduced therein, illustration number 3.[10] In 1923, soon after Adler's collection was sold to the JTS and transferred to New York, B. M. Lewin of Haifa published a poor transcription of a portion of the

---

[7] Schechter's departure to New York reduced his potential as a publisher of Genizah texts. On Schechter, see N. Bentwich, *Solomon Schechter: A Biography* (Philadelphia, 1938); A. S. Oko, *Solomon Schechter: A Bibliography* (Cambridge, 1938); S. C. Reif, 'Jenkinson and Schechter at Cambridge: an expanded and updated assessment', *Jewish Historical Studies: Transactions of the Jewish Historical Society of England* 32 (1990–92), pp. 279–316 and 'One hundred years of Genizah research at Cambridge', *Jewish Book Annual* 53 (1995–96), pp. 7–28.

[8] For a brief description of the Cambridge fragment, see N. Danzig, *Introduction to Halakhot Pesuqot* (Hebrew; New York and Jerusalem, 1993), p. 190, n. 73, which was written before I had the opportunity of analysing the text more fully.

[9] On the dating of the oldest items in the Genizah, see Danzig, *Catalogue* (see n. 1 above), particularly pp. 4–5, 33–34. See also M. Beit-Arié *et al*, *Codices Hebraicis Litteris Extrati quo Tempore Scripti Fuerint Exhibentis* (Brepols, Paris and Jerusalem, 1997).

[10] *Catalogue of Hebrew Manuscripts in the Collection of Elkan Nathan Adler* (Cambridge, 1921), p. 30.

text of ENA 4053, under the title קדיש עתיק מימי הגאונים.[11] Lewin saw the text as being a record of the *qaddish* (that is, the doxology; literally, 'the consecration') recited at the investiture of a certain Exilarch, whose name Lewin read on the leaf as יצחק. This text includes a blessing on behalf of the Exilarch and the Geonim, in which the names of two specific Geonim are mentioned, namely, Ṣemaḥ ben Palṭoi, Gaon of Pumbedita (872–890), and Ṣemaḥ ben Ḥayyim, Gaon of Sura (879–885), while the Exilarch remains unnamed (see below, at n. 33). The text of the Adler fragment must have been written during the period in which these two Geonim simultaneously headed their academies, that is to say between 879 and 885, since during the tenure of any other Geonim, it would have been the names of the latter that would have been recited.[12] Thus, the first publication of this important text.

In his review of that volume in the literary journal *Ha-Tor*, S. Assaf republished the same passage, based upon Lewin's transcription. He did not see the original but presumably consulted the facsimile in Adler's catalogue. Assaf's justification for the republication was primarily to dispel the notion that the name יצחק was mentioned therein (as indeed it is not), and thus to conclude that the event reflected in the text was not the ceremony for the Exilarch. He offered no alternative explanation as to the specific nature of the event.[13] Thus, the second publication of that leaf. In his review of Lewin's volume, J. N. Epstein made two important points. First, he argued that one line in the text resembles the invocation found in several of the *She'iltot*, a volume containing lectures that were delivered by the Babylonian Geonim in the academies, weekly on the sabbath, and on festivals. These weekly lectures or homilies (singular *pirqa*, plural *pirqey*)[14] focused on a halakhic theme but also

---

[11] *Ginze Kedem* 2 (1923), pp. 46–48.

[12] The chronology and dating of the various Babylonian Geonim appear in several modern lists (e.g., *Encyclopaedia Judaica*, vol. 7, cols 319–20), which are in turn based on the account in Sherira's famous epistle; see אגרת רב שרירא גאון [=*IRSG*], ed. B. M. Lewin (Haifa, 1921). Compare also *Toratan shel Ge'onim*, ed. I. Yudelov and S. Z. Havlin (Jerusalem, 1993), vol. 1, pp. 31–39.

[13] *Ha-Tor* 4/6 (24 *Marḥeshvan* 5684 [1923]).

[14] The institution of the *pirqa* dates back to the talmudic period, see L. Zunz and C. Albeck, הדרשות בישראל (Jerusalem, 1974), pp. 166, 463; S. K. Mirsky, introduction to vol. 1 of his edition of the *She'iltot* (Jerusalem, 1960); D. Goodblatt, *Rabbinic Instruction in Sassanian Babylonia* (Leiden, 1975), pp. 171–96; A. S. Amir, *Institutions and Titles in the Talmudic Literature* (Hebrew; Jerusalem, 1977), pp. 133–49; I. M. Gafni, 'Public sermons in talmudic Babylonia: the *pirqa*' in *Knesset Ezra. Literature and Life in the Synagogue. Studies Presented to Ezra Fleischer*, eds S. Elizur, M. D. Herr, G. Shaked and A. Shinan (Hebrew; Jerusalem, 1994), pp. 121–28; see also Maimonides, *Mishneh Torah*, שאלה ופקדון, 2.4. Regarding the specific time at which the *pirqa* was delivered, see below, n. 123. One of the early codes of the geonic period, the *She'iltot,* is a collection of these *pirqa* lectures that were delivered on the sabbath and in connection with most festivals, each one focusing on a legal issue that is somehow related to the Torah reading of the week, or to the festival (see Mirsky's introduction). Each of these lectures had to be delivered with a specific internal sequence, and used certain stylized and formulaic expressions. It is likely that the structure and formulaic language facilitated the memorization of the material; see Danzig, *Introduction to Halakhot Pesuqot* (see n. 8 above), pp. 15–16 for this point and p. 198 on the

incorporated an aggadic section. The relevant *she'ilta* passage is quoted below (at n. 87) and confirms the fact that the Genizah text relates to a *pirqa* lecture. Epstein's second point related to the identity of this יצחק, claiming that while the identification remained dubious, it was perhaps a reference to the head of the academy in the Land of Israel.[15]

Some three months after Lewin's publication, Arthur Marmorstein, professor of rabbinics at Jews' College, London, and the unnamed editor of Adler's catalogue, published the same text in a subsequent issue of *Ha-Tor* but added several snippets from the other sections of those three leaves. Marmorstein claimed that Lewin had seen the item while it was in Marmorstein's hands, and had published it without his knowledge or permission.[16] Thus, the third publication. At that same time, in 1924, Marmorstein published a fuller treatment of the three Adler leaves and, in that more extensive study, transcribed as much as he could read of the entire text, with his comments. He also put an end to the יצחק question and corrected Lewin's readings in many other places.[17] Thus, the fourth publication. Not to be outdone, Lewin published the same text again in 1925, adding little apart from admitting the יצחק error, and correcting some mistakes in Marmorstein's transcription.[18] All told, there had been five publications of basically the same Genizah fragment within a period of two or three years.

One last publication must be mentioned in this regard. In 1927, C. Duschinsky (a rabbi turned businessman in London) published a seminal study on the *yequm purqan* prayer recited in synagogues on the sabbath after the Torah reading. In the accepted Ashkenazi rite the prayer is recited in two versions, first on behalf of the leaders, teachers and students (who are mentioned in the third person since they are not present), followed by a second blessing that addresses the members of the congregation at hand (who are mentioned in the second person since they are present). This text is perhaps the most famous vestige of geonic prayer to be found in the sabbath liturgy. In that essay, Duschinsky published and analysed several lines from Adler's fragment (which he claimed to have copied as early as 1917) and correctly deduced a relationship between this blessing on behalf of the Exilarch and the

---

evidence for the oral recitation of the *She'iltot*. The sources gathered by Goodblatt and Amir also demonstrate that the talmudic *pirqa* was not necessarily delivered in the academy, and was attended by lay people. On the terms *pirqa* and *pereq* in geonic and medieval literature, see below, n. 66. A similar term, ריגלא, refers to the assembly convened once a year by the Exilarch (on the sabbath in which the Torah portion לך לך was read) at which he preached; see *IRSG* (see n. 12 above), p. 91; and on the talmudic sources for that event, see the studies listed at the beginning of this note and M. Beer, *The Babylonian Exilarchate in the Arsacid and Sassanian Periods* (Hebrew; Tel Aviv, 1976), pp. 129–36. The event that Nathan described (see below, at n. 28) also revolved around a *pirqa* lecture, as evidenced by the phrase **מתחיל בבעיא ואומר ברם צריך את למילף** the last four words of which constitute the formulaic beginning of the בעיא (rhetorical query) posed in each *she'ilta*.

15 *Devir* 2 (1923), pp. 333–34.

16 *Ha-Tor* 4/18 (19 *Shevaṭ* 5684 [1924]).

17 A. Marmorstein, 'Mitteilungen zur Geschichte und Literatur aus der Geniza', *MGWJ* 68 (1924), pp. 150–60.

18 'שרידים עתיקים ממחזור הישיבה בפומבדיתא', *Ginze Kedem* 3 (1925), pp. 50–55.

Babylonian Geonim and the *yequm purqan* prayer. His thesis was that Adler's text predated a *qaddish* that was recited after Torah study (see below, section II), and that the *qaddish* bifurcated into two traditions, the so-called *qaddish de-rabbanan* and the *yequm purqan*. Duschinsky's theory will be further discussed below.[19]

During the more than seventy years that have since passed, the Adler text, though mentioned many times in scholarship devoted to the geonic period, has neither been re-edited nor re-interpreted. My discovery of the joining piece in the Cambridge collection has presented me with the opportunity not only of transcribing and publishing the new part but also of using it to shed light on the nature of the item as a whole.[20]

The item in question is a kind of handbook written for use in a synagogue, something akin to a *lu'aḥ* in which are listed various liturgical customs, talmudic texts and traditions, and the required Torah readings for the festivals. Although it covers much of the annual cycle of festivals, it is not a *siddur* or a *maḥzor,* since it does not contain the texts of the regular prayers.[21] When joined together, the combined text of the ENA and Cambridge leaves contains the following:

1. A collection of various talmudic sources, some of them abbreviated or in variant versions, regarding dream interpretation and the days on which bloodletting is permitted. This section of the text is partially obliterated.
2. A list of the months, beginning with Nisan, stating which are 'whole' (מלא) and which are 'defective' (חסר).
3. Various liturgical instructions regarding Day of Atonement that falls on the sabbath. These generally agree with similar instructions found in *Seder Rav Amram Gaon* [=*SRAG*], an important *siddur* from this period.[22]

---

[19] C. Duschinsky, 'The Yekum Purkan (יקום פורקן)', *Livre D'Hommage à la Mémoire du Dr. Samuel Poznanski* (Warsaw, 1927), pp. 182–98, especially pp. 187–89. Duschinsky claimed (see his n. 1), in error, that ENA 3564 is not part of the same text. For other theories regarding the *yequm purqan*, see the literature cited below in nn. 37, 45, 55. On the similarity between *yequm purqan* and the blessing found in Nathan's report, see below, n. 31.

[20] Though a brilliant scholar and rabbi, Marmostein is renowned as a poor copyist of Genizah texts, and for this reason alone the ENA portion of the text deserves to be republished.

[21] Various types of liturgical works, including those from the Genizah, are comprised of instructional material interwoven with the texts of the prayers and may also contain lists of Torah readings for festivals and the like. An overview of liturgical texts from the Genizah and the early medieval *siddurim* may be obtained from S. C. Reif, 'Codicological aspects of Jewish liturgical history', *Bulletin of the John Rylands University Library* 75 (1993), pp. 116–31; see also his *Judaism and Hebrew Prayer* (Cambridge, 1993), pp. 141–206. On the anthological nature of the *siddur* throughout the ages, see J. Tabory, 'The prayer book (siddur) as an anthology of Judaism', *Prooftexts* 17 (1997), pp. 115–32.

[22] D. Goldschmidt, סדר רב עמרם גאון (Jerusalem, 1971) [=*SRAG* below]. Amram Gaon is not the author of that work; see the review of scholarly opinions in T. Kronholm, *Seder R. Amram Gaon: Part II* (Lund, 1974), pp. XXIII ff.; R. Brody, 'The enigma of Seder Rav 'Amram' in *Knesset Ezra* (see n. 14 above), pp. 21–34; and compare my comments in *Introduction to Halakhot Pesuqot* (see n. 8 above), pp. 110, 184–85, 276.

4. A comprehensive list of Torah and *hafṭarah* readings for the year, beginning with Passover. This section, which bears the title זה סידור שלשנה מה קורין בתורה, covers much of one side of the strap and continues on the obverse. The text represents a reformulation, expansion and translation of a similar list found in several early codes from the geonic period. The list was originally composed in Aramaic but the version in this fragment is in Hebrew. Although the witnesses to the original list already sometimes differ from each other, the fact that the customs mentioned in the present list differ from any form of the original version rule out the possibility that it is an original composition, suggesting rather that it drew directly on one of those older texts. The most likely source was the *Halakhot Pesuqot*, a code written near the end of the eighth century.[23]

5. Various verses from the Prophets and Hagiographa listed for recitation on several festivals, and one verse ל[ריש] גלותא ('for the Exilarch'). This entire section bears the title (as I have reconstructed it) א[גדת]א דפירקא ('the *aggadah* of the *pirqa*'), a reference to the *pirqa* type of lecture delivered in the Babylonian academies and in some local congregations on the sabbath and festivals. This section provides a list of verses to be used, I believe, by the lecturer in the homiletic segment that concluded the lecture.

6. The next sections contains several components related to the beginning and conclusion of that *pirqa* lecture. They include:[24]

A standard invocation with which to begin the *pirqa*;

A formula, intertwined with phrases from the *qaddish*, with which to conclude the *pirqa*;

A blessing on behalf of the Babylonian Geonim and the Exilarch;

The continuation of that blessing on behalf of the supporters of Torah study;

A concluding benediction; and

An instruction to say the *qaddish de-ḥadata,* a special longer version of *qaddish* recited following the public study of Torah.

7. The fragment continues with an assortment of brief talmudic passages, with no unifying theme. The topics include food preparation by a Gentile on a Jewish festival, the invitation of a Gentile for a meal on the sabbath or festival, the prohibition against neutering an animal, the blessings recited at the circumcision of a

---

[23] The original list appears in the following works (in order of publication): Ch. M. Horowitz, תורתן של ראשונים, vol. 1 (Frankfurt am Main, 1881), pp. 38–44; ספר הלכות פסוקות או הלכות ראו, ed. A. L. Schlossberg (Versailles, 1886), pp. 132–35 [in a different Hebrew translation]; הלכות גדולות, ed. E. Hildesheimer (Berlin, 1892), pp. 617–23; ספר הלכות פסוקות, ed. S. D. Sassoon (Jerusalem, 1950), pp. 180–87 [republished edition, Jerusalem, 1998, cols 449–64]. Regarding the dating of this list, see Danzig, *Introduction to Halakhot Pesuqot* (see n. 8 above), pp. 126–27, 142, *et passim*. This list was subsumed in *SRAG* (see n. 22 above), pp. 98–99, 105, 106–7, 125–27, 131, etc. The basis for the Torah and *hafṭarah* readings for the festivals in the Babylonian tradition is a *baraita* in BT, *Megillah* 29a, into which are interpolated several Babylonian customs; cf. M. Bar-Ilan, לפירושה של ברייתא בעניין קריאת התורה, *Sinai* 112 (1993), pp. 126–34.

[24] These passages will be quoted throughout this study.

slave, the blessings for the redemption of a first-born son (including a suggested poetical prayer), the blessings and procedure for the redemption of the first-born donkey (Exodus 13:13), and end with the blessings and procedure for the redemption of 'fourth-year fruits' (Leviticus 19:24).

8. The last passage on the leaf is a petitional prayer written in Aramaic. This section is written by a different hand, clearly not a professional one, and presumably that of the author. The prayer was added on what was previously an unused part of the strap and is not related in any way to the text just described.[25] With that the text concludes.

Based on an overall examination of the style and language of the liturgical and instructional sections of the text – which are, incidentally, written in Hebrew rather than in Aramaic – as well as of parallel materials in other geonic sources, I have little doubt that this text served as a kind of ritual guide for a community synagogue in Babylonia during the ninth century and is in no way directly related to the geonic academies themselves (see below).[26] Thus, the prayer on behalf of the Exilarch and the Geonim, as well as the *pirqa* lecture that preceded it, were a regular part of the congregation's sabbath and festival service. We may assume that this unit followed the Torah reading of the day; its position following the list of festival readings supports such an assumption.

The text is very rich and lends itself to examination from several angles: liturgical, legal, homiletic and historical. I have chosen two aspects to discuss: the history of the *yequm purqan* prayer, and the *qaddish de-ḥadata* that was recited as a conclusion to the *pirqa* lecture.

---

[25] The prayer (as well as its vocabulary and orthography) is worthy of a separate study. The practice of writing on unused portions of leaves, especially on vellum, is well known; see, for example, my comments in *PAAJR* 54 (1987), Hebrew section, pp. 22–24. This phenomenon differs from liturgical fragments in the Genizah in which certain texts are compiled at the end of the liturgy, as those seem to be a product of intentional compilation (and are thus written by the same hand as the prayers); an example of a Babylonian *siddur* ending with a collection of aggadic texts is T-S H10.10. On such compilations in the Genizah, in general, see M. B. Lerner. 'דף מתוך ספר ליקוטים מן הגניזה' in *Ish Bi-Gevurot: Studies... Alexander Safran*, ed. M. Ḥallamish (Hebrew; Jerusalem, 1990), p. 107, n. 3.

[26] Several of the passages in sections 1 and 7 of this text are found in two other Genizah fragments. Some of these passages are identical, while some appear in varying forms or in Aramaic, but it is clear that all three texts shared a similar source (i.e., none of the three is the direct source of the other two). These two fragments are T-S F10.5, published by L. Ginzberg, *Geonica* (New York, 1909), vol. 2, pp. 400–401 (compare Danzig, *Introduction to Halakhot Pesuqot* (see n. 8 above), p. 190), and Russian National Library (St. Petersburg), Antonin 954. Both items appear to be collections of laws appended to *siddurim* and they share some of the material found in the ENA/T-S text (each also containing different material). The Torah and *hafṭarah* readings and other liturgical customs in the ENA/T-S text are clearly Babylonian, as is the prayer appended to the text, section 8. All the evidence points to its composition in a Babylonian community. On the Babylonian and Palestinian congregations in Fustat, see E. Bareket, *The Jewish Leadership in Fustat* (Hebrew; Tel Aviv, 1995).

I. The *yequm purqan* prayer

Woven into an expanded version of *qaddish*, the blessing on behalf of the Exilarch and the Geonim found in the Adler fragment reads as follows:[27]

> על נשיאינו פל[וני] ראש גל[ות] דכל יש[ראל] חמוד נשי[אנו] פל[וני] ר[אש] ג[לות] דכל ישר[אל] מלך
> ברחמיו יחוס עליו... אמ[ן] כן תהי רעוא מן קוד[מא] ד׳ק׳ב׳ה׳ו׳א׳.
> על אדונינו צמח ראש ישיבת ג[און] יע[קב] חמוד אדונינו פלטוי ראש ישיב[ת] ג[און] יע[קב] כבודינו
> והדרינו נזר ראשינו ועטרת תפארתינו שלא יפול לעולם... אמן כן תהי רעוא מק[ודמא] דק[׳ב׳ה׳].
> על אדונ[נו] צמח ר[אש] יש[יבת] ג[און] יע[קב] חמוד אד[וננו] חיים כב[ודינו] הד[רינו] נזר רא[שינו]
> ותפ[ארתינו] שלא יפ[ול] לעולם...

What has always made this part of the Adler fragment so historically interesting is that it seems to corroborate and flesh out what was previously known from an eye-witness account penned in the middle of the tenth century by Nathan Ha-Bavli ('Nathan the Babylonian') regarding a similar blessing. According to Nathan, the two heads of the academies graciously deferred to each other. After the Exilarch had given his lecture, the head of one academy, Sura, rose and preached, and was followed by the head of the other academy, Pumbedita, who did the same. Nathan's account is thus a detailed description of a *pirqa* lecture delivered with great pomp and circumstance, at the centre of which the following is stated:[28]

> וכשהוא גומר מתחיל בבעיא ואומר ׳ברם צריך את למילף׳ ועומד זקן א[חד] חכם [ונבון] ורגיל ומשיב
> בענין, ויושב ועומד החזן ואומר קדיש. וכשמגיע בחייכון וביומיכון אומר בחיי **נשיאנו ראש גלות**
> ובחייכון ובחיי דכל בית ישראל. **וכשגומר הקדיש מברך ראש גלות ואח״כ מברך ראש ישיבות.**
> וכשהוא גומר את הברכה עומד ואומר ׳מדינה פלוני וכל בנותיה כך וכך יבא מהן׳ וזוכר כל המדינות
> שהן משלחות לישיבה ומברך אותם, ואח״כ מברך האנשים שבהם שמתעסקין בנדבה עד שתגיע
> לישיבות. ואח״כ מוציא ס[פר] ת[ורה] וקורא כהן...

The gist of this paragraph is that the Gaon of Sura began his lecture (a *pirqa*), after which the *ḥazzan* arose and intoned the *qaddish*, in which he incorporated the name of the Exilarch.[29] He then proceeded to intone a blessing, first on behalf of the Exilarch, then for the Geonim. After that blessing, he announced the donations from the various communities for the benefit of the academies, and blessed those who had sent the funds. He then blessed the agents who had collected the funds and insured

---

[27] This passage appears in all the publications listed in nn. 11–18 above.

[28] A. Neubauer, *Medieval Jewish Chronicles,* vol. 2 [=*MJC*] (Oxford, 1895), p. 84. On Nathan's account, see M. Ben-Sasson, 'The structure, goals and content of the story of Nathan Ha-Babli' in *Culture and Society in Medieval Jewry,* eds M. Ben-Sasson, R. Bonfil and J. R. Hacker (Jerusalem, 1989), pp. 137–96; for a brief overview, see Brody, *Geonim* (see n. 2 above), pp. 26–30, 72–76.

[29] On the inclusion of names of leaders in the *qaddish*, see below, n. 78. A blessing on behalf of the Exilarch is not known from earlier sources; see Beer, *Exilarchate* (see n. 14 above), p. 177.

their safe arrival at the academies.[30] After this, they read that week's Torah portion.

Nathan was witness to a prayer, the text of which he did not record, and scholars have assumed that the text in the ENA fragment reflects the version that Nathan heard. What I, however, believe is that the text contains a version of that prayer *as it was recited in a Babylonian synagogue* and not in one of the two geonic academies.[31] We may speculate that the custom of reciting this prayer was practised by other congregations within the precincts of Babylonia and in nearby lands, and that it is not

---

[30] It was an ancient custom for charitable donations to be declared in synagogue on the sabbath; see Tosefta, *Shabbat* 16 (17).22, ed. Lieberman, p. 79 (and parallels) and *Terumot* 1.10, p. 109. These donations were announced by the *ḥazzan*; see *Leviticus Rabbah* 16.5 (ed. M. Margaliot (reprinted, Jerusalem, 1972), p. 357), with a parallel in *Ecclesiastes Rabbah* 5.5. Regarding inscriptions with names of donors, see below, n. 76. This custom seems to be in disagreement with BT, *Megillah* 28b, where חשבונות are forbidden in synagogue (on any day) due to the sanctity of the place; see, however, Menaḥem Ha-Meiri's commentary on that passage: וחשבונות של צבור יש מתירין שכל שהוא צורך צבור אין בו קלות ראש, and *Sefer Ha-Manhig* quoted below in n. 123. The custom seems to have prevailed in the East during the Middle Ages, given the number of lists of donors that survived in the Genizah, many of which were written for the purpose of being read aloud in the synagogue; see S. D. Goitein, *A Mediterranean Society*, vol. 2 (Berkeley, Los Angeles and London, 1971), pp. 106, 162, 471–510, etc. It would, however, seem that Sa'adya did not approve of the custom of declaring charity at all on the sabbath, because of the sanctity of the day; see his commentary on Exodus published recently by Y. Ratzaby (Hebrew; Jerusalem, 1998), p. 188. In early Ashkenazi communities charity was declared in synagogues on the Day of Atonement after the Torah reading; see *Maḥzor Vitry* [=*MV*], ed. S. Hurwitz (Berlin, 1889–93) [based on a MS in the British Museum], pp. 392–93 and ספר ראבי״ה, ed. V. Aptowitzer (reprinted, Jerusalem, 1964), vol. 2, p. 192. This was also the early custom in France; see Nathan b. Judah, ספר המחכים, ed. J. Freimann (Cracow, 1909), p. 41. Similarly, *MV* (pp. 309–10) records a justification for declaring charity on the three pilgrim festivals. This custom was later extended to each and every sabbath; see שבלי הלקט השלם, §81, ed. S. K. Mirsky (New York, 1966), pp. 311–12. In some communities it was done after the Torah reading even on Monday and Thursday; see Judah b. Yaqar, פירוש התפילות והברכות, ed. Sh. Yerushalmi (Jerusalem, 1979), vol. 1, pp. 78, 107. In the Rhineland, the custom was to recite a blessing on behalf of one reading from the Torah on the sabbath and to include the phrase בעבור שית[ן] נדבה לכבוד התור[ה]; see ספר מנהגים דבי מהר״ם ב״ר ברוך מרוטנבורג, ed. I. Elfenbein (New York, 1938), p. 14. Despite all this evidence, *Sefer Ḥasidim* objects to the custom of publicizing the names of the donors to synagogues at all; see ed. J. Wistinetzki (Berlin, 1891), §1528, p. 374. It would appear that the generic מי שברך prayer, in which no specific names are listed, was composed from that perspective; on the development of that prayer, see A. Ya'ari, 'תפלות מי שברך: השתלשלותן, מנהגיהן ונוסחאותיהן', *Kiryat Sefer* 33 (1958), pp. 118 ff. On donations of houses and other property to synagogues and charity (*heqdesh*), see M. Gil, *Documents of the Jewish Pious Foundations from the Cairo Geniza* (Leiden, 1976).

[31] S. J. Rapaport already alluded to a similarity between the blessing mentioned in Nathan's report and the *yequm purqan*; see *Kerem Ḥemed* 3 (1838), p. 46. It is likely that aspects of the prayer in the Genizah fragment may be similar to the prayer that was offered in the academies but we have no witness to the wording of that prayer; see below. The prayer recited in the local congregations may have developed along the lines of its academic counterpart, mimicking parts of the version that was heard by students and visitors to the academies.

unique to the one synagogue from which this fragment survived.[32] In any event, we need not accept Lewin's theory that since the Pumbeditan Ṣemaḥ is mentioned first, the fragment must be a remnant of a Pumbeditan *maḥzor*.[33] Interestingly, the name of the Exilarch is left out in the text, as the prayer reads: על נשיאינו פל[וני] ראש גל[ות] דכל יש[ראל] חמוד נשי[אנו] פל[וני] ר[אש] ג[לות] דכל ישר[אל]. This line is odd and self-contradictory since it grandly mentions the Exilarch as 'Head of all the Diaspora', while at the same time omitting his name and replacing it with a humble פלוני [בן] פלוני, something that would never have been done had this prayer been recited in the geonic academy. The absence of the Exilarch's name must have been the result of confusion on the part of that community as to who was the Exilarch at that time, if not merely witness to an interregnum between two Exilarchs. This itself corroborates what we know from other sources about the decline of the role of the Exilarch that began in the second quarter of the ninth century.[34]

Regarding the *yequm purqan* prayer, it is, as Duschinsky demonstrated, reminiscent of the type of prayer found in the ENA leaf in which the Exilarch and Geonim are blessed, although Duschinsky could not point to any specific passage in our *yequm purqan* that is directly taken from the older Genizah text. Duschinsky found a rather long version of the *yequm purqan* in several Yemenite prayer-books in which there are indeed more significant parallels, and from which he attempted to

---

[32] Specific cities and precincts in Babylonia and Persia were allied with one of the two academies and with the Exilarch (their רָשׁוּת), and were so designated primarily for the collection of funds and the appointment of local judges. A list of these geographic areas appears in Nathan's account; see Neubauer, *MJC* (see n. 28 above), pp. 85–87 and Gil, *Ishmael* (see n. 2 above), pp. 90–93.

[33] *Ginze Kedem* 3 (1925), p. 51. Lewin's theory is to a degree based on the assumption that the Gaon of Sura would normally receive preference and be mentioned first; since he is not, the blessing must have been written in Pumbedita. Sura's formal prominence is attested to in several geonic sources, especially in the document preceding Nathan's account, entitled אלה המעלות שנתעלה בהם ישיבת סורא על [ישיבת] פומבדיתא; see Neubauer, *MJC* (see n. 28 above) pp. 77–78 and Brody, *Geonim* (see n. 2 above), pp. 28–29. This hierarchy is also reflected in Nathan's own description, where the Gaon of Sura lectures first and sits to the right of the Exilarch (*MJC*, p. 84), and in the fact that the Suran academy was often proudly called ישיבה של ימין. The truth be told, I have no clue as to why the Pumbeditan Gaon should be mentioned first, especially since the two Ṣemaḥs presided over the academies before the decline of Sura, which set in around the beginning of the tenth century; see *IRSG* (see n. 12 above), pp. 116–18.

[34] The matter of the chronology and dating of the Exilarchs during the geonic period is still confused and even the latest treatment of this topic finds that precision is far from feasible; see Gil, *Ishmael* (see n. 2 above), vol. 1, pp. 93–101, 113–14 (no specific Exilarch is known from the period of the Ṣemaḥs) and Ch. Tykochinsky, 'בוסתנאי ראש הגולה', *Devir* 1 (1923), pp. 174–77. A collection of all pertinent sources (except chronologies) may be found in A. Grossman, *The Babylonian Exilarchate in the Gaonic Period* (Hebrew; Jerusalem, 1984). On the decline of the power of the Exilarch, see Gil, pp. 102–8, Grossman, pp. 53 ff. and Brody, *Geonim* (see n. 2 above), pp. 80–82. The story told by Sherira about the Exilarch needing to join the Gaon of Sura and his academy to convene a *rigla* (*IRSG* (see n. 12 above), pp. 91 ff.) is corroborated by geonic responsa; see *'Oṣar Ha-Ge'onim* to *Megillah*, §116 and R. Brody, תשובות רב נטרונאי בר הילאי גאון (Jerusalem, 1994), p. 302.

prove his theory. The Yemenite prayer was, however, recited only on Simḥat Torah and would appear to be a later elaboration of *yequm purqan*.[35]

The earliest witnesses to the text of *yequm purqan* are *Maḥzor Vitry* [=*MV*] (twelfth-century France) and *Ḥibbur Berakhot* [=*ḤB*] (twelfth-century Italy). *MV* and other early French *siddurim* contain only one version of the prayer wherein all the persons and institutions are blessed together,[36] while in *ḤB* two versions of the prayer already appear (as became the custom in the later Ashkenazi rite), the first addressing only the attending congregation and the second directed toward the communities and their leaders in the Land of Israel and in Babylonia (the two prayers being introduced as *alternative* texts: ויש נוהגין לומר כך... ויש שנוהגין לומר כן).[37] The third early witness to

---

[35] See Duschinsky (see n. 19 above), p. 194: 'it is not impossible that this prayer was the original form from which the Yekum Purkan was afterwards derived in an abridged form'. The Yemenite prayer was published on pp. 195–97 and again (from additional MSS) by A. Ya'ari, תולדות חג שמחת-תורה (Jerusalem, 1964), pp. 181–85. I have found the long prayer in other *Tiklal*s, including JTSA MS 3038. Duschinsky's theory as to this being the origin of the prayer is implausible, as already indicated by Ya'ari, p. 181, n. 2 (and foot of p. 185), and his 'תפילות מי שברך' (see n. 30 above), p. 119. Nevertheless, we see that the prayer travelled to Yemen at a fairly early date, as the JTSA MS was written in the first half of the fifteenth century.

[36] *MV* (see n. 30 above), pp. 172–73; *yequm purqan* is also mentioned there on p. 99 and p. 393, the text of the prayer appearing in the section on the festivals, see below, at n. 48. The prayer appears in *MV*, JTSA MS 8092 ('Reggio'), with very few variants; see D. Goldschmidt, *On Jewish Liturgy* (Hebrew; Jerusalem, 1980), p. 74. The prayer is already included in the earlier layer of *MV* and is not merely one of its many later accretions. Regarding *MV,* see I. Ta-Shma, 'על כמה עניני מחזור ויטרי', *Alei Sefer* 11 (1984), pp. 81–89 and A. Grossman, *The Early Sages of France* (Hebrew; Jerusalem, 1995), pp. 395–403. In my opinion, the entire matter of the authorship of this work requires further examination. According to Goldschmidt (p. 80, n. 1), the French rite consistently has one version of the prayer while the German rite has two (as similarly in the two French MSS cited below in n. 55). This is borne out by another important witness to *yequm purqan* in the commentary on the *siddur* by the German rabbi, Eleazar b. Judah of Worms (*c.*1165–*c.*1230); see פירושי סידור התפילה לרוקח, eds M. and Y. Hirshler (Jerusalem, 1992), vol. 2, pp. 560–61. Although his reading is closest to *MV* (see below, before n. 56, but he lacked the 'gloss' in *MV*; see below, n. 39), he nevertheless had the prayer in two versions, as did Abraham b. Nathan (ראב״ן); see the volume entitled סידור רבנו שלמה, ed. M. Hirshler (Jerusalem, 1972), pp. 173–74. (On the correct identity of this work, see A. Grossman, *The Early Sages of Ashkenaz* (Hebrew; Jerusalem, 1981), pp. 346–48 and Ta-Shma's comment, p. 82, n. 2.) The version that addresses the local congregation is similar in style to the מי שברך prayer said after the Torah reading, which was far more widespread that the *yequm purqan*; see Ya'ari's article cited above in n. 30. It is interesting to note that the author of *Seder Troyes* attaches *yequm purqan* to the יהי רצון prayer said following the reading of the Torah at *minḥah* on Shabbat (see *MV*, p. 179; the prayer was later moved to Mondays and Thursdays), and includes the following phrase: כל חכמי ישראל, הם ונשיהם ובניהם ובנותיהם ותלמידיהם ותלמידי תלמידיהם בכל מקומות מושבותיהם. According to that author, both prayers are recited only when there is no *musaf* sacrifice with which to atone; see M. Z. Weiss, סדר טרוייש (Frankfurt am Main, 1905), p. 14 (similarly in JTSA MS 8259, p. 163b).

[37] JTSA MS 8402 (which is Solomon Schechter's personally transcribed copy of *Ḥibbur Berakhot* [=*ḤB*], the original MS having been burnt in a fire in Turin). On this work, the MS

the prayer (although the text is not quoted) is in a responsum of Qalonymos b. Isaac ('the Elder'), who survived the First Crusade in Mainz (Mayence) and moved to Speyer (d. 1126). Although we find the prayer simultaneously attested in France, Italy and Germany in the twelfth century, the potential evidence of its inclusion in the liturgy of Mainz is of great importance, given the Italian origins of the rabbinic

---

of which was not available to Duschinsky, see A. Schechter, *Studies in Jewish Liturgy* (Philadelphia, 1930); part of this passage is quoted there on p. 70. A. Schechter attributed the work to Menaḥem b. Solomon, author of the *Sekhel Tov* (see below, n. 114), but this still requires some clarification; see I. Davidson's review of A. Schechter's book, *JQR* NS 21 (1930–31), pp. 241–79. In any event, the work does seem to be from the twelfth century. Although that *siddur* is definitely Italian, the prayer is not formulated according to the regular Italian rite, as, for example, in *Maḥzor Roma*; see Goldschmidt, *On Jewish Liturgy* (see n. 36 above), p. 154 (in a note) and p. 164. In A. Schechter's quotation of the passage, the prayer is quoted incorrectly and no mention is made of the first version on behalf of the attending congregation; see Marx's quotation from this MS, at n. 59 below). While we may assume that the 'original' text did indeed exist in a single version only, as in *MV*, the fact that *ḤB* records two versions does not preclude it from being witness to an equally old formulation of the prayer.

There are abundant theories about the origin of the prayer and the relationship between its two versions but, however elegant and simple each may sound, there is no hard proof to support any of them. Several opinions share a relatively *late* dating for the composition of the prayer: according to Tal, *MV* records the single version because the academies and Exilarchate were then still active, while by the mid-twelfth century the shift to two versions reflects the decline of those institutions at that very time; see Sh. Tal, פרי חיים (Tel Aviv, 1983), pp. 60–62. A. L. Frumkin suggested that the prayer was composed either in Babylonia before Amram's time, but that he did not include it in his *siddur* so as not to obligate the Jews in Spain to recite it [*sic*], or later, during the time of Sherira and Hai, to bolster the waning support for the geonic academies; see the note to his edition of *SRAG*, סדר רב עמרם השלם, vol. 2 (Jerusalem, 1912), pp. 75–76. Similarly, Hildesheimer suggested that the prayer was composed in Babylonia, but not until the twelfth century, during the tenure of Samuel b. Ali; see E. Hildesheimer, 'לחקר על היכלאי בתקופת הגאונים' in *Festschrift Dr. Jakob Freimann* (Berlin, 1937), Hebrew section, pp. 10–12 (where the phrase רישי מתיבתא is taken to refer to heads of *yeshivot* at large, not to the Babylonian Geonim). According to A. Ya'ari, a single version was composed in Babylonia on behalf of the Geonim only and did *not* include any mention of the local communities, necessitating the creation of a second version for the local leaders, also composed in Babylonia (Ya'ari, 'תפילות מי שברך'; see n. 30 above), a theory that is disproved by the T-S text quoted below, at n. 40. A certain rabbi Frankel claimed that the prayer was composed at a time when the sabbath sermon ceased; see K. A. Frankel, 'תפלת יקום פורקן בשבת', *Ha-Qerem* 1:1 (1955) pp. 18–24, especialy p. 20. Z. Karl suggested that the Babylonian prayer was not said in Spain (given that the *SRAG* was assumed to have been sent from Babylonia to Spain), as the Spanish communities already said the *qaddish de-ḥadata* after the sermon, which included mention of the rabbis; see Z. Karl, הקדיש (Lvov, 1935), pp. 67–68. Foerster, however, suggested that *yequm purqan* was not composed in Babylonia, as the blessings for the Exilarch and the Geonim would already have been included in the *qaddish*; see G. Foerster, 'כתובות מבתי-הכנסת העתיקים וזיקתן לנוסחים של ברכה ותפילה', *Cathedra* 19 (1981), p. 30. This would be in direct opposition to Duschinsky's theory; see above, nn. 19, 35). The proponents of the origin of the prayer in the Land of Israel are listed below, in n. 45; compare also n. 55.

leadership of that community.[38] Although I have not collated all the extant versions in medieval manuscripts (which remains a *desideratum*), an examination of the subtle differences between the *MV* and the *ḤB* versions is illustrative. (The quotation given here is of the second of the two prayers in *ḤB*, with line 11 added from the first prayer.)

	מחזור ויטרי	חיבור ברכות
1		לכל קהלייא קדישייא
2	למרנן ורבנן חבורתא קדישתא	
3	די בארעא דישראל ודי בבבל	די בארעא דישראל ודי בארעא דבבל
4		ודי בכל ארע גלוותהון
5	רישי כלי	לריש כלה
6		ולרבני חברותא
7	ורישי מתיבתא דייני דבבא	ולרישי מתיבתא ולדייני דבבא
8	ודייני דמתא ולכל תלמידי חכמים	
9	ולכל תלמידיהון ולכל תלמידי תלמידיהון	ולכל תלמידיהן ולכל תלמידי תלמידיהון
10	ולכל מאן דעסקין באורייתא	ולכל מאן דעסקין באוריתא
11	ולכל קהלא קדישא הדין	[לכל קהלא קדישא הדין]
12	רברבייא עם זעירייא טפלייא עם נשיא	
13	מלכא דעלמא יפיש חייהון	מלכא דעלמא יברך יתהון ויפיש חייהון
14	ויסגי יומיהון	ויהא ארכא לשניהון
14	ויפרוק וישיזיב יתהון מכל עקא ומכל עקתא	וישתיזבון ויתפרקון מכל עקן
15	ומכל מרעין בישין	ומכל מרעין בישין
16	מרן דבשמיא יהא בסעדהון	מראן דבשמיא יהא בסעדהון
17	וישמע בקול צלותהון ויתן יתהון	

[38] The responsum was published by M. Hirshler, גנוזות, vol. 2 (Jerusalem, 1985), p. 126, from Vatican MS 487 (not '478' as printed by Hirshler). The title of the responsa identifies them as: 'ואילו שאילות מאת מורי הרב ר' קולונימוס' (I have corrected on the basis of the MS), but there is no further indication of which Qalonymos is intended. I agree with Hirshler's identification of the author (p. 125) as Qalonymos b. Isaac, in view of the fact that several traditions in other parts of the text (pp. 125–29) are elsewhere quoted in relation to Samuel he-Ḥasid b. Qalonymos. This passage states: לפיכך אנו אומ[רים] קדיש בשבת תכף הקרייה, ולא לסמוך על אותו קדיש שלפני מוסף, לפי שיש להפסיק בנתיים ולומר **יקום פורקן** ודברים אחרים. I presume that דברים אחרים refer to מי שברך and יהי רצון; see above, n. 36. Qalonymos was the grandson of Eliezer b. Isaac ('the Great') who, in turn, was a student of Gershom Me'or Ha-Golah (both of whom also lived in Mainz; Gershom probably migrated there from Italy). On the leaders of the Mainz community during the eleventh century; see Grossman, *Sages of Ashkenaz* (see n. 36 above), pp. 27 ff., including a reference to the Italian connections, as well as pp. 1–9, and the addenda to the second edition, p. 441. I see no evidence that this is the famous Qalonymos of Lucca, or Qalonymos b. Moses, both of whom have even stronger ties to Italy. The influence of halakhic sources and traditions from both the Land of Israel and Babylonia on the early German rabbis, especially those of Mainz, has been much debated recently by Grossman and Ta-Shma (see Grossman, pp. 424–35, and addenda to the second edition, p. 448). It is very tempting to draw a parallel between that issue and the mention of both centres in *yequm purqan* (see below, n. 45). See also below, n. 63, regarding mention of the the heads of the academies in *reshut* poems.

18 לחינא ולחסדא קדם כורסי יקר מלכותיה
19 וקדם שלטונייא דארעא
20 ויקיים זכוותהון דכל ישראל[39]
21 בכל זמן ועידן ונאמר אמן בכל זמן ועידן ונאמר אמן

Before I proceed with my analysis of the *yequm purqan* prayer, I must first note the importance of the T-S leaf for confirming Duschinsky's basic thesis as to the precursor of *yequm purqan*. The T-S leaf continues from where the ENA fragment leaves off, and at the very beginning of the new folio we have the conclusion to that long blessing on behalf of the Exilarch and the Geonim, which reads as follows: [...] דקבה [...] על תלמידי ת[למידיהו]ן גבריא נשיא וטפלא דאית אתו לבית מדרשא הויין למישמע ולמילף פיתגמי אריתא קיד׳ב׳ה׳ו יברך יתכון ויפיש ויסגי יתכון. Several biblical verses are then quoted and the section concludes with the refrain אמן כן תהי רעוא.[40] The phrase just quoted is strikingly similar to the *yequm purqan* prayer (especially in the *MV* version, as given above, lines 9–14). Although part of the phrase is not unique to this text and occurs in Targum Jonathan on Judges 5:2 (ועל נסא ופורקנא [!] דאתעביד להון לישראל בכן תבו חכימיא למתב בבתי כנישתא בריש גלי **ולאלפא ית עמא פתגמי אורייתא**; the phrase פתגמי אוריתא being extremely common in Onqelos!),[41] and part of the passage is obliterated, we nevertheless have sufficient evidence in the surviving text to confirm Duschinsky's thesis regarding the direct correlation between this Genizah text and the *yequm purqan* prayer.

From the text of the T-S leaf, we also see that the original intent of that phrase was to serve as a blessing for women and children, together with the adult males. Despite the explicit reference to attendance in 'the house of study' (דאית אתו לבית מדרשא), the blessing appears not to be a general reference to the support of Torah study, but rather refers to the attendance at the Torah reading on the sabbath and the ensuing *pirqa* lecture (whether in the academy or in the synagogue), an act praised here as a demonstration of devotion to Torah study (see also the Targum Jonathan passage quoted in the previous paragraph).[42] The reward for women and children hearing the Torah reading and sabbath sermon in the synagogue is stressed in the following passage from *Midrash Ha-Gadol*: נשיכם. אע״פ שאינן יודעין הן באין לשמוע ולקבל שכר. מלמד שכל הנכנס לבית כנסת ושומע דברי תורה אע״פ שאינו יודע זוכה ומקבל שכר.[43]

---

[39] Although it is reminiscent of a gloss, lines 17–20 are indeed found in all the French witnesses to the prayer that I have checked.

[40] This section of the text is discussed below, following n. 98.

[41] בריש גלי is Onqelos's translation of ביד רמה (Exodus 14:8, Numbers 15:30, 33:3).

[42] The reference to פיתגמי אריתא is not intended as a general statement, given that the text later states: פיתגמא דהוא רב ועילאי ויקיר מכולא ולית בר מיניה, which is a clear reference to the Torah reading and lecture that have just taken place.

[43] *Midrash Ha-Gadol* to Deuteronomy 29:10, ed. S. Fisch (Jerusalem, 1975), p. 639. A specific association between women's attendance at sabbath services and the reading aloud of the Targum is found in *Soferim* 18.5–6 (ed. M. Higger (New York, 1937), pp. 316–17), where the reason given for translating the Torah reading on sabbath is so that women and children may comprehend it. The fact that women attended synagogue on the sabbath is also

Mentioned, as Duschinsky points out, by only a handful of medieval rabbis, the *yequm purqan* is unknown to many medieval codifiers such as Maimonides and, more significantly, is lacking in the two major prayer-books of the geonic period, namely, the one attributed to Amram Gaon, and the one composed by Sa'adya.[44] To my knowledge, it has also not been found in any prayer-book in the Genizah, neither of the Babylonian nor the Palestinian rite. Although several scholars have argued that the *yequm purqan* prayer as we know it was composed in the Land of Israel, I suggest that in all likelihood it is a product of the Diaspora, composed as it is from the perspective of a community removed from the two centres and reflecting loyalties to both, as well as to their own leaders. Although it is difficult to specify the precise community, Southern Italy comes to mind as a candidate (see above at n. 38).[45]

---

known from BT, *'Avodah Zarah* 38a–b and *Soferim* 18.6 (pp. 317–18); cf. S. Safrai, 'The Synagogue', in *The Jewish People in the First Century*, vol. 2 (Assen/Maastricht and Philadelphia, 1987), pp. 919–21. On the attendance of children (both boys and girls) at services, see *Soferim* 18.7–8 (pp. 319–20), and *Tosafot,* BT, *Soṭah* 3a, s.v. כדי ליתן. In the T-S fragment, women are listed after men and before children (as we would expect), and the reversed sequence in *MV* is somewhat puzzling, although it may merely be influenced by the cadence of the pattern: רברבייא עם זעירייא, טפלייא עם נשיא [MS JTSA: טפלא עם נשייא]. Compare the phrase הם ונשיהם ובניהם ובנותיהם in the מי שברך prayer, similar to what is found in *Seder Eliyahu Rabbah*, ch. 4 (ed. M. Friedmann (Vienna, 1902), p. 19).

44 See Duschinsky 'Yekum Purkan' (see n. 19 above), pp. 189–90 (to which one may add the sources mentioned below to which he had no access), as against Rapaport who assumed that the prayer was indeed in *SRAG* (which was still unpublished in his day); see *Kerem Ḥemed* 3 (1838), p. 46. The absence of the prayer in *SRAG* is all the more puzzling, given that many additions to the prayers, derived from various places and periods, were added in the MSS of that work. This phenomenon has been noted by many scholars, e.g. N. Wieder, *The Formation of Jewish Liturgy in the East and West* (Hebrew; Jerusalem, 1998), pp. 53, 264, *et passim*, and above, n. 22.

45 The proponents of the origins of the prayer in the Land of Israel are, among others: A. Schechter, *Studies* (see n. 37 above), p. 70; B. Dinur, ישראל בגולה, 1/1 (Tel Aviv, 1926), p. 266, n. 65; Tal, *Peri* (see n. 37 above), pp. 55–63. I suggest Southern Italy (rather than North Africa) for the same reason that I offered regarding the composition of *Sefer Ḥefeṣ*, see N. Danzig, 'The First Discovered Leaves of *Sefer Ḥefeṣ*', *JQR* NS 82 (1991), pp. 51–136, especially pp. 100–109. Here too, the evidence converges on a European community, rather than a Mediterranean one. On works that bridged the traditions of Babylonia and the Land of Israel during that period, see also J. Sussmann, 'The Ashkenazi *Yerushalmi* MS – Sefer Yerushalmi', *Tarbiz* 65 (1996), pp. 37–63, especially the concluding paragraph. On the liturgical influence of the Land of Israel on Italy during this period, see the preliminary study of A. Schechter, *Studies* (see n. 37 above), pp. 26–40, *et passim*; see also E. Fleischer's comments in *Sefunot* 1[16] (1980), pp. 42–43, and in *Ha-Sifrut* 30/31 (1981), pp. 131 ff. and pp. 141 ff. On the shifting allegiance of the Italian rabbinate toward Babylonian *halakhah*, see R. Bonfil, 'בין ארץ-ישראל לבין בבל', *Shalem* 5 (1987), pp. 1–30, a shorter version of which appeared originally as: 'Tra Due Mondi', *Italia Judaica* (Rome, 1983), pp. 135–58; see also A. Grossman, 'When did the hegemony of Eretz Israel cease in Italy?', *Mas'at Moshe: Studies in Jewish and Islamic Culture Presented to Moshe Gil*, eds E. Fleischer, M. A. Friedman and J. L. Kraemer (Jerusalem, 1998), pp. 143–57. See also Gil, *Ishmael* (see n. 2 above), pp. 200–205. On relations between these two Diaspora communities, see M. Ben-Sasson, 'Italy and Ifriqia from the ninth to eleventh century', *Les Relations Intercommunautaires Juives en Mediterranée Occidentale* (Paris, 1984), pp. 34–50; compare

Although the prayer is written in a 'classical' Aramaic style, it bears no evidence of the live influence of Western (Palestinian) Aramaic, since its language seems to be intentionally composed in an archaic style, closer to the language of the Targumic translations. Its language would not therefore point to its composition in the Land of Israel.[46] Its style was chosen either for the purpose of elevating the language of the prayer, or perhaps to mimic the language of the Targum, given that the Targum was read together with the Torah and *hafṭarah* portions in the synagogue and that several phrases in the *yequm purqan* prayer are indeed common to the targumic translations.[47] (Interestingly, in the printed *MV*, the *yequm purqan* is quoted immediately after the Aramaic translations of the *hafṭarot* for the festivals and the poetical elaborations, written in Galilean Aramaic, on the *hafṭarot* recited on those days, but that is unique to the manuscript on which the printed edition is based, and in other manuscripts the prayer is written for the sabbath.[48]) The phrase in the Cambridge fragment יברך יתכון

---

above, n. 26. While suggesting a general theory as to the composition of *yequm purqan*, I am not suggesting a specific time for such; it must have been no later than the first half of the eleventh century in order to have appeared in the three communities mentioned above at n. 38, and probably somewhat earlier, Hai having died in 1038.

[46] I have not seen this point mentioned in the literature on this topic, except for the note of S. Baer, סדר עבודת ישראל (reprinted, Tel Aviv, 1957), p. 229; for the proponents of the Land of Israel theory, see the previous note. The very term יקום פורקן is not itself Eastern (Babylonian) Aramaic; compare ופורקנא in *qaddish de-rabbanan* in the Ashkenazi rite, and in *qaddish titqabel* in the Sephardi rite, although פורקן does appear in Hebrew in the על הנסים prayer recited on Ḥanukkah (see Baer, p. 100). The only use of יקום in the Babylonian Talmud is in an old dictum used in the Land of Israel, recorded in BT, *'Avodah Zarah* 11b: ווי לדין כד יקום דין (so too in MSS); see J. N. Epstein, *A Grammar of Babylonian Aramaic* (Hebrew; Jerusalem, 1960), pp. 13–14 (דין being dealt with on pp. 23–24). Note that the Jonathan Targum on Ezekiel 29:21, as quoted in Qimḥi's commentary there, has ביומא ההוא **אקים פורקן** לבית ישראל, whereas the printed edition has איתי פורקן (the Reuchlin MS reading altogether differently: אצמיח קרן; see ed. A. Sperber, Leiden, 1969). Both יקום and פורקן are common in Onqelos (Exodus 8:19, 21:30, 30:12, and elsewhere), although פורקנא also appears (Exodus 14:13 and elsewhere). See also M. Sokoloff, *A Dictionary of Jewish Palestinian Aramaic of the Byzantine Period* (Ramat Gan, 1990), s.v. פורקן; D. de Sola Pool, *The Old Jewish-Aramaic Prayer: The Kaddish* (Leipzig, 1909), p. 37. On יקום, see G. Dalman, *Grammatik des Jüdisch-Palästinischen Aramäisch* (Darmstadt, 1960), p. 320.

[47] The first option is in a similar vein to what Ch. Rabin has written regarding the language of the Hebrew prayers; see his overview 'The linguistic investigation of the language of Jewish prayer' in *Studies in Aggadah, Targum and Jewish Liturgy in Memory of Joseph Heinemann,* eds J. J. Petuchowski and E. Fleischer (Jerusalem, 1981), Hebrew section, pp. 163–71. On the targumic style of *yequm purqan*, see above after n. 40, as well as the previous note, and below, n. 51. J. Heinemann (*Prayer in the Talmud* (Berlin and New York, 1977), pp. 265–66) cites the opinion, shared by Zunz and Bacher, that Aramaic prayers such as *qaddish* (which would also include *yequm purqan*) were said in Aramaic as they followed the sermon which was itself delivered in that language, as already implied by *Tosafot, Berakhot* 3a, s.v. ועונין. The influence of the Targum on *qaddish* was noted by de Sola Pool, *Kaddish* (see n. 46 above), pp. 12, 15, 23–24, and this would indeed account for the classical Aramaic in which that prayer was composed.

[48] Compare above, n. 36. On these poems, see M. Sokoloff and J. Yahalom, *Jewish Palestinian Aramaic Poetry from Late Antiquity* (Hebrew; Jerusalem, 1999).

ויפיש ויסגי יתכון indicates that the archaic form יתכון, common in Targum and in tractate *Nedarim* of the Babylonian Talmud, already appears in the older version of the prayer, and is not a product of its later reworking in Europe.[49] By the second half of the eleventh century, with the passing of Hai Gaon, the Babylonian Geonim were no longer leaders of the Diaspora communities in any sense, certainly not in Europe and barely so on their own turf. The retention of the prayer for the academies in the medieval liturgy remains something of an enigma.

In truth, however, although I have demonstrated the correctness of Duschinsky's theory of Babylonian influence on the prayer, that position must be somewhat amended. We now know that the antecedent to the *yequm purqan* prayer is not merely in the Genizah text containing the blessing for the Geonim, since there is also something of a parallel to the *yequm purqan* prayer in a phenomenon that pre-dates the geonic period and whose roots lie in the Land of Israel. I refer to dedicatory inscriptions found in synagogues in Israel from the Byzantine era, specifically those that contain blessings written in Aramaic honouring those who contributed to the building of that synagogue, and that begin דכיר/דכירין לטב and name those people to whom the community owes its thanks.[50] These inscriptions demonstrate that the *yequm purqan* continues a history shared with aspects of the synagogal customs of both Babylonia and the Land of Israel, and that the prayer as we know it is really an amalgam of aspects of both traditions.[51]

---

[49] Although it is possible that the overall archaic language of the prayer is merely representative of what is known as 'geonic Aramaic', a 'dialect' that exhibits several older characteristics (see Epstein's *JQR* article cited below in n. 55), I do not believe that this would account for the specific choices of language attested here and in the previous notes. The phrase יפיש ויסגי appears in Onqelos on Genesis 28:3: ואל שדיי יבריך יתך ויפשינך ויסגינך (compare Onqelos on Genesis 8:17: וייפשון ויסגון), but it is an idiom also found in BT, *Yoma* 88a: כי אתא רב דימי אמר מפיש חיי סגי ומסגי (see Rashi's comment: סגי ומסגי: בבנים ובני בנים). The term יסגי is found in royal greetings (see Daniel 6:26: שלמכון ישגי) and in R. Gamliel's epistle to the Jewish communities (BT, *Sanhedrin* 11b, and parallels).

[50] See especially, G. Foerster, 'כתובות'(see n. 37 above), pp. 12–40. Foerster refers to the inscriptions mostly according to their inclusion in J. Naveh, *On Stone and Mosaic* (Jerusalem, 1978), *passim*; see also *Ancient Synagogues Revealed*, ed. L. I. Levine (Jerusalem and Detroit, 1982), pp. 85, 93, 122, 126–27, 137–38 (and plates I–II), and pp. 140–45 (on the En Gedi inscription). Many of these inscriptions were included in J. B. Frey, *Corpus Inscriptionum Iudaicarum* (2 vols; Rome, 1939 and 1952), *passim*. See also ספר היישוב, ed. S. Klein, vol. 1 (reprinted, Jerusalem, 1977), pp. 46 (photo opposite p. 48), 109–10, 141 and his תולדות היישוב בארץ ישראל (Tel Aviv, 1935), pp. 263–64, 266, 268. The inscriptions listed above are all written in Aramaic and employ the דכיר/דכירין לטב formula. Dedications to donors were also written in Greek, as for example in the synagogue at Ḥammath Tiberias; for the social implications of that phenomenon, see L. I. Levine, *The Rabbinic Class of Roman Palestine in Late Antiquity* (Jerusalem and New York, 1989), pp. 176–81. It may be of interest to note that dedicatory inscriptions were apparently not limited to floors and lintels of synagogues but were also made on ritual objects, such as a menorah; see PT, *Megillah* 3.2, 74a.

[51] See above at n. 45. Foerster stresses ('כתובות', p. 15; see n. 37 above for various aspects of the matter) that the *yequm purqan* and similar prayers have the same roots as the

An important example of this phenomenon is the inscription in the Bet She'an synagogue that states דכירין לטב כל בני **חבורתא קדישתה** דהנון מתחזקין בתקונה דאתרה ק[די]שה..., a reference to the general membership of that community who erected (or refurbished?) the synagogue, and not a reference to the rabbinic leaders of that community. This becomes especially clear when a comparsion is made with a similar inscription in Jericho that reads דכירן לטב יהוי... כל קהלה ק[די]שה רביה וזעוריה דסייע יתהון... ועבדון פסיפסה..., the phrase קהלה ק[די]שה being parallel to חבורתא קדישתה.[52] This may explain the original intention of the phrase in *yequm purqan* (at least in the *ḤB* version) לריש כלה **ולרבני חבורתא** ולרישי מתיבתא ולדייני דבבא, where לרבני חבורתא refers to the local rabbinic leaders of the community who are blessed together with the heads of the *kallah* and before the prayer mentions the heads of the academies. It should be added that חבורתא here is not, as many have assumed, a reference to the academy in

---

inscriptions; note especially the דכירן לטב liturgical text from Kaffa and Cochin, which he cites on p. 24, with a further analysis by A. Horovitz on pp. 41–43. The text was originally cited by Zunz, and published by de Sola Pool, *The Kaddish* (see n. 46 above), p. 16; see further in this note. The inscriptional evidence comes from the Land of Israel, and it is likely that similar inscriptions were made in Babylonian synagogues, the lack of parallel data being due merely to modern political circumstances. Thus, it is *possible* that, despite the lack of evidence, the phrase חבורתא קדישתא may also have been used in Babylonia but I think this unlikely (see below, n. 53) and disagree with Foerster who claims (without proof, p. 27) that the phrase is also linked to Babylonia and refers to groups of Torah scholars there.

The phrase רברבייא עם זעיריא טפלא ונשיא which appears in *MV* (but not in *ḤB*), appears to me to be a blending of two traditions. The first part (רברבייא עם זעיריא) harks back to terms not found in the Babylonian talmudic tradition but specifically in the *Yerushalmi* where the juxtaposition between רברבייא and זעירייא appears several times (PT, *Berakhot* 2.7, 5b; *Mo'ed Qaṭan* 3.5, 82d; and *Bava Meṣi'a* 6.2, 8b). The very word רברבייא is common in Onqelos and the *Yerushalmi* (see Jastrow, *Dictionary*, s.v. רברבא). Note also the phrase in PT, *Bava Batra* 9.6, 17a, referring to two classes of scholars: חברייא רברבייא אמרי...חברייא זעיריא אמרי (on חברייא, see below, n. 53). The appearance of the phrase לכל קהלא קדישא הדין מרברביכון ועד זעירכון in the Kaffa and Cochin text does not negate its roots in the tradition of the Land of Israel (for either part of that phrase); if anything, the parallel in the Jericho inscription confirms such origins. I also do not believe that the phrase רברבייא עם זעיריא is Babylonian, as there is no direct parallel to it in the Babylonian Talmud. In BT, stature in Torah knowledge is alluded to by the use of such phrases as גדולי הדור (*Pesaḥim* 49a, *Qiddushin* 71a, and especially *Bava Batra* 91a) or אדם גדול (*'Avodah Zarah* 4a, regarding R. Abbahu), and even גברא רבא in Aramaic (=one who knows Scripture and law as in *Bava Meṣi'a* 84a; or a preacher as in *Pesaḥim* 53b), etc., but never as a designated group רברבייא or זעירייא. On the other hand, although the phrase גובריא ונשיא וטפלא is the Onqelos translation for האנשים והנשים והטף (Deuteronomy 31:12), this part of the prayer was borrowed from the Babylonian prayer in the Genizah text quoted above.

[52] This Bet She'an inscription is found in Levine, *Ancient Synagogues* (see n. 50 above), pp. 84–85. The one from Jericho is published by Naveh (see n. 50 above), pp. 103–105; by Foerster (see n. 37 above) and only as a photograph on p. 138 of Levine. One cannot, however, exclude rabbinic participation in the upkeep of local synagogues and their related communal institutions; see Levine, *The Rabbinic Class* (see n. 50 above), pp. 162–67. The phrase אתרה קדישה also appears in the synagogue at Ḥammath Tiberias (Levine, *Ancient Synagogues*, p. 67), and is certainly reminiscent of the phrase in the *qaddish de-rabbanan*.

the Land of Israel. [53]As to the *MV* version, which reads **למרן ורבנן חבורתא קדישתא די בארעא דישראל ודי בבבל**, רישי כלי ורישי מתיבתא דייני דבבא ודייני דמתא, this is further discussed below. The inclusion of the *resh kallah* prior to the Exilarch has puzzled many scholars, from Rapaport onwards,[54] but it is clear that the reference in this context is to local scholars whose title was bestowed upon them by the Geonim.[55]

---

[53] The association with the Land of Israel is apparent in the declaration of the New Moon according to the Romanian rite: כמה דגזרו מרנן ורבנן חבורא קדישא דהוו יתבין בארעא דישראל (as quoted by Goldschmidt, *On Jewish Liturgy* (see n. 36 above), p. 135, and Wieder, *Formation* (see n. 44 above, p. 89). The term חברייא in the *Yerushalmi* refers to a specific group of scholars in the Land of Israel; see M. Beer, *Bar Ilan Annual*, 20–21 (1983), pp. 76–95, with a reference to this source on p. 95. In later sources the term חבורה refers to the academy in the Land of Israel (see M. Gil, *Palestine During the First Muslim Period (634–1099)* (Hebrew; Tel Aviv, 1983), vol. 3, index, p. 672), as implied in its honorific titles, e.g. שלישי שבחבורה; see: A. Marmorstein, 'Solomon ben Judah and some of his contemporaries', *JQR* NS 8 (1917–18), pp. 27–28 and J. Mann, *The Jews in Egypt and in Palestine Under the Fatimid Caliphs* (Oxford, 1920–22), vol. 1, p. 272. Despite all that, my position regarding the use of the term in the *yequm purqan* prayer is in consonance with other sources cited by Gil, vol. 1, p. 410–11, n. 733 (as in the phrase חבורת צדק quoted below, n. 63).

[54] See S. J. L. Rapaport, 'רב חפץ בן יצליח', *Jeschurun* [Kobak] 8 (1875), p. 64, reprinted in תולדות, vol. 2 (Warsaw, 1913), pp. 126–27. For more recent scholars, see the following note, and Tal, *Peri* (see n. 37 above), p. 60.

[55] My position is *somewhat* similar to that of S. K. Mirsky who suggested that the *resh kallah* was mentioned first as he was the one who regularly delivered the *pirqa*, and was thus present at the time of the blessing (see his introduction to the *She'iltot* (see n. 14 above), p. 10); see also Tal, *Peri* (see n. 37 above), p. 60. Although the term *resh kallah* had nothing inherently to do with the sermon during the geonic period, an equation of the two was assumed for the talmudic period; see Rashi's commentary on *Bava Batra* 22a: ריש כלה: דורש ברבים בשבתות. Thus, Rapaport (in the article cited in the previous note) already suggested that the רישי כלי in the *yequm purqan* were preachers in *the* Land of Israel; similarly, S. Krauss, 'ביאור מושג ירחי כלה', *Tarbiz* 20 (1949), pp. 131–32, but this position has been refuted by Epstein as noted below. Much has been written about the terms כלה and ריש כלה; for a review of opinions on this issue, see K. F. Tchorsh, ירחי דכלה בהלכה, באגדה ובספרות הגאונים (Israel, n.d.), pp. 45, 55–59, and Hildesheimer's study cited above in n. 37, pp. 3–16. However, the only philologically viable explanation remains that of J. N. Epstein, 'Notes on post-talmudic-Aramaic lexicography', *JQR* NS 12 (1921–22), pp. 369–73; see, more recently, I. M. Gafni, *The Jews of Babylonia in the Talmudic Era* (Hebrew; Jerusalem, 1990), pp. 198–200, with references to some of the previous literature. Within the geonic academies, the title 'head of the *kallah*' referred to one of seven colleagues, each of whom presided over a row of ten students; this position was alternatively called אלוף. See Nathan's account in Neubauer, *MJC* (see n. 28 above), p. 87, and Sherira's letter to Jacob b. Nissim published by Sh. Abramson, במרכזים ובתפוצות בתקופת הגאונים (Jerusalem, 1965), p. 111, and explained on p. 44; a list of *'allufim* appears in another letter, cited there on pp. 18–19. The title was, however, also bestowed honorifically, even on scholars in far-away communities who did not preside in the academies; see, especially, S. Poznanski, 'ענינים שונים הנוגעים לתקופת הגאונים', *Ha-Qedem* 3 (1909), pp. 91–113 (also in book form (Warsaw, 1909), pp. 45–67). There is much to add to that list from more recently published material; see for example, M. Gil, 'The Babylonian Yeshivot and the Maghrib', *PAAJR* 57 (1990–91), pp. 69–120, *passim.* Although most of the scholars who were granted the title *'alluf* or *resh kallah* lived in North Africa, some also lived in Spain, including Ḥisdai ibn Shapruṭ (Poznanski, pp. 100–101), and I know of two in

Apparently, Eleazar b. Judah of Worms also understood this title as referring to local scholars and explained it thus: לרישי כלי: ראשי דרשות... ריש כלה: ראש הדרשה.

From the fact that the list of leaders is recorded in various textual readings in these versions of the prayer, one receives the impression that the reason for the variants is the distance, in both space and time, from the institutions mentioned in the prayer. The Exilarch is not mentioned in either *MV* or *ḤB*, but he is already mentioned by Eleazar b. Judah of Worms. While Eleazar's text is close to that of *MV*, he nevertheless reads לרישי כלי **ולרישי גלוותא** ולדייני דבבא. Apparently, he did not have רישי מתיבתא anywhere in his text, and therefore offers the explanation רישי גלוותא: ראשי גאונים שבגלות, understanding רישי גלוותא as referring to the Geonim rather than the Exilarch! Both in an early French *siddur* (written in 1294), as well as in a manuscript of the Romanian rite, the prayer reads לרישי **גלי** ולרישי מתיבתא ולדייני דבבא ולדייני דמתא, with the Exilarch replacing the *resh kallah*. It would therefore seem that the eventual inclusion of all the names in the later tradition (לרישי כלי ולרישי גלוותא ולרישי מתיבתא ולדיני די בבא) is a conflation of the majority of these witnesses, as already suggested by A. Berliner in 1909 with regard to the *resh kallah*. It should also be noted that in both the French *siddur* and the manuscript of the Romanian rite, only one version of the prayer exists, and the local congregation is not mentioned at all.[56] Despite the difficulty in establishing the 'earliest' witness to the prayer, *ḤB* represents the clearest

Italy, namely, Shabbetai b. Moses (Poznanski, pp. 109–111); (see Grossman, *Sages of Ashkenaz* (see n. 36 above), p. 350) and Abraham b. Isaac of Bari (B. Klar, 'פיוט ארמי לפייטן איטלקי קדמון', *Leshonenu* 21 (1958), pp. 212–18). In this connection, mention should be made of Ḥushiel (father of Ḥananel) and his three compatriot travellers in Ibn Daud's story of the 'Four Captives', who at the time of their capture were travelling from Bari (Italy) to Babylonia to attend a *kallah* convocation; see G. Cohen, *The Book of Tradition (Sefer Ha-Qabbalah) by Abraham ibn Daud* (Philadelphia, 1967), p. 64, with Hebrew text on p. 46. Despite the fable-like nature of the story and its historical inaccuracies, what we perhaps have here is evidence of an association between Italian rabbis and the Babylonian *kallah*.

[56] On Eleazar b. Judah, see above, n. 36. The line quoted here is from the Romanian rite, MS Vatican 320, as copied by Goldschmidt, *On Jewish Liturgy* (see n. 36 above), p. 150, and the prayer does not appear in other MSS or the printed editions. The French *siddur* is JTSA MS 4460 which reads רישיה [!] גלי; on that MS, see A. Marx, *JQR* NS 19 (1928–29), pp. 10–11. However, in another French *siddur*, JTSA MS 8259, the phrase reads: רישי כלי (as, among others, does *MV*). The French version also appears in the old English rite as copied by Jacob Ḥazzan of London and there too the reading is רישי כלי; see his עץ חיים, ed. I. Brodie, vol. 1 (Jerusalem 1962), pp. 108–9, and D. Kaufmann's earlier comments in *JQR* OS 4 (1892), pp. 31, 50. Berliner's suggestion appears in his *Randbemerkungen zum täglichen Gebetbuch*, vol. 1 (Berlin, 1909), p. 65 [=*Selected Writings*] (Hebrew; Jerusalem, 1969), vol. 1, p. 62; the idea was based upon the reading in *MV* alone. Berliner also suggested that the prayer entered Europe via France, but compare above at n. 38. For another example of confusion among medieval rabbis between ריש כלה and ריש גלותא, see *OHG* [='*Oṣar Ha-Ge'onim*] to *Giṭṭin*, §155 and n. ב, and to *Ketubbot*, p. 4. See also *Sefer Pitron Torah*, ed. E. Urbach (Hebrew; Jerusalem, 1978), p. 135, which reads וראש הישיבה in place of ואב בית דין. On the Geonim who followed Hai (d. 1038), see S. Poznanski, *Babylonische Geonim im nachgaonäischen Zeitalter* (Berlin, 1914); Gil, *Ishmael* (see n. 2 above), pp. 446–66. On the Exilarchate from the eleventh century (to the fourteenth century), see Gil, pp. 109–13, 431–45.

Euro-centred version in that it moves consistently from near to far, mentioning first the local rabbinic leadership, then proceeding to distant institutions. In any case, none of the versions are similar to the Babylonian lists of leaders and functionaries, whether in the academy or in the communities, further demonstrating that the prayer as we know it has changed a great deal from its Babylonian antecedent.[57]

Many scholars have commented on the unusual order in the two lines of our *yequm purqan,* according to which the leaders and scholars are listed in an order that places the Babylonian Geonim second from last and places the rabbis of the Land of Israel *before* those of Babylonia (as in *MV* and similar witnesses): למרן ורבנן חבורתא קדישתא **די בארעא דישראל ודי בבבל**. This proved particularly perplexing to scholars who noted the Babylonian roots of the prayer (an identification already assumed in the Middle Ages by Abraham b. Nathan (ראב״ן) and by Eleazar b. Judah of Worms).[58] Again the

---

[57] In legal documents issued by the Geonim the rabbinic leadership of local Babylonian communities was described as consisting of רבננא ודייני וראשי כנישתא ובני בי [!] כנישתא וסופרי ופרנסי ופלחין חרי ומקרי דרדקי; see V. Aptowitzer, 'Formularies of decree and documents from a gaonic court', *JQR* NS 4 (1913–14), p. 26, items 3 and 4. The full address is abbreviated in the other documents; see Aptowitzer's commentary on pp. 41–42, where the documents are written in Aramaic. In a similar text the list appears as follows in Hebrew: חכמים וראשי כנסיות וזקנים ולבלרין ופרנסים or variations thereof; see *OHG* (see n. 56 above) to *Mashqin*, p. 17 and n. 9. The list of functionaries in the academies varies from text to text, as per the following example from Amram Gaon: ...ריש מתיבתא... דיינא דבבא... רישי כלי... חכמים הסמוכים... בני קיומי [=סיומי]... שאר חכמים ותנאים ותלמידי חכמים שבישיבה; see J. Mussafia, *Geonic Responsa* (Lyck, 1864), no. 56, and J. Mann, *JQR* NS 11 (1920–21), p. 446, n. 11. The list in Sherira appears as: ...ריש מתיבתא... ראשי כלי וראשי מדרשי וראשי פירקי... רבנן דדרא רבא... רבנן [ד](ו)סיומי... רבנן תנאי... כל מתיבתא; see Assaf, *Geonic Responsa,* מדעי היהדות 2 (1927), p. 39. See also the examples cited by Poznanski (see previous note), pp. 91–94, and by D. Rosenthal, 'רבנן דסיומא ובני סיומי', *Tarbiz* 49 (1979), pp. 52–61. On ריש פירקא, see n. 66. All told, I am not certain whether the phrase דייני דמתא in *MV* and other French *siddurim* refers to local judges, or communal judges in Babylonia.

[58] Abraham b. Nathan: יקום פורקן. כבר אמרנו סדר תפילות בבבל התקינו, ותיקנו לאומרו בלשון ארמית כדי שיבינו הכל שמתפללין על חיי בעלי תורה, ויתנו לב לעסוק בכל התורה. Similarly in Eleazar b. Judah's commentary: הנה זאת התחינה הוסדה בבבל על כן מתורגמת כמו שבחיה וקדיש (on both, see above, n. 36). See also: Judah Löw Kircheim, מנהגות וורמייזא, ed. I. M. Peles (Jerusalem, 1987), p. 71; Isaac Tyrnau, ספר המנהגים (Warsaw, 1869), fol. 6a. The fact that *yequm purqan* was, as the *qaddish*, written in Aramaic and not in the Hebrew of the standard prayers needed to be explained by these medieval rabbis; see for example: *Tosafot, Berakhot* 3a, s.v. ועונין; *MV* (see n. 30 above), p. 99; אור זרוע (Zhitomir, 1862), vol. 2, fol. 12a (§50); Eleazar b. Judah, *Commentary on the Siddur*, p. 242; *Siddur of R. Solomon ben Samson of Garmaise*, ed. M. Hershler (Hebrew; Jerusalem, 1971), pp. 77, 96; Judah b. Yaqar (see n. 30 above), vol. 1, pp. 19–22; and compare I. Schepansky, התקנות בישראל (Jerusalem, 1992), vol. 3, pp. 84–85. The acceptance of the notion of writing prayers in Aramaic does, however, presuppose the principle that petitionary prayers may be couched in that language, especially those said in public; see Menaḥem Ha-Meiri's commentary on BT, *Shabbat* 12a (quoted in *OHG* to *Shabbat*, second section, §26). A different tack was taken by Sherira in his responsum to Qayrawan; see A. Harkavy, *Responsen der Geonim* (Berlin, 1887), no. 373 [=*OHG*, first section, §16]. When asked about the talmudic tradition that petitionary prayers should not be said in Aramaic (BT, *Shabbat* 12b and *Soṭah* 33a), he responded that this stricture applies only to prayers addressed to angels, whereas prayers to God may be said in any language.

ḤB version appears to solve the riddle, as the previous line there reads לכל **קהילייא קדישייא** די בארעא דישראל ודי דבבל ודי בכל ארע[א] גלוותהון.[59] Here, the blessing first addresses the far-flung Jewish communities, and then turns to the leaders of those communities. In this version, the explicit inclusion of Israel before Babylonia does not reflect the leadership hierarchy of the two lands but is a demonstration of the affinity and religious devotion to the Land of Israel and its people.

That having been said, the *MV* reading as it stands is consistent with the medieval custom of Jews living in the European Diaspora who paid homage to the religious leadership of the Land of Israel *before* that of Babylonia. This is already demonstrated in the tenth century by Paltiel, an Italian Rabbi who, after the Torah reading on the Day of Atonement, announced as his monetary donation אלף **לראש הישיבה** ולחכמים... ואלף **לבבל לישיבת הגאונים**, ואלף אל הקהילות..., a donation later repeated as ואל **הישיבה** לתלמידים ולתנאים, **ולחכמי בבל לישיבת הנשיאים**.[60] The expression ראש הישיבה undoubtedly refers to the head of the academy in the Land of Israel, and assuming that the record of these donations is accurate, we learn that the donations to the academy in the Land of Israel were announced prior to those for the academy in Babylonia and that the Exilarch was included in the second passage.[61] This sequence also appears unselfconsciously in the response to Ḥisdai ibn Shapruṭ attributed to Joseph, King of the Khazars: ואנחנו עינינו אל ה' אלהינו ואל חכמי ישראל, [ואל] **הישיבה שבירושלים** ואל **הישיבה שבבבל**, ואנו רחוקים מציון.[62] The priority given to the Land of Israel is an expression of the deep-seated love felt by Jews in the Diaspora for their spiritual homeland, and should not be construed as a declaration of support for the religious authority of one centre over the other since both are indeed mentioned in these sources.[63]

---

[59] A. Marx quoted this line in *JQR* NS 1 (1910–11), p. 63, n. 1, but in a form that made it refer to the leaders. The passage is quoted correctly by A. Schechter, *Studies* (see n. 37 above), p. 70. See also ספר הישוב, eds S. Assaf and L. Mayer, vol. 2 (Jerusalem, 1944), p. 90, n. 9.

[60] B. Klar, *Megillat 'Aḥima'aṣ* (Jerusalem[2], 1974), pp. 35, 37. On Aḥima'aṣ, see Bonfil, cited above in n. 45.

[61] On ראש הישיבה see *Megillat 'Aḥima'aṣ* (see n. 60 above), p. 14, line 21, and p. 17, line 1. The priority accorded here to the Land of Israel over Babylonia was already noted by S. Klein, תולדות הישוב היהודי בארץ-ישראל (Tel Aviv, 1935), pp. 92–93.

[62] There has been much debate (as yet without resolution) as to whether the correspondence between Ḥisdai and Joseph is pseudepigraphic. If the letter turns out to be a forgery, we may at least say that the phrase quoted reflects the attitude of an anonymous author who probably lived in Spain prior to the eleventh century since the letter was known to Abraham ibn Daud and Judah b. Barzilai of Barcelona. The text is printed at the beginning of several editions of Judah Halevi's *Kuzari* (I used the Warsaw, 1880 edition, p. 8), and improved by P. Kokovtsov, *Evreisko-khazarskaya perepiska v X veke* (Leningrad, 1932), p. 25.

[63] This appears be the intent in an anonymous *reshut* poem: ומרשות **סנהדרי גדולה** קדושה ובחירה, ומרשות **ראשי ישיבות** ואלופי התורה, ומרשות זקנים ונערים יושבי השורה. This poem appears in *MV* (see n. 30 above), p. 457; see also: I. Davidson, *Thesaurus of Medieval Hebrew Poetry* (New York, 1924–33), vol. 3, no. מ/2473 and D. Goldschmidt and J. Fraenkel, מחזור סוכות שמיני עצרת ושמחת תורה (Jerusalem, 1981), pp. 442–43. In another MS, the text reads: ומרשות סנהדרין הקדושה והנבחרה...; see M. Zulay, 'לחקר הסידור והמנהגים', *Sefer Assaf*, eds M. D. Cassuto, J.

But beyond its specific language in both the Genizah text and the later *yequm purqan*, this prayer must be fundamentally understood as a demonstration of the reciprocal blessings that were pronounced during the geonic period, on the one hand by the Geonim on behalf of their supporters and the communities, and on the other by the local congregations on behalf of the Geonim and the academies. In addition to Nathan's testimony regarding the blessing for the communities, we find that the Geonim expressed their concern for the welfare of the Diaspora in epistles they sent to these communities. An example is found in a letter written by an anonymous Gaon to Yemen, in which he expresses his thanks for the efforts made in better arranging the collections for the academy, and adds וצוינו וברכו אותך על שער הישי[בה] וחכמי סנהדרין והתנאים ותלמידיהם כלם ענים אמן בקול רם וערב.[64]

Especially significant are Sa'adya's words in his first epistle to Egypt: ובכל **הפרקי[ם]** אשר קבענו, נשאנו תפלה ותחנה לפני יי׳ צבאות אלהינו בעד השארית הנמצאת לראות את ענים ולקבץ נדחם וליסד אדמתם ולקומם חרבותם, וכן יעשה וכן ימלא כאשר הבטיחנו רנו שמים וגילי ארץ פצחו הרים רנה, כי גאל יי׳ יעקב ובישר[אל] יתפאר [Isaiah 49:13 and 44:23].[65] Similar references to blessings recited by the Geonim on behalf of leaders of the communities are found in at least four additional sources, and each one specifies that the blessing is given at the *pirqa*.[66] The Babylonian custom differs from that of the Land of Israel,

Klausner and J. Guttmann (Jerusalem, 1953), pp. 310–11. The academy in the Land of Israel is not, however, mentioned in every such text; see, for example, the *reshut* poem by Menaḥem b. Makhir: מרשות... מלומדיה גאוני יעקב... כליל דוד נשיא... ראשי ישיבות ראשי גולה... ומרשות חבורת צדק... זקנים ונערים.... That poem was first published by M. Stern, in *Festschrift zum siebzigsten Geburtstage A. Berliner's* (Frankfurt am Main, 1903), Hebrew section, p. 115 and is cited by Gil, *Palestine* (see n. 53 above), vol. 1, p. 411, n. 733; see also Davidson, *Thesaurus*, מ/2499, and Goldschmidt, *Maḥzor*, pp. 453–55). On Menaḥem b. Makhir, see Grossman, *Sages of Ashkenaz* (see n. 36 above), pp. 361–86, and above, n. 38. The yearning of European Jews for the Land of Israel is demonstrated by those who came as pilgrims and as *'olim*; see E. Reiner, 'Pilgrims and Pilgrimage to Eretz Yisrael, 1099–1517' (doctoral dissertation at the Hebrew University, Jerusalem, 1988). In their letters and greetings to the Diaspora communities, the Babylonian Geonim themselves expressed their hope for the redemption and ingathering of the exiles to Jerusalem; see for example, S. Assaf, *Gaonic Responsa* (Hebrew; Jerusalem, 1928), p. 144, also mentioned by J. Mann, *JQR* NS 11 (1920–21), pp. 446–47, n. 9. This does not, however, signify in any sense a capitulation to, or reverence for, the Gaonate of the Land of Israel. The relationship enjoyed by the two centres with each other and with the Diaspora communities during this period is the theme of a monograph that I am currently preparing.

64 *Ginze Kedem* 3 (1925), p. 22, ll. 14–15, p. 19, l. 15 and p. 23, l. 21. According to S. Assaf, the author of that letter was Nehemiah b. Kohen Ṣedeq; see his review in *Kiryat Sefer* 2 (1925), p. 182.

65 This is the Sa'adya's 'second epistle' to Yemen, published by B. Revel, *Devir* 1 (1923), p. 184, reprinted in Yudelov and Havlin, *Toratan* (see n. 12 above), vol. 1, p. 92, and reset in paragraph format on p. 99. I am not certain whether this is merely a coincidence, but the verse that Sa'adya quotes (although in the original form, Isaiah 44:23) is also found in the ENA fragment, where it is recited immediately preceding the blessings for the Exilarch and the Geonim (*Ginze Kedem* 3 (1925), pp. 53–54).

66 Three of the additional sources are listed by J. Mann, *Texts and Studies in Jewish History and Literature*, vol. 1 (Cincinnati, 1931), pp. 84–85, n. 66, and by Abramson, במרכזים (see n. 55 above), p. 44. The fourth is Sherira's letter recently published by Gil, *Ishmael* (see n. 2

where special merit was given to blessings that were recited outside the Temple Mount gates, particularly those said with great pomp and circumstance once a year on Hosha'nah Rabbah on the Mount of Olives, the Babylonian Geonim having no parallel to this annual ceremony, short of a blessing at the semi-annual *kallah* gathering.[67] In Nathan's account cited above, a very special assembly was described for the investiture of an Exilarch, at which he and the heads of the two academies, Sura and Pumbedita, were all involved, and at that time a blessing was said for the Exilarch, the Geonim and their academies, and on behalf of the communities. Since Sa'adya's comment indicates that the prayer for the communities was said in the academy at the *pirqa* (ובכל הפרקי[ם] אשר קבענו), we may deduce that it was performed on a regular basis, most likely on each and every sabbath.[68]

An endearing expression of the concern that the Babylonian Gaon had for the welfare of all Jewish communities, including those in the Diaspora, is found in the a poem written by Hai: וכתבתי חרוזתי באהב...להקרא בכל אפסי אדמה... ובצבי ובספרד ורומי ומצרים... וחנני בצורך כל עדתי במזרחה ומערבה מכורה.[69] The Geonim regularly appended to their responsa their blessings for the communities[70] and also attempted to cultivate the loyalty of wealthy Diaspora communities (such as those in North Africa) in other ways, primarily by bestowing honorific titles upon the religious leaders of those communities (as did their counterparts in the Land of Israel).[71] The interests of the

---

above), vol. 2, p. 92. For further discussion of this topic, see *Appendix 1*, pp. 120–21 below.

[67] Entrance to the Temple Mount was forbidden to Jews. Reference to the blessing on the Mount of Olives for Babylonian Jewry is found in Aaron b. Meir's letter to Babylonia; a text published several times, from various Genizah fragments; see Ḥ. Y. Borenstein, מחלוקת רב סעדיה גאון ובן מאיר (separate printing, Warsaw, 1904), pp. 48–49. Honorific titles were also bestowed in absentia upon the Diaspora leaders on the Mount of Olives, and that was the site where the Gaon of the *yeshivah* of the Land of Israel read the famous proclamation renouncing the Karaites. See, most recently, M. Gil, 'The Jewish Community' in *The History of Jerusalem: The Early Muslim Period (638–1099)*, ed. J. Prawer and H. Ben-Shammai (Hebrew; Jerusalem^2, 1996), pp. 177–81, with references to earlier literature.

[68] From the material gathered, it may safely be assumed that if the *pirqa* was delivered in the academies every sabbath, then the blessings of the Geonim would have also been given weekly. There is, however, no direct evidence as to the frequency of the blessings.

[69] J. Schirmann, *New Hebrew Poems from the Genizah* (Hebrew; Jerusalem, 1965), p. 73.

[70] These blessings and personal statements were not copied in the later medieval collections of geonic responsa but they do remain in several Genizah fragments; see e.g. S. Assaf, *Gaonic Responsa* (Hebrew; Jerusalem, 1928), pp. 46, 144, and Harkavy, *Responsen* (see n. 58 above), at the end of nn. 77, 328, 344, 418 and 452.

[71] See Mann, *Jews* (see n. 53 above), vol. 1, pp. 259–80; Goitein, *Mediterranean Society*, vol. 2 (see n. 30 above), pp. 22–40, 196–99; Bareket, *Jewish Leadership* (see n. 26 above), pp. 34–42. M. Ben-Sasson has written much on the relationship between the Gaonate and the Diaspora communities in North Africa; see his *The Emergence of the Local Jewish Community in the Muslim World: Qayrawan, 800–1057* (Hebrew; Jerusalem, 1996), pp. 401–24, with further bibliography on p. 506 and, more recently, Gil, *Ishmael* (see n. 2 above), *passim*. On the titles *'alluf* and *resh kallah*, see above, n. 55. By the eleventh century, even the ancient title ריש פירקא had also become solely honorific and was bestowed upon *ḥazzanim* and *payyeṭanim*; see Bareket, pp. 40, 166. On Nehemiah *resh pirqa* b. Abraham *ha-'alluf he-ḥaver*, note also Hai's greeting published by M. A. Friedman, *Te'uda*

Geonim were driven by their need for financial support for the upkeep of the academies and many of the letters that survived from the later Geonim are simply pleas for money couched in lofty and sentimental language.[72] But Sa'adya expressed it differently in his second *Epistle to Egypt*, where that craving for support from the communities is expressed in the bluntest of terms: כי אם אין צבא אין מלך, ובאפס תלמידים אין הוד לחכמים.[73] Without the support of the Rabbanite population at large, in Babylonia as well as in the Diaspora, the Geonim would have been shepherds with no flocks to tend.

Whatever the motivation of the Geonim for blessing the communities at the weekly *pirqa* – according to Nathan's report, only the communities whose monies were received by the academies were mentioned! – there was undoubtedly a reciprocal expression of loyalty and obeisance on the part of the communities for the leaders of the academies. We have evidence of a blessing recited in a far-flung community on behalf of the academies. In the ninth century, the scholars of Qayrawan wrote an extensive query to one of the two Ṣemaḥs mentioned in the Genizah text regarding the famous heroic figure, Eldad the Danite. In his responsum, Ṣemaḥ dealt with one of the issues raised by those scholars as follows:[74]

> ושאמר אלדד שהם מתפללים על חכמי בבל בראשונה ואחר כך על כל הגלות, יפה הם עושים מפני שעיקר החכמים והנביאים לבבל גלו, והם יסדו את התורה וקבעו ישיבה בנהר פרת מימי יהויכין מלך יהודה ועד היום... והתחזקו במה שהחכמים דורשים לכם, ואל תטו ימין ושמאל מאחרי כל דבריהם.

Although we do not know which parts of Eldad's tales regarding the Jews of Ethiopia and the 'Ten Lost Tribes' are factually accurate, what we at least have here is evidence of a prayer already recited in the ninth century by communities for the Babylonian Geonim and for the general welfare of the Diaspora which is certainly in consonance with the style of the later *yequm purqan* prayer. Additional evidence for

---

3 (1983), pp. 73, 166, 178. On the roots of this title, see also A. Ya'ari, שלוחי ארץ ישראל (Jerusalem, 1951), pp. 191–92. At times, conflicts arose between the two centres over the bestowing of such titles on one and the same person, the tendency of some individuals being to accept these titles with no other intent than to demonstrate their allegiance to the two centres. Among the scholars in Fustat (Egypt) who maintained dual titles were: Ephraim b. Shemariah (see Bareket, *Jewish Leadership* (n. 26 above), pp. 119–20), Shemariah b. Elḥanan (pp. 147–49, 156–61), Sa'adya b. Ephraim (pp. 167–70), and Sahlan b. Abraham (pp. 175–76).

[72] Many texts may be cited in this regard; for a fair sample, see M. Ben-Sasson, 'Fragmentary letters from the Genizah', *Tarbiz* 56 (1987), pp. 171–209. This practice of the Geonim to plead for funds was mocked by Daniel al-Qumisi the Karaite; see פתרון שנים עשר, ed. I. D. Markon (Jerusalem, 1957), pp. 57, 66.

[73] Abramson, במרכזים (see n. 55 above), p. 40.

[74] First printed in Mantua, c. 1474. The text of the Constantinople 1516 edition was published by A. Jellinek, *Bet ha-Midrasch*, vol. 2 (reprinted, Jerusalem, 1967), p. 113, and that of the Rome edition by A. Epstein (with full annotation) in אלדד הדני סיפוריו והלכותיו (Pressburg, 1891), p. 8 [= כתבי אברהם אפשטיין], vol. 1 (Jerusalem, 1950), pp. 40–41. This part of the query that Qayrawan posed to Ṣemaḥ is lacking (only the response having been preserved).

the prayers of the local communities is found in a letter to the Maghreb written by Daniel b. Azariah (a Babylonian native, descendant of the Exilarchate family, appointed Gaon of the *yeshivah* of the Land of Israel in the eleventh century) in which he states: והתפלה עלינו בכל המדינות והעירות. The blessing on Daniel's behalf by the communities is also attested in a letter written to Joseph, son of Samuel ibn Nagrela: כי בעת אתפלל על אדונינו דניאל ה[נ]ש[יא] וה[גאון] אור העולם יחי לעד בעת אתפלל עליך אור יש[ראל] והקהל עומדים כולם והם אומרים אמן בקול רם.[75]

This type of cultural memory on the part of the Geonim and the academies, in Babylonia and in the Land of Israel, was also expressed at that time in the form of lists (found in the Genizah) that were read aloud in the synagogue and that began with the phrase דוכרן טב (literally, 'we remember for good'), and mentioned the Geonim together with other scholars and leaders. The *dukhran ṭav* list as such may have originated not exclusively as a 'memorial' prayer (the phrase itself not necessarily referring to the deceased) but as a testimony to the leaders of the day. It did, however, develop into a memorial prayer and would seem to be the precursor of the later Ashkenazi *yizkor* prayer. What is not clear is when these lists were recited, whether at specific times, such as the Day of Atonement, or more regularly every sabbath.[76] Such prayers on behalf of the geonic academies are found in petitionary prayers *(seliḥot)* written in Aramaic, of the רחמין genre, as in the following unpublished example from the Genizah:[77]

---

[75] Daniel's letter: Mann, *Jews* (see n. 53 above), vol. 2, pp. 215–16 [= Gil, *Palestine* (see n. 53 above), vol. 2, pp. 679–80]. Letter to Joseph: Mann, *Jews*, p. 222, and on the warm relationship between Joseph and Daniel Gaon, see Gil, *Palestine*, vol. 1, p. 593. See also Elḥanan b. Shemariah's letter (to Damascus?) published by Mann, *Jews*, p. 40: ואליכם מתפ[לל]ים; but, according to Abramson, the phrase reads ואליכם מתפשטים (במרכזים) (see n. 55 above), p. 108, n. 17).

[76] See already I. Elbogen, *Jewish Liturgy: A Comprehensive History,* translated by R. Scheindlin (Philadelphia, 1993), p. 162. See also Mann, *Jews* (see n. 53 above), vol. 2, pp. 50–51, 210–211 (a Karaite memorial list); his *Texts* (see n. 66 above), vol. 1, pp. 452–53, 466–72; his article in *JQR* NS 11 (1920–21), pp. 419–20, for another type of memorial list of Babylonian Geonim that included the dates of their demise; A. David, 'רשימת זכרון לחכמים בישיבת ארץ-ישראל', *Shalem* 1 (1974) pp. 75–80 (the beginning formula is missing); and S. D. Goitein, 'Prayers from the Geniza for Fatimid Caliphs', in *Studies in Judaica, Karaitica and Islamica Presented to Leon Nemoy on his Eightieth Birthday*, ed. S. R. Brunswick (Ramat Gan, 1982), pp. 47–57 (where he claims that the list was recited on the Day of Atonement). See also Goitein, *A Mediterranean Society*, vol. 2 (see n. 30 above), p. 163 and nn. 28–30 on p. 554. A generic prayer beginning with this formula is known from the rites of Aleppo, Persia and Cochin; see Wieder, 'כתובת יריחו והליטורגיה היהודית', *Tarbiz* 52 (1987), pp. 557–63 [= *Formation* (see n. 44 above), pp. 126–132]. See also above, n. 53, where the formula דכיר לטב is noted as appearing in synagogues in the Land of Israel with reference to donors.

[77] ENA 3295.4. Ginzberg's publication is in *Genizah Studies in Memory of Doctor Solomon Schechter* (New York, 1929), vol. 2, p. 158. The genre of רחמין was common during the geonic period. Sa'adya included a collection of such prayers in his *Siddur* (pp. 343 ff.) and others of this type were published from the Genizah by S. Assaf, 'פיוטים וסליחות מתקופת הגאונים', *Kiryat Sefer* 2 (1925), pp. 145–49; B. M. Lewin, *Ginze Kedem* 4 (1930), pp. 65–76; and Y. Ratzaby, *Sinai* 115 (1995), pp. 193–216 and 117 (1996), pp. 218–34. Many of the

רחמ[נא] הב לח[מ]א לאינשא ועסבא לבעירא ויסגי טובא בארעא
רחמ[נא] ויודון כולא לישבחון קדמך על רווחות מזוני
רחמ[נא] ופרוס עלן ברחמך מטלית [שלמ]א
רחמ[נא] וזרע שלמא רבא בעמך ישראל
רחמ[נא] וזרע ש[למא] רבה **בתרתין מתיבתא**
רחמ[נא] וזרע שלמא רבה **בארץ ישראל**
רחמ[נא] וזרע שלמא רבה ב[לומד]י? אוריתא
רחמ[נא] וזרע ש[למ]א רבה בכולי שתא [=בכנישתא?] דישראל.

Here, 'the Merciful One' is asked to 'spread peace', that is, prosperity and well-being, upon the two geonic academies, upon the Land of Israel, upon those who study Torah and upon all the Jewish people. A parallel to this passage is found in another Genizah text published by Louis Ginzberg, where the order and language are different. The variants between the two texts attest to the existence of a general typology for this blessing, rather than a single fixed version. These prayers are the closest parallels found in the Genizah to the *yequm purqan* prayer, other than the older text earlier discussed. They are witness to the expression of allegiance to the Geonim and concern for their welfare, and in both versions the Babylonian Geonim are mentioned first.

From several other sources, primarily from the Land of Israel, we know of the custom to mention the rabbinic leaders either in the *qaddish* following the Torah reading, or in the blessing preceding the Torah reading as in Nathan's description, or at some other juncture in the prayer service, such as, for example, before the *yoṣer* section of *shaḥarit*. There is evidence that the Muslim caliphs were also sometimes mentioned in a custom that is continued to this very day in the prayer for the welfare of the government.[78] As attested by Naḥmanides, the custom in Yemen was to invoke

prayers begin with the word רחמנא. These old petitions continued to be retained in the Yemenite rite; see Y. Ratzaby, מגנזי שירת הקדם (Jerusalem, 1991), pp. 288–89. Many of these prayers are written in alphabetical acrostic form but not the one quoted here.

[78] Note Maimonides's statement in his responsum (ed. J. Blau (Jerusalem, 1960), no. 329, p. 599): כדרך שמזכירים שם ראשי הגליות וראשי ישיבות ושאר השרים והגאונים במועדות או בשבתות או בעת קבוץ רבים. Evyatar Ha-Kohen is mentioned in a special *qaddish,* first published by S. Schechter, 'נוסחא בקדיש', *Gedenkbuch zur Errinerung an David Kaufmann*, eds M. Brann and F. Rosenthal (Breslau, 1900), Hebrew section, pp. 52–54; see also E. Fleischer, *Eretz-Israel Prayer and Prayer Rituals* (Hebrew; Jerusalem, 1988), p. 245 and Wieder, *Formation* (see n. 44 above), pp. 264, 274. That *qaddish* was recited before the *yoṣer* section of *shaḥarit*; see Fleischer, pp. 243–49. Similarly, a *qaddish* in honor of an Exilarch was said at that same juncture in the service; see *Ginze Kedem* 3 (1925), p. 56. The blessing added within *qaddish* is known from other sources, e.g.: ואמרו לחזני[ם] הוציאו ס[פר]י תורה וברכו בשם כ׳גיקי מ׳ורי אברהם הכהן... וכב[ר ה]וצ[יאנו ס]פרי תורה וכל העם עומדים על עמדם וכל הקהל מתפללי[ם ל]אלהי[ם]... שיאר[יך] ימיך וח[ייך]; see Mann, *Jews* (see n. 53 above), vol. 2, pp. 113–14. Similarly, in Solomon b. Judah's letter to Abraham b. Sahlan: ועל כן הכל יתאוו לשמוע ולענות אחריו אמן וקדוש וברוך בתפלות; see Mann, *HUCA* 3 (1926) pp. 269–70 [= Gil, *Palestine* (see n. 53 above), vol. 2, p. 182]. In some cases, it seems that the claim regarding regular blessings in the service is intentionally exaggerated, e.g.: ובכל תפילה שאני מתפלל לפניו במדרש אני מתפלל עליכם בברכות מעולות, והוא [=הגאון] שמח באהבתכם; see Gil, *Palestine*, vol. 3, pp. 349–50. In any event, this type of *qaddish* is to

the name of Maimonides in the *qaddish* pronounced every sabbath.[79]

It is my opinion that the academies were indeed mentioned in the prayers of the various local communities in Babylonia during the geonic period, although not in the language of the later *yequm purqan.* This long blessing (as evidenced in the Genizah text) would have been said only in congregations where and when a *pirqa* lecture was delivered, whether on the eve of the sabbath, or in the morning after the Torah reading, or in the afternoon, following the *minḥah* service, whichever period would draw the largest crowd in that community.[80] The blessing for the academies was, first and foremost, a sort of 'request for permission' (נטילת רשות) on the part of the lecturer who nominally deferred to the Geonim as the sole bearers of the permission to deliver the *pirqa.*[81] But, beyond that, it presented an opportunity to reinforce in the congregation the importance of the Geonim and their academies, and to reciprocate for the blessings pronounced by the Geonim in the academies at that very same time.[82] Since the *pirqa* lecture was not delivered in all (most?) local synagogues, even in

---

be understood within the framework of the *reshut*; see M. A. Friedman, 'R Yeḥiel b. Elyakim's responsum permitting the *reshut*' in *Mas'at Moshe* (see above, n. 45), pp. 328–67; especially pp. 344–45, on the Evyatar *qaddish*. See also: P. Fenton, 'תפילה בעד הרשות ורשות בעד התפילה', *Mi-Mizraḥ Umi-Ma'arav* 4 (1984), pp. 7–21; Wieder, *Formation,* p. 100; Goitein, *A Mediterranean Society*, vol. 2 (see n. 30 above), pp. 19–22, 164. Note also Ephraim b. Shemariah's comment in a poetical letter written to Nathan b. Abraham Gaon: תפלות לו קבעתי בכל מועד, as published by E. Bareket, *The Jews of Egypt 1007–1055* (Hebrew; Jerusalem, 1995), p. 88, l. 10. Blessings for the caliphs were also pronounced at special occasions in the liturgy; see the *dukhran ṭav* published by S. D. Goitein, 'Prayers from the Geniza' (see n. 76 above), pp. 47–57, but Goitein surmises (p. 50) that the prayer was read on the Day of Atonement. On a blessing said on Purim for two rival Geonim, see Goitein, *Palestinian Jewry* (see n. 66 above), pp. 66–67, and explained on p. 61. As already suggested by Foerster (see above, n. 37), the inclusion of the blessing in the *qaddish* precludes the recitation of *yequm purqan*.

[79] See Ḥ. D. Chavel, כתבי רבינו משה בן נחמן (Jerusalem, 1963), vol. 1, p. 341, corrected by M. A. Friedman, 'בחייכון וביומיכון ובחיי דרבנא משה', *Zion* 72 (1997), pp. 75–78 (with references there to previous literature). Friedman demonstrates that it was already the custom in Yemen two generations earlier than Maimonides to mention the head of the Egyptian academy in their prayers.

[80] See below, n. 122.

[81] See Mirsky's introduction to the *She'iltot* (see n. 14 above), p. 7. The association with נטילת רשות may be alluded to in the words of Zeraḥya Ha-Levi, ספר המאור on *'Eruvin*, chapter 5 (fol. 17b): ורגילין היו ליטול רשות מן הנשיא כל מי שהוא דורש ברבים ולברך את הנשיא בכל שבת ושבת. כמו שרגילין לומר עכשו יקום פורקן מן שמיא וכו'. As Zeraḥya resided first in Narbonne, then in Lunel, and later in Gerona, it may be inferred that the *yequm purqan* was recited in one of those communities; it is not, however, mentioned in the liturgical guide to the customs of Marseilles and Montpelier composed by Moses b. Samuel, JTSA MS R515a. Regarding the prerogative to deliver the lecture, see above, nn. 66, 78. This was also the prerogative of the Gaon in the Land of Israel and is included among the items for which he claimed authority; see Goitein, *Palestinian Jewry (*see n. 66 above), pp. 57–58.

[82] See above. The liturgical nature of the geonic blessings in the academies on behalf of the communities is attested in Nathan's description (see above, at n. 28), in the geonic epistle to Yemen (at n. 64), and in Sa'adya 's epistle to Egypt (at n. 65).

Babylonia,[83] and since the blessing would have been recited only by the preacher as part of his lecture, the blessing was never accepted on its own as an integral part of the liturgy of those communities, and thus is not in the geonic *siddurim*, nor in Genizah prayer-books. The *darshan* concluded the blessing following the *pirqa* by reciting the *qaddish de-ḥadata* and, to a large degree, this practice also fell into desuetude when the *pirqa* no longer existed, as I will explain below. But, then again, this makes the inclusion (and retention) of the *yequm purqan* prayer in the Ashkenazi rite all the more remarkable.[84]

II. The *qaddish de-ḥadata* (יהא שמיה רבא דאגדתא) concluding the *pirqa* lecture

The sermon alluded to in the ENA/T-S text and preceding the blessing just described is undoubtedly a *pirqa* lecture, as delivered on the sabbath and festivals in a Babylonian synagogue. More specifically, we can transcribe the formulaic blessings and aggadic sources that were recited at the conclusion of the homiletic section of the

[83] The fact that the *pirqa* lecture was delivered on the sabbath in cities in Babylonia during the geonic period, but not in all of them, is evidenced by the following law in *Halakhot Gedolot*: ...ושארי למירהט בשבתא לפירקא בתוך התחום, אבל חוץ לתחום כגון דאיכא פירקא במאתא אחריתי (ed. E. Hildesheimer, vol. 1 (Jerusalem, 1971), p. 249). That passage probably refers to a lecture at *minḥah,* rather than in the morning, requiring only a one-way trip on the sabbath; see below, n. 123. This law originally appeared in an earlier code, *Halakhot Pesuqot*, as attested in its Hebrew translation in *Siddur Rashi* (ed. Buber-Freimann (Berlin, 1911), p. 233) in which פירקא is translated as מדרש של תורה. This section occurs in a gap between two Genizah fragments of the Aramaic original; see Danzig, *Introduction to Halakhot Pesuqot* (see n. 8 above), p. 553; and also *Sefer Ve-Hizhir*, ed. I. M. Freimann, vol. 1 (Leipzig, 1873), fol. 11a, where the word is translated merely as פרק. The inclusion of the *pirqa* as part of the normal sabbath routine is also documented in the first *she'ilta* to Genesis (ed. Mirsky (see n. 14 above), vol. 1, p. 7). The absence of a sabbath sermon in the morning service in certain congregations may be inferred from the statement in *Soferim* 12.6 (ed. Higger (see n. 43 above), p. 230): ואם היה בשבת מתורגמן או דורש; see also 13.15 (ed. Higger, p. 250): בשלא תירגמו ושלא דרשו, and compare J. Mann, *Tarbiz* 1:3 (1930), foot of p. 6. See also *Sefer Ha-Manhig*, quoted below in n. 104. The absence of the *pirqa* may be the result of a lack of qualified personnel, although, when necessary, a scholar who was not of top rank might deliver a sermon; see BT, *Ta'anit* 16a, regarding a sermon delivered at the declaration of a public fast. As for Babylonia during the geonic period, we may assume that a suitable *pirqa* lecture was delivered in communities where appointed judges presided. On the scope of judges appointed throughout the land, see Nathan's report in Neubauer, *MJC* (see n. 28 above), pp. 85–86; the document of appointment is discussed by Hai in Harkavy, *Responsen* (see n. 58 above), no. 180, and see *OHG* (see n. 56 above) to *Mashqin*, pp. 23–24. On the power and procedures of these courts, see J. Mann, 'The Responsa of the Babylonian Geonim as a Source of Jewish History', *JQR* NS 10 (1920), pp. 335–65. The cities in Babylonia and Persia in which Jews were known to have lived during this period are discussed by Gil, *Ishmael* (see n. 2 above), pp. 487–528. The current estimates of the Jewish population in these countries at that time run as high as 2,500,000; see Danzig, *Catalogue* (see n. 1 above), pp. 4–5, n. 4*.

[84] I have not attempted to chart the proliferation of *yequm purqan* in various rites, as the basic pattern was already described by Duschinsky and others. A thorough examination of MSS is, however, still a desideratum.

pirqa, known in the *She'iltot* as the דרשה.[85] The lecture wound down with the following proclamation, a passage probably recited before the aggadic conclusion to the lecture (see below):[86]

> בריך שמיה ד׳ק׳ב׳ה׳ [דבח]ר בהון בצדיקיא ויתרעי בעובדי ידיהון [...] ויהב לנא אורייתא ומצואתא על יד [משה] רבנא לאלפא עמיה בית ישראל בריך הוא [ובריך?] יהי שמיה רבא. ועונין ציבור יהי שמיה רבא מ׳ ל׳ ול׳ עלמיא ולעלמי עלמיא. ויתברך וישתבח ויתפאר ויתרומם ויתנש׳ ויתהדר ויתע׳ ויתק׳ שמיא דק׳ב׳ה׳ו׳א׳. אלף אלפי אלפין וריבי ריבי ריבוון עד דלית לא מיניני׳ ולא שיעורא ולא סכא לעילא לעילא לעילא מכל ברכא׳ שיר׳ תשב׳ ונח׳ דאמירן ודמתאמרן לעלמא ולעלמי עלמיא.

Firstly, as demonstrated by J. N. Epstein (see above, at n. 14), the opening phrase found here is similar to the formula that appears in several of the *she'iltot* preceding the דרשה section, the *she'ilta* formula reading as follows:[87] בריך שמיה דקודשא בריך הוא דיהיב לנא אורייתא ומצותא על ידי משה רבנא לאלפא לעמיה [או: עמיה ד]בית ישראל, כך תנו חכימייא... Both these formulas (the Genizah text and the *she'iltot*) are similar to the declaration pronounced immediately following the Aramaic translation of the *hafṭarah* on the sabbath and festivals, as recorded in *Maḥzor Vitry*, this passage preceding the *yequm purqan* prayer in the printed edition: וקודם שיתחיל המפטיר ברכה אחרונה יאמר המתרגם: על דא יתברך וישתבח שמיה דמריה כולא ויתרעי בנבייא צדיקיא, ויהב לנא אורייתא על ידי משה רבנא לשבוחי ולברוכי שמיה דקודשא בריך הוא, ואמרו אמן... A similar, but briefer, statement was recited in many other rites, including Yemen, at that juncture in the service: על דא יתברך וישתבח שמיה רבא קדישא די לעילא חיא וקיימא מברך הוא לעלם ולעלמי עלמיא... We are not here dealing with a medieval custom specific to Ashkenaz, but with an older practice, one that signaled the inception of the sermon that was to follow the recitation of the *hafṭarah*;[88] hence the similarity to the declaration in the

---

[85] We can best appreciate the style of a 'classic' *pirqa* lecture by examining the *She'iltot* (see above, n. 14); for a brief overview of these texts, including their structure, see R. Brody, *The Textual History of the She'iltot* (Hebrew; New York and Jerusalem, 1991), English foreword, pp. VII–XIX, and the more extensive analysis that appears in Mirsky's introduction to the *She'iltot*. For further discussion of this topic, see *Appendix 2* on pp. 121–22 below.

[86] The reader may refer to the transcription of the ENA leaves published by Lewin, *Ginze Kedem* 3 (1925), p. 53. I have reproduced the text exactly as it appears in the Genizah fragment, without completing the abbreviated words.

[87] See: Epstein, *Devir* (see above, n. 15); 'Notes on Post-talmudic-Aramaic Lexicography', *JQR* NS 12 (1921–22), pp. 309–10. The connection between these sources was also noted by Liebreich (see below, n. 89). This formula appears in full in the first *she'ilta* to Genesis, and in other manuscript *she'iltot*, especially from the Genizah; see Abramson, *'Inyanot* (see n. 85 above), pp. 9–10. In one such fragment, the phrase ends בריך הוא (Abramson, p. 329), similar to the wording in the ENA text. This phrase was later abbreviated to בריך שמיה דקוב״ה, or simply בריך שמיה.

[88] *MV* (see n. 30 above), p. 172; the Yemenite custom is mentioned by Y. Qafiḥ, הליכות תימן (Jerusalem, 1963), p. 68. For other references, see de Sola Pool, *The Qaddish* (see n. 46 above), p. 9, n. 46. See also L. Liebreich, 'The Benedictory Formula in the Targum to the Song of Songs', *HUCA* 18 (1943–44), pp. 182–83, n. 20, who also cites the abbreviated form as it appears in the Italian rite (*Maḥzor Roma*). Similarly, I have found it in Italian MSS, e.g. JTSA MS 4814: על דא יתברך וישתבח שמא דאלהא רבא וקדישא לעלם ולעלמי עלמיא.

pirqa format... The *pirqa* formula was not itself an invention of the geonic period, as the practice dates back to talmudic times, or even to tannaitic times, and apparently served as a form of blessing over the Torah (ברכת התורה) prior to the sermon.[89] From the evidence presented here, it becomes clear that the ENA/T-S text is witness to the aggadic conclusion of a *pirqa* lecture, and that the lecture followed the *hafṭarah* reading in the synagogue or, according to Nathan's description, preceded the Torah reading. There is other evidence that the benedictory phrase בריך שמיה דקודשא בריך הוא דיהיב לנא אורייתא... was employed in similar sabbath lectures composed in the oriental communities of the medieval period.[90]

I believe that we may in this light interpret what appears in the ENA leaves in the form of a list of verses from the Prophets and Hagiographa, preceded by the phrase

---

[89] *Siphre ad Deuteronomium*, §305 (ed. L. Finkelstein (New York, 1969), p. 324): ויש אומרים שהעמידו (את יהושע) מן הארץ והושיבו בין ברכיו, והיו משה וישראל מגביהים ראשם לשמוע קול דבריו של יהושע. ומהו אומר? **ברוך אשר נתן תורה לישראל על ידי משה רבנו**. כך דבריו של יהושע. See King Solomon's declaration in Targum to Song of Songs 1:2: בריך שמיה דהי׳ דיהב לן אורייתא על ידוהי דמשה ספרא רבא; Liebreich (see n. 88 above), pp. 177–97, especially pp. 183–86; J. Heinemann, *Prayer* (see n. 47 above), p. 254 and *Studies in Jewish Liturgy*, ed. A. Shinan (Hebrew; Jerusalem, 1983), p. 26; Abramson, *'Inyanot* (see n. 85 above), p. 10. A similar formula appears at the beginning of a homily from the Land of Israel dated to the eighth century; see N. Wieder, 'שלוש דרשות לתענית גשמים מן הגניזה', *Tarbiz* 54 (1985), p. 50, and explained on p. 36 [=*Formation* (see n. 44 above), pp. 540, 527]. It is also known at the beginning of several other geonic texts, functioning there as a prelude to a homily in praise of Torah (דרשה בשבח התורה). Several scholars (including Liebreich, Heinemann and Wieder) refer to the famous passage in *Tanḥuma*, *Noaḥ*, §3, which is actually from Pirqoi b. Baboi's early ninth-century text; see B. M. Lewin, 'משרידי הגניזה', *Tarbiz* 2 (1931), pp. 394–96. A similar formula appears at the beginning of the story of Eldad the Danite in its various recensions (see כתבי אברהם אפשטיין, vol. 1 (see above, n. 74), pp. 50, 69, 75, 378, 382), and in מדרש יתברך, ed. S. A. Wertheimer, בתי מדרשות, vol. 1 (Jerusalem[2], 1980), p. 181 (these two sources being mentioned by Liebreich).

[90] I refer to כתאב אלתפאחה, MS Oxford Huntington 115 (Neubauer 1009), which contains a collection of extensive lectures in *halakhah* and *aggadah*, composed in Judaeo-Arabic for the weekly Torah portion; there are also fragments of this work in the Genizah and a partial MS is held by JTSA, R1803. The work was probably composed in Egypt or North Africa in the first half of the twelfth century. The benedictory phrase appears in full in the first lecture but is abbreviated in the subsequent sections. Although it is arguable that this work is a literary composition and reflects no actual homiletical practice, each lecture ends with the phrase (again, written in full in the first occurrence, and abbreviated thereafter) שיאמר בעל הרחמים לקרב העת להושיענו מגלותינו וישלחנו הגואל אוכיי״ר, which is the standard conclusion to a genuine homily (see below, n. 131). On this work, see M. Steinschneider, 'Zur Geschichte und Literatur der jüdischen homiletik: Arabische Predigten', in *Homiletisches und literarisches Beiblatt als Unhang zur Bibliothek jüdischer Kanzelredner* (Berlin, 1872), 'Homiletische und literarische Beilage, No. 3'; compare Sh. Abramson, 'רב יוסף ראש הסדר', *Kiryat Sefer* 26 (1950), pp. 72–95. This benediction is not, however, employed by Isaac Gaon in his מטה עוז, a collection of homilies in Judaeo-Arabic composed during the years 1210–32 (MS Oxford Huntington 241, Neubauer 1001). On the latter, see: I. Z. Langerman, 'ספר ׳מטה עוז׳ לר׳ יצחק גאון', *Sinai* 98 (1986), pp. 215–22; M. Saperstein, *Jewish Preaching: 1200–1800* (New Haven and London, 1989).

that is partially obliterated but that I have reconstructed as א[גדת]א דפירקא.[91] Under that heading, a selection of verses is supplied for Tisha B'Av, Rosh Ha-Shanah, Sukkot (the text is partially obliterated), Ḥanukkah and Purim. This section ends with a verse under the heading ל[ריש] גלותא[92] which is either 2 Samuel 22:51 or Psalms 18:51, and refers to the Davidic Messiah, an obvious allusion to the lineage claimed by the Exilarchs. This would appear to signal the concluding theme in the homily that promises the coming of the Messiah (see below, regarding the *qaddish de-ḥadata*).[93] The purpose of this list of verses was to provide the homilist with the opportunity of referring to those talmudic and midrashic passages that make use of them in the context of the particular festival. This increases the number of possible passages beyond those associated with the verses already included in the Torah reading for the festival.[94] No verses are supplied for the weekly sabbath Torah reading and we can surmise that the homilist had enough options to locate appropriate texts that deal with the Torah portion, given that the sections read in the annual (Babylonian) cycle are usually fairly lengthy. This is to be further understood in light of the fact that the bulk of the text in the ENA/T-S fragment is devoted to listing the Torah and *hafṭarah* readings for the festivals.

A 'classic' *pirqa*, that is, one that would have been delivered in the geonic academies, as evidenced in the *she'ilta* format, included a section devoted in part to *aggadah* (the דרשה) but did not usually conclude with that section.[95] The ENA/T-S text would, however, indicate that the homilist outside the academies did indeed conclude the lecture with an aggadic discourse (the אגדתא דפירקא), thus leaving the congregation with an uplifting thought and enabling those assembled to answer to the *qaddish* that followed the sermon (the יהא שמיה רבה דאגדתא, see below).[96] Several scholars have already suggested that the lectures inside the academy differed in nature

[91] Lewin was unable to read the first word; see *Ginze Kedem* 3 (1925), p. 52.
[92] See Lewin, as cited in the previous note. A text containing verses in praise of the Exilarch (in this case, Ḥasdai b. David), intended for recitation at his inauguration, was published by S. Assaf, *Ginze Kedem* 4 (1930), pp. 63–64.
[93] Neither this, nor the anonymous mention of the Exilarch earlier in the blessing, is testimony to the Exilarch's presence at the delivery of the lecture; see n. 34 above. The claim of Davidic lineage for the Exilarchs (similar to that made for the Patriarchs in the Land of Israel) is alluded to in BT, *Sanhedrin* 38a; see Beer, *Exilarchate* (see n. 14 above), pp. 11 ff. and *IRSG* (see n. 12 above), p. 73.
[94] See Lewin's article mentioned in n. 85 above.
[95] See n. 85 above.
[96] Mirsky, introduction to the *She'iltot* (see n. 14 above), p. 22. The extensive *derashah* in the first *she'ilta* to Genesis deals with aspects of the sabbath (see above, nn. 85, 87) but curiously concludes with sources relating to the recitation of אמן יהא שמיה רבה (ed. Mirsky, vol. 1, pp. 18–19). This is further proof of the homilist's intention to lead into the recitation of *qaddish*. Note also the words בחייכם אמן at the end of a section in a Genizah fragment of (apparently) a commentary in Judaeo-Arabic on *hafṭarot*, an obvious allusion to the homilist's concluding phrase in which he would mimic the words of *qaddish* and cue the response of the congregation; see J. Mann, *The Bible as Read and Preached in the Old Synagogue*, vol. 1 (Cincinnati, 1940), Hebrew section, p. 146.

from those delivered in synagogues outside the academy and this text would seem to support such an hypothesis.[97] Although I have little additional proof to this effect, I believe that in local synagogues the aggadic דרשה portion of the *pirqa* lecture concluded with an extemporaneously created aggadic homily, rather than with the dry recitation of talmudic passages found in the classical *she'ilta* format. This was the section preceded here by the benediction ...בריך שמיה דקב״ה (see above) and with that the *pirqa* concluded.[98]

---

[97] See: Z. Jawitz, תולדות ישראל, vol. 9 (London, 1942), p. 121; Mirsky, introduction to the *She'iltot* (see n. 14 above), pp. 11–12; J. Heinemann, דרשות בציבור בתקופת התלמוד (Jerusalem, 1970), pp. 17 ff.; G. Alon, תולדות היהודים בארץ-ישראל בתקופת המשנה והתלמוד (Jerusalem[6], 1977), vol. 1, pp. 305–6; S. Safrai, 'Education and the Study of Torah' in *The Jewish People* (see n. 43 above), vol. 2, pp. 966–68; A. Oppenheimer, *Cathedra* 18 (1981), pp. 45–48. Jawitz saw the halakhic prelude as a reflection of the practice in the Land of Israel, according to which a small halakhic discourse was added at the beginning so that *halakhah* should not be forgotten; see *Pesiqta de-Rav Kahana* 12.3, ed. B. Mandelbaum (New York, 1962), p. 205: א״ר יצחק בראשונה היתה הפרוטה מצויה היה אדם מתאוה דבר משנה ודבר תלמוד. ועכשיו שאין פרוטה מצויה, וביותר שאנו חולים מן המלכיות, אדם מתאוה לשמוע דבר מקרא ודבר אגדה (compare *Song of Songs Rabbah* 2.5 and *Soferim* 16.3, ed. Higger (see n. 43 above), p. 286). See Zunz-Albeck, *Ha-Derashot* (see n. 14 above), pp. 170, 467, and especially A. Rosenthal, 'תורה שבעל פה ותורה מסיני – הלכה ומעשה' in *Meḥqerey Talmud,* eds J. Sussmann and D. Rosenthal, vol. 2 (Jerusalem, 1993), pp. 458–60. Nevertheless, there seem to be precedents for both types of lecture (*halakhah* first, as in the *Yelamdenu* type, or *aggadah* first); see already BT, *Bava Qamma* 60b and *Shabbat* 30a. The order of these lectures has been much discussed; e.g. by M. B. Lerner at the Tenth World Congress of Jewish Studies held in Jerusalem in 1989, the issue being related to the type of material that preceded the recitation of the *qaddish* (see below, n. 128). Many other sources may be cited to demonstrate the attitudes of the rabbis toward *aggadah*; see Y. M. Guttmann, מפתח התלמוד, vol. 1 (Csongrád, 1906), pp. 450–81.

[98] It is possible that one such homily, on Ḥanukkah, did survive in the Vatican MS of the *She'iltot* and was published in Mirsky's edition (see n. 14 above) as no. 27 (vol. 1/2, pp. 175–90). The text lacks several of its component sections, and the lengthy דרשה (pp. 182 ff.) is not merely a collection of talmudic passages but is composed in the style of an authentic, original homily in which various sources are interwoven. The first part is rich in verses from Prophets and Hagiographa (the homily beginning with a verse from Ecclesiastes), and the second part is a retelling of the story of Judith and Holophernes. A portion of this text, in a more complete version, survives in a Genizah fragment, T-S NS 215.27. The Genizah witness also confirms the existence of this very homily outside the Vatican MS, and beyond the parallels in the midrash for Ḥanukkah referred to in Mirsky's notes. In his commentary (p. 183), Mirsky contends that this long homily is the result of the lecturer's having resumed the aggadic portion at the end of the *pirqa*. While one may argue with Mirsky's premise that this is indeed a *pirqa* lecture, I suggest that it is the type of lecture that would have been delivered in a local synagogue, and thus differs considerably from the standard format. In the academies, the attitude of the Babylonian Geonim toward aggadic texts outside the Babylonian Talmud would have prevailed, vastly reducing the options for appropriate aggadic texts. Compare another 'pseudo-*she'ilta*' published by B. M. Lewin, 'שאילתא לחנוכה', *Sinai* 6 (1940), pp. 68–72. On the position of the Geonim in that regard, see *OHG* (see n. 56 above) to *Ḥagigah*, p. 60, and the sources cited by Y. Horovitz, 'יחסי הגאונים לאגדה', *Mahanaim* 7 (1994), pp. 122–29. See also D. Sklare, *Samuel ben Ḥofni Gaon and his Cultural World* (Leiden, New York and Köln, 1996), pp. 41–48. See also above, n. 85.

The lecture alluded to in this text ends with the blessing for the congregation and community who support the Geonim and the study of Torah. That section follows with the recitation of several verses that refer to blessing, productivity, and protection from drought and famine (Deuteronomy 1:11; Isaiah 60:22, 65:23, 65:22, 49:10), and concludes with the following passage (from the unpublished T-S fragment):

> פיתגמא דהוא רב ועילאי ויקיר מכולא ולית בר מיניה יהי שמיה רבא מבי לעי ולעי עלמיא בחייכון וביומיכון ובחיי דכל בית ישראל [ב]עגלא ובזמן קריב ואמרו אמן. יתגדל ויתקדש [שמ]יה רבא. בעלמא דברא כרעי **דעתיד לחדתא** כו['].

The interesting credo פיתגמא דהוא רב ועילאי ויקיר מכולא ולית בר מיניה[99] appears as a declaration of faith and returns the listener (as does a proem) to what was stated at the beginning of the sermon: בריך שמיה דקב״ה. This credo is followed by one phrase from *qaddish* that begins יהי שמיה רבא מבי לעי ולעי עלמיא בחייכון וביומיכון ובחיי דכל בית ישראל [ב]עגלא ובזמן קריב ואמרו אמן and was pronounced (by the congregation) as an affirmation of that credo.[100] Then the entire proceedings conclude with no more than one line that serves as an instruction to end with yet a second *qaddish*. This final line reads: יתגדל ויתקדש [שמ]יה רבא. בעלמא דברא כרע[ותיה] **דעתיד לחדתא** וכו׳. The last line is a reference to what is known as the *qaddish de-ḥadata*,[101] and, although only its first words appear in the fragment, it is clear that the sermon and blessing are formally concluded with the recitation of the entire version.[102] This *qaddish* begins with the

[99] Compare Daniel 4:14: בגזירת עירין פתגמא, ומימר קדישין שאילתא. It seems that this line cues the 'spontaneous' response that follows; see also n. 100 below.

[100] Note the theories of de Sola Pool and Karl regarding the refrain recited by the congregation during and after the sermon (see n. 117 below), which are perhaps supported by the repeated phrases in the Genizah text. It is possible that the phrase פיתגמא דהוא רב ועילאי... may be read as פיתגמא דהוא, רב ועילאי..., where הוא represents God, since the *qaddish*, according to several medieval commentaries, addresses the theological status of the Divine Name. On the early use of הוא as a Divine epithet (also in Islam) and its significance in the *qaddish*, see N. Wieder, 'צעקת ״הוא״ בימים הנוראים', *Sinai* 89 (1981), pp. 6–41, especially pp. 22–25 [=*Formation* (see n. 44 above), pp. 395 ff.]. Wieder discusses other types of credos that were exclaimed aloud in prayer (in both Judaism and Islam), and the declaration in this text could be of that type. See also examples of congregational responses to homilies and lectures quoted by Heinemann, *Prayer* (see n. 47 above), pp. 252–56, and compare de Sola Pool, *The Kaddish* (see n. 46 above), pp. 46 ff. In another study, Wieder collected evidence of a declaration of praise for the teacher or preacher offered by the listeners at the conclusion of the lecture; see his 'המנהג ״לפאר״ את הדרשן בסיום דרשתו', *Sinai* 63 (1968), pp. 187–89 [=*Formation*, pp. 555–57].

[101] I transliterate the term as it is known in the geonic texts, in Maimonides, and in the Sephardi rite in general; in the Ashkenazi rite the reading is דאתחדתא (see below). In any event, the form is not Babylonian Aramaic but is found in the Targum; see Onqelos to Deuteronomy 32:12, as cited by Jastrow, *Dictionary*, p. 428, s.v. חדית, חדת.

[102] According to the testimony of Nathan the Babylonian, the *qaddish* and the accompanying blessings were intoned by the *ḥazzan* but I cannot say for sure whether the homilist or the *ḥazzan* pronounced the blessings and the *qaddish* in the local synagogues. In the geonic academies, and even more so at the special lecture that Nathan witnessed, various scholars

following passage, quoted from a modern Ashkenazi *siddur*, Maimonides's version being quoted further below:

> יתגדל ויתקדש שמיה רבא. בעלמא די הוא עתיד לאתחדתא ולאחיאה מתיא ולאסקא יתהון לחיי עלמא, ולמבנא קרתא דירושלים ולשכללא היכלה בגוה, ולמעקר פולחנא נוכראה מן ארעא, ולאתבא פולחנא די שמיא לאתריה, וימליך קודשא בריך הוא במלכותיה ויקריה, בחייכון וביומיכון...

The *qaddish* then proceeds with what has become the standard *de-rabbanan* version, including the passage: על ישראל ועל רבנן ועל תלמידיהון ועל תלמידי תלמידיהון ועל כל מאן דעסקין באורייתא די באתרא הדין ודי בכל אתר ואתר, יהא להון ולכון שלמא רבא.... The striking parallel between this passage and the *yequm purqan* prayer has already been noted by several scholars.[103] The long *qaddish de-ḥadata* was known to have been recited only on two occasions, that is, following a eulogy at the time of burial, and after a sermon. The connection between these two events is noted in an anonymous geonic responsum regarding whether one may recite *qaddish* following an interment, in which the Gaon replied:[104] הוי יודע כי קדיש שהוא יתגדל לא מצאנו לו עיקר על המת אלא לאחר המספד או לאחר צידוק הדין, **שכל מקום שיש שם דברי תורה עונין אחריהם אמן יהא שמיה רבא**, וכן הספד וכן צידוק הדין.

The custom of reciting the *qaddish de-ḥadata* after burial is known from several sources, such as *SRAG*,[105] although the earliest appearance is in *Soferim* 19.9, where its recitation is designated for a prayer service offered on the sabbath in a mourner's house, upon the death of a student or a preacher: אין אומרים בעלמא דעתיד לחדתא אלא על התלמיד ועל הדרשן.[106] Subsequently, the *qaddish* probably became associated with the

---

delivered different parts of the *pirqa*; see at n. 28 above. It would appear that these special reciters of one section of the *she'ilta* (other than the Gaon) were called רבנן פשטאי דשאילתא; see Danzig, *Introduction to Halakhot Pesuqot* (see n. 8 above), p. 13, n. 55. Here too, I do not presume that this was so for a local *pirqa*, which was probably delivered by one rabbi (who did not employ a *meturgeman*).

103 See especially de Sola Pool, *The Kaddish* (see n. 46 above), pp. 90–91; Tal, *Peri* (see n. 37 above), pp. 55–56. Tal concluded that the *yequm purqan* derived from an extended *qaddish* in which the Geonim were blessed.

104 D. Cassel, *Die Rechtgutachten der Geonim* (Berlin, 1848), no. 94 [=*OHG* (see n. 56 above) to *Mashqin*, §139]. Although דחדתא is not specified, it is obvious that the reference is to that word.

105 Ed. Goldschmidt (see n. 22 above), p. 187: וכשמסיימין לקבור את המת לאחר שאומר צדוק הדין אומר השליח: יתגדל ויתקדש שמיה רבא. בעלמא דהוא עתיד לחדתא [קטע-גניזה: לאתחדתא] ולאחאא מתיא ולשכללא היכלא [חסר בקטע-גניזה; בכ״י אוקספורד נוסף: ולמבני קרתא דירושלים] ולמיעקר פולחנא נוכראה מארעיה....

106 Ed. Higger (see n. 43 above), pp. 336–37. There is some confusion as to the reading in this phrase, as documented by the variants recorded there. I selected the reading that best fits the context. This is the reading in *MV* (see n. 30 above), p. 715 and Higger (p. 73) also preferred it. Similarly, Naḥmanides reads here על תלמיד דרשן (see his תורת האדם in Chavel (see n. 79 above), p. 155) but explains that this law refers only to the passage beginning בעלמא דאעתיד לחדתא (which is recited for a scholar) whereas the rest of the *qaddish* would indeed be recited for everyone. He explains the rationale for this as follows: וטעמא דמילתא שאין מזכירין עולם חדש אלא למי שמעשיו מוכיחין עליו שהוא בן תחיית המתים, אבל לסתם בני אדם לא. See also n. 107 below.

burial of a preacher or learned person and then spread to all funeral ceremonies, as it speaks of the future resurrection of the dead.[107] In fact, from Sa'adya 's comment in his *siddur* we see that the custom of reciting the *qaddish de-ḥadata* at a funeral was viewed with some disdain. After providing the text of the blessings that are recited every morning over the Torah, Sa'adya notes the custom of saying אילו דברים שאין להם שיעור (a combination of two talmudic texts) and then states (in the Hebrew translation):[108]

> והיחיד לא יברך אחרי גמר הקריאה והלימוד, אבל אם היו עשרה לומדים יאמרו בגמרם 'ברוך אלהינו' וקדיש יתגדל ומוסיפים בו 'דעתיד לחדתא עלמא ולאחאה מיתיא ולמיבני קרתא ירושלים...' ויתר קדיש. ויש אנשים שאומרים קדיש זה בקבורת המת, ואין זה מן העיקר.

Sa'adya 's attempt to limit the *qaddish de-ḥadata* exclusively to Torah study was apparently not accepted and, as the custom of reciting it at funerals became widespread, an anonymous copyist erased the dissenting comment from a manuscript of the *siddur*.[109] Here, Sa'adya also refers to a prayer entitled ברוך אלהינו that is to be said after the study session, prior to the *qaddish*. In his note on that passage, S. Assaf suggests that while this may merely be a reference to קדושא דסידרא (see below), it is more likely a reference to a special benediction that was recited on the conclusion of the daily lecture at the end of the *shaḥarit* service. That prayer is mentioned by Nissim b. Jacob of Qayrawan in a query addressed to Hai Gaon regarding a custom that his students imported from Egypt:[110]

---

[107] So too de Sola, *The Kaddish* (see n. 46 above), p. 116. The printed edition of *Soferim* reads על התלמוד ועל הדרש and on that basis Karl concluded that this *qaddish* originated with the sermon and was later transferred to the funeral ceremony; see his הקדיש (see n. 37 above), pp. 66, 71–76. This is also my conclusion, but the statement in *Soferim* does not prove it, since the reading in the printed edition seems to be incorrect (see n. 106 above). It may be noteworthy that the custom at the time of the Geonim was to deliver the eulogies for scholars and teachers in the very academy where they taught: חכם ואלוף וגאון מכניסין אותו לבית המדרש ומניחים את המטה במקום שהיה דורש (*OHG* (see n. 56 above) to *Mashqin*, §137). For a geonic parallel to the theme of this *qaddish*, see n. 132 below.

[108] *Siddur R. Saadya Ga'on*, eds I. Davidson, S. Assaf and B. I. Joel (Jerusalem³, 1970), pp. 358–59.

[109] See the variants there and Wieder, *Formation* (see n. 44 above), p. 568.

[110] *OHG* (see n. 56 above) to *Shabbat*, §320. Assaf suggests, in the name of J. N. Epstein, that the anonymous Egyptian rabbi is none other than Shemariah b. Elḥanan. Epstein further concluded that the prayer originated in the Land of Israel and reached Egypt via Italy, a claim for which there is no evidence. This prayer is apparently attested in the Oxford MS of *SRAG*, ed. Goldschmidt (see n. 22 above), p. 82: ותנין בני אוריאן וגרסי כל חד וחד כפום דבעי, וכד גמרינן הלכתייהו קאים חד בר בי רב ואמר ברוך אלהינו וענו כלהו ברוך אלהינו שבראנו לכבודו וכו' וקדיש כולו ומיקם בי ציבורא כולהו וענו כולהו בקלא נעימא ובסימא יהא שמיה רבה מברך; I copied the text according to A. Marx, 'Untersuchungen zum Siddur des Gaon R. Amram', *JJGL* 5 (1907), Hebrew section, p. 15, and compare *OHG* (see n. 56 above) to *Pesaḥim* §265. The language of the benediction is strikingly similar to a passage in *Siphre*, §53 (ed. Finkelstein (see n. 89 above), pp. 120–21): יש לך אדם שניתן לו חלקו ואינו שמח בחלקו, אבל ישראל מודים מפויסים [כתב-יד: מקלסים] שאין חלק יפה כחלקם ולא נחלה כנחלתם ולא גורל כגורלם, והם מודים ומשבחים על כך.

> עד שבאו מקצת תלמידים ממצרים ואמרו שהרב במצרים חבר דבר שיאמר אחר הפרק בכל יום קודם זו השמועה [=אמר ר׳ אלעזר אמר ר׳ חנינא]... 'ברוך אלהינו אשר נתן לנו חלק טוב וחלק יפה וגורל נעים ונחלה יפה שאין חלק כחלקנו ולא גורל כגורלנו ולא נחלה כנחלתנו...'

The text of this blessing is also found in a Genizah *siddur*, where it follows the synagogal reading of the second chapter of Mishnah *Shabbat* on Friday evening.[111] Although there is no instruction in that Genizah fragment to recite the *qaddish de-ḥadata* following the mishnaic text, such a practice is suggested by Judah b. Barzilai al-Bargeloni in his *Sefer ha-'Iṭṭim* (twelfth-century Spain): ונאה למימר **עליו קדושא דאגדתא**.[112]

The *qaddish de-ḥadata* is also included by Maimonides in the text of the prayers included in his *Mishneh Torah*, with the following instruction (quoted in full in order to convey adequately its messianic message):[113]

> קדיש דרבנן. כל עשרה מישראל או יתר שהיו עוסקין בתלמוד תורה שבעל פה ואפילו במדרשות או בהגדות, כשהן מסיימין אומר אחד מעומד קד[יש] בנוסח זה: יתגדל ויתקדש שמיה רבה דעתיד לחדתא עלמא ולאחאה מיתיא ולמפרק חייא ולמבני קרתא דירושלם ולשכללא היכלה קדישא ולמעקר פולחנא נוכראה מן ארעא ולאתבא פולחנא דישמיה לאתריה בזיויה וביקריה וימליך מלכותיה ויצמח פורקניה ויבע משיחיה ויפרוק עמיה, בחייכון וביומיכון... על ישראל ועל רבנן... וזהו הנקרא קדיש דרבנן.

No mention is made of this text in that part of Maimonides's code dealing with a funeral. To sum up, I believe that all the evidence supports the conclusion that, despite its language which stresses the rebirth of the dead, the association of the *qaddish de-ḥadata* with the burial ceremony is due only to the fact that a homily is delivered at a funeral, in the form of a eulogy.[114] Thus, the original context of that

---

[111] See N. Wieder, 'ברכה בלתי ידועה על קריאת פרק ׳במה מדליקין׳ מתוך הגניזה', *Sinai* 82 (1978), pp. 220–21 [=*Formation* (see n. 44 above), pp. 346–47].

[112] Ed. J. Schorr (Cracow, 1903) p. 279, as cited by Wieder (see n. 111 above). Wieder also cites an instruction in the Yemenite *Tiklal*: ואומר קדיש דרבנן משום המשנה, והוא דעתיד לחדתא. The expression קדיש דרבנן was apparently borrowed from Maimonides; see below. In another *Tiklal* (JTSA MS 3038, fifteenth century), a similar instruction written in Judaeo-Arabic also betrays Maimonides's influence and the *qaddish de-ḥadata* is there required for all תורה שבעל פה. See, however, another Yemenite passage quoted below in n. 128.

[113] So the Oxford MS of the *Mishneh Torah*; see Goldschmidt, *On Jewish Liturgy* (see n. 36 above), pp. 203–4 and *Mishneh Torah*, Book II, ed. N. Rabinovitch (Jerusalem, 1984), p. 1329. For a comparison of the basic readings in this *qaddish,* see de Sola Pool, *The Kaddish* (see n. 46 above), p. 79 with an explanation of the text following on pp. 80–89.

[114] This may also be inferred from a passage in מדרש שכל טוב to Genesis, ed. S. Buber (Berlin, 1900–1901), vol. 1, p. 334: ונהוג רבנן כי אמרי פסוקים של צידוק הדין והספידות על הקבר, מוכי הדרי אפייהו אמר קדיש הכי. The *qaddish de-ḥadata* is then quoted in full and the prayer thus associated with the eulogies, and not with the burial *per se*; note that the need for the *qaddish* is consequent on the recitation of biblical verses, and see n. 128 below. It appears that this passage is a reference to some earlier tradition but I have found no parallel to these exact words or to various other passages on that page; compare, however, *SRAG* (see n. 22 above),

qaddish was the conclusion of a sermon or talmudic lecture (see also below, following n. 131).

In the Babylonian Talmud itself, a *qaddish* related to Torah study is alluded to in a famous passage at the end of tractate *Soṭah* (49a), where a statement in the Mishnah that since the destruction of the Temple all days are cursed elicits the following talmudic comment:

> אמר רבא בכל יום ויום מרובה קללתו משל חבירו...ואלא עלמא אמאי קא מקיים, **אקדושא דסידרא ואיהא שמיה רבה דאגדתא**, שנאמר 'ארץ עפתה כמו אופל צלמות ולא סדרים' [איוב י,כב], הא יש סדרים תופיע מאופל.

In the passage just quoted, reference is made to יהא שמיה רבא דאגדתא and to a seemingly related phenomenon, the קדושא דסידרא (literally translated as 'the sanctification of the portion'), the latter being a reading from the Prophets that is followed by the recitation of biblical verses, especially קדוש קדוש קדוש (Isaiah 6:3), ברוך כבוד ה' ממקומו (Ezekiel 3:12), and ה' ימלוך לעולם ועד (Exodus 15:18). This concatenation constitutes the 'Trisagion' or 'Sanctus' normally recited during the repetition of the *'amidah*, and partially during the *yoṣer* section of the morning service, but in the *qedusha de-sidra*, the Pseudo-Jonathan Targum to those verses is also included. Regarding the יהא שמיה רבא דאגדתא, Rashi already explained that it refers to the refrain said after the sabbath homily: וכן יהא שמיה רבה מברך שעונין אחר הגדה שהדרשן דורש ברבים בכל שבת היו נוהגין כך. In the *Tosafot*, the phrase appears as יהא שמיה רבא **דבתר** אגדתא, that is, the *qaddish* that the homilist recites *following* the aggadic discourse.[115] Indeed, in some rites the *qaddish de-ḥadata* was recited daily following the *qedushah de-sidra*.[116]

In BT, *Sotah* 49a, there is no inherent indication that a full *qaddish* text was recited

---

p. 187, and *Halakhot Gedolot* (see n. 83 above), vol. 1, pp. 446–48. Abraham Maimuni explains the custom of standing for the *qaddish* at a burial as arising out of the emotion of the moment and dismisses the custom; see ספר המספיק לעובדי השם, ed. N. Dana (Ramat Gan, 1989), p. 79. Note also the position implied by several rabbis, including Rashi, namely, that *qaddish* is said at a funeral in response to verses recited in association with צידוק הדין; see *MV* (see n. 30 above), p. 244; I. Elfenbein, תשובות רש"י (New York, 1943), p. 209; ספר מעשה הגאונים, eds A. Epstein and J. Freimann (Berlin, 1910), p. 49; *Sepher Ha-Pardes*, ed. H. L. Ehrenreich (Budapest, 1924), p. 262. Compare, however, שו"ת הרי"ף, ed. Z. Biednowitz (Bilgoraj, 1935), §27 and Cassel, *Rechtgutachten* (see n. 104 above), §118 (Qalonymos b. Moses).

115 *Tosafot, Berakhot* 3a, s.v. ועונין. This is not the Tosafist's reading of the text in *Soṭah* but was added for clarity; see תוספות הרא"ש there as well as Asher b. Saul's formulation at n. 125 below. On *qedusha de-sidra*, see Elbogen, *Jewish Liturgy* (see n. 76 above), pp. 55, 61–62, 70–71, 101. See also J. Mann, 'Changes in the Divine Service…', *HUCA* 4 (1927), pp. 261–77 (although his thesis regarding the 'original' meaning of the phrase is untenable). Much is yet uncertain regarding the origin of the *qedushot* in the liturgy, especially as regards their mystical connection and their parallels in the *Hekhalot* literature. See bibliography in R. Elior, 'From Earthly Temple to Heavenly Shrines', *Tarbiz* 64 (1995), p. 354 n. 36 and M. Bar-Ilan, 'קוי יסוד להתהוותה של הקדושה וגיבושה', *Da'at* 25 (1990), pp. 5–20.

116 See עץ חיים (n. 56 above), p. 126

in conjunction with the sermon since the words יהא שמיה רבה may simply be the congregational affirmation of the sermon. In the following post-talmudic sources, we do, however, find the יהא שמיה רבה response in the context of a *qaddish*, and in some of these sources the occasion is specifically identified as the sabbath sermon:[117]

a. *Midrash Mishley*, a midrash to Proverbs composed during the geonic period, in the following passage:[118]

> בא מי שבידו חומשים, הקב״ה אומר לו: בני, הגדה למה לא שנית? שבשעה שחכם יושב ודורש, אני מוחל עונותיהם של ישראל. ולא עוד אלא שבשעה שהן עונין יהי שמו הגדול מברך [כתבי-יד: **אמן** יהא שמיה רבה מבורך] אפילו גזר דינו שלכמה שנים אני מוחל ומכפר.

In a later chapter of that same midrash, the tradition regarding the refrain to the homilist's *qaddish* is recorded in the name of the second-century Tanna, R. Ishmael. It would, however, appear that the attribution is pseudepigraphical as the impression given in these midrashim seems to reflect the *sitz im leben* of the post-talmudic period and certainly not the tannaitic era.[119]

---

[117] The suggestion regarding the talmudic reference was made by Karl, הקדיש (see n. 37 above), p. 60, n. 2. De Sola Pool suggested that the refrain אמן יהא שמיה רבא may have been said several times by the congregation throughout the course of a sermon; see *The Kaddish* (see n. 46 above), p. 50 (see also n. 100 above). The origin of *qaddish* in a praise of God recited at the conclusion of a sermon was already surmised by L. Zunz (Zunz-Albeck, *Ha-Derashot* (see n. 14 above), pp. 180–81, and p. 483, n. 64), and this view is shared by others, e.g. Heinemann, *Prayer* (see n. 47 above), pp. 256, 266–67; see also n. 133 below. Karl (p. 66) goes so far as to suggest that the phrase בחייכון וביומיכון refers to the homilist and his *meturgeman*. That position is untenable since the present plural refers to the congregation, as already noted in שו״ת הרשב״א, vol. 5, §54. In a slightly different vein, S. J. Rapaport suggested that the earliest form was the *qaddish de-rabbanan* recited following a eulogy; see *Kerem Ḥemed* 3 (1838), pp. 46–47. Most of the following references have already been cited in earlier work, e.g. Zunz-Albeck, *Ha-Derashot,* pp. 467–68 and de Sola Pool, pp. 8–9.

[118] Ch. 10, ed. B. Visotzky (New York, 1990), pp. 83–84; compare BT, *Shabbat* 119b: אמר ריב״ל כל העונה אמן יהא שמיה רבה בכל כחו, קורעין לו גזר דינו של שבעים שנה. A similar passage appears in *Ecclesiastes Rabbah* (ch. 9, ed. Vilna, fol. 25c, on Ecclesiastes 9:14–15): שבשעה שהזקן יושב ודורש ועונין אחריו אמן יהי שמו הגדול מבורך, אפילו יש לו שטר נזירות [צ״ל: גזירות] של מאה שנה הקב״ה מוחל לו על כל עונותיו.

[119] Ch. 14, ed. Visotzky (see n. 118 above), p. 112: ר׳ ישמעאל אומר בשעה שהן נאספין לבית המדרש ושומעין דבר הגדה מפי החכם, ואחר כך עונים יהי שמו הגדול מבורך, באותה שעה הקב״ה שמח ומתעלה בעולמו ואומר למלאכי השרת, בואו וראו עם שיצרתי לי כמה הם משבחים אותי... This passage is also quoted in *SRAG,* ed. N. Coronel (Warsaw, 1856), p. 12, but is an addition absent in other witnesses; see ed. Goldschmidt (see n. 22 above), p. 38, line 37. Even the reference in BT, *Soṭah* is apparently by the 'anonymous' Talmud and is not part of Rava's comment, as already noted by Mirsky in his commentary to *she'ilta* (see n. 14 above), no. 1, p. 19, and by Mann, 'Changes' (see n. 115 above), p. 275. Note especially the phrasing in Naṭronai's responsum: אמרו חכמים **האידנא** לא מקיים עלמא אלא אקדושה דסידרא ואמן יהא שמיה רבא מברך דאגדתא (*OHG* (see n. 56 above) to *Soṭah*, §148; Brody, *Naṭronai* (see n. 34 above), p. 148), although this seems to be a paraphrase (see Brody). In *SRAG*, p. 41, the passage is quoted as it appears in our Talmud. Nevertheless, Naṭronai's paraphrase may allude to the institution in his day.

b. *Seder Eliyahu Rabbah,* chap. 2 (ed. M. Friedmann, p. 11): אילו האגדות שמקדשין את שמו בגדול בהן. This reference is not to the content of the homilies but to the response made after their recitation.[120]

c. *Midrash Avkir,* a lost tenth-century work, as quoted in *Yalquṭ Shim'oni* to Exodus 35:1:

אמר הקב״ה עשה לך קהילות גדולות ודרוש לפניהם ברבים הלכות שבת, כדי שילמדו ממך דורות הבאים להקהיל קהילות בכל שבת ושבת, וליכנס בבתי מדרשות ללמד ולהורות לישראל דברי תורה, איסור והיתר, כדי שיהא שמי הגדול מבורך מתקלס בין בני.

d. In *Midrash Ha-Gadol,* a similar version of that midrashic text reads: ... ולהכנס **בבתי כנסיות** ובבתי מדרשות **לשמוע דברי תורה** ולקדש את שמי הגדול.[121]

e. And, lastly, אלפא-ביתא דרבי עקיבא, another midrash of the geonic era:[122]

עתיד הקב״ה שהוא יושב בגן עדן ודורש... וכיון שמגיע להגדה [ילקוט: **שמסיים ההגדה**] עומד זרובבל בן שאלתיאל על רגליו ואומר יתגדל ויתקדש... וכל באי עולם עונין אמן.

---

[120] See also the beginning of ch. 11 (p. 52): שהם משכימין ומעריבין לבית הכנסת ולבית המדרש ועונין אמן ומברכין את הקב״ה באמן, which may be a reference to the same. Study in the academy (בית המדרש) is one of the prevalent themes of that work, and the refrain from *qaddish* is also woven into many passages, see Friedmann's introduction (see n. 43 above), p. 79. *Seder Eliyahu* may date from the ninth century; see H. L. Strack and G. Stemberger, *Introduction to the Talmud and Midrash* (Edinburgh, 1991), pp. 369–70. Some scholars suggest that it may have been composed in Italy; see H. J. Zimmels, 'Scholars and Scholarship in Byzantium and Italy', *The Dark Ages*, ed. C. Roth (New Brunswick, 1966), pp. 186–88.

[121] See *Yalquṭ* to ויקהל, §407, quoted also by Mirsky, introduction to the *She'iltot* (see n. 14 above), p. 3. Part of this passage is quoted anonymously in ספר רוקח, §55, and compare *Midrash Ha-Gadol* to Exodus, ed. M. Margaliot (Jerusalem, 1976), p. 722. See M. Kasher, תורה שלמה, vol. 23 (Jerusalem, n.d.), p. 2, §ה, and note to §ה*. On the *Avkir* passage, see now A. Geulah, מדרש אבכיר: מבואות ומובאות (MA dissertation at the Hebrew University, Jerusalem, 1998), p. 169, and introduction, p. 36. Compare also Rashi's comment quoted below, after n. 127.

[122] A. Jellinek, *Bet ha-Midrasch*, vol. 3 (reprinted, Jerusalem, 1967), pp. 27–28; also in Wertheimer, בתי מדרשות (see n. 89 above), vol. 2, p. 368 [=J. Even-Shemuel, מדרשי גאלה (Tel Aviv, 1953), p. 347, with variants on p. 437; compare a different version there on pp. 349–50]. The passage is quoted in *Yalquṭ Shim'oni* on Isaiah 26, §429, with the variant noted above. In Eleazar b Judah's *Commentary on the Siddur* (see n. 36 above), p. 435, the reading is as the former (see pp. 555 and 583), while in *Siddur of R. Solomon* (see n. 58 above), p. 116, this tradition is cited in the name of פירקי ר' אליעזר. See also *Seder Eliyahu Zuṭa*, ch. 20, ed. Friedmann (see n. 43 above), p. 33, n. 44; and on Zerubbabel in the heavenly academy, see Jellinek, *Bet ha-Midrasch*, p. 75. This passage continues with reference to Gehinnom and seems to allude to the recitation of the *qaddish* at a funeral; see Karl, הקדיש (see n. 37 above), pp. 74–75. According to C. Albeck, *Alphabet of R. Akiva* was probably composed in the ninth or tenth century (Zunz-Albeck, *Ha-Derashot* (see n. 14 above), pp. 333–34), but others date it somewhat earlier; see Strack-Stemberger, *Introduction* (see n. 120 above), p. 381.

Among the five sources just cited, only in *Midrash Avkir* and *Midrash Ha-Gadol* (c+d) is there an overt reference to the lecture having been delivered on the sabbath. From elsewhere in the Talmud we can, however, deduce that the *pirqa* was a part of the sabbath service, delivered between *shaḥarit* and *musaf* (i.e., following the Torah reading). In BT, *Berakhot* 28b, we are told of R. Aviya who felt faint and did not attend the *pirqa* of R. Joseph and the reason proposed for his weakness is that he subscribed to R. Huna's position that one is forbidden to eat prior to the *musaf* prayer; thus, the *pirqa* was apparently delivered prior to *musaf*.[123] A direct connection between this *qaddish* and the sabbath sermon (following the Torah reading) is found in *Sefer ha-'Iṭṭim* of Judah b. Barzilai al-Bargeloni (p. 279):[124]

ולאחר שמפטירין בנביא ומתרגמינין, או איכא דרושא דדריש בדברי תורה שפיר דמי למידרש מקמי דליהדר ס[פר ת]ורה] למקומה... והדר מפטיר **בקידושא דאגדתא** והדר פתח בתהלה לדוד ומהדרה

---

[123] See Rashi: לא על לפרקא דרב יוסף: שהיה ראש הישיבה בפומבדיתא והיה דורש בשבת קודם תפלת המוספין ולאחר הדרשה היו הולכים לבית הכנסת ומתפללים תפלת המוספין. According to Rashi, the *pirqa* lecture was delivered in the academy, following which the rabbis adjourned and recited *musaf* in the synagogue. See also Abraham b. Nathan, ספר המנהיג, ed. Y. Raphael (Jerusalem, 1978), vol. 1, p. 167: ולבתר דקרו אפטרתא ואית להו עסקי דצבורא או למפסק צדקה או למימר פירקא או דרשא באתרא דרגיל שפיר דמי. On the law of not eating before *musaf* and the talmudic episode mentioned above, see S. Lieberman's comment in Ch. Z. Taubes, לקוטי ר' יצחק בן יהודה אבן גיאת (Zürich, 1952), pp. 82–83 (cited by Raphael). In both *Sefer ha-'Iṭṭim* and *Sefer Ha-Manhig*, the sermon follows the Torah reading and *hafṭarah*. In some congregations, however, or under certain circumstances, the sermon preceded the Torah reading, as is apparent from Nathan's account and in a question posed to Maimonides, ed. Blau (see n. 78 above), no. 110, pp. 189–91. Based on that responsum, Goitein remarks that in those days the sermon preceded the Torah reading but that a second lecture may have followed *musaf* if there was a special lecturer present, or for an invited audience (*A Mediterranean Society*, vol. 2 (see n. 30 above), p. 158 and p. 553, n. 15). I find this assumption difficult to accept, given that the sermon that followed the Torah reading on the sabbath in local communities is an ancient institution (see Luke 4:16–22 and Acts 13:15) and would be likely to have continued in that specific position throughout the ages. See also Zunz-Albeck, *Ha-Derashot* (see n. 14 above), pp. 167, 465–66; Mirsky, introduction to the *She'iltot* (see n. 14 above), pp. 2–3. See also above, nn. 66, 83 and 128, and at nn. 102–3. However, J. Heinemann has indeed argued that the sermon was given as an introduction to the Torah reading – see *idem*, 'The Proem in the Aggadic Midrashim: A Form-critical Study', *Scripta Hierosolymitana* 22 (Jerusalem, 1971), pp. 110–11. J. Fraenkel contends, in general, that most of what is found in rabbinic sources refers to academic lectures, even when the lectures are given בציבורא, whereas congregational homilies (and information about them) have been all but lost; see his דרכי האגדה והמדרש (Jerusalem, 1991), pp. 17–23. Regarding the time of the academic *pirqa* during the talmudic era, see Amir (see n. 14 above), p. 139, n. 37.

[124] While the passage is written in Aramaic and is followed by Judah's disagreement (ואנן לעניות דעתן חזי לן...), it would nevertheless appear that it is his own formulation and represents the custom in his day, that is to say, it does not stem from an older, geonic source. Duschinsky (see n. 19 above; p. 191) misinterpreted the phrase קידושא דאגדתא and assumed that it refers to *yequm purqan* while it is in fact a reference to *qaddish de-ḥadata* (as correctly established by Davidson, *Thesaurus*, vol. 2, p. 424, note). Another mention of this *qaddish* in *Sefer Ha-'Iṭṭim* is quoted above at n. 112.

סנפר] תנורה] למקומו. ואיכא מקומות טובא דנהגי שלוחא דצבורא לברוכי לצבורא בסנפר] תנורה]
ולמבעי עליהון רחמי כפי הזמן והצורך.

In a similar vein, Asher b. Saul of Lunel calls this *qaddish* קידושא דבתר דרשא, and Samuel b. Ali, the Baghdadi Gaon and contemporary of Maimonides, also speaks of a קידוש השם following the *pirqa* lecture, an apparent reference to the very same *qaddish de-ḥadata*.[125]

The theological grounds for the significance of declaiming אמן יהא שמיה רבה and the Divine response to that blessing are already established in a *baraita* (BT, *Berakhot* 3a) that tells of the *bat qol* heard by R. Yose, as he reported it to Elijah the Prophet:[126]

> ולא זו בלבד אלא בשעה שישראל [כי"י: עושין רצונו של מקום ו]נכנסין לבתי כנסיות ולבתי מדרשות ועונין יהא שמיה הגדול מבורך [כי"י: רבא מברך] הקדוש ברוך הוא מנענע ראשו ואומר אשרי המלך שמקלסין אותו בביתו כך.

In the later midrashic passages, however, the opportunity of glorifying God's name is specifically connected to the aggadic sermon, a point that is not suggested in the talmudic antecedent. Although, as we would expect, the exact wording of the *qaddish* is not found in any of these sources, the later texts are referring to the *qaddish de-ḥadata* version, which first and foremost served as a conclusion to the sermon, and only later became associated with a funeral eulogy, as already indicated.[127]

A final point needs to be made regarding the *pirqa* lecture and the recitation of *qaddish* at its conclusion. From the phrase איסור והיתר in *Midrash Avkir*, it would appear that the sabbath lecture dealt with *halakhah* only, and not with *aggadah*. While that phrase may have been used in the light of the theme of the passage (ודרוש

---

[125] Asher b. Saul, ספר המנהגות, published by S. Assaf, ספרן של ראשונים (Jerusalem, 1935), p. 142. Samuel b. Ali's passage is quoted above, n. 66.

[126] Most medieval quotations of this passage (a least among Ashkenazi *rishonim*) have the refrain here in Hebrew, e.g. *Tosafot* (see n. 115 above), although in other talmudic passages, as in *Soṭah* 49a, and in MSS and all early editions it appears in Aramaic; see R. N. Rabbinovicz, דקדוקי סופרים , vol. 1 (Munich, 1868), on that passage, n. כ. According to M. Friedmann, the *baraita* demonstrates that the original version of *qaddish* was Hebrew; see his introduction to *Seder Eliyahu Rabbah (*see n. 43 above), pp. 78–80. Similarly, Karl in הקדיש (see n. 37 above), pp. 63–65, *et passim*, but this theory has no basis; compare de Sola Pool, *The Kaddish* (see n. 46 above), p. 19. According to Judah b. Qalonymos, the two linguistic versions arise out of the two lands of origin: ונראה כי בארץ ישראל היו אומרים יהי שמו הגדול מבורך בלשון עברי, ובבבל בתרגום; see יחוסי תנאים ואמוראים, ed. M. Blau (Brooklyn, 1994), vol. 1, p. 40. As a curiosity, we find this *baraita* in the early English liturgy for *shaḥarit*, where it is meant to be recited by one praying alone who has not heard the *qaddish*; see עץ חיים (see n. 56 above), p. 82 and compare *JQR* OS 4 (1892), p. 38.

[127] Curiously, Elbogen, in his German work, made no mention of *de-ḥadata* after homilies but this was corrected in the Hebrew and English translations; see *Jewish Liturgy* (see n. 76 above), p. 81. Similarly, L. Hoffman merely states: 'recited primarily at the graveside after burial' in his *Canonization of the Synagogue Service* (Notre Dame, 1979), p. 191.

הלכות שבת לפניהם ברבים), it would appear that the lecture need not have dealt with *aggadah* to qualify for the recitation of that *qaddish*. This would appear to be the interpretation of this midrashic text as refracted through Rashi's commentary on BT, *Shabbat* 115a, s.v. בין: ובשבת היו דורשין דרשה לבעלי בתים... **ובתוך הדרשה היו מורין להן הלכות איסור והיתר**. Similarly, Sa'adya , Maimonides, and especially *Sefer ha-'Iṭṭim* (quoted above at n. 112), stress that the *qaddish de-ḥadata* is said after any form of Torah lecture. But this would appear to be a later halakhic development, since the earlier texts repeatedly refer to the talmudic precedent of יהא שמיה רבה **דאגדתא**. In this vein, אלפא-ביתא דרבי עקיבא (above, '**d.**') returns to the original intent of this tradition, as it states **וכיון שמגיע להגדה**...(ו)אומר יתגדל ויתקדש and this is stressed even more in the *Yalquṭ* reading וכיון **שמסיים** ההגדה. Thus, the optimal choice for the lecturer (at least on the sabbath) was to conclude with *aggadah* (as discussed below). In this regard it may be worth noting that the *qaddish de-ḥadata* was said not only on sabbath after the morning sermon but also by some on sabbath afternoon after the study of a section from *Pirqey 'Avot* (Mishnah) that followed the afternoon service.[128] The ENA/T-S

---

[128] This is attested in a passage found in the JTSA MS of *SRAG* (ed. Goldschmidt (see n. 22 above), p. 80 and cited also by Heinemann, *Prayer* (see n. 47 above), pp. 262–63): ולאחר ששונין אבות מקדשין יתגדל ויתקדש שמיה רבא. ויש שמוסיפין בעלמא דהוא עתיד לחדתא ולאחא מתיא ולמפרק חייא ולמבני קרתא דירושלים ולמעקר פולחנא נוכראה מן ארעא ולאתבא פולחנא דשמיא לאתריה וימליך קב״ה בחייכון וביומיכון כו׳. וכך נהגו לאמר אחר צדוק הדין; the study of *'Avot* was known at that time to have been a custom practised in the geonic period. Several medieval rabbis note that *qaddish* is recited following any reading from Scripture, the oral Torah or *aggadah*, and this has basically become the prevalent custom; see רבינו אברהם ב״ר יצחק... שאלות ותשובות, ed. J. Qafiḥ (Jerusalem, 1962), no. 181: אחרי קריאת מזמור או פרק או אגדה או משנה שרגילין לקרות במקצת מקומות, and שבלי הלקט, ed. Mirsky, p. 150. This responsum is actually by Abraham b. David; see now S. Emmanuel, *Newly Discovered Geonic Responsa and Writings of Early Provençal Sages* (Hebrew; Jerusalem, 1995), pp. 35–37. We do, however, see in some places a vestige of the older custom, such as in a marginal note beside the chapter קנין תורה in a Yemenite *Tiklal*: אומרים זאת האגדה אחר כל פרק ופרק, והטעם לפי שאין אומרים קדיש על המשנה אלא על האגדה; see G. Margoliouth, 'Gleanings from the Yemenite Liturgy', *JQR* OS 17 (1905), p. 703 but compare also the quotation from another Yemenite text in n. 112 above. An old Ashkenazi tradition records that *qaddish* (in this case, even the basic 'half' *qaddish*) is recited only following the recitation of Scripture; see Qalonymos's responsum cited above in n. 38; Eleazar b. Judah's *Commentary on the Siddur* (see n. 36 above), pp. 496, 555 (and the sources cited there by Hirshler, p. 496, n. 114); *Siddur of R. Solomon* (see n. 58 above), p. 116. In the literature דבי-רשי, however, the tradition being recorded reflects either Scripture or *midrash* of Scripture, in according with BT, *Soṭah* 49a; see *Sepher Ha-Pardes* (see n. 114 above), pp. 301–2; *MV* (see n. 30 above), pp. 74–75 (and other parallels) and see n. 115 above. These rabbis explain that the addition of רבי חנניא בן עקשיא אומר at the end of each chapter of *'Avot* is in order to conclude the Mishnah with a *verse* (Isaiah 42:21), for the same reason that passages are added to Mishnah *Shabbat* 2 on Friday night, and to פיטום הקטורת. A different reason is, however, provided in the commentary on *'Avot* attributed to Rashi (on *'Avot* 6.15): נאה נהגו כל העם לאומרו בסוף כל פרק ופרק לפי שא״א קדיש אלא על האגדה (and see מסורת הש״ס there), namely, that the passage is added because of its 'aggadic' theme, not because of the verse with which it ends, in a similar vein to the Yemenite gloss quoted above; on the original context of Hananiah's saying, see J. N. Epstein, מבוא (see n. 66 above), pp. 977–78, but compare J. Sussmann, 'פרקי ירושלמי', in *Meḥqerey Talmud* 2 (see n. 97 above), pp. 256–

Genizah text is witness to the recitation of *qaddish de-ḥadata* immediately following the aggadic conclusion to the *pirqa* lecture.

Returning to the *qedushah de-sidra* mentioned in BT, *Soṭah* 49a, we find that this liturgical passage itself has an interesting history. In all likelihood, this section is a vestige of a practice to recite portions of the Hagiographa at the sabbath afternoon service, the portion read being called the סדר (Aramaic: סידרא).[129] If so, its appearance in the daily liturgy concluding the *shaḥarit* service would then be a later development. Naṭronai does, however, suggest an opposite history, that is, one that relates the *qedushah de-sidra* to the custom of reciting biblical verses, Targum and rabbinic texts immediately following the daily *shaḥarit* service. Once that lengthy procedure was abandoned for lack of time, an abbreviated and standardized format remained at the end of the service in the form of the *qedushah de-sidra*.[130] In Naṭronai's explanation, the common denominator between the *qedushah de-sidra* and the יהא שמיה רבא דאגדתא is that they both relate to Torah study.

The connection between the *qedushah de-sidra* and the conclusion of a homily is also thematic, since both include expressions of 'words of consolation' (דברי נחמות), and such a connection was already noted by Eleazar b. Judah of Worms in his commentary on the *siddur* (compare the problematic word ונחמתא in *qaddish*).[131] It is

---

70. Again, these sources refer either to the 'half' *qaddish*, or to *qaddish de-rabbanan* (see also *Abudraham*, ed. A. J. Wertheimer (Jerusalem, 1963), p. 68), but not *de-ḥadata*; similarly in *Ḥibbur Berakhot* (see at n. 37 above), following *Piṭṭum ha-Qetoret*: ואומ[ר] קדיש, ואין אומ[רים] תתקבל צלותהון... וכן אחרי כל פרק ומגילה ודרש ופסוקי שאומרין. The custom recorded in the MS of *SRAG* of reciting *de-ḥadata* after Mishnah does, however, reflects the use of that *qaddish* as a conclusion to an aggadic homily, and it is for this reason that several passages were added to Mishnah *'Avot.* That practice is also documented in several old Mishnah MSS; see Sh. Sharvit, 'מנהג הקריאה של אבות בשבת ותולדות הברייתות שנספחו לה בעקבותיו', *Bar-Ilan Annual* 13 (1976), pp. 169–88 and 'משנה מזרחית מן המאה הי״ב', *Alei Sefer* 17 (1993), pp. 5–17. Nevertheless, *qaddish* after *halakhah* may be implied from a different passage in *Seder Eliyahu Rabbah* (see n. 43 above); see Mann, 'Changes' (see n. 115 above), p. 267, n. 51. See also n. 97 above.

129 BT, *Shabbat* 116b: בנהרדעא פסקי סידרא דכתובים במנחתא דשבתא. See: Z. Jawitz, מקור הברכות (Berlin, 1910), p. 79; Y. Ofer, 'סדרי נביאים וכתובים', *Tarbiz* 58 (1989), pp. 166–69.

130 *OHG* (see n. 56 above) to *Megillah*, §152 and to *Soṭah*, §150; Brody, *Naṭronai* (see n. 34 above), pp. 146–47. See also *OHG* (see n. 56 above) to *Shabbat*, §314; *Siddur of R. Solomon* (see n. 58 above), pp. 121, 123. Other Geonim and medieval rabbis provided different explanations; see: Ginzberg, *Genizah Studies* (see n. 77 above), vol. 2, pp. 100, 106; Mann, 'Changes' (see n. 115 above), pp. 267–69; Karl, הקדיש (see n. 37 above), pp. 69–71. On Torah study into the early hours of the morning, before prayers, see Naṭronai's responsum in *OHG* (see n. 56 above) to *Berakhot*, §41; Brody, *Naṭronai*, p. 130.

131 Eleazar b. Judah's *Commentary on the Siddur* (see n. 36 above), p. 428: על כן אומרים ובא לציון בכל יום, כמו במדרש אבכיר בסוף כל דרשה דברי נחמות וסופו אמן במהרה [אולי: בימינו?] כן יהי רצון, וכן בילמדינו בסוף כל דרש דברי נחמות, על כן בסוף כל תפילה אנו מתפללים ובא לציון גואל. See also the phrase quoted above in n. 90. The eschatological message of *qedusha de-sidra* is apparent and was noted by other rabbis; see especially the formulation by Manoaḥ of Narbonne in *Sefer Ha-Menuḥah,* ed. E. Hurvitz (Jerusalem, 1970), p. 147: לפי שהוא מדבר על ביאת הגואל ועל תחית המתים ועל רוח הקדש ועל התורה שלא תפסק ממנו ועל הקדושה שנקדיש להקב״ה ועל מלכותו שתתחדש. According to de Sola Pool, the word נחמתא refers to 'the praises and Messianic consolations brought by the preacher in his Aggada'; see *The Kaddish* (see n. 46 above), p. 64 and on that word in

for that reason that the recitation of *qaddish de-ḥadata* serves as the formulaic conclusion to the sabbath homily, since it is the ultimate expression of faith in the rebirth of the dead, the restoration of Jerusalem and the crowning of the Divine glory. This is also the rationale for beginning the *qedushah de-sidra* with the verse ובא לציון גואל (Isaiah 59:20). According to the tradition explained above, the *qaddish de-ḥadata* was a natural choice as a formula with which to conclude the sabbath homily, as it affirmed the belief in the coming of the Messiah and the resurrection of the dead.[132] This origin for the *qaddish* would account for the messianic and eschatological sentiments expressed therein, such elements being noted by several medieval rabbis and also expressed in the sections common to all its versions.[133]

---

general, pp. 62–65. A direct connection between the thematic element of the sermon on sabbath afternoon and *qedusha de-sidra* is made by Judah b. Yaqar, פירוש התפילות והברכות (see n. 30 above), vol. 1, pp. 75–76: ואיפשר לפי שהיו דורשין בכל שבתות וימים טובים קודם תפילת המנחה ורגילות הוא לדבר בעינייני גאולה ובפסוקים בסוף הדרשה; see, similarly, *Abudraham* (see n. 128 above), p. 122; *Siddur of R. Solomon* (see n. 58 above), ed. Hirshler, p. 181; Eleazar b. Judah's *Commentary on the* Siddur, p. 583.

[132] It is interesting to note in Hai's responsum on redemption the following parallel to the *qaddish de-ḥadata* of the concluding benediction: ויבנה דבירכם וישכלל היכלו בחייכם ויבנה ביתו בימיכם ויקרב קץ גאולתכם ויחיש במהרה מבוא משיחכם ויקבץ נפוצותיכם מבין אויביכם...; see A. Ashkenazi, טעם זקנים (Frankfurt am Main, 1865), p. 60. Themes from this *qaddish* are also woven into the long Yemenite *yequm purqan* cited above in n. 35.

[133] My intention has not been to lead us to the conclusion that the long text of *qaddish de-ḥadata* could have been the original version of *qaddish*, representing the יהא שמיה רבה דאגדתא. I assume as a rule of thumb that briefer liturgical formulas normally precede more elaborate ones (a rule for other texts as well), and what I have intended is to prove that during the *post-talmudic* era the *de-ḥadata* was the *qaddish* said after the lectures. Those who saw the *qaddish* originating with the sermon, understood the talmudic references to יהא שמיה רבה דאגדתא as relating to a shorter ('original') *qaddish*, or to the refrain alone (not in the context of a full *qaddish*); see at n. 116 above. The *qaddish de-ḥadata* would then have been a later development (but prior to *Soferim*); see de Sola Pool, *The Kaddish* (see n. 46 above), pp. 8, 21, and especially p. 26; see also his conclusion (p. 80): '…it [=*itḥadata*] was amplified in the study house with the comforting Messianic praises and hopes that recur again and again at the close of Aggadic study'. The messianic and eschatological tone of the basic *qaddish* was noted by many rabbis, including Hai Gaon; see his responsum published by Ginzberg, *Genizah Studies* (see n. 77 above), vol. 2, pp. 164–65. Note also Abraham b. Nathan's succinct declaration: ויעמוד החזן ויאמר קדיש להזכיר קץ הימים והגאולה... כי עיקר הקדיש על עניין הגאולה נוסד במלחמת מלך המשיח... (*Sefer ha-Manhig* (see n. 123 above), p. 56, with parallel sources cited by Raphael, in a note to line 70), and see the commentaries listed by Wieder, as cited above in n. 100. Note of course the phrase in the Sephardi tradition: ויצמח פורקניה ויקרב משיחיה; compare de Sola Pool, *The Kaddish* (see n. 46 above), pp. 37–40. Many of the *hafṭarah* readings were chosen because of their messianic message, and this also would have lead into the theme of the homily that followed.

I am grateful to Professor Stefan C. Reif for hosting me at Cambridge in December 1998, and to the University Library staff for assisting me during my brief visit. My thanks also go to the Reverend Dr Andrew Macintosh and the Reverend Professor William Horbury for their kind words preceding and following my lecture. The present study has retained the format of that lecture but I have added some information and footnotes and omitted a brief review of the various legal texts of the geonic period discovered in the Genizah.

In conclusion, we have demonstrated how the blessing on behalf of the Geonim and the *qaddish de-ḥadata* were once connected to the *pirqa* lecture delivered after the reading of the Torah on the sabbath and festivals in Babylonian congregations during the geonic period, and have noted that in the Genizah text the material connected to the *pirqa* follows the list of Torah and *hafṭarah* readings for the festivals. The prayer for the Exilarch and the Geonim affirmed for the congregation the validity of those institutions and served as a public declaration of allegiance to those leaders, in spite of the weakening of the Exilarchate. That blessing was reciprocal and was recited virtually at the very same time that the Geonim themselves were to deliver their blessings on behalf of the communities and local leaders. The prayer read by the local *ḥazzan* (or the homilist himself) also served as a formulaic request by the homilist for permission to deliver the local lecture, a prerogative of the Geonim. The *yequm purqan* prayer that later evolved combined elements of the communal version of the Babylonian prayer with traditions and language common to other benedictions from the Land of Israel, this amalgam probably occurring in Europe, where the two centres were equally venerated. The *yequm purqan* also addressed the local communities and their leaders and blessed them, before turning to the Geonim and others who presided over the far-away centres.

The *pirqa* lecture on the sabbath and festivals in local Babylonian synagogues concluded with an aggadic homily that began with a formulaic benediction and concluded with the recitation of the *qaddish de-ḥadata*. The *qaddish* (and probably elements of the aggadic homily too) stressed the coming of the Messiah and the ultimate redemption. Both prayers were important parts of the Babylonian liturgy during the geonic period but were dropped from the formal liturgy when the specific type of Babylonian lecture, the *pirqa*, was no longer delivered in local communities. Due to the themes that it expresses, the *qaddish de-ḥadata* survived mainly as an addition to the funeral service, and the blessing for the Geonim found its way into the Ashkenazi rite in the form of the *yequm purqan* prayer.

The combined ENA/T-S fragment is witness to these Babylonian customs and traditions from the ninth century. The text serves as an important marker for the development of the liturgical practices of that period, and, together with other historical, literary, legal and documentary evidence from that time, helps us better understand the important role played by the Geonim of Babylonia, in various and different ways, in the establishment of these practices. As in many other areas of custom and law, the traditions from the early medieval communities of the East were transmitted to the centres of Jewish life in Europe, in whose rites and practices they developed and flourished, and by way of whom they have survived to this very day.

Appendix 1 (to n. 66 above)

For the fourth source see Sherira's letter in which the following is stated: ומאחרי גאון אבי אבינו נוחו עדן אחזנו מנהגו לברכך בשבת [בשער] הישןיבה]... וכי ברך נברכך בתדר בקרב ישיבתנו וכין בפרקים ועצרו[ת]... This passage attests to this practice during the days of Judah, Sherira's grandfather, who reigned in Pumbedita some thirty years after Ṣemaḥ. According to Mann, 'on special occasions public meetings were held… at which prayers were recited for the Diaspora's welfare and for the hastening of the Messianic age' (foot of p. 85; and see also p. 195). Similarly, M. Gil argues that the phrase refers to a general assembly convened in the synagogue (not a lecture); see *Ishmael,* vol. 1, pp. 129–30. But, as I argued above, these are not occasionally held meetings convened for a specific purpose (a phenomenon for which I know of no other evidence), but rather the weekly *pirqa*, as already argued by Mirsky in his introduction to the *She'iltot* (see n. 14 above), p. 6. Obviously, the term פירקי (literally, 'chapters') may also indicate general talmudic lessons; see J. N. Epstein, מבוא לנוסח המשנה (Jerusalem, 1948), pp. 898–900; E. S. Rosenthal, 'למילון התלמודי', *Tarbiz* 40 (1971), pp. 193–200; Danzig, *Introduction to Halakhot Pesuqot* (see n. 8 above), p. 24, n. 35, and pp. 137–38, n. 99. Nevertheless, in many occurrences in geonica and related material, the terms *pirqa* and *pirqe* are used, in the context of rabbinic authority, in the sense of the right to deliver a lecture in the academy, which was the sole prerogative of the Gaon or one whom he entrusted with that authority; see Sherira's description of the tripartite role of the Gaon: למיקבע פירקא, ולאתובי מתיבתא, ומדבר מנהג גאונים (*IRSG* (see n. 12 above), p. 99). The phrase מדבר מנהג גאונים is to be understood in the light of similar usage by the Geonim of the Aramaic verb דבר in the sense of 'the right to lead'; see J. N. Epstein, 'Philologisch-historische Miszellen', *MGWJ* 63 (1919), pp. 253–59, and the geonic commentary quoted in *OHG* (see n. 56 above) to *Ta'anit* §139: פי' אדבריה... כלומר שם בפיו שידרוש כן בדרשא שידרוש על הציבור בפרק. Note also the passage attributed to an early geonic source: (פעם אחת הלך... מרשות ראש גולה שלא ברשות ראש ישיבה לקבוע פרק [כתב-יד: פרקא]) and quoted by Judah b. Qalonymos, יחוסי תנאים ואמוראים, ed. J. L. Maimon (Jerusalem, 1942), p. 99; see also addenda to *IRSG*, p. XIX, and Ch. Tykochinsky, *Devir* 1 (1923) p. 173. Regarding the permission needed from the Gaon, see also above, n. 81, and M. A. Friedman in *Maimonidean Studies* 1 (1990), p. 6, n. 24. Such is the simple and obvious meaning of the statement by Samuel b. Ali: ונתנו לו רשות... ולדרוש תורה ברבים ולקבוע פרקים ולהעמיד מתורגמנין, ולומר קודם מדרשו: 'שמעו מאי דסברה', ואחר מדרשו קידוש השם; see S. Assaf, *Tarbiz* 1:2 (1929), pp. 61–62, and note also the reference to *qaddish* that followed the lecture; compare at n. 106 above. Similarly, the phrase refers to the authority vested in a sage to deliver the lecture in a local community, as in the statement describing the activity of Elḥanan b. Shemariah: וגם נס כי קבע פרק וכי ברהון עמד על ראשו בהגדה ושבועה כי כל יושבי האדמות ההמה לא ידעו מנהג הפרקים קל וחומר מנהג הישיבה; see Abramson, pp. 110–11, Gil, *Palestine* (see n. 53 above), vol. 2, pp. 44–45, and Mann, pp. 195–99 and p. 201, n. 9. In another letter, describing a different episode, Elḥanan is again described as having delivered a sabbath sermon: וירד יום השבת אל המקום אשר יתפללו בו ודרש ופתח. This is quoted by Bareket, *Jewish Leadership* (see n. 26 above), p. 161 and indicates that the other source regarding Elḥanan also refers to a sabbath lecture. On Elḥanan's travails, see M. R. Cohen, 'Administrative relations between Palestinian and Egyptian Jewry during the Fatimid Period', *A Millenium of Association (868–1948)*, ed. A. Cohen and G. Baer (Jerusalem, 1984), pp. 122–24, with reference to the first episode. Similarly, this right was granted by the Gaon of the Land of Israel to communal leaders under his jurisdiction, as per the letter published by S. D. Goitein, *Palestinian Jewry in Early Islamic and Crusader Times,* ed. J. Hacker (Hebrew; Jerusalem, 1980), p. 178 [= Gil, *Palestine* (see n. 53 above), pp. 40–41]. In a responsum attributed to Naṭronai, the phrase לפתוח פרק בקהל refers to a talmudic lesson in the synagogue on Friday night; see *OHG* (see n. 56 above) to *Shabbat*, §20 and Brody, *Naṭronai* (see n. 34 above), p. 195 and p. 52 regarding the attribution. But others do not indicate when on the sabbath the lecture was given; see above, n. 122. In medieval halakhic literature, פרק usually refers to a chapter of Mishnah; see above, n. 128.

Appendix 2 (to n. 85 above)

We need concern ourselves here with only one noteworthy aspect. I refer to the דרשה section in which designated talmudic passages, in *halakhah* and *aggadah*, are collected in order to be recited in conjunction with the topic of the lecture. Over time, most of these *derashot* were omitted from the written records (i.e. the printed edition, MSS and Genizah fragments) of the *She'iltot*, but sometimes just a few words survived (particularly in MSS), beginning with the word דרשה and containing a brief clue as to one or two of those passages; see Mirsky's introduction to the *She'iltot*, pp. 20–22, 25–38. It would appear that despite the rigid formula of the *pirqa* as a whole, the lecturer was permitted to improvise and embellish his lecture by adding to the aggadic (only!) part of the דרשה section, as long as he remained within certain given boundaries. In some cases, there were multiple *derashot* from which the lecturer could make his selection; see especially Sh. Abramson, עניינות בספרות הגאונים [= *'Inyanot*] (Jerusalem, 1974), pp. 10–20 and compare the extensive דרשה on the subject of the sabbath in the first *she'ilta* to Genesis, ed. Mirsky, pp. 7–18. An important clue as to the nature of the aggadic discourse in the *she'ilta* was uncovered in a Genizah fragment where, following the quotation in full of a lengthy selection of aggadic passages (in this case regarding *Sukkot*), the following instruction to the lecturer appears: ואמר אגדתא כמה דניחא ליה, והדר אמר; see J. N. Epstein, 'שרידי שאילתות', *Tarbiz* 6 (1935), p. 495, and his explanation on p. 465; this text was later incorporated in Mirsky's edition, vol. 5/2, p. 106. In some cases, the thematic elements that unite the sources in the aggadic portion of the *she'ilta* relate to verses in the Torah reading; see B. M. Lewin, 'לחקר שאילתות רב אחאי גאון', *Jüdische Studien Josef Wohlgemuth* (Frankfurt am Main, 1928), Hebrew section, pp. 4–5. The unfettered nature of an aggadic discourse may also to be inferred from Sherira's (unrelated) comment: וכן הוא אומר בעל הגדה כיון שהכל רצין אחריו מפני שמושך את לב העם כמים בפתרוניו והגדותיו **ויכול להרבות דברים ומדרשות**, דומה הוא לעשיר שעשרו דברים ארוכים ורחבים ועצומים בעצמם ואין דמיהן יקרים...; see BT, *Ḥagigah* 14a; H. Kis, *Gáoni Responsumok* (Budapest, 1912), p. 12; גנזי ירושלים, ed. A. J. Wertheimer (Jerusalem, 1981), p. 31, no. 41. On Geonim and *aggadah*, see above, n. 98. Although reference to the דרשה section appears at the end of the *she'ilta*, this was done by copyists, while in the live recitation of the lecture this section normally appeared in the penultimate position, and the *pirqa* ended with a return to the halakhic discussion at hand (ולענין שאילתא דשאילנא קדמיכון). The following is, however, recorded in a marginal note written in Judaeo-Arabic on a leaf of a *she'ilta* in the Genizah: תרתיב הדה אלשאלות: יקול שאלתא. תם יקול ברם. תם יק[ול] בריך. תם יק[ול] ולענין. תם יק[ול] דרשא (Ginzberg, *Geonica*, vol. 2 (see n. 26 above), p. 366): 'this is order of the *she'iltot*... then say *derashah*'. This is an instruction for a reciter of the text to deliver the lecture in that order, with a return to the דרשה section at the conclusion; see Ginzberg, vol. 1, p. 91, n. 2, and S. Poznanski's comments in his review of *Geonica*, *JQR* NS 3 (1912–13), pp. 422–23, and foot of p. 405. This interpretation differs from that of Abramson, who claimed that the mention of the *derashah* at the end of the note is merely an 'error', as the scribe was swayed by the order of the written text of the *She'iltot*; see *'Inyanot*, pp. 10–11. I believe that this demonstrates that, on some occasions, the דרשה was delivered at the end of the *pirqa* – this would be the 'non-academic' format of the lecture – and that would certainly apply to the aggadic portion.

6

Judah Halevi: Records of a Visitor from Spain

JOSEPH YAHALOM

In his account to the *Times* newspaper of London in 1897, Solomon Schechter recorded his lively impression of the newly discovered Genizah, describing it as 'a battlefield of books'. Regarding the poetic material in the Genizah, the situation is even more complicated, since many of the poorly preserved leaves were originally written for actual recitation, and never comprised more than a quire or two, hardly amounting to real books. Many of them included contemporary compositions that would never have survived, had it not been for the fact that they were consigned to the Genizah. The poets active during the classical Genizah period, namely, the eleventh and twelfth centuries, were actually most productive and, according to one estimate, at least forty per cent of the Genizah matcrial consists of poetry.[1] Although these manuscripts originated in the eastern communities, our concern here is with western Hebrew poetry, particularly that of Andalusian Spain.

Until the tenth century, the history of Hebrew poetry is fairly clear. The poets of the classical period flourished mainly in the Land of Israel and their extant works are liturgical. The complexion of Hebrew poetry was dramatically transformed with the emergence of the Andalusian school and the appearance of secular poetry. For the first time, the quantitative metres of Arabic were adapted for use in Hebrew. Dunash ben Labrat, who was active in Cordova, initiated Arabic genres, forms and images. He wrote – in an almost apologetic manner – the first secular poems and succeeded in effecting one of the most remarkable developments in the history of Hebrew culture. Within a few decades, the holy language submitted to, and then quickly mastered, the new Andalusian techniques.

Isaac ibn Ḥalfōn (c.1000) was one of the first representatives of the Spanish school who turned his private emotions and feelings into poetic themes. In addition, he was the first professional court poet who made his living through writing, travelling from place to place in search of patrons. When disappointed, he knew how to vent his feelings in poetic satire. In one of his poems, he even complains that instead of the promised wine he has had to make do with a gift of cheese. Being one of the first in a long line of such poets, Ibn Ḥalfōn exerted much influence on his successors, among them some of the greatest and most famous of this school, such as Samuel Ha-Nagid, a younger contemporary. We have, of course, to take into account that the great medieval poets had to be not only naturally gifted, but also well educated. In order to

[1] See T. Carmi, *The Penguin Book of Hebrew Verse* (Harmondsworth, 1981), p. 23.

write poetry, they had to acquire the specific skills of classical writing: well established themes and motifs, a fixed prosody, and a set of poetic embellishments. As for the origins of such special skills and the special training they required, the great poets must have acquired them not only from outstanding Arabic compositions but also from those Hebrew poets who preceded them. The importance of a poet like Ibn Ḥalfōn lies in the fact that, although he became relatively unimportant in future generations, he stands at the centre of developments in his own day.

It is not surprising that the edited collection of his poems, his *diwān*, compiled during his life, was not transmitted with other medieval Hebrew texts into the modern period. The *diwān* of Ibn Ḥalfōn is mentioned in a list of books dating from the twelfth century, and it is specifically requested at the start of that century in an Arabic letter from Damietta in Egypt. But already at that time, the writer complains that the only copy available to him has been borrowed by someone who has absconded to Yemen. The only reason that we have an edition of Ibn Ḥalfōn's poetry, comprising 75 items, is thanks to the discoveries in the Cairo Genizah. Here, fragments of eight very different copies of his *diwān* have been preserved.[2]

One of the most mature representatives of the Andalusian school, perhaps the finest, was Judah Halevi. His poetry may be characterized as urban and elegant, and he delighted in ornate metaphors. Moreover, the figure of Judah Halevi towers above the Hebrew poets of medieval Spain as that of a vibrant intellectual, deeply involved in the public affairs of his own day. His philosophical-theological *chef d'oeuvre* is known as the *Kuzari*. The Khazars were a Turkic people the members of whose nobility had embraced Judaism at some time in the early Middle Ages. The book is in the form of a dialogue between a king of the Khazars, first with a philosopher, then a Christian, a Muslim, and finally with a *ḥaver*, or Jewish scholar. The exposition is very lively, which also perhaps ensured the popularity of the book. According to the *ḥaver*'s contention, Israel was endowed with a unique religious sense, appropriate for development in a country particularly selected for that purpose, namely, the Holy Land.[3] The same idea is to be found in many of Halevi's poems. His love for the Holy Land was expressed in a longing for the return of God's presence there, and for the places sanctified by his revelations. Halevi's poems are indeed numerous, totalling approximately one thousand, and manuscript copies of his poems are equally abundant. In addition to two complete *diwān*s, there exist more than a thousand Cairo Genizah fragments reflecting not only the poet's productivity but also the admiration he enjoyed among his Egyptian followers.

An important manuscript of a *diwān* of Halevi was acquired by the famous Italian scholar, Samuel David Luzzatto, in Tunis in 1839. Within twenty-five years, Luzzatto

[2] *Itzhak Ibn Khalfun: Poems*, ed. A. Mirsky (Hebrew; Jerusalem, 1961), pp. 52–58, 174–75.

[3] *Kitāb Al-Radd Wa-'l-Dalīl Fī 'l-Din Al-Dhalil*: *Al-Kitāb al-Khazarī: The Book of Refutation and Proof on the Despised Faith by Judah Halevi*, eds D. H. Baneth and H. Ben-Shammai, (Jerusalem, 1977).

managed to publish two collections of poems based on this manuscript.[4] Altogether, Luzzatto published no fewer than one hundred texts from the *diwān*. Following his death, the manuscript changed hands and reached the Bodleian Library in Oxford.[5] Publication of a complete edition of Halevi's poems remained buried among the projected schemes of *Mekizei Nirdamim,* a society dedicated to the publication of medieval Hebrew literature at the close of the nineteenth century. Then, the trustees of the society discovered a talented young man – none other than Heinrich Brody, eventual Chief Rabbi of Prague – who undertook the publication of the *diwān*. Thus it came about that the first part of the edition appeared in print in Berlin in 1894.[6] Since then, however, not much additional work has been done in the area of scholarly redaction, and this neglect, it must be admitted, represents no small injustice to the greatest of medieval Hebrew poets. Yet at the same time, these hundred years have witnessed remarkable progress in research on the poet's life and times, much of it based on Genizah sources.

In the late thirties, a new immigrant to the Land of Israel named Jefim Schirmann, fresh from Berlin and a pupil of Brody, began publishing in Jerusalem a series of articles under the short and modest title, 'The Life of Judah Halevi'.[7] Schirmann built his research on a meticulous reading of the poems themselves, and of the Arabic rubrics heading each poem that described the circumstances surrounding each composition. A supplementary contribution to the realm of biography was made by the gifted historian, S. D. Goitein. While immersed in research on the documentary material from the Cairo Genizah, Goitein discovered autograph Arabic letters of Judah Halevi, as well as letters emanating from his circle of friends and acquaintances about his visit to Egypt, cradle of the Genizah. Goitein began publishing his discoveries in a series of articles in Jerusalem over forty years ago.[8]

All these documentary materials have come directly or indirectly from one source, the archives of a Cairene businessman, public figure, and scholar. He was called Abū Sa'īd Ḥalfōn b. Nethanel Halevi al-Dimyāṭī. Ḥalfōn was a traveller and often visited Spain. The letters addressed to him, as well as those written by him, demonstrate that he was on familiar terms with everybody of consequence in Jewish Spain. It is therefore not surprising that Ḥalfōn, on his repeated visits to Spain, should have made the acquaintance of Judah Halevi, and embarked on what became a lasting friendship. Goitein discovered and published five autographs of Halevi, all written while the poet

---

[4] *Virgo Filia Jehudae sive Excerpta ex inedito celeberrimi Jehudae Levitae* (Prague, 1840); *Diwan Yehuda Halevi* (Lyck, 1864).

[5] A. Neubauer, *Catalogue of the Hebrew Manuscripts in the Bodleian Library*, vol. 1 (Oxford, 1886), cols 656–60, no. 1971.

[6] *Dîwân des Abû-l-Hasan Jehuda Halevi*, ed. H. Brody, vol. 1 (Berlin, 1894).

[7] J. Schirmann, *Studies in the History of Hebrew Poetry and Drama*, vol. 1 (Hebrew; Jerusalem, 1979), pp. 247–341. The original article was published in *Tarbiz* 9 (1938), pp. 35–54, 219–40, 284–305.

[8] S. D. Goitein, 'The last phase of Rabbi Yehuda Hallevi's life in the light of the Geniza papers', *Tarbiz* 24 (1954), pp. 21–47; 'Did Yehuda Halevi Arrive in the Holy Land?', *Tarbiz* 46 (1977), pp. 245–50.

was still in Spain. One of them is of the highest importance for the poet's biography. In it he explains to his friend, Ḥalfōn, how he was induced to write his classic, the *Kuzari*. He had written that book as a reply to questions he had been asked by a Karaite from Christian Spain. The circumstances that gave the impetus to the composition are still discernible in the book as we have it. Proof of the truth of the Jewish faith, according to Halevi, is to be found not in any argument but in the uninterrupted Jewish tradition, an aspect of history glossed over by the Karaites.[9] His clear-cut, nationalistic tendency is revealed in the concluding part of the *Kuzari*, where he expresses his desire to emigrate to the Holy Land. Similarly, in his letter on the subject of the *Kuzari*, Halevi reiterates to his friend Ḥalfōn that he has no other wish than that already expressed to him orally, namely, to move eastwards.

It is, however, only thanks to Genizah material that we actually know the details of Halevi's journey to the East. It is a letter written by Ḥalfōn's brother-in-law and business representative in Alexandria, in which he announces the arrival of the poet in that town on board the Sultan's new ship on 24 Elul (8 September) 1140).[10] The arrival of the great poet must have had considerable consequences for the intellectual history of Egyptian Jewry. At the same time, things were also changing rapidly in the West. The mid-twelfth century is an important turning point for the history of western Jewish culture in Arabic Spain. In 1140, the regiments of the North African Almohads invaded Spain, imposing Islam by the sword. The major source of Jewish literary production was abruptly cut off and a new centre had to be established in the north of Spain, which had been recovered from the Muslims by the Christian *Reconquista*. The polished and lyrical Hebrew verse was soon transformed and never regained its original beauty. The poetic productivity itself was destined to end some 200 years later with the increase in the activities of the Inquisition and the eventual expulsion of the Jews. Original *diwān*s did not remain in Spain, and those taken by the Jews to their newly established centres were not numerous.[11] In fact, we lack even a single specimen of Andalusian Hebrew poetry written in an Andalusian manuscript, and the *diwān*s of the great poets are known only from copies produced much later. Even the classical *diwān* of such a poet as Judah Halevi reached us in only one late manuscript.[12]

This situation is redressed by the early material found in the Cairo Genizah. This material is particularly valuable since the remnants of the authentic Jewish culture of Andalusia should be sought in a geographic area that preserved a cultural continuity with Muslim Spain and the Genizah manuscripts did indeed originate in a Muslim

---

[9] S. D. Goitein, 'Autographs of Yehuda Hallevi', *Tarbiz* 25 (1956), pp. 393–412; *A Mediterranean Society: The Jewish Communities of the Arab World as Portrayed in the Documents of the Cairo Geniza*, vol. 5: *The Individual* (Berkeley – Los Angeles – London, 1988), pp. 448–50, 464–65.

[10] *A Mediterranean Society* (see n. 9 above), p. 454 (n. 10).

[11] M. Beit-Arié, 'The Hebrew script in Spain: its development, offshoots and transformations' in *Moreshet Sepharad: The Sephardi Legacy,* ed. H. Beinart (Hebrew; Jerusalem, 1992), pp. 224–58.

[12] Neubauer, *Catalogue* (see n. 5 above), cols 641–56, no. 1970.

environment similar to that of Andalusia, namely, that of North Africa and Egypt. In fact, even the compiler of the large, classical *diwān* of Judah Halevi may have lived in Cairo in the generation following Halevi's visit, and was known as R. Ḥiyya al-Maghribī.[13] It is not therefore surprising that many fragmentary leaves of one copy of this *diwān* are to be found in the Genizah and that we know of another thousand fragments containing Judah Halevi's poetry in the same source.[14] Halevi was of great interest to the Jews of Egypt as he arrived there at the peak of his fame and while on a pilgrimage to the Holy Land. Some of his best poems were composed on the banks of the Nile and others were penned during the sea voyage. Of his extant poems, fifty were written during his stay of less than eight months in Egypt. Twelve of these are not to be found in the classical *diwān* of Ḥiyya al-Maghribi but were recovered by the later Cairene editor of the *diwān* who was active some 100 years after the death of the poet. The efforts of this editor to retrieve as many of the poems as possible is evident from the appendix to his *diwān*. Here, he adds some of the Egyptian poems, in addition to others that he inserts in their respective places throughout the *diwān*.[15]

Another three Egyptian poems, seemingly unknown even to the later Cairene editor, were published by Schirmann on the basis of the New Series material of the Taylor-Schechter Collection in Cambridge.[16] These poems belong to the large group that relate to the exchange between Halevi and his host in Alexandria, Aaron ibn al-ʿAmmānī, the Chief Justice of the Jewish community. He himself was a scholar and a poet, in addition to earning his living as a prosperous physician. He and his five sons did all they could to make Halevi's stay in Alexandria a joyful one. Halevi reciprocated by dedicating to the *dayyan* and his entourage numerous verses, many of which were certainly improvised and composed simply as an act of courtesy. Documentary finds in the Genizah indicate that this group of poems was even more extensive than previously thought. An Arabic letter in the Genizah provides us with a lively account of their composition.

The details are included in an urgent letter sent to the poet – now already in Cairo – by an Alexandrian admirer. The letter concludes in a very unusual way, with a short Arabic note in Arabic letters. This is contrary to the usual practice of writing Arabic in Hebrew characters and assumes that the Arabic script is a better medium for concealment. The Arabic note requests that the reader should destroy the letter immediately after reading it. The writer must have realised that it contained socially

[13] E. Fleischer, 'Yehuda Halevi – Remarks Concerning his Life and Poetical Oeuvre' in *Israel Levin Jubilee Volume: Studies in Hebrew Literature* I, eds R. Tsur and T. Rosen (Hebrew; Tel Aviv, 1994), pp. 273–76.

[14] Catalogued at the Institute for the Research of Medieval Poetry in the Genizah, at the National and University Library, Jerusalem, under the direction of Professor E. Fleischer.

[15] J. Yahalom and I. Benabu, 'Towards a history of the transmission of secular Hebrew poetry from Spain', *Tarbiz* 54 (1985), p. 249.

[16] J. Schirmann, *New Hebrew Poems from the Genizah* (Hebrew; Jerusalem, 1965), pp. 237–38.

contentious issues. The pressures surrounding the hosting of the poet in Alexandria were apparently considerable.[17]

In an earlier letter sent to Ḥalfōn, he is informed of the great excitement caused by the arrival of the poet in Alexandria. People have made the utmost efforts to host him in their homes. The writer recounts that when he himself wanted to meet Halevi, he did not invite the poet to his house, in order not to embarrass him, but took his own dinner along every evening to the poet's place, in order to share his distinguished company. By doing this, he hoped to avoid making other people envious of his success in enjoying the company of Halevi. One man apparently had no problem in obtaining the poet's agreement to visit him in his palatial residence. This was Ibn al-'Ammānī, the *dayyan*. Halevi was to be found there on most sabbaths and festivals, and spent even the most holy of days, the Day of Atonement, with the *dayyan*. As expected, the major part of the poet's literary production in Egypt was dedicated to Ibn al-'Ammānī.[18]

An urgent letter sent to Cairo for Halevi informs him of what occurred in the aftermath of his visit to Alexandria. The *dayyan* was not content with having the autograph poems in his private possession but was anxious to disseminate the fact widely. To that end, he compiled a small *diwān,* commemorating the poet's visit. The *diwān* comprised, of course, not only Halevi's poetic works, but also his literary interchanges with the *dayyan*. As was traditional in *diwāns*, rubrics in Arabic were added to the poems. The rubrics include introductory remarks such as 'This is Judah Halevi's Poem on the Pool' and there are similar introductions to verses on fountains, on the gift of chickens, and even on razor blades, as well as on other subjects. It appears that most of the poems written on that occasion are extant and although they seem to deal with trivial matters, they were preserved as a token of admiration for their author. It is certain, however, that there were other Egyptian poems that have not reached us and, considering the fact that the Judaeo-Islamic society of the East was less refined than that of Spain, this is not surprising.

The Genizah has not only provided us with texts otherwise unknown, but has also provided information about poems (such as the one on razor blades?) that will presumably never reach us. Moreover, from the letters themselves, we learn how literary collections came to be arranged and compiled. Additionally, we gain first-hand information about the socio-cultural environment in which the mere publication of Halevi's poems caused great turmoil. Not much time was to pass before the dispute left the personal domain and became ideological. People raised eyebrows and asked how poems of such jovial content came to be written by someone setting out on a sacred pilgrimage. It is not clear, however, that Halevi's pilgrimage was primarily intended as an act of personal repentance, even if every such journey has an element of

---

[17] S. D. Goitein, 'Letters about R. Yehuda Hallewi's stay in Alexandria and the collection of his poems', *Tarbiz* 28 (1959), pp. 343–61; J. Yahalom, 'Poetry and society in Egypt: their relationship as reflected in the attitude towards the secular poetry of Judah Ha-levi', *Zion* 45 (1980), pp. 286–98.

[18] S. D. Goitein, 'Stay in Alexandria' (see n. 17 above); *A Mediterranean Society* (see n. 9 above), pp. 458–60.

seeking forgiveness. Indeed, one of Halevi's disciples reports that in his old age the poet repented, vowing that he would never again use Arabic metre and write secular poetry.[19] It is fortunate for the history of Hebrew poetry that the poet apparently did not keep his alleged promise, and that in the spring of 1141, on the banks of the Nile, while in his sixties, he penned some of his best poems on nature. The opposition in Alexandria gained momentum. There were those who even accused him of going up the Nile to Cairo, instead of making for his stated destination, the Holy Land.

Testimony as to what actually occurred in that case is to be found in a newly discovered Arabic rubric to a poem that he wrote in Cairo on 10 Ṭevet (29 December) 1141. According to the title, the poet set out on his pilgrimage but had to return. This attempt was evidently by the land route via Cairo. In the poem itself, dedicated to his great benefactor Ḥalfōn, the poet praises him for having changed a day of disaster into a day of feasting and joy. It is clear that some major problem had beset the pilgrimage[20]. The question arises why the poet did not in the first place choose the sea route via Alexandria. It seems that the land route via Sinai to Gaza and Jerusalem was the regular route for Spanish pilgrims in those days. Judah al-Ḥarīzī used the same route at the start of the thirteenth century, and others did the same.[21] Among its advantages was the continuous settlement of Jews in both Cairo and Gaza, a fact that softened the impact of the change from Muslim to Crusader domains. The poet had been preparing the trip and this particular route for a number of years, and his previous contacts with the scholar-businessman Ḥalfōn, who was stationed in Cairo, symbolised this route and his intentions. Halevi, of course, came into contact with the head of the Jewish community in Egypt, who resided in Old Cairo, and especially with his secretary, Nathan b. Samuel he-Ḥaver, who was in contact with the heads of the Jewish community in the wider Palestinian region.[22] After all these preparations, Halevi found himself having to turn back in disappointment; this left him with the seafaring option, not a particularly ideal one in the month of December.[23]

---

19 *Salomonis ben Abrahami Parchon Aragonensis Lexicon Hebraicum*, ed. S. G. Stern (Pressburg, 1844), p. 5r.

20 J. Yahalom, 'Diwan and Odyssey: Judah Halevi and the Secular Poetry of Medieval Spain in the Light of New Discoveries from Petersburg', *Miscelánea de Estudios Árabes y Hebráicos: Sección de Hebreo* 44 (1995), pp. 23–45.

21 Y. Ratzaby, 'An Arabic Maqama by Alharizi', *Criticism and Interpretation* 15 (1980), pp. 10–11, 18, 34; *The Tahkemoni of Judah al-Ḥarizi*, English translation by V. E. Reichert (Jerusalem, 1973), vol. 2, ch. 46, p. 304 and ch. 50, pp. 419–20; S. D. Goitein, *Palestinian Jewry in Early Islamic and Crusader Times in the Light of the Geniza Documents,* ed. J. Hacker (Hebrew; Jerusalem, 1980), pp. 239, 252, 327.

22 S. Abramson, 'R. Judah ha-levi's Letter on his emigration to the Land of Israel' (with facsimile), *Kiryath Sefer* 29 (1953), pp. 133–44, 287.

23 No commercial ships undertook voyages in the autumn and winter months between October and the end of March. On the Syro-Palestinian coast, the end of the season was the Coptic Feast of the Cross, which was celebrated on 26–27 September; see Goitein, *A Mediterranean Society* (see n. 9 above), vol. 1 (1967), pp. 316–17, and A. L. Udovitch, 'Time, the sea and society: duration of commercial voyages on the southern shores of the Mediterranean during the high Middle Ages', *La navigazione mediterranea nell'alto*

The winter storms making the sea passage impossible, Halevi had no choice but to wait in Cairo for more agreeable weather in the spring. At this point, the Alexandrian opposition became more vocal and started to ask pointed questions. Why should the pilgrim go up the Nile to Cairo? Is he minded to describe the ripening of the corn in the spring and the beautiful girls on the banks of the Nile? This description is to be found in the prologue to a poem dedicated to the secretary of the Nagid, Nathan.[24] The polemical poem that Halevi wrote in reaction to the Alexandrian criticism is included in the appendix to the *diwān* compiled by a later Cairene compiler, Yeshu'ah ben Elijah Halevi. The poet sings the praises of historical Cairo. This is the city where great miracles were performed in the past; the place where Moses, the leader of the nation, was born; and the place where he prayed, according to tradition, in a synagogue named after him in Dammūh, a village near Cairo. In the place where Moses stood in prayer, Halevi now stands and declares that, although this place is holy, Jerusalem is the most holy.[25]

With the arrival of spring and the end of the winter storms, Halevi returned to Alexandria. He arrived in time to board a ship going east on Thursday, 8 May, but, owing to unfavourable winds, the ship was still in port on Sunday, 11 May. This was three days before the festival of Pentecost. It is interesting to note that, while on board, the poet left a strongly worded message for a relative of his whom he expected to follow him, indicating that he should not go up to Cairo, but proceed directly from Alexandria to the Holy Land.[26] It seems that the poet was not without experience in attempts to reach the Holy Land; the question is whether he ever achieved his goal.

According to a historiographical work of the fifteenth century, Judah Halevi reached the gates of Jerusalem, where he rent his clothes, fell to the ground mourning the destruction of the holy city, and recited the famous passage 'for thy servants hold her stones dear and they have pity on her dust' (Psalms 102:14).[27] This verse appears in many of his poems, especially in his famous 'Zionide' *Will You not Ask after the Welfare of your Captives*, which subsequently became one of the mainstays of the Ninth of Av service commemorating the destruction of Jerusalem, and which Halevi

---

meolioevo: Cèntro Italiano di studi sull'alto medioevo, Settimane di studio, 25 (1977), p. 532. See also L. Casson, *Travel in the Ancient World* (London, 1974), p. 150.

[24] *Dîwân Halevi* (see n. 6 above), pp. 112–15.

[25] *Dîwân Halevi* (see n. 6 above), vol. 2, pp. 180–82 ('*Miṣr*' in the rubric undoubtedly refers to Cairo); E. Ashtor, *The History of the Jews in Egypt and Syria under the Mameluks*, vol. 1 (Hebrew; Jerusalem, 1944), pp. 245–46; M. Gil, *Documents of the Jewish Pious Foundation from the Cairo Geniza* (Leiden, 1976), pp. 99–100, 259–62 (a decision taken in the court of the Nagid, Samuel b. Ḥananiah, appointing a general administrator of the properties belonging to the *qodesh*, including the synagogue of Dammūh and its plantations).

[26] S. D. Goitein, 'The Last Phase' (see n. 8 above), pp. 32, 44.

[27] Gedaliah ibn Yaḥya, *Sefer Shalshelet ha-Qabbalah* (Venice, 1587), p. 40; A. David, 'Gedalia Ibn Yahia, auteur de Shalshelet ha-Qabbalah', *Revue des Études Juives* 153 (1994), pp. 101–32.

allegedly recited at the gates of Jerusalem[28]. According to the fifteenth-century report, an Arab horseman rode over Halevi, causing his death. In the atmosphere of the nineteenth-century Romanticism, this story aroused great excitement. The German poet of Jewish origin, Heinrich Heine, described the event, and the dirge recited by Halevi on that occasion, in his famous poem *Yehudah ben Halevy*:

This rare song of teardrop pearls
Is the famous lamentation
Sung in all the tents of Jacob
Scattered through the universe,

Each year on the Ninth of Ab
On the anniversary day
Of Jerusalem's destruction
By Vespasian's bloody legions.

Yes, it is the song of Zion,
which Yehudah ben Halevy,
Dying in the holy ruins
Of Jerusalem, intoned –

....

And his song's wild notes of grief
Almost tamed the featherd creatures,
And the vultures fluttering nearer
Listened, almost sympathetic –

But there came a saucy Arab
Galloping along the road,
Rocking high upon his stallion,
Brandishing a shiny lance – [29]

That was Heine. A rather different view was held by the Jewish scholar, Samuel David Luzzatto, who first discovered the later Egyptian *diwān*. In his opinion, this legend was a well publicized untruth, given the impossibility of a Muslim horseman in Crusader Jerusalem. And even if a single Muslim horseman somehow appeared there, would he have dared to commit a murder at the gates of the city? Thus far Luzzatto.[30]

---

[28] *Seder ha-Qinot le-Tish'ah be'Av (Ashkenazi Rite),* ed. D. Goldschmidt (Jerusalem, 1968), pp. 124–26.
[29] *The Poetry and Prose of Heinrich Heine,* eds F. Ewen and A. Kramer (New York, 1948), pp. 293–94.
[30] *Virgo Filia Jehudae* (see n. 4 above), pp. 25–26.

Depriving the Muslim of his part in the story apparently destroyed the whole tradition. Luzzatto claimed that Halevi never succeeded in reaching the Holy Land. But scholarship did not end with Luzzatto's critical opinion.

A small fragment found by Goitein some twenty years ago in the Additional Series of the Cambridge Genizah changed the whole picture. In a letter to Ḥalfōn, the writer announces that Halevi's ship set sail on Wednesday, the first day of Pentecost (14 May, 1141). We therefore know that Halevi set out for the Holy Land, and Goitein supposes that he also arrived there safely, since even a small sailing boat could make Acre or Ashkelon, the two main ports, from Alexandria within ten days. And since Halevi died, as we deduce from another letter to Ḥalfōn, in July (the Hebrew month of Av), he had at least the full month of June in which to wander between the port where he disembarked and Jerusalem.[31]

In another Cambridge Genizah document, a letter written by the scribe, Nathan b. Samuel he-Ḥaver, we find details of Halevi's last journey.[32] Nathan was well connected with the leaders of the Palestinian community, to be found at that time living in and around Damascus. This was probably also his place of origin and the place where his family lived. After the death of the last of the priestly gaonic lineage, R. Maṣliaḥ, Nathan had emigrated from Damascus leaving behind him his mother, a sister and a brother-in-law. While he was gone, a successor was elected, namely the Gaon, R. Abraham b. Mazhir. This was during the latter part of the third decade of the twelfth century. Nathan had, in the meantime, settled in Egypt. Two years later, in October, 1141, Nathan is worried about having lost contact with the family he left behind. He now writes to an old friend, complaining that he has not heard from him for two years. Obviously not confident that his old friend would respond, Nathan also penned another letter in the same month, addressed to the new Gaon himself. Nathan emphasises in his letter that he has acquired an important position in his new home, Cairo, and that he is well loved by both the community and the Nagid. There then follows the main body of the text. The letter, informative and functional as it is, stands out in its use of Hebrew as the linguistic medium, and indeed a learned Hebrew, with occasional rhymed prose. Its scholarly author belonged to the wider Palestinian Jewish community which used Hebrew for more than liturgical purposes. Unfortunately, it is the main part of the letter which is also the most damaged. According to the first line on the reverse, which apparently concludes the section that most interests us, Nathan is recommending that a certain person should be honoured and accompanied wherever he goes. The reason for the recommendation is given in a statement similar to that of the Queen of Sheba when she expressed her awe at the wisdom of Solomon: 'Behold, I was not told the half of it' (1 Kings 10:7).

Unfortunately, what had been reported to Nathan about such a person has not fully survived. We must therefore attempt to reconstruct that part of the story. The writer

---

[31] S. D. Goitein, 'Did Yehuda Halevi arrive in the Holy Land?' (see n. 8 above).

[32] J. Mann, *The Jews in Egypt and in Palestine under the Fatimid Caliphs* (New York^2, 1970), vol. 1, p. 224, n. 1; vol. 2, pp. 279–80; S. D. Goitein, A *Mediterranean Society* (see n. 9 above), p. 455 (no. 22).

first refers to the sage, 'our Rabbi, Judah Halevi, the righteous, the pious, may his holy memory be a blessing....' Apart from what his teachings testify about him, it is especially his deeds, and those that Nathan himself was witness to, that are important for the writer. Judah Halevi is here referred to as 'the righteous, the pious', or, somewhat later, as 'the righteous and the martyr'.[33] It is about him that Nathan writes in his letter that 'his image...the fields of Egypt alight...may he rest in peace'. After some five fragmentary lines, Nathan continues his heroic description of how Halevi had 'experienced the Shekhinah and the appearance of the Divine Presence at the gates of Jerusalem...', providing the most important information in these last few words of the sentence. While the descriptions might be fragmentary, the message that the writer wishes to convey seems clear, and is addressed in bold tones to the Gaon himself: '...these visions of God should awaken you and should press you to action...'

It would appear that Nathan is using the saga of the pious and holy Judah Halevi in order to recommend to the Gaon someone who was in some way involved in it. The best candidate for this recommendation must be the poet Isaac, Halevi's son-in-law, and the son of another famous poet, Abraham ibn Ezra, who came to Alexandria along with Judah Halevi. While in Egypt, Isaac already converted to Islam.[34] It is possible that Judah Halevi wanted his son-in-law to escort him to Crusader Palestine in order to return there officially to the Jewish fold. Since apostasy from Islam was punishable by death, Isaac had to travel for his second change of religion to a Christian country.[35] It is about him that Nathan presumably writes in his letter, saying that Judah Halevi was successful 'in enticing him to the resting place of his [God], so that he would walk into Eden, the garden of the Lord'. Isaac took part in the spiritual voyage of Halevi and witnessed its dangers and pitfalls. In the top margin of our letter, it says of him that 'he carried the standard of greatness and of his outstanding deeds and... will sing out his praises'. He joined Judah Halevi on his journey to Cairo, was involved in the failed attempt to undertake the pilgrimage, and remained there after Halevi departed.[36] In poems written after Halevi's death, Isaac complained of his misery and loneliness.[37] The scribe at the rabbinical academy in Cairo was not the only one interested in Isaac's fate; others were also worried about him. In a letter to Cairo, written on Sunday, 12 April, 1142, there are still enquiries concerning Isaac and his fate.[38] We know now that a friendship later developed between the poet, Isaac, and the recipient of the letter

[33] S. D. Goitein, 'The Last Phase' (see n. 8 above), p. 34.

[34] S. D. Goitein, A *Mediterranean Society* (see n. 9 above), p. 459; S. Stroumsa, 'On Jewish intellectual converts to Islam in the early Middle Ages', *Pe'amim* 42 (1990), pp. 61–75.

[35] A *Mediterranean Society* (see n. 9 above), vol. 2 (1971), p. 303.

[36] S. D. Goitein, 'The Last Phase' (see n. 8 above), p. 36, and 'Stay in Alexandria' (see n. 17 above), p. 348.

[37] *Isaac ben Abraham ibn Ezra: Poems*, ed. M. H. Schmelzer (Hebrew; New York, 1980), pp. 11, 28.

[38] S. D. Goitein, 'The Last Phase' (see n. 8 above), p. 34.

of recommendation, the Gaon R. Abraham. About a year after the letter was sent, the Gaon was writing to take leave of the poet (2 November, 1142).[39]

Returning to Halevi, it is now clear that even if he did not manage to spend more than a month or so in the Holy Land, and even if his pilgrimage began and ended in Acre (where pilgrims sojourned at that time), he must have succeeded in reaching the gates of Jerusalem. In his imagination, he had often seen himself falling to the ground and kissing the dust of the Land. This is at least how he describes the event in his poetry, dwelling on his desire to see, taste and even kiss the dust. Since there was barely a Jewish presence in Jerusalem during the Crusader period, his pilgrimage to the Holy City would necessarily have been brief.[40] The Temple Mount itself could be seen only from the heights of the Mount of Olives, where the Church of the Ascension, with a large rock at its centre, is situated. It was to there, legend has it, that the Divine presence removed itself before completely abandoning Jerusalem after its destruction (*Lamentations Rabbah*, *petiḥta* 25). When Halevi in his poems longs to taste the dust of the burial place of the Ark, he apparently has in mind this large rock, often referred to as the Stone of the Divine Presence.[41] The location gained in importance after the Temple Mount became off limits for Jews in Crusader Jerusalem and, according to a tradition found in contemporary Ashkenazi pietistic works, if 300 priests were to stand on the Mount of Olives and recite the priestly benediction the Messiah would come.[42] In a Hebrew epistle of rhymed prose, written by Halevi on his way to Cairo and only recently discovered in the Firkovich collection in St. Petersburg, he describes the aims of his pilgrimage accordingly: 'to bow down in proximity, in the priestly presence, and near the hidden Ark, and to say before the Lord, Thou wilt arise and have pity on Zion; it is the time to favour her; the appointed time has come; for thy servants hold her stones dear and they have pity on her dust.'[43] So, how are we now to understand the late story surrounding Halevi's death? The quick disappearance of the one 'who bowed and fell on his face' was easily connected with the presence of

[39] *Isaac ben Abraham* (see n. 37 above), p. 9.

[40] During his pilgrimage, Maimonides stayed in Jerusalem for only four days (6–9 Marḥeshvan, 1165); see M. Sacks, *Ḥiddushey ha-Rambam la-Talmud* (Jerusalem, 1963), pp. 58–60; I. Ta-Shma, 'Maimonides' Commentary to the Talmud', *Shenaton ha-Mishpaṭ ha-'Ivri* 14–15 (1988–89), pp. 299–305.

[41] M. Gil, *Palestine during the First Muslim Period (634–1099)*, vol. 2 (Hebrew; Tel-Aviv, 1983), p. 6 (a guide for pilgrims dating from the eleventh century); and see also 'Epistle by Samuel ben Samson from 1211', in A. Ya'ari, *Letters from the Land of Israel* (Ramat Gan, 1971), no. 16, p. 78; and E. Reiner, 'Pilgrims and Pilgrimage to Eretz Yisrael 1099–1517' (doctoral dissertation, Hebrew University of Jerusalem, 1988), pp. 189–92.

[42] *Commentary of the Roqeah on the Torah*, eds Sh. Y. H. Kanievsky and J. Klugmann (Bnei Brak, 1980), vol. 2, p. 156; J. Dan, 'Ashkenazi "Gates of Wisdom"', in *Hommage à Georges Vajda*, eds G. Nahon and C. Touati (Louvain, 1980), pp. 183–89; 'An anonymous biblical commentary attributed to R. Eleazar of Worms', *Kiryath Sefer* 59 (1984), p. 644.

[43] S. Abramson, 'R. Judah ha-levi's Letter' (see n. 22 above), and MS Firkovich II, EBp. 206.41 (to be published by J. Yahalom, in 'Imagination and reality in the pilgrimage story of Judah Halevi', *Shalem* 7 (forthcoming)).

cavalry in Crusader Jerusalem, later metamorphosed into an Arab horseman. His famous dirge, *Zion, will you not ask after the welfare of your captives,* was subsequently connected with his death in the month of Av and was thus included in the collection of dirges recited on the national day of mourning on the ninth day of that month. In this dirge, he addresses the Holy Land, saying:

> I would bow down, my face on your ground;
> I would love your stones;
> Your dust would move me to pity.[44]

The above reconstruction is also supported by the presence of similar peaks of emotion in some of his more informative short poems, and it is fitting to conclude here with one of the most famous:[45]

> My heart is in the East and I am at the edge of the West
> Then how can I taste what I eat, how can I enjoy it?
> How can I fulfil my vows and pledges while
> Zion is in the bonds of Edom, and I am in the bonds of Arabia?
> It would be easy for me to leave behind all the good things of Spain;
> It would be glorious to see the dust of the ruined Shrine.

[44] T. Carmi (see n. 1 above), p. 348.
[45] T. Carmi (see n. 1 above), p. 347.

7
Medieval History and Religious Thought

HAGGAI BEN-SHAMMAI

Introductory remarks

a) It seems to me that the term 'Genizah' should be used and understood as a generic term. There is (or rather was) more than one Genizah. In Cairo alone there was apparently more than one such storage, or deposit place, for old, worn-out writings, mostly, but not exclusively, in Hebrew script. An important Genizah was at a Karaite synagogue and was apparently the source of much of the material that came to be known as the Firkovich Collection, housed in the Russian National Library in St. Petersburg.[1] There were additional such deposits in Aleppo and Damascus and also possibly in other places. Consequently, in the following discussion the term Genizah will not necessarily refer to the one found in the Ben Ezra synagogue in Cairo; occasionally the term 'Genizah-type material' will be used.

b) With regard to all areas and genres of material, no Genizah is an organised and comprehensive archive or deposit library. Genizahs are not therefore representative of the daily or spiritual life of their users. On the other hand, they are more representative than any private archive or collection of books. In the absence of comprehensive archives and deposit libraries the importance of the Genizahs lies in their randomness. It is this randomness that makes the contents of Genizahs so varied and rich, and that kept for us organised family archives of those who were not immortalised in 'classical' sources (cf. below), together with haphazardly preserved documents of an official nature relating to communities, persons or properties no longer in existence or of any interest. This same randomness also preserved for posterity complete or fragmentary literary works that at some point seem to have lost

[1] See P. B. Fenton, 'Leningrad treasures', *Genizah Fragments* 10 (1985), pp. 2–3; M. Ben-Sasson, 'Firkovich's second collection: remarks on historical and halakhic material', *Jewish Studies* 31 (1991), pp. 47–67 (in Hebrew), and the recent communication by G. Khan, 'Documents support Firkovitch theory', *Genizah Fragments* 28 (1994), p. 2. See now also the survey by T. Harviainen, 'The Cairo *Genizot* and other sources of the Second Firkovich Collection in St. Petersburg' in E. J. Revell (ed.), *Proceedings of the Twelfth International Congress of the International Organization for Masoretic Studies* (= *Masoretic Studies* 8), 1995, pp. 25–36 (with references to several recent publications). Harviainen's description is based on close acquaintance with Firkovich's personal archives housed in St. Petersburg. The archives include many detailed records, written by Firkovich himself, of his acquisitions and their sources. It seems reasonable to conclude from the information about these records cited by Harviainen that the Karaite synagogue in Cairo was a major source of the Firkovich Collecton.

their attraction or importance for their owners in particular, for the reading public in general, or for book collectors and dealers.

c) As is the case in many other areas of knowledge, a large portion of the material relevant to both history (represented by documents) and to religious thought (represented by literary works) is in Judaeo-Arabic. This is especially true (at least for the present discussion) with respect to Jewish thought. Since all Genizahs were found in Arabic-speaking countries, and contain texts that originate mainly from that environment, it is not surprising that there is very little from such sources that is written in Hebrew and deals with Jewish thought. The history of such a subject did, after all, begin in the Middle Ages in works written in Judaeo-Arabic, and developed for centuries in that language. As is well known, from the last third of the twelfth century there was an increasingly intense effort to translate many important Jewish and Muslim philosophical works from Arabic into Hebrew. This effort is scarcely reflected in any Genizah. To my knowledge, Genizah collections contain few fragments of such translations.[2] From discoveries in the Genizah, it seems that the admonitions of al-Ḥarīzī in his Arabic introduction to his *Maqāmas*[3] had little effect on his oriental Jewish contemporaries, who continued to use Judaeo-Arabic for their literary and scientific pursuits.

History

When one looks back at the evolution of the modern historiography of the Jews in Islamic countries, one realises that this discipline is nowadays unimaginable without the Genizah. The first decades after the discovery of the Genizah brought a flurry of publications that presented the material as curiosities, or constituted haphazard selections of 'sensational' findings. The authors were important scholars and included Schechter himself, as well as the likes of Gottheil, Bacher, Poznanski and many others.

It took another generation or so before the first appearance of an organised book of history, covering the Jewish communities in a given geo-political entity and span of time and based to a large extent on Genizah documents. This was the *The Jews in Egypt and in Palestine under the Fatimid Caliphs* by Jacob Mann, published in 1922. This history revealed a whole new gallery of personalities, communal offices, institutions, and processes. A further, similar attempt was Mann's *Texts and Studies*, published in 1932–35. Both these large works of Mann, together with a long series of articles, brought to light thousands of Genizah documents and literary fragments. They gave researchers of Jewish medieval history a sense of making contact with events as they occurred, and offered them a collection of primary sources of unparalleled, unprecedented vividness, creating a feeling of real life, of actual persons

[2] One such rare example is T-S NS 223.37, a fragment, in two leaves, of Judah ibn Ṭibbon's translation of Sa'adya's *Kitāb al-Amānāt* (*Book of Beliefs and Convictions*), belonging to parts 4–5.

[3] For a translation and discussion of the context, see R. Drory, 'Literary contacts and where to find them', *Poetics Today* 14 (1993), pp. 277–302.

in flesh and blood. Mann's works made reference for the first time to many persons and institutions that had not previously been known, mainly with respect to the Palestinian arena, but also with respect to other areas, and recorded such events as the attempts to revive ancient Jewish institutions in twelfth-century Iraq.[4] Mann was a talmudic scholar turned self-taught philologist, with no historical training, and only a limited acquaintance with non-Jewish (in this case mainly Islamic) historical sources.[5] Considering these deficiencies, his pioneering achievement is indeed astonishing. Despite the real pioneering importance of Mann's works, which guided generations of historians, and despite his awareness of the uniqueness of these materials in comparison with sources of Jewish history previously known, and his enthusiasm to publish this wealth of materials, he nevertheless saw this history primarily as a rather formal record of documentary texts, and not a chronicle of concrete social activities and processes.

The most important accomplishment in the field of Genizah history is without doubt the monumental work of S. D. Goitein. Goitein was initially educated in a combination of deep-rooted Jewish tradition and nineteenth-century German humanism. He was then trained as a philologist, with the leading Islamicist Joseph Horovitz in Frankfurt, in the rigorous methods so typical of German universities. He later turned his attention to Islamic historical sources, and still later made another turn, to Genizah studies, mainly in the area of documentary material. In his works, the extent to which the Genizah has shaped our picture of the medieval history of Jewish communities in the East reached its fullest expression.[6] The uniqueness of his research can, and should, be understood as a result of the uniqueness of the material, namely, of the fact that here we have at our disposal direct sources that shed light not only on the actions and the views of communal leaders, but also, or perhaps mainly, those of many individuals that made up the communities' rank and file. Already in

---

[4] A unique collection of documents relevant to this topic was published at that stage of Genizah studies (in 1929–30) by S. Assaf, another pioneer in the field, namely, the collection of letters of Samuel ben Ali (probably from his chancery), the head of the Baghdad Yeshivah in the second half of the twelfth century; see *Tarbiz* 1/1 (1929), pp. 102–30, 1/2 (1930), pp. 43–84, and 1/3 (1930), pp. 15–80.

[5] On Mann's works and their background, see S. D. Goitein, 'Preface and Reader's Guide' in the reprint of Mann's *The Jews in Egypt and in Palestine under the Fatimid Caliphs* (New York, 1970); G. D. Cohen, 'The reconstruction of gaonic history: introduction to Jacob Mann's *Texts and Studies*' in the reprint of Mann's *Texts and Studies*, vol. 1 (New York, 1972).

[6] Several appraisals of Goitein's personality as a scholar and of his works (some of them obituaries) have appeared; see the booklet *Shelomo Dov Goitein 1900–1985* published by the Institute of Advanced Study in Princeton (1985), with contributions by A. L. Udovitch, F. Rosenthal, Y. H. Yerushalmi; see also M. A. Friedman, 'Goitein on the India Route', *Genizah Fragments* 21 (1991), pp. 3–4. See in Hebrew M. A. Friedman, 'A note on the contribution of S. D. Goitein to the interdisciplinary study of Judaeo-Arabic culture', *Sefunot* NS 5[20] (1991), pp. 1–20; J. L. Kraemer, 'Goitein and his *Mediterranean Society*', *Zemanim* 34–35 (1990), pp. 6–17 (all with references to previous publications).

his early Genizah studies, Goitein paid special attention to the light shed on the social structure of the communities by the Genizah documents. He focused his attention on individuals whose personalities and activities could not have been known from the formal, literary sources. Such was his study of Ibn 'Awkal, a rich North African Jewish merchant who settled in Cairo in the early eleventh century, conducted from there his international commercial ventures, and became a prominent figure in the local community.

Already in the early stages of his work on the Genizah documents, Goitein also encouraged his students to work on individual personalities from the Genizah. Even at that stage, it became clear that certain segments of the Genizah documents were not just randomly disposed of by their owners, but constituted entire family archives, or at least parts of such archives, while others were parts of court archives, mainly from Cairo. This recognition led Goitein and his students to pursue the remains of such archives. The first such archive that served as a subject of a doctoral thesis (by Murad Michael[7]) was that of Nahray b. Nissim, another North African Jewish merchant, who settled in Cairo in the middle of the eleventh century. From there he directed his merchant-banking activities that stretched virtually over three continents, from Spain, through North Africa and Egypt, to the Fertile Crescent, and further through Yemen, as far as India. When Michael finished his work on the archive over thirty years ago, he was able to trace about 260 documents. Since then over a 100 additional documents from that archive have come to light, and enabled us to draw a fascinating picture of commercial and postal connections; banking practices of the High Middle Ages; transportation routes in the Mediterranean Basin; the varying prices of a wide range of commodities; the communal and family ties of the Cairene merchant-banker and his agents who were stationed in many major ports and commercial centres, as well as in some important communities such as Jerusalem. This is just one example of studies focused on individuals or families on the basis of their family archives, deposited by later generations in the Genizah. I would mention briefly just three other examples, namely, the archive of Ḥalfōn b. Nethanel (see Yahalom's article above, and later in this article, on Judah Halevi); the Genizah material on the Tustari family of Jewish politicians, bankers and savants;[8] and the documents relating to the Maimonidean family.

Goitein's approach paved the way for comprehensive historical studies that illuminated specific sections of the material, such as those that revolve around geographical foci (the most important one to date is by Moshe Gil on Palestine[9]), or

---

[7] Submitted to the Hebrew University of Jerusalem, 1968.

[8] M. Gil, *The Tustaris: The Family and the Sect*, (Hebrew; Tel Aviv, 1981).

[9] *Palestine during the First Muslim Period (634–1099)*, vols. 1–3 (Hebrew; Tel Aviv, 1983); *A History of Palestine 634–1099* (Cambridge, 1992). To these one may add the collections of annotated documents that are appearing in the *Oriens Judaicus* series of the Ben-Zvi Institute: M. Ben-Sasson, *The Jews of Sicily 825–1068* (Hebrew; Jerusalem, 1991); E. Bareket, *The Jews of Egypt 1007–1055* (based on documents from the 'archive' of Ephraim b. Shemariah) (Hebrew; Jerusalem, 1995).

social ones (such as the studies of Menahem Ben-Sasson on the beginnings of communal organisation in North Africa in the ninth century[10]), or social and halakhic ones (the most important to date being M. A. Friedman's studies on marriage documents and practices[11]). Such works resulted from a synthesis of the unique, primary Genizah documents and the well-known literary materials from a wealth of Jewish and non-Jewish sources. On the solid basis of Goitein's research and publications, it is possible to identify many diverse sections of activity that can shed light on every imaginable aspect of Jewish life and culture in the Middle Ages. As examples, one may quote Joel Kraemer's projects to edit new collections of letters by women[12] and by Maimonides[13] preserved in the Genizah. In fact, Goitein's first published book on the Genizah was such a study of education.[14]

Goitein's concluding publication in the field was the five-volume *A Mediterranean Society*.[15] When he started this work, he had already made considerable progress with his studies of economic, social and cultural history. This fact had a decisive impact on the structure and plan of this gigantic opus. It is basically planned along social lines, its five volumes corresponding to five social levels:

A: Economic foundations.
B: The Community.
C: The Family.
D: Daily Life.
E: The Individual (see below).

It is interesting to note that Goitein did not intend to write the history of *the* Mediterranean society but of *a* Mediterranean society. He did not think that there was a uniform Mediterranean society reflected in the Genizah. But he was of the opinion that the Genizah conveys the reality of one important segment that was typical of the Mediterranean individual in his, or her, social context; and that the Jewish individual and society as depicted in the Genizah documents have much in common with their Mediterranean environment.

Perhaps more than other students of medieval Jewish history, Goitein realised the uniqueness of the Genizah documents, not only in absolute terms, but also from a comparative perspective. As an example, let us compare the history of the Jews in

---

[10] M. Ben-Sasson, *The Emergence of the Local Jewish Community in the Muslim World – Qayrawan, 800–1057* (Hebrew; Jerusalem, 1996).

[11] Such as his *Jewish Marriage in Palestine*: *A Cairo Geniza Study* (Tel Aviv – New York, 1980–1981).

[12] J. L. Kraemer, 'Spanish ladies from the Cairo Geniza', *Mediterranean Historical Review* 6 (1991), pp. 237–67.

[13] See for instance his 'Six unpublished Maimonides letters from the Cairo Genizah', *Maimonidean Studies* 2 (1991), pp. 61–94.

[14] *Jewish Education in Muslim Countries Based on Records from the Cairo Geniza* (Hebrew; Jerusalem, 1962).

[15] Berkeley – Los Angeles – London, 1967–85. A sixth volume of indices was prepared by Goitein and Paula Sanders and appeared in 1993.

Islamic countries to the history of the Jews in medieval Germany. The least formal source of the latter is probably the responsa, where the circumstances of ordinary people are sometimes described in some detail (if and when they are not eliminated), and the personal views and feelings of the respondent are occasionally expressed.[16] Such a degree of reliable, primary detail, as found in so many thousands of Genizah documents, is probably impossible in German Jewish documents.

Other, no less important, aspects of the uniqueness of the data preserved in the Genizah material had first been uncovered and discussed by scholars associated with the early stages of Genizah studies, even shortly after the discovery of the treasure-trove.[17] Their full meaning was not, however, revealed and expounded until this was done by Goitein. A noteworthy example is the theme of leadership and communal institutions. The important institution of the Jerusalem *yeshivah*, which enjoyed full jurisdiction over all the communities of Palestine, Egypt and Syria during the ninth to twelfth centuries, came to light only as a result of the discovery of the Genizah. Goitein's studies gave new dimensions to the personalities of some of the communal leaders who were until then almost, if not completely, unknown, because they did not leave much in writing. They were not part of the literary or textual history mentioned above. This is particularly truewith regard to the heads of the Jerusalem *yeshivah*, the Palestinian Geonim, and may be convincingly illustrated by the energetic figures of Solomon ben Judah and Daniel ben Azariah. The former was a North African of Babylonian origin who was imported, as it were, to the post of leader of the Jerusalem *yeshivah*. The latter was a Babylonian who captured the leadership of Palestinian Jewry in the middle of the eleventh century, and whose activities may have contributed considerably to the acceptance of the Babylonian Talmud at the expense of the old Palestinian traditions.[18] Solomon b. Judah was involved in a political dispute that affected the whole communal fabric of the Jewish communities of the Eastern Mediterranean for a number of years. The dispute resulted from the attempt of Nathan b. Abraham, the president (*av*) of the Jerusalem court, to challenge Solomon's tenure of the position of Gaon. Considerable sections of the correspondence of these figures, otherwise totally unknown, have been preserved in the Genizah. From these documents, we are able to obtain a close acquaintance with such personalities; we can almost see them and hear them, with all their ambitions and personal pursuits, in many of their political manoeuvrings. This is changing the

---

[16] See for instance the *Responsa: Rashi: Solomon ben Isaac*, ed. I. S. Elfenbein (New York, 1943).

[17] See n. 4 above.

[18] On Solomon b. Judah and Daniel b. Azariah, see now Gil, *A History of Palestine* (see n. 9 above), pp. 672–739. For Goitein's comprehensive studies, especially on Daniel, see his article 'New sources on Daniel B. Azarya, Nasi and Gaon' in *Shalem* 2 (1976), pp. 41–102 (in Hebrew; reprinted in *Palestinian Jewry in Early Islamic and Crusader Times in the Light of the Geniza Documents* (Hebrew; Jerusalem, 1980), pp. 132–87 and, more generally, *A Mediterranean Society* (see n. 15 above), Index, s.v.

entire picture and perception of Jewish history under medieval Islam, or in the Mediterranean Basin.

So much for the impact of the Genizah on our knowledge of the communal and spiritual leadership. But its impact on the medieval history of ordinary individuals and families, and their everyday life, is even deeper; it relates to merchant-bankers, local traders, communal officers of various ranks, shopkeepers, artisans, craftsmen, teachers, housewives, and even beggars. It is the lives of these people that the Genizah treasure-trove preserved for eternity, and that Goitein, in his unique study *A Mediterranean Society,* brought to the fore of historical research.

The testimony of the Genizah documents regarding individuals is sometimes amazing in the degree of detail and vividness that they reveal. A highly instructive example is a letter preserved in the Genizah collection of the Jewish Theological Seminary in New York, ENA 2727, fol. 28. On both sides of one long sheet, we find two letters written in Judaeo-Arabic by a certain Aaron.[19] The first letter is to his father, the second to his mother. The addressees probably lived in Cairo. The two letters differ in several respects, and the differences are rather revealing. The letter to the father occupies only about one third of the sheet, while the letter to the mother occupies the remaining two-thirds. The style of the first letter is fairly formal, and besides greetings and some brief, understated complaints about previous letters not being answered, contains mainly business information (with one detail particularly important for the dating of the document, namely, the 'Nāṣiriyya' dirhams, which can refer only to Saladin's coins). There is very little of personal feeling or experience in this letter. Not so in the letter to 'Mum'. Here, one finds much more personal matter, and the interesting testimony of the writer that he had heard '[the Crusaders'] talk', and that 'our bread was coloured with blood',[20] with further impressions and with descriptions of the hardships during the Crusader siege of Ayyubid Acre. Here, we also have some interesting details about the personal status of the writer in the entourage of the Sultan, as well as additional personal matters, such as a request to send him a pharmaceutical[?] treatise written in his own hand, that only he and the housewife addressee will know where to find, and that may be an indication of the writer's occupation.

I would like to mention another fragment of a single leaf whose fate sheds light on a whole range of topics, events, places and persons in medieval Jewish history. The

[19] A partial English translation of the document is found in Goitein, *A Mediterranean Society* (see n. 15 above), vol. 1, p. 132. On the basis of various data in the document, it seems that the dating suggested by Goitein should be corrected from 1104 to 1191, and that the writer is referring to the re-conquest of Acre by the knights of the Third Crusade. The full text of the document will be published by E. Reiner (with my Hebrew translation) in *Sefer Ha-Yishuv* III [a comprehensive collection of sources on the history of the Jews in Palestine during the Crusader, Ayyubid and Mameluk periods], section *'Reẓef ha-Yishuv'*, entry 'Acre', no. 10 (year 1191 <?>). I also intend to publish with Dr Reiner a detailed discussion of this document and others relating to the history of the Crusader period in Palestine.

[20] Goitein, *A Mediterranean Society* (see previous note).

fragment in question is T-S 12.722. It is the first leaf of Sa'adya's commentary on Isaiah. The *recto* is a title page with a number of inscriptions, and the *verso* is the beginning of the text of Sa'adya's introduction. It was first published by Schechter.[21] This publication was typical of the early stage of Genizah studies, when mainly 'sensational' pieces were published. Schechter's publication was most important, because it ascertained the existence of Sa'adya's introduction to Isaiah, even if the damaged remnants of the text were only partly legible, and did not provide much intelligible content. The text did at least provide additional evidence for the subsequent publication of the full text.[22] It was mainly the inscriptions on the title-page that later attracted the attention of several historians.[23] The dated inscription of the first[24] owner was seen to be that of Yoshiyya b. Aaron, who acquired the manuscript in Acre in 1030/1, was himself a scribe, as well as a learned and qualified member of the Jerusalem *yeshivah*, and ultimately settled in a provincial town in Lower Egypt.[25] A second ownership inscription by Jacob, son of Ayyub, does not reveal much, since this person is not known from anywhere else.[26] But the third inscription on the same page was highly instructive, consisting as it does of three Latin words that are barely legible, but that can be reconstructed as *<inter>p<re>tacio esaye prophete*. Kedar rightly suggested that Acre was the original location of the manuscript and that it had been appropriated there by a Crusader knight, in the course of the city's capture by the European conquerors. The anonymous knight had even enquired about the contents of the writing that had come into his possession, and made the brief Latin note of three words. It was then ransomed from the Crusader knight(s) in the transaction attested in a fascinating document originally written by Karaites and published by Goitein.[27] At that stage,

---

[21] *Saadyana* (Cambridge, 1903), pp. 54–56.

[22] H. Ben-Shammai, 'Saadya's introduction to Isaiah as an introduction to the books of the Prophets', *Tarbiz* 60 (1991), pp. 371–404, and again by Y. Ratzaby, *Saadya's Translation and Commentary on Isaiah Collected and Edited with Translation and Notes* (Hebrew; Kiryat Ono, 1993), pp. 151–56 and 245–51.

[23] For details see S. C. Reif, *Published Material from the Cambridge Genizah Collections: A Bibliography 1896–1980* (Cambridge, 1988), p. 243.

[24] According to Schechter (see n. 21 above). Most of the following discussion is based on B. Z. Kedar, 'A commentary on the book of Isaiah ransomed from the Crusaders', B. Z. Kedar and Z. Baras (eds.), *Jerusalem in the Middle Ages: Selected Papers* (Hebrew; Jerusalem, 1979), pp. 107–11. The inscriptions were published again with further comments by Gil, *Palestine* (see n. 9 above), vol. 2, pp. 408–9 (no. 221); he thinks that Yoshiyya was the second owner.

[25] Goitein, *A Mediterranean* Society (see n. 15 above), vol. 2, pp. 50–51.

[26] It is still possible to argue the following: if Yoshiyya settled in Lower Egypt before 1035, and the manuscript stayed behind in Acre until it eventually came into the hands of the Crusader knight (in 1099), it stands to reason that Jacob was the later owner, and it was either he or one of his descendants who may have encountered the Crusaders in person.

[27] Goitein, *Palestinian Jewry* (see n. 18 above), pp. 231–40 (introduction), 240–50 (the letter's text and Hebrew translation). An annotated English translation of the full text of the document, with references to recent publications, is in *A Mediterranean Society* (see n.15

the manuscript could still have been complete, or nearly so, and may have then, perhaps at a much later time, been so worn out that it was discarded in the Genizah. The fragment thus tells us something about the history of Sa'adya's writings and their distribution; about the intellectual pursuits of Jewish residents of eleventh-century Acre; about Jewish court scribes in the eleventh century and their qualifications;[28] about the vicissitudes of Jewish manuscripts in the turbulent times of the First Crusade; and, finally, about the formation of the Genizah. The fragment is also a fine example of the inter-relationship between Genizah fragments. The brief Latin note vividly illuminates the ransoming of document(s), while the latter give(s) actual meaning to an inscription that would otherwise have remained a senseless jotting. In short, the fragment, interesting as it may be by itself, makes a real contribution to medieval Jewish history only in the context of several other documents and sources; in this sense it encapsulates the contribution of the Genizah to the study of history, not as isolated findings – fascinating as those may be – but *in toto*.

Religious Thought

I would like to start this section with some general remarks.

a) 'Religious Thought' is used here in a rather broad sense, less committing than the term 'Religious Philosophy' or 'Theology'. It may also include works that belong to genres other than those strictly defined as philosophical or theological, such as biblical exegesis. The term 'religious thought' is used to avoid the term 'philosophy', which may have a more limited technical connotation, referring to the Aristotelian system or its Neoplatonic medieval versions.

b) The contribution of the Genizah to the textual history and to the grand historical picture of the 'classical' Jewish medieval philosophers[29] is relatively small. The complete texts of such 'classics' were attested in manuscripts, of both Judaeo-Arabic originals and medieval Hebrew translations,[30] without, or before the Genizah. The Genizah has, however, contributed to a number of areas in this field.[31] In several

above), vol. 5, pp. 372–79. Not surprisingly, Goitein's discussion of the document concludes his chapter on Karaism. Concerning the ransoming of Karaite and other books from the Crusaders, see Gil, *A History of Palestine* (see n. 9 above), pp. 834–35. Gil refers there to a Karaite colophon that mentions a ransom of books from Baldwin, the first king of Crusader Jerusalem, in the year 1105. The document has been considered a late forgery, but it may well be that it is authentic, and that the reference to Anan there is actually to Anan II; see my remarks in 'Between Ananites and Karaites: observations on early medieval Jewish sectarianism', *Studies in Muslim-Jewish Relations* 1 (1993), pp. 19–29.

[28] See Goitein, *A Mediterranean Society* (see n. 15 above) vol. 2, p. 565, n. 6.

[29] The reference is mainly to the ones who wrote in Judaeo-Arabic since, as already indicated above, Hebrew philosophical material has very meagre representation in the Genizah.

[30] Sometimes only such translations have survived, as is the case with *The Exalted Faith*, the philosophical work of Abraham ibn Da'ud, the first Jewish Aristotelian, which even survived in two Hebrew translations (one entitled *Emunah Ramah*, the other *Emunah Nissa'ah*), with no trace found to date of the original Arabic text, in the Genizah or elsewhere. This may be an indication that the work never reached the East.

[31] This is mentioned here in general terms; the details will be further discussed below.

cases it has enriched, sometimes considerably, the textual basis of the original texts; it has brought to light works, sometimes whole sections, of medieval Jewish religious thought that were considered lost (this is true mainly of works from the geonic period); it has added important information about the historical circumstances of certain works (see also the next paragraph). In addition, through the sheer number of fragments, the Genizah supplies interesting data about the acceptance and distribution of certain works.[32] This may be illustrated with a few examples. We find that Baḥya ibn Paquda's *Duties of the Hearts*, originally a book of ethics rather than a philosophical treatise, was a very popular work. Of Sa'adya's *Beliefs and Convictions* a fairly large number of fragments also survived (see below). Another popular work was Maimonides's introduction to the tenth chapter of the Mishnah tractate of *Sanhedrin*, including his famous discussion of the thirteen articles of faith.[33]

c) Since the present discussion comprises both the documentary, historical aspect of the Genizah material and its ideological, literary aspect, it may be of interest to mention that Goitein dealt with various questions relating to religious thought in the last volume of his *magnum opus*, as though this matter belonged entirely to the world of the individual. Thus, the Karaite ideology and important sections of the history of the sect's centre in Jerusalem are discussed in this volume,[34] followed by a lengthy discussion of Sa'adya a as a person and his contribution to answering questions asked by individual Jews and by the community at large during the tenth, eleventh and twelfth centuries.[35] I would like to remark here that the inclusion of these chapters in the volume entitled 'The Individual', is understandable against Goitein's humanistic background, according to which, one's faith was a private matter. In the Genizah world, however, the Karaite 'Reformation', and even doctrinal decisions made by Sa'adya, were certainly of paramount importance to their communities at large. Further in Goitein, we find a section entitled 'Seven Portraits'.[36] Some of these are especially relevant to the topic under discussion: the detailed portrait of 'Judah ha-Levi – Poet laureate, religious thinker, communal leader';[37] 'Interconfessional learned

---

[32] Some statistics are quoted in my 'Fragments yield surprises', *Genizah Fragments* 20 (1990), pp. 3–4.

[33] This discussion was then condensed into a Hebrew prose text of confession (with the title borrowed from its opening words *ani ma'amin*), that appears in many versions of Jewish prayer-books at the end of the morning service, and into a liturgical poem (entitled *yigdal* after its opening word), that appears in many versions of Jewish prayer-books at the beginning of the morning service. The most recent edition of this introduction (I. Shilat, *Haqdamot ha-Rambam la-Mishnah* (Jerusalem, 1992), pp. 360–74, with the Hebrew translation, preface and comments on pp. 127–223) does not demonstrate much interest in the Genizah material since, as in previous cases, the editor had at his disposal Maimonides's autograph for virtually the entire text.

[34] Goitein, *A Mediterranean Society* (see n. 15 above), vol. 5, pp. 358–79.

[35] Goitein, *A Mediterranean Society* (see n. 15 above), vol. 5, pp. 379–91, (the chapter is entitled 'Schism and Counterreformation').

[36] Goitein, *A Mediterranean Society* (see n. 15 above), vol. 5, pp. 426–96.

[37] Goitein, *A Mediterranean Society* (see n. 15 above), vol. 5, pp. 448–68.

contacts' – a translation and analysis of a deathbed declaration of a certain Abu 'l-Faraj, in which Maimonides is mentioned with the Cairene judge Ibn Sanā' al-Mulk (famous for their theological discussions with Saladin's chancellor al-Qāḍī al-Baysānī) as creditors;[38] 'A Perfect Man with a Tragic Fate: Abraham Maimuni'.[39]

Let us turn now to the interesting case of a 'classic' of Jewish medieval thought that may serve here as a test case in miniature as it were, Sa'adya's *Book of Beliefs and Convictions* (in Arabic *Kitāb al-Amānāt wa-'l-I'tiqādāt*).[40] It is true that the first critical edition of the Arabic text of this early work of medieval Jewish religious thought was possible without any reference to Genizah material.[41] This edition did, however, make it clear that there were actually two versions of the Arabic text (the difference was especially conspicuous with regard to the seventh part of the work), and that the medieval Hebrew translation made by Judah ibn Ṭibbon (in 1186) was closer to one of them (St. Petersburg, Russian National Library, Ev.-Arab. 1:127). The editor considered the latter inferior, and therefore based his edition on the other MS, Bodl., Poc. 148 (Neubauer, no. 1222).[42] No convincing solution was proposed to account for the difference between the versions. But now it seems that such a solution is to be found in the Genizah fragments.[43] So far (in the course of many years), fifty fragments have been identified as parts of this work. They are of different sizes, between one torn leaf, and up to ten leaves. For some sections of the book, there is the testimony of a number of parallel fragments. I estimate that all the fragments together cover well over 50% of the text. Thirty of them are kept at Cambridge University Library, and the remainder in no less than six libraries throughout the world (including five in the Firkovich Collection in St. Petersburg).

It seems that virtually all the fragments are closer to the version of the Firkovich ('Leningrad') manuscript and the Ibn Ṭibbon translation than to the Oxford manuscript. This is true with respect to all parts of the work, including part 7. So far, one exception to this rule has been positively identified: CUL, T-S Ar. 25.27, which consists of two torn leaves, one belonging to the end of part 6, the other to part 7. The solution to the difference between the versions is provided by the Genizah material. Even if we accept that the fifty fragments represent a lesser number of

---

[38] Goitein, *A Mediterranean Society* (see n. 15 above), vol. 5, pp. 443–48; the text is the Genizah fragment in the Bodleian Library, Oxford, MS Heb. f. 56, fol. 45.

[39] Goitein, *A Mediterranean Society* (see n. 15 above), vol. 5, pp. 474–96.

[40] Cf. Goitein's remark in the course of his discussion of Sa'adya (see n. 35 above, p.389): 'Saadya's *Book of Beliefs and Opinions* makes fascinating reading.' For a detailed discussion of the relationship between the two manuscript versions of the Arabic text of Sa'adya's work and the Genizah material, see my paper 'Textual problems in Saadya's *Kitāb al-Amānāt*', presented to the seventh conference of the Society for Judaeo-Arabic Studies (held in Strasbourg in July, 1995), the proceedings of which, edited by P. B. Fenton, are scheduled to be published in a future issue of *Studies in Muslim-Jewish Relations*.

[41] This was the edition by S. Landauer (Leiden, 1880).

[42] A similar course was followed by the editor of the second edition (Y. Qafiḥ, Jerusalem, 1970), who consulted only a handful of Genizah fragments.

[43] Those obviously originate in various Genizahs, as already explained above.

codices, the total number of codices represented by the fragments is still fairly large (to the extent that numbers count here) and constitute an overriding consideration. This consideration appears to lead to the inescapable conclusion that there is a real need for a new, definitive edition of *Kitāb al-Amānāt*. Such an edition may be based on the Firkovich manuscript as its primary source; it should, however, also reflect the spirit of Goldziher's critique[44] and, above all, pay due consideration to the rich harvest of Genizah fragments, as well as to the excellent work of Judah ibn Ṭibbon.[45]

Another famous 'classic' of Jewish medieval religious thought is Judah Halevi's *Kuzari*. The contribution of the Genizah to research on the Arabic original text[46] is much less decisive than in the previously mentioned case. Thirteen fragments[47] cover less than a third of the text, and show that early copies of the work probably had better readings than the single almost complete manuscript, which is rather late. The Genizah has, however, had a different impact on the study of the *Kuzari*. No less than five letters, written in Halevi's own hand, have been recovered from the Genizah, in addition to a large number of documents relating to the poet. This documentary wealth all came, without doubt, from the archive of Ḥalfōn ben Nethanel, a Cairene merchant with international connections who was a faithful friend of Halevi.[48] One of these letters contains an explicit reference to the *Kuzari* and supplies an important clue to the actual motive for the composition of the work. Apparently, the first stage, or version of the book, had been written in response to questions, or to a challenge from a Karaite who resided in a Christian country, probably northern Spain.[49] As is well known, a large section of the third part of the work is indeed devoted to the dispute with the Karaites. An argument for an anti-Karaite motivation (among others!) for the composition of the *Kuzari* could well have been defended on textual and contextual grounds, but the discovery of the autograph letter has given solid ground for such an argument. The theory of a gradual development of the *Kuzari* through a number of stages or versions has thus become widely accepted in general terms, while scholars still differ with respect to the

---

[44] In his review of Landauer's edition, published in *Zeitschrift der Deutschen Morgenländischen Gesellschaft* 35 (1881), pp. 773–83.

[45] I have already gathered material for such an edition and completed parts of it. I hope to be able to publish it at some later stage.

[46] *Kitāb Al-Radd Wa-'l-Dalīl Fī'l-Din Al-Dhalīl*: *Al-Kitāb al-Khazarī*: *The Book of Refutation and Proof on the Despised Faith* by Judah Halevi, eds D. H. Baneth and H. Ben-Shammai (Jerusalem, 1977), introduction.

[47] This number does not include two additional fragments that have so far been identified in the Firkovich Collection; these are Russian National Library, Ev.-Arab. 1:751 (7 leaves, from the beginning of the book); 3087 (7 leaves, from part 4)

[48] The entire matter has been discussed in Goitein's portrait of Halevi; see above, n. 34.

[49] The document in question is in the Jewish Theological Seminary in New York, ENA NS 1; a full English translation is found in Goitein, *A Mediterranean Society* (see n. 15 above) vol. 5, p. 465; it was first published with Hebrew translation and annotation and a photostatic reproduction in *Tarbiz* 25 (1956), pp. 408–12.

details.[50] The strong sentiments expressed in the (hastily written) letter about the prospective trip to the Holy Land[51] also add a unique, personal dimension to the concluding paragraphs of the *Kuzari*, where the Jewish sage expresses a similar feeling to the Khazar king.

In general, the philosophical works of the most important Jewish thinker of the Middle Ages, Maimonides, have not seen great advantage from the discovery of the Genizah. This generalization applies even to autographs of the *Guide*.[52] The intellectual legacy of the Maimonidean family and their contemporaries has benefited more from the Genizah, especially with respect to works on ethics, asceticism and mysticism (Jewish Sufism), as is attested in several learned publications by Paul Fenton.[53]

I would like to mention here one case in which the Genizah has enriched our knowledge and understanding of a specific work of the great master himself, namely, his *Epistle on Resurrection*. It has been long been known that this work, as many of its kind, was not composed for purely academic or intellectual reasons, but rather as a response to some polemic challenge. Now that the texts of an actual controversy between Joseph b. Judah, a North African scholar who became an enthusiastic disciple of Maimonides and settled eventually in Aleppo, and Samuel b. Ali, the head of the Baghdad *yeshivah* (see above), have been identified in Genizah-type manuscripts,[54] one can understand and fully appreciate the clear background to

---

[50] Y. Silman, *Thinker and Seer* (Hebrew; Ramat Gan, 1985), especially pp. 103–47.

[51] Genizah-type materials have also made a new, important contribution to an understanding of the complex chapter of the final stage in Halevi's life, namely, his sojourn in Egypt and his trip to Palestine; see J. Yahalom, 'The Leningrad treasures and the study of the poetry and life of Yehuda Halevi', *Pe'amim* 46–47 (1991), pp. 55–74; see also his 'Anthology of Ha-Levi poems', *Genizah Fragments* 30 (1995), p. 4; 'Diwan and Odyssey: Judah Halevi and the secular poetry of Medieval Spain in the light of the new discoveries from St Petersburg', *Miscelanea de Estudios Arabes y Hebraicos* 44 (1995), pp. 23–45; and his contribution to this volume; E. Fleischer, ' "The essence of our land and its meaning" – Towards a portrait of Judah Halevi on the basis of Geniza documents', *Pe'amim* 68 (1996), pp. 4–15 (Heb.); J Schirmann, *The History of Hebrew Poetry in Muslim Spain*, ed. E. Fleischer (Jerusalem, 1995), pp. 421-80.

[52] See S. Hopkins, 'An unpublished autograph fragment of Maimonides's *Guide for the Perplexed*', *Bulletin of the School of Oriental and African Studies* 50 (1987), pp. 465–69, with references to several previous publications.

[53] To mention just a few examples: 'Daniel Ibn al-Māshiṭa's *Taqwīm al-Adyān*: new light on the oriental phase of the Maimonidean controversy' in *Genizah Research after Ninety Years: The Case of Judaeo-Arabic*, eds J. Blau and S. C. Reif (Papers read at the third congress of the Society for Judaeo-Arabic Studies = *University of Cambridge Oriental Publications* 47; Cambridge, 1992), pp. 74–81; 'The literary legacy of David ben Joshua, last of the Maimonidean Negidim', *JQR* 75 (1984–85), pp. 1–56; 'A Pietist Letter from the Genizah', *Hebrew Annual Review* 9 (1985), pp. 159–67; 'A mystical treatise on prayers and the spiritual quest from the pietist circle', *Jerusalem Studies in Arabic and Islam* 16 (1993), pp. 137–75.

[54] For a preliminary discussion, see S. Stroumsa, 'On the Maimonidean controversy in the East: the role of Abu 'l-Barakat al-Baghdadi' in *Hebrew and Arabic Studies In Honour of*

Maimonides's *Epistle*. This background also concerns the spiritual world of the old, indigenous Jewish communities of the East in the High Middle Ages (represented here by Samuel b. Ali), about which not much is known.

I would now like to turn to an earlier stage in the development of medieval Jewish religious thought. A feature common to the fields of history and religious thought is that in both areas the discovery of the Genizah, or, to be sure, Genizah-type material, has had a deep, one would even tend to say revolutionary impact on our knowledge of the geonic period. Were it not for the Genizah, important aspects of that period would have been almost lost to Jewish history. Without the Genizah-type material, our concept of Jewish religious thought in the geonic period was limited (and would have remained so) to Sa'adya's theological *summa* (see above) in the Rabbanite camp, and to unpublished Karaite works of theology and biblical exegesis, laden with difficult textual problems. Biblical exegesis of the geonic period is especially important here, since several such commentaries that have survived in their entirety in well preserved manuscripts contain extensive theological discussions.[55] It is thus clear that fragments that belong to the genre are most likely to contain important theological or philosophical discussions.

To the geonic period belongs the earliest medieval Jewish philosopher, Da'ūd b. Marwān al-Muqammiṣ. His work, entitled *Twenty Chapters*, has become known from quotations and the partial publication of selections from a unique, inaccessible manuscript in the Firkovich Collection. The recent publication of the text on the basis of all available manuscript materials,[56] is accompanied by a first-hand appreciation of the work. The Genizah fragments used in this edition change former conceptions of the work and have shown that it is more relevant to Jewish thought than had previously been imagined.

Sa'adya's philosophical work has earlier been discussed and mention has been made of his commentaries with important theological elements. But other works of Sa'adya were less fortunate and survived only in fragments, in Genizah-type conditions, which means that they are now dispersed over several libraries in America, England, Russia and elsewhere. So, for instance, is his commentary on Isaiah,[57] and, indeed, large sections of his commentaries on those parts of the

---

Joshua Blau , ed. H. Ben-Shammai (Hebrew; Jerusalem – Tel Aviv, 1993), pp. 415–22; *The Beginnings of the Maimonidean Controversy in the East* (Hebrew, with English introduction; Jerusalem, 1999); the Hebrew version of Samuel b. Ali's treatise will be published by Z. Langerman, see his description in *Kiryat Sefer* 64 (1992–93), pp. 1431–32; see also Fenton's study on Ibn al-Māshiṭa mentioned in the previous note.

[55] Such is, for instance, Sa'adya's commentary on Job; see L. E. Goodman, *The Book of Theodicy: Translation and Commentary on the Book of Job by Saadiah ben Joseph Al-Fayyumi* (New Haven and London, 1988).

[56] S. Stroumsa, *Dāwūd ibn Marwān al-Muqammiṣ's Twenty Chapters* (Leiden, 1989). On possible fragments of his commentary on Genesis, see my remarks in 'Genesis fragment yields a surprise', *Genizah Fragments* 15 (1988), p. 3, and S. Stroumsa, 'The impact of Syriac tradition on early Judaeo-Arabic Bible Exegesis', *Aram* 3 (1991), pp. 83–96.

[57] See above, nn. 21–23.

Pentateuch that he chose to interpret. Zucker's edition of Sa'adya's commentary on the first half of Genesis[58] is virtually a jigsaw puzzle of fragments, whose identification is not always certain. Sa'adya's 'Commentary on the Ten Songs', which is actually an appendix to his commentary on Exodus 15, and is attested in geonic literature and in several Genizah fragments, has already turned out to contain important theological elements, such as the earliest list of articles of faith.[59] The present discussion is not an exhaustive list; several more cases that are already known could have been mentioned, while others are still hidden in uncatalogued manuscripts and may surface later.

Another case in point is that of Sa'adya's younger North African contemporary, Dunash b. Tamim. He was active in Qayrawān, the capital of the province Ifrīqiya (present-day Tunisia), towards the middle of the tenth century, where he was a disciple of Isaac Israeli, one of the earliest Jewish medieval philosophers, and there composed his commentary on *Sefer Yeṣirah*, in response to Sa'adya's commentary on the same work.[60] Dunash wrote his commentary, one of the earliest representatives of Jewish medieval Neoplatonism, in Judaeo-Arabic, but for centuries the original Judaeo-Arabic text remained lost, and the work was known only in a medieval Hebrew version that was in many places incomprehensible or corrupt. Grossberg's ostensibly critical edition[61] did very little to improve the condition of the text. Goldziher, who also (or, shall we say, even?) tried his hand at Genizah studies, identified in the Kaufmann collection in Budapest two short fragments of the Judaeo-Arabic text.[62] When G. Vajda started his studies of this text, he was still confronted by the difficulties of the Hebrew version.[63] Later, he discovered large and important sections of the original text in Genizah collections. Thanks to these fragments, the text has come to occupy the place it deserves in the history of medieval Jewish religious thought.[64] The situation has recently changed again, since most of the Judaeo-Arabic text is now available, thanks to Fenton's identification of an early manuscript in St. Petersburg.[65]

---

[58] M. Zucker, *Saadya's Commentary on Genesis* (Hebrew; New York, 1984).

[59] See my 'Saadya Gaon's Ten Articles of Faith', *Da'at* 37 (1996), pp. 11–26.

[60] See Ben-Sasson, *Qayrawan* (see n. 10 above), pp. 252–53.

[61] London, 1902.

[62] I. Goldziher, 'Fragment de l'original arabe du commentaire sur le S. Yeçirah par Isak Israéli' (*Mélanges Judéo-Arabes* 28), *REJ* 52 (1906), pp. 187–90.

[63] G. Vajda, 'Quelques notes sur le commentaire kairouanais du Sefer Yesîra', *REJ* 105 (1940), pp. 132–40; 107 (1946–47), pp. 99–156; 110 (1949–50), pp. 67–92; 112 (1953), pp. 5–33.

[64] 'Nouveaux fragments arabes du commentaire de Dunash b. Tamim sur le "Livre de la Création"', *REJ* 113 (1954), pp. 37–61; 119 (1961), pp. 159–61; 122 (1963), pp. 149–62.

[65] P. Fenton, 'New Fragments from the Arabic Original of Dunash b. Tamim's Commentary to *Sefer Yezira*', *Alei Sefer* 15 (1988–89), pp. 45–55.

A central figure in the intellectual history of the Geonic period is Samuel ben Ḥofni. Once A. E. Harkavy published his short monograph on him,[66] it became clear that the history of Samuel ben Ḥofni's career and the contents of his literary legacy would have to be recovered and reconstructed from Genizah-type fragments. This was further confirmed by Jacob Mann's studies, and has now been very convincingly presented, with ample documentation, in the recent and most comprehensive monograph by David Sklare,[67] which is based largely on Genizah-type material. Relevant for the present discussion are fragments of his theological monographs and compendia, as well as fragments of his commentaries on sections of the Pentateuch. The former are especially important because this is the only case known to date of a Rabbanite scholar who closely followed a specific school of the Islamic theological system known as Kalam, namely the Basran school as it developed during the second half of the tenth century. His doctrinal views are known from a number of works of which only fragments have survived, among them a theological compendium, entitled *Kitāb al-Hidāya* (*The Book of Guidance*). Nevertheless, these fragments suffice for understanding the structure and important details of his system. They also indicate the depth of his influence on contemporary and subsequent Karaite theologians who followed the same theological principles.[68]

In sum, the impact of Genizah-type manuscripts may seem less revolutionary for the study of medieval Jewish religious thought than for the study of history. This difference results, in part at least, from the characteristics of the material, or more broadly stated from the difference between the documentary and the literary Genizah. The range of the latter is much vaster, and the process of piecing together fragments that to all appearances seem to be unrelated, is much slower. The corpus of medieval Jewish literature in general, and the Judaeo-Arabic section of it in particular, is constantly building up, and this is indeed due in no small measure to the Genizah. The opening up of Russian libraries, with their rich collections of Jewish manuscripts, to unrestricted research adds new assignments and challenges of impressive dimensions, and underlines the fact that the corpus of Jewish literature is far from being closed. It may fairly be expected that our knowledge of the several fields and trends in medieval Jewish religious thought that Genizah-type materials have already highlighted and brought to the forefront of scholarship, will be enriched and augmented by many more surprises.

---

[66] *Leben und Werke des Samuel Ibn-Chofni* (*Studien und Mittheilungen* 3; Hebrew; St. Petersburg and Leipzig, 1880).

[67] D. E. Sklare, *Samuel ben Hofni Gaon and his Cultural World* (Leiden – New York – Köln, 1996), accompanied by many texts, in the original and in translation.

[68] See my survey 'Kalam in Jewish Philosophy', in D. H. Frank and O. Leaman (eds), *The History of Jewish Philosophy*, (London–New York, 1997), pp. 115–48; D. E. Sklare, 'Yūsuf al-Baṣīr: theological aspects of his halakhic works', in D. H. Frank (ed.), *The Jews of Medieval Islam* (Leiden – New York – Köln, 1995), pp. 249–70.

8

Jewish-Muslim Relations in the Medieval Mediterranean Area

PAUL B. FENTON

There is practically no area of Jewish studies that has not been fundamentally revolutionized and enriched by the discovery of the Genizah. The diligent investigation of its withered contents has brought to life voices from the distant past, bearing messages often of relevance to our modern times. One such area on which new light has been shed is that of interfaith relations in the Middle Ages, a subject of increasing significance in our own pluralistic society. Although Genizah documents reflect what are mainly internal Jewish concerns, they nevertheless have much to contribute to our understanding of the relationship between Jew and Muslim in the society of medieval Egypt and other Middle Eastern countries. Their study has in this respect yielded a host of information in the economic, social, intellectual and religious contexts.

A great deal of knowledge about interfaith relations in the economic and social spheres has become available thanks principally to the monumental efforts deployed by the late S. D. Goitein, whose *magnum opus, A Mediterranean Society*,[1] has unravelled the complicated mysteries concealed in the Genizah documents. Importantly, these remarkable texts inform us that the unfortunate principles of seclusion and discrimination inculcated by religious bigotry were often countered by the kind of economic and social realities that nurtured more tolerant attitudes. Unlike their brethren of medieval Europe who were mainly confined to a few unproductive occupations, the Jews of Egypt enjoyed freedom in the choice both of their residence and – with the exception of certain government services – their craft. Thus, since there was no exclusively Jewish quarter in Old Cairo, Jews had neighbours and even tenants who were Muslims. Interestingly, a letter from Minyat Zifta tells of a house jointly owned by a Muslim *qāḍī*, or judge, and the son of a rabbi.[2] On the economic front, the Egyptian Jews were represented in almost every profession, including agriculture, although they were especially active in textiles and dyeing. Since business tended to be international, the Jews of Arab lands played a vital role in the world-wide trade of the Muslim empire during its commercial heyday. Their widespread contacts and their knowledge of languages made them indispensable links in overseas business, and they were particularly prominent in the India trade-route.

---

[1] *A Mediterranean Society: the Jewish Communities of the Arab World as Portrayed in the Documents of the Cairo Geniza*, 6 vols including the index volume prepared with the assistance of Paula Sanders (Berkeley, Los Angeles, London, 1969–93).

[2] T-S 8.4; Goitein, *A Mediterranean Society* (see n. 1 above), vol. 2, p. 292.

Though in principle excluded from government office, there were Jews, as has been surprisingly revealed in the Genizah, who were employed by the strictly orthodox Ayyubid administration to a larger degree than by the more 'liberal', sectarian Fatimids.

While there was a general preference to keep business dealings within the religious groups, transactions were often entrusted by Jews to Muslims and vice-versa.[3] Partnership constituted the most common form of investment in those days, and Genizah letters mentioning Jewish-Muslim partnerships indicate that the business world knew no social or religious boundaries.[4] Indeed, the great philosopher and jurist, Moses Maimonides (1138-1204) declared legal an arrangement described in a query, according to which a business jointly owned by Jews and Muslims remained open on the sabbath. Profits made on Friday accrued to the Jews while those made on Saturday went to their Muslim colleagues.[5] Commercial correspondence widely refers to Muslim partners and conveyers. There is even an instance of a Jew sending an Arabic letter written in Hebrew characters to a Muslim associate, presumably to be read to him by another Jewish acquaintance.[6] It was not uncommon for Muslims to provide capital for Jewish enterprises.[7] When the Jew Abū l-Faraj ibn al-Kallam died in 1182, monies were returned from his estate to his Muslim creditors, the *qāḍī* Ibn Sanā' al-Mulk and the jurisconsult, Ibn Sawla.[8]

Documents show that dealings with Muslims were enacted with a deep sense of ethical responsibility and co-operation. Moreover, in his code of Jewish law, the *Mishneh Torah*, Maimonides strictly condemns double standards of business ethics when dealing with members of other faiths.[9] If legal corners were cut, it was sometimes with the assistance of Muslim associates. One rather amusing form of co-operation was the dispatching of Jewish goods with Muslim agents so as to avoid paying the double rate of custom duties imposed on Jews as a discriminatory measure. Thus, the writer of a letter from Alexandria advises his brother, trading with India, to confide his merchandise to Muslims in order to save the oppressive taxes.[10]

Such supplementary taxes were indeed part of the harsh measures enforced by Islam on *dhimmis*, – members of the 'protected' religious minorities. Such measures included, amongst other things, the wearing of distinctive clothing and the prohibition to build or renovate their places of worship. It would appear from certain Genizah

---

[3] In one single instance, T-S 20.180, a Jewish merchant from Qayrawan, makes mention of four different consignments of his being conveyed by Muslims; Goitein, *A Mediterranean Society* (see n. 1 above), vol. 2, p. 295.
[4] Goitein, *A Mediterranean Society* (see n. 1 above), vol. 2, pp. 294–95.
[5] Maimonides, *R. Moses b. Maimon Responsa*, ed. J. Blau (4 vols; Jerusalem, 1957–86), no. 204, p. 360.
[6] T-S 8J18.33; Goitein, *A Mediterranean Society* (see n. 1 above), vol. 2, p. 294.
[7] Goitein, *A Mediterranean Society* (see n. 1 above), vol. 2, pp. 294–95.
[8] Goitein, *A Mediterranean Society* (see n. 1 above), vol. 5, pp. 444–47.
[9] *Mishneh Torah* XII, *Hilkhot Mekhirah*, 18.1.
[10] T-S 13J.28.15; Goitein, *A Mediterranean Society* (see n. 1 above), vol. 2, p. 295.

documents that constant efforts were deployed, mainly in the form of bribes, to circumvent these measures. Thus, Jews did not always wear a specific attire and this obligation was periodically renewed, for instance at the time of the fanatical Fatimid caliph al-Ḥakim who reigned from 996 to 1021.[11] When a Muslim judge declared illicit the construction of a new synagogue in eleventh-century Hebron, the problem was solved when the edifice, now deftly described not as a synagogue but as a 'home', was erected on land bought from the selfsame judge.[12]

As a minority, even less numerous than the Christians, Jews were especially vulnerable to exploitation and even assault, particularly in times of general hardship. According to the principles of the *dhimmah*, Jews were required to be subservient. Public display of their faith, such as funeral processions, was invariably harassed by the Muslim population. On one occasion in 1101, a great multitude of Jews had assembled to render the last honour to a popular cantor. On the way to the cemetery, the cortège was attacked and abused by a Muslim mob. Twenty-three of the more prominent members of the community were arrested amid the jeers of fanatical crowds, hauled off to prison and condemned to death.[13] Genizah documents attest that such molestation also took place in Jerusalem and Ramla.[14] There is even an instance of Jewish ritual slaughter being prohibited in Old Cairo.[15] The Genizah documents often echo the hostility to which Jews were subjected on the part of the Muslim population. The Genizah writers even employ a special Hebrew word designating hostility directed specifically against Jews by Muslims, namely, *sin'ūt*, 'hatred'. Though not apparently a ubiquitous phenomenon, outbursts of *sin'ūt* were especially frequent in Alexandria, where the situation of the Jews, subjected to false accusations, was particularly precarious.[16] Nowhere is this oppression more poignantly expressed than in connection with the poll-tax imposed upon non-Muslims, the annual payment of which constituted a toilsome burden for the poorer classes. Some, relentlessly pursued by Muslim tax-collectors, were thrown into prison, where, if unransomed, they were sometimes induced by the threat of execution to convert to Islam.

Apostasy was otherwise a relatively rare occurrence, principally motivated by duress or, in the exceptional case of certain dignitaries, a matter of pragmatic expedience. Apostates to Islam periodically appear in litigations about inheritance.[17] Abraham Maimonides discusses the case of a converted couple who sought to have

---

[11] S. A. Aldeeb Abu-Sahlieh, *L'Impact de la Religion sur l'Ordre Juridique: Cas de l'Egypte: Non-Musulmans en Pays d'Islam* (Fribourg, 1979), p. 104.

[12] T-S Arabic 18(2).4, published by S. Assaf, *Texts and Studies in Jewish History* (Jerusalem, 1946), pp. 46–48.

[13] J. Mann, *The Jews in Egypt and in Palestine under the Fatimid Caliphs* (2 vols; Oxford, 1920–22; New York², 1970), I, pp. 30–31.

[14] Goitein, *A Mediterranean Society* (see n. 1 above), vol. 2, p. 285.

[15] Goitein, *A Mediterranean Society* (see n. 1 above), vol. 2, p. 282.

[16] Goitein, *A Mediterranean Society* (see n. 1 above), vol. 2, p. 279.

[17] Goitein, *A Mediterranean Society* (see n. 1 above), vol. 2, p. 301.

their son circumcised according to Jewish custom.[18] On the other hand, the mention of converts to Judaism occurs far more frequently in the documents. These, however, originated mainly from Christian backgrounds, since a Muslim renegade was liable to the death penalty. Sporadic cases did nevertheless occur, as we learn from Maimonides's responsa to the pious Obadiah the Muslim proselyte, which also inform us that such converts were obliged to leave the country.[19]

In the area of social relations, contacts on a personal level, especially among the middle-class, were often quite intimate, despite official segregation. Documents report that Jews would visit Muslims on their holdays, and the converse no doubt was also the case.[20] An instance is recorded about a particularly ceremonious reading of the Esther scroll on the Jewish feast of Purim, which had also been attended by Muslims.[21] Purim was not the only occasion for partaking of wine. It is known that drinking parties were a common feature of social life and the Genizah has even preserved some ancient drinking songs.[22] Such gatherings did, of course, take place in the privacy of the home but, even then, they were not without risk. From a contemporary responsum by Maimonides, it may be assumed that such receptions were occasionally attended by Muslims.[23] One particularly revealing letter from early thirteenth-century Aden relates an incident which occurred at such a party, imprudently held by three Jewish notables at the time of the Muslim feast marking the end of Ramadan. A Muslim musician who had been present reported the event to the local *qāḍī*, whereupon the Jewish offenders were set upon, beaten up and subjected to a heavy fine.[24] Such drinking-parties, say the rabbis, lead to intermarriage.[25] While intermarriage of any kind is proscribed by Jewish law, Islam does permit the union of a Muslim and a Jewess. It is nevertheless surprising that not a single case of a mixed marriage is recorded in the Genizah archives, although it seems likely that there were individual occurrences, possibly under duress.

On other levels, too, amicable relations were maintained with Muslim friends. On occasion, formal letters by Jewish officials would convey regards to Muslim colleagues.[26] In one instance, the Palestinian Gaon, Elijah Ha-Kohen, induces a Jewish court physician to intervene with the Muslim governor on behalf of a Muslim

---

[18] *Abraham Maimuni Responsa*, eds A. Freimann and S. D. Goitein (Jerusalem, 1937), no. 53, pp. 54–55.

[19] Maimonides, *Responsa* (see n. 5 above), vol. 2, no. 293, pp. 548–50; no. 448, pp. 725–28.

[20] T-S 13J17.11, published by S. D. Goitein, *Tarbiz* 36 (1967), pp. 388–90.

[21] ENA 4020.6, published by J. Mann, *The Jews* (see n. 13 above), vol. 1, p. 150 and vol. 2, p. 172.

[22] D. Pagis, 'Wine Songs Preceding the Spanish Period', *Qoveṣ Meḥqarim* [*Dov Sadan Jubilee Volume*], eds S. Werses, N. Rotenstreich and Ch. Shmeruk (Hebrew; Jerusalem and Tel Aviv, 1977), pp. 245–55.

[23] Maimonides, *Responsa* (see n. 5 above), vol. 2, no. 269, pp. 515–16; Goitein, *A Mediterranean Society* (see n. 1 above), vol. 5, p. 40.

[24] Goitein, *A Mediterranean Society* (see n. 1 above), vol. 5, p. 40.

[25] BT, *'Avodah Zarah* 31b and the commentary of Rashi there.

[26] Kaufmann Collection VI; Goitein, *A Mediterranean Society* (see n. 1 above), vol. 2, p. 298.

acquaintance.[27] This kind of solidarity in higher circles was especially conspicuous among religious dignitaries and scholars. In the judicial realm, Muslim courts would sometimes refer cases to their Jewish counterparts, and vice-versa, when matters were considered to be of a denominational character. The responsa of Maimonides also record such cases.[28] In Alexandria we find the chief *qāḍī* informing his Jewish counterpart of an accusation leveled against him in government circles by members of the Jewish community.[29]

The early Ayyubid period witnessed an intellectual revival which perhaps favoured contacts between members of different faiths. A text, published by Franz Rosenthal, records that Ibn Sanā' (1155–1211), chief *qāḍī* of Egypt and a renowned poet who had eulogized Maimonides in a famous poem, and other Muslim intellectuals participated with Maimonides in a debate on the topic of speculative theology (*'ilm al-kalām*).[30] Through their professional contacts, jurists like Ibn Sanā' and Maimonides, as well as physicians such as Ibn Abī Ūṣaybī'a and Maimonides's son Abraham, who at times worked in the same hospital, evidently established personal relationships. Of special significance in this respect is another document dated 1182 showing Moses Maimonides, the *qāḍī* Ibn Sanā', the Jewish physician Ibn Jumay' and other Muslim and Jewish intellectuals jointly involved in a business transaction, and therefore seeming to suggest that they enjoyed close relations.[31]

While religious pursuits were limited to members of the same faith, the medical profession and scientific studies were inter-denominational, though confined to restricted circles. Jewish doctors held appointments and were regularly called upon to do their rounds at Muslim hospitals. In a letter to a disciple in 1235, Abraham Maimonides apologizes for his absence from his correspondent's wedding, his having been on duty that day at the Bimaristan, the government hospital.[32] It is recorded that Jewish physicians, such as Nethanel b. Moses, could gain personal access to eminent Muslim men of power or courtiers who employed them.

Intellectual pursuits also blurred denominational barriers. Unlike the Arabic-speaking Jews of later centuries who were confined to limited habitats and

---

[27] T-S 13J14.5, published by Mann, *The Jews* (see n. 13 above), vol. 1, pp. 84–85 and vol. 2, p. 83.

[28] Maimonides, *Responsa* (see n. 5 above), vol. 1, no. 90, p. 145 (two sisters refer a sale of property to a Muslim judge); vol. 2, no. 191, pp. 347–48 and no. 211, pp. 373–75 (cases judged by a *qāḍī* referred to Maimonides); vol. 2, no. 196, pp. 352–54 (a mother requests a *qāḍī* to pressure a Jewish court into giving a decision).

[29] T-S 16.272; Goitein, *A Mediterranean Society* (see n. 1 above), vol. 2, p. 298.

[30] F. Rosenthal, 'Maimonides and a Discussion of Muslim Speculative Theology' in *Jewish Tradition in the Diaspora: Studies in Memory of Professor Walter J. Fischel*, ed. M. M. Caspi (Berkeley, 1981), pp. 109–12.

[31] S. D. Goitein, 'The Moses Maimonides – Ibn Sana' al-Mulk Circle', in *Studies in Islamic History and Civilization in Honour of Professor David Ayalon*, ed. M. Sharon (Jerusalem and Leiden, 1986), pp. 399–405. See also Goitein, *A Mediterranean Society* (see n. 1 above), vol. 5, p. 477.

[32] T-S 10J14.5, published by S. D. Goitein, 'Documents on Abraham Maimonides and his Pietist Circle', *Tarbiz* 33 (1963–64), pp. 192–95.

occupations as well as to their Hebrew religious culture, the Jews of Fatimid Egypt knew neither geographical nor intellectual ghettos. Numerous children's exercises scattered throughout the Genizah demonstrate that from early youth school-children simultaneously learnt the Hebrew and Arabic scripts and that the better-educated amongst their elders were acquainted with the scientific and literary accomplishments of their Muslim environment. The book-lists and catalogues, of which a fair number have survived in the Cairo trove, bear witness to the intellectual interests of their Jewish owners and buyers. Besides books on Muslim theology and philosophy, *belles-lettres* and even magic, medical works also figure conspicuously. This comes as no surprise, considering that Jews were very prominent in the medical profession, and their services were eagerly sought by Muslim patients. An oft-quoted statement by a Muslim visitor to Egypt in the mid-thirteenth century tells us that most of the prominent Christians and Jews of that country were either government officials or doctors.[33] The historian of Arabic medicine, Ibn Abī Ūṣaybī'a, tells us that Ephraim ibn Zaffān, a medical celebrity but also a prodigious bibliophile, sold about ten thousand volumes of his library to al-Malik al-Afḍal, viceroy of Egypt (1096-1121).[34] Letters from businessmen, who were often men of considerable learning, also evince keen interest in Arabic literature. That this interest was widespread is, moreover, borne out by the Genizah's rich variety of manuscript remnants of religious and secular Muslim literature, written both in Arabic and in Hebrew characters. These fragments, coupled with the above-mentioned book-lists, allow the partial reconstruction of their owners' libraries and intellectual options.

Among the books to be found in one such library belonging to a doctor was a fundamental text of Neoplatonic thought, the so-called *Theology of Aristotle*.[35] This work, which is, in reality, an Arabic paraphrase of Plotinus's *Enneads*, was one of the bedside books of the Isma'īlī doctrine. Copies of it have been discovered in the Genizah, copied and annotated in Hebrew characters. It must be recalled that the Isma'īlī dynasty of the Fatimids showed a more tolerant attitude to their non-Muslim subjects and even manifested concern about their educational and administrative system. Not only did they afford a financial allowance to the talmudical academy in Fustat[36] but they also endowed the Egyptian Jewish community with an institutional framework by creating the office of *nagid*, 'Head of the Jews'.[37] No wonder then that the Genizah has yielded other Shi'ite texts, such as an extensive fragment in Hebrew

---

[33] Ibn Sa'īd al-Maghribī, cited in Maqrizī's *Khiṭaṭ* (ed. Būlāq; Cairo, 1853), vol. 1, p. 367. See also S. D. Goitein, 'The Medical Profession in the Light of the Cairo Geniza Documents', *HUCA* 34 (1963), pp. 177–94 and *A Mediterranean Society* (see n. 1 above), vol. 2, pp. 240–61.

[34] M. Meyerhof, 'Medieval Jewish Physicians in the Near East', *Isis* 28 (1938), pp. 442–43.

[35] D. H. Baneth, 'A Doctor's Library in Egypt at the time of Maimonides', *Tarbiz* 30 (1960–61), pp. 176–78.

[36] See Goitein, *A Mediterranean Society* (see n. 1 above), vol. 2, p. 202.

[37] See S. D. Goitein, 'The Title and Office of the Nagid: a Re-examination', *JQR* 53 (1962–63), pp. 93–119.

characters of the caliph ʻAli's ethical will to his son Ḥusayn, as well as an Arabic letter of an Ismaʻīlī missionary to a chief *qāḍī*.[38]

The most remarkable testimony to the deep interest Jews took in the religious beliefs of their Muslim neighbours is, however, the presence in the Genizah of Islamic mystical and pietistic texts. These manuscripts were not just an indication of intellectual curiosity. They were studied in earnest by the members of a circle of Jewish pietists who practised a sort of Judaic mysticism akin to Islamic Sufism, which by that time had struck firm roots in Egyptian soil, in the form of organized brotherhoods.[39] The Jewish pietists recognized a spiritual model in Sufism, some of whose practices, they claimed, had originated in Jewish sources. That this trend was no marginal phenomenon in the Egyptian-Jewish community is attested by the status of its leaders, some of whom came from the family of Maimonides. Foremost among them was his son Abraham (1186–1237), who officiated as *nagid*. It seems that he endeavoured to revitalize the Judaism of his time by adopting certain Sufi customs. Thus, for instance, he sought to re-introduce the custom of kneeling and bowing in Jewish worship, in imitation of Muslim practice. Paradoxically, a further expression of the congenial relations between Jews and Muslims is to be found in a letter sent by the Jewish community to the Muslim authorities after the *nagid*'s death. It enquires about the lawfulness of these practices, which, their opponents claimed, were contrary to Jewish custom. The Muslim rulers, members of the conservative Sunni Ayyubid dynasty, saw themselves not only as defenders of the Islamic faith but also as being responsible for the ritual orthodoxy of the religions under their protection. The letter, which is one of the most curious documents ever to come to light in the Genizah, in effect asks the Muslim authorities to intervene and to adjudicate a specifically Jewish dispute. The enquirer emphasizes that prostration – the disputed issue – constitutes the revival of an ancient practice, his assumption being that the Ayyubid jurisconsult would find these liturgical innovations lawful:

> In the name of God, the merciful and compassionate.
>
> What do our lords, the jurisconsults, the *imāms*, *imāms* of the faith and paragons of the Muslims, may God grant them success for their obedience and assist them to gain His satisfaction, say concerning the following: A group of Jews whose word is authoritative, namely the head of the Jews and those of their sages who are his followers, have established the practice of genuflection and prostration in their worship. They have stated that this was an ancient practice and that they have revived an aspect of their religion which had fallen into disuse. They established and practiced it over a protracted period of approximately twenty years. When the head (of the Jews) passed away, an individual who was not a scholar arose and spoke against the earlier (opinion) of their sages in disapproval of genuflection and prostration. What action should be taken with

[38] S. M. Stern, *Studies in Early Ismāʻīlism* (Jerusalem and Leiden, 1983), pp. 243–45. See Goitein, *A Mediterranean Society* (see n. 1 above), vol. 5, p. 399.

[39] On the Jewish pietist movement, see P. Fenton, *Treatise of the Pool*: *Al-Maqāla al-Hawdiyya* (London², 1995).

> regard to him on account of his opposition, if he opposes (the practice)? Grant us your opinion, may God have mercy upon you.[40]

Apparently, relations between communal leaders in both camps extended into the mystical domain. Indeed, a few generations later, in the fifteenth century, a letter addressed by a woman to the last scion of the Maimonidean dynasty, David II ben Joshua (who died about 1415), implores the *nagid* to intervene on her behalf with the sheikh Muḥammad al-Kurānī, the spiritual leader of a Sufi order, in order to retrieve her husband, who was threatening to abduct his children and go and live in a dervish monastery in the Muqattam hills above Cairo. Supposedly, the Jewish *nagid*, who himself had mystical leanings, was on friendly terms with the Sufi sheikh.[41]

This is yet another instance of how these remnants, long embalmed in the ancient pages of the Genizah, bear witness to the dynamic interaction between the Jewish and Muslim communities of medieval Cairo, on both the material and the spiritual planes. They resonate from the depths of the past with a message that beckons to the peoples of the present to rebuild a new Mediterraean society based on mutual respect and friendship.

---

[40] T–S AS 182.291. The text was published by G. Khan, *Arabic Legal and Administrative Documents in the Cairo Genizah Collections* (Cambridge, 1993), pp. 293–94.

[41] See S. D. Goitein, 'A Jewish Addict to Sufism in the Time of the Nagid David II Maimonides', *JQR* 44 (1953–54), pp. 37–49.

9

On Marital Age, Violence and Mutuality in the Genizah Documents

MORDECHAI A. FRIEDMAN

During the first half-century of Genizah research, scholars showed little interest in the socio-economic conditions of the middle and lower middle classes represented in the papers from the so-called classical Genizah period, covering the tenth to thirteenth centuries, and preferred to devote their efforts to publishing important literary works and select documents that illuminated significant historical events as well as the lives and works of famous people. This state of affairs was reversed by the late S. D. Goitein's researches, published in several volumes and hundreds of articles, the apex of which is his magisterial *A Mediterranean Society*. Its third volume, which appeared in 1978, is devoted to the family. It is divided into four main sections: the extended family, marriage, the nuclear family and the world of women. This seminal study is invaluable not only for research on the Jewish family in medieval Islam but also for understanding, more generally, socio-economic conditions in the Islamic world and in the Mediterranean basin.[1] For the foreseeable future it will remain definitive as the comprehensive work on the family as reflected in the Genizah documents. Subsequent studies will, essentially, elaborate, complement and refine specific issues already discussed by Goitein. The abundant, multifaceted materials presented and interpreted in the third volume of *A Mediterranean Society* do not lend themselves even to a brief summary in this limited context. I therefore consider here only three distinct topics, two of which have been the subject of some debate in recent scholarly literature.

The age of the bride and groom at marriage, especially that of the bride, is a decisive factor in their relationship and the course it takes throughout their married life, and it is only to be expected that the Genizah documents would shed light on this issue. I believe that the first publication to consider the question was a preliminary study of mine that appeared twenty-five years ago.[2] A few years later, Goitein discussed the age at marriage in *A Mediterranean Society*.[3] Most recently, Abraham Grossman of the Hebrew University has reassessed the relevant material and revised Goitein's conclusions.[4] Given the

---

[1] See M. A. Friedman, Review of S. D. Goitein, *A Mediterranean Society (= Med. Soc.)* III (Berkeley, Los Angeles, London, 1978) in *JAOS* 100 (1980), pp. 128–31.

[2] M. A. Friedman, 'The Ethics of Medieval Jewish Marriage' in *Religion in a Religious Age*, ed. S. D. Goitein (Cambridge, Mass., 1974), pp. 86–87, 98–99.

[3] Goitein, *Med. Soc.* III (see n. 1 above), pp. 76–79, 442–43.

[4] A. Grossman, 'Child Marriage in Jewish Society in the Middle Ages until the Thirteenth Century', *Pe'amim* 45 (1990), pp. 108–25.

importance of this matter for understanding the status of women and the marriage institution, I would like to open the question for further discussion.

In order to place the phenomenon, as it occurred in the Jewish society of medieval Islamic lands, in a broader perspective, the situation in talmudic Judaism must first be briefly highlighted. For the talmudic sages, the age of the bride and groom at marriage was a matter of legal, social and moral consequence but, as in other areas, the sages did not always speak with one voice. A minor might not contract a marriage. For purposes of marriage, a boy remained a minor until he reached puberty or, as usually assumed, the age of thirteen. In theory, neither he nor his father could contract a marriage for him before that age. Afterwards, he was legally independent, and his father's role was limited to serving as his agent in formalizing the betrothal, and then only if he was appointed by the son to serve in such capacity. The adage 'the eighteen year old goes to the marriage chamber' (שמונה עשרה לחופה) is a late addition to tractate *Avot* (5.21) that seems to have had no influence on talmudic society.[5] Some sages encouraged their students to marry in their teens so that they could devote themselves to their studies without the disturbance of sexual fantasies; others advised their students to finish their studies before taking on the financial burden of a wife and family. In practice, the predominant age seems to have been closer to twenty or thereabouts.[6]

The legal situation concerning girls was somewhat more complicated. On reaching her majority, six months after the first signs of puberty or, as usually defined, the age of twelve and a half,[7] she too was considered to be completely independent for marital purposes, and her father could contract a betrothal for her only if she appointed him to serve as her agent. Before that age, she was theoretically in his sole jurisdiction, and were he to give her in marriage, the act was binding, whether or not she consented. At least as of the early third century, betrothing one's minor daughter was distinctly discouraged, and Rav declared: 'One is forbidden to betroth his minor daughter, but must wait until she matures and says, "I want to marry so and so." ' All agreed that were a father to ignore this teaching, the betrothal had full validity, and later authorities debated whether 'one is forbidden' was intended to have the full force of a prohibition or denoted only undesirable behaviour.[8]

A minor girl, orphaned from her father, could be married off by her mother, brother or other close relative. Although one who married such a child bride was permitted to engage

---

[5] On this as an addition to the Mishnah, see Y. D. Gilat, *Studies in the Development of the Halakha* (Hebrew; Ramat Gan, 1992), pp. 19–20.

[6] See A. Schremer, 'Men's Age at Marriage in Jewish Palestine of the Hellenistic and Roman Periods', *Zion* 61 (1996), pp. 45–66, and his ' "Eighteen years to the *Ḥuppah*"? The Marriage Age of Jews in Eretz Israel in the Second Temple, Mishna and Talmud periods' in *Sexuality and the Family in History*, eds I. Bartal and I. Gafni (Hebrew; Jerusalem, 1998), pp. 43–70.

[7] See the (incomplete) sources and literature cited in M. A. Friedman, *Jewish Marriage in Palestine: A Cairo Geniza Study* I–II (=*JMP*) (Tel Aviv and New York, 1980–81), I, p. 217, n. 3.

[8] BT, *Qiddushin* 41a, 81b. See Friedman, 'Ethics' (see n. 2 above), pp. 86, 99; see also Friedman, *JMP* (see n. 7 above), I, pp. 216, 222. According to Judah b. Qalonymos, *Yiḥuse Tanna'im Va-Amora'im*, ed. J. L. Maimon (Jerusalem, 1963), p. 216, if one's minor daughter desires sex, her father may marry her off.

in sex with her, the marriage was only provisional. It was considered permanent only after she reached majority and expressed no objection (*me'un*) to the arrangement. Were she to express her disapproval, the marriage would be annulled retroactively, and no bill of divorce was required. Some sages discouraged the use of such annulments, presumably because they rendered the previous sexual relationship tantamount to fornication, which in fact it was (as verbalized by R. Eliezer in M. *Yevamot* 13.2: 'the [sexual] act of a minor girl is just as if she were seduced'). In a relatively late talmudic passage, the authority of the orphan girl's relatives to marry her off is explained as the result of a rabbinic enactment intended to protect her from being taken advantage of sexually by strangers.[9] From our current point of view, marrying off a minor daughter or sister to a paedophile hardly seems an effective way to protect her from sexual abuse.

In general, the sages discouraged marriages where there was a significant age difference between the bride and groom, arguing that they would end in marital strife. Marrying off one's young daughter to an old man was regarded as equivalent to making her a prostitute, on the assumption that she would turn to others for sexual satisfaction.[10]

As to the Genizah material, I adduced, in my preliminary study, direct and indirect evidence that the marriage of child brides was not prevalent, and referred to the three Genizah fragments relevant to that practice with which I was then familiar. In a subsection of his book on the family entitled 'child marriage', Goitein cited two of these and adduced six additional manuscripts, as well as two responsa by Maimonides. At the beginning of his discussion he wrote: 'The Geniza records reveal that child marriages, although quite exceptional, did occur.' And he concluded: 'It was an insignificant social phenomenon, but I have treated it at some length because it is indicative of the near absolute paternal authority, that was equally operative with regard to the mature virgin who was legally independent.'[11]

---

[9] On the marriage of the minor orphan girl and the annulment, see Y. Dinari, 'The History of *Meyyun* [!]', *Diné Israel* 10–11 (1981–83), pp. 319–45. The assessment of 'relatively late' is dependent on an anonymous passage in BT, *Yevamot* 112b, שלא ינהגו בה (מנהג) הפקר, 'so that people do not treat her as if she were free for the taking' (see *The Babylonian Talmud with Variant Readings... Yebamoth*, ed. A. Liss, I–IV (Jerusalem 1983–96), IV, p. 245), that uses the same terminology as Bet Shammai in M. *Yevamot* 13.1, אין בנות ישראל הפקר, 'the daughters of Israel are not free for the taking', and is perhaps an extension of it. The latter phrase, as explained in BT, *Yevamot* 107 by Rabba and R. Joseph and in PT, *Yevamot* 13.1 (13b), means that marital sex with an orphaned minor was considered – retroactively, after the annulment – tantamount to fornication. On R. Eliezer's dictum, see Z. Falk, *Mavo Le-Dine Yisra'el Bime Ha-Bayit Ha-Sheni* (Tel Aviv, 1971), p. 267.

[10] See BT, *Sanhedrin* 76a and Rashi. We might argue that giving her in such a marriage was in itself commensurate with selling her for prostitution but it is doubtful whether this was the intention. See S. Lieberman, *Tosefta Ki-Fshuṭah* 8 (New York, 1973), p. 915. Age difference at marriage is also discouraged as something that may lead to domestic strife in *Sifre on Deuteronomy*, ed. L. Finkelstein (New York, 1969), §290, p. 309.

[11] Goitein, *Med. Soc.* III (see n. 1 above), pp. 76, 79.

Goitein's conclusion that this was an insignificant social phenomenon is based, notes Grossman, on an argument from silence (*a silentio*).[12] Grossman adds to the discussion by adducing and discussing several sources outside the Genizah, mainly from the responsa literature, emanating from Jewish communities in Islamic countries (our concern here), and in Ashkenazi circles, and in doing so he has certainly made a noteworthy contribution. In his opinion, marriage of child brides, whether minors or young teenagers, who were physically and intellectually immature, was rather frequent, and he discusses its negative ramifications.

What number of Genizah documents concerning a specific socio-economic phenomenon represents a widespread practice rather than exceptions to the rule is a valid question for which there is no simple answer. The evidence for each case must be carefully analysed and considered on its merits. Furthermore, on the question of child brides as reflected in the Genizah documents, additional manuscripts are relevant to our discussion. Let us briefly review the material.

Four of the documents involve engagements or match agreements (or betrothals), one from Damascus in 933 CE, one from Fustat, that is, Old Cairo, from about the second quarter of the eleventh century, and two from the Egyptian town of Bilbays, from the early thirteenth century. One was explicitly contracted by the girl's father, one, a fragment, implicitly so, and two involved orphans. In the documents from Fustat and Bilbays, it was agreed that the wedding itself would be delayed for several years – three, five and seven years respectively – until the girl matured. The fragmentary eleventh-century document specifies that the marriage arrangement would be concluded only if the girl, upon reaching her majority, consented to the match arranged by her father. The waiting period before performing the wedding of a minor orphan girl is not specified in a betrothal contract registered in the court book of the Babylonian Jewish community of Damascus in 933.[13]

---

[12] Grossman, 'Child Marriage' (see n. 4 above), pp. 108–9, where it is suggested that the conclusions in my preliminary study are also based on an argument from silence. To be more precise, in both cases the argument is based not only on the paucity of documents that mention child brides but also on the fact that such information is absent from innumerable documents where it would have been relevant. Furthermore, in my preliminary study, I adduced evidence that the bride was usually of legal age.

[13] (1) ENA NS 1.89a (L146a) (Cairo, wedding delayed for 7 years); see Goitein, *Med. Soc.* III (see n. 1 above), pp. 78, 443, n. 33. The act that took place between the parties is described (l. 2) by the verb *amlakū*, which probably denotes here 'engaged' (*shiddᵉkhū*) but could mean 'betrothed' (*ērᵉsū*); for the ambiguity, see M. A. Friedman, 'Matchmaking and Betrothal Agreements in the Cairo Geniza' (Hebrew), *Proceedings of the Seventh World Congress of Jewish Studies: Studies in the Talmud, Halacha and Midrash* (Jerusalem, 1981), p. 158; M. A. Friedman, *Jewish Polygyny in the Middle Ages: New Documents from the Cairo Geniza* (Hebrew; Jerusalem, 1986), pp. 232–33, and the sources and literature cited there (note that *mumlaka* is also used by Sa'adya and by Qirqisani for 'a betrothed woman'). In l. 12, I read אבוהא, 'her father', rather than אכוהא, 'her brother', obviously Goitein's reading. The fragment mentions the date 13[.]7 Sel. (either the date of writing or the date of the marriage), and since it is in the handwriting of the Fustat scribe Japheth b. David, from whom dated documents between 1020 and 1057 have been preserved, this is equivalent to 1025/6, 1035/6, 1045/6 or 1055/6 CE.

(In the centuries following the classical Genizah period, Egyptian Jews did not always postpone marriage until the bride reached her majority. A late, fragmentary engagement contract contains a clause, known from sixteenth-century literary sources, that anticipates the bride's marriage before she reaches childbearing age.)[14]

In an early thirteenth-century letter to the judge Elijah [b. Zachariah], an Alexandrian writes about the problems he has encountered in marrying the daughter of Bū Zikrī b. Nethanel 'the great prince' (that is, the holder of a government office) b. Hillel. Though the bride was still a minor when engaged, her mother promised the writer that he could marry the girl a month later, presumably when she would have reached her majority. But at the public betrothal ceremony, Bū Zikrī declared: 'not less that one year'. The writer requests the judge's intervention and quotes the talmudic ruling (BT, *Ketubbot* 57b): 'A match agreement may not be made to marry a minor girl when she is still a minor, but it may be made to marry her after she reaches her majority.'[15]

A bizarre story involving an abuse of paternal authority is described in a court record from Alexandria, dated 1042. After the death of his daughter and a dispute with his son-in-law over ownership of the dowry, a bereaved father contracted a betrothal between the young man and another daughter, seven-year-old Sitt al-Dār ('Lady of the House'), and the

---

(2) T-S 8.112 (Bilbays; wedding delayed for 5 years); see Friedman, 'Ethics' (see n. 2 above), pp. 87, 99, n. 27; Goitein, *Med. Soc.* III, pp. 78, 443, n. 32. This is an engagement deed, the bride 'not yet of age, a minor in her father's jurisdiction', wedding postponed 5 years. *Verso* is a page from a copy of Genesis (41:8–12). For a description of this page, see M. C. Davis, *Hebrew Bible Manuscripts in the Cambridge Genizah Collections* I (Cambridge, 1978), p. 311, where lines 3–6a of *recto* are also quoted (correct there והשוע for והושע). This page allows us to place the document in Bilbays, early thirteenth century, since other pages of this copy of Genesis are written on the reverse sides of documents from there: ENA NS 13.34 (1208 CE); CUL Add. 3339ab (1217/1219).

(3) T-S 8J9.13 (Bilbays, 1218; wedding delayed for 3 years); see Goitein, *Med. Soc.* III, pp. 77, 442, n. 29. An engagement of an orphan, 9 years old.

(4) T-S AS 146.66 (Damascus, 933); part A, ed. Friedman, *JMP* (see n. 7 above) II, pp. 430–34 (for the girl's status as an orphan, see my comments there to lines 2 and 6, and I, pp. 227–28). In a similar deed from the same place and time, T-S 16.181, part C, ed. Friedman, *JMP* II, pp. 415ff., the bride was an orphan described as a *na'ara* probably between the ages of 12 and 12½; see Friedman, *JMP* I, p. 227.

[14] ENA NS 1.9 (L45); see Friedman, 'Ethics' (see n. 2 above), pp. 87, 99, n. 26; *Polygyny* (see n. 7 above), pp. 45, 346.

[15] Mosseri IV,3 (L7), cited briefly in Friedman, 'Ethics' (see n. 2 above), p. 99, n. 28 (add this reference to *Catalogue of the Jack Mosseri Collection*, Jerusalem, 1990, p. 73). According to Goitein, *Med. Soc.* III (see n. 1 above), pp. 114, 450, n. 80, the document concerns postponement of the marriage due to insufficient funds but, as far as I can see, this is not mentioned. The writer has a handsome hand but wrote in haste and omitted some letters and words. In l. 16, שהר חתי ואמהא כאנת תועדני בדלך, 'a month until — and her mother promised me this'. Presumably the word תבלג, 'she reaches her majority', was omitted. Reference is made to סיידנא, 'our lord', and this seems to refer to Abraham Maimonides (as noted in the *Catalogue*, where the reference to 'Nagid' is incorrect), who apparently instructed that the talmudic principle is binding law. But the text is fragmentary; and it could refer to Moses Maimonides (d. 1204), since Elijah was already active as a judge in Alexandria at least from 1204 (Goitein, *Med. Soc.*, II (Berkeley, Los Angeles, London, 1971), p. 515).

marriage was set for three years later. When Sitt al-Dār was ten, another married sister of hers died, and her father then wanted to marry her without delay to his newly widowed son-in-law, evidently because she was needed to care for the young orphans. Bystanders objected that this could not be done because of the previous betrothal, but testimony was produced that the first contract had been conditional, and since the condition had not been fulfilled, the act was invalid. This resolution must have been considered suspect by some people, and they questioned whether it was 'kosher'. This explains the note in Arabic on the *verso* that registers that the Jewish judge and cantor testified before the *qāḍī* of Alexandria concerning the first, conditional betrothal.[16]

Five years later (1047), a fragmentary court record from Fustat tells the story of an orphan girl who had been married before she was eleven years old. She refused to engage in sex with her husband, and it was decided to let her live with her brother for fourteen months, when she would turn twelve. A query or request for a legal opinion written in the early thirteenth century describes a somewhat similar case. After two years of marriage, an eleven-year-old orphan still could not endure sex with her husband, and both wanted a divorce.[17]

The head of Egyptian Jewry in the late eleventh century, R. Daniel b. David b. Azariah, discussed in a responsum two separate cases of child brides, one an orphan girl and the other a minor whose father had contracted her marriage. It is not clear whether these refer to full marriages or betrothals. They speak respectively of זוגתה זוגת and אב יזוגהא, normally translated 'his wife who was married' and 'a father who marries her'; but the verb *zawwaj* is also used in Judaeo-Arabic for 'contract betrothal' (*qiddushin*) and *zawja* can mean 'betrothed'. R. David instructed his correspondent, obviously a local judge, that he had no choice but to permit the marriage (or betrothal), and assured him that he 'had nothing to fear'. Goitein, followed by my distinguished colleague at Tel Aviv University, Moshe Gil, who subsequently published the manuscript, explained that the questioner had expressed concern over the possibility of a negative reaction on the part of the Muslim authorities, and that the jurisprudent had assured him that they would not interfere, since Islamic law also permitted such marriages.[18] Muslim authorities did supervise unusual

---

[16] T-S 13J8.31; see Friedman, 'Ethics' (see n. 2 above), pp. 87, 99, n. 28; Goitein, *Med. Soc.* III (see n. 1 above), pp. 78–79, 443, n. 34; other references are in S. C. Reif, *Published Material from the Cambridge Genizah Collections: A Bibliography 1896–1980* (Cambridge, 1988), p. 158.

[17] Court record: T-S Ar. 47.244; see Goitein, *Med. Soc.* III (see n. 1 above), pp. 77, 442, n. 29, l. 6, מן אלוטי, 'from sexual intercourse; l. 14, נאשז ען זוגהא, 'recalcitrant towards her husband.' The document was issued in Adar I, 1047, and it was agreed that the girl would stay in her brother's house until Passover of the following year. In l. 11 her age is given as 'less' than 11, with the word 'less,' דון, written between the lines, which suggests that she was probably almost 11. Query: T-S 12.242, lines 13–21, translated in Goitein, *Med. Soc.* III, p. 77, and edited in Friedman, *Polygyny* (see n. 7 above), pp. 153–55.

[18] ENA 1822A.23; see M. A. Friedman, ' "Is there no Balm in Egypt; is there no Physician in Cairo?" (A Kohen Divorces his Wife in Eleventh Century Egypt)', *Diné Israel* 5 (1974), p. 208, n. 6 (where it was incorrectly interpreted as referring to one case, a minor orphaned from her mother); S. D. Goitein, 'New Sources on Daniel b. Azarya, Nasi and Gaon', *Shalem* 2 (1976), p. 94 (= *Palestinian Jewry in Early Islamic and Crusader Times*; Hebrew; Jerusalem, 1980), p. 173);

cases, as we have seen in the affair involving the *qāḍī* of Alexandria,[19] but marriages of child brides among Muslims must have been commonplace, and I assume that their permissibility in Islamic law was well known.[20] I propose that the document reflects doubt about whether officiating at marriages (or betrothals) of child brides was acceptable in Jewish tradition. As Goitein already suggested, concern that the bride is of legal age is probably reflected in a fragmentary court record from 1049/50, in which several witnesses testify to a girl's age.[21] Support for this interpretation of the line in question may be adduced from the following item.

A Babylonian Gaon, that is, head of a talmudic academy in Iraq, rules in an almost complete responsum preserved in a Genizah fragment published by B. M. Lewin, that marrying a child bride, though not forbidden by the Torah, is considered מכוער, 'ugly' or 'reprehensible', clearly a parallel to the Islamic category of *makrūh*. The responsum cites the talmudic dictum (BT, *Niddah* 13b): '[...] Those who play with little girls delay the advent of the messiah,' which is interpreted there as 'those who marry little girls' not yet of childbearing age. A father's right to marry off his minor daughter was considered by the sages to be a biblical principle, and, according to the Gaon, was subsequently permissible.

> But it is improper to perform such a betrothal for an orphan. [Our] regular practice [and that of] our [ancestors], in accordance with the words of the sages, is to demand proof that an orphan girl [is of age] when she comes to have a betrothal performed. And if a judge officiates at the betrothal of a minor orphan girl, we rebuke him and castigate him, because we consider it reprehensible. But we do not declare it forbidden, nor do we force her to leave [her husband].[22]

Med. Soc. III (see n. 1 above), pp. 76, 442, n. 25 (where only the second case in mentioned); M. Gil, *Palestine during the First Muslim Period (634–1099)* I–III (Hebrew; Tel Aviv, 1983), III, pp. 335–36, no. 536. I suggest translating והי יתימה in l. 4, as an apodosis: '(as concerns ...) she is an orphan' (see J. Blau, *A Grammar of Mediaeval Juaeo-Arabic* (Hebrew; Jerusalem², 1980), p. 194); and in l. 6, instead of אל[שער]את, perhaps read: [ע]לאמאת. For *zawwaj* in the sense 'contract a betrothal,' see, e.g., *azwaj* in T-S Ar. 50.197, l. 9, ed. M. A. Friedman, 'Government Intervention in Qayrawān in the Divorce of a Betrothed Girl', *Michael* 5 (1978), p. 225, concerning the case of a betrothed girl: אזוג אבנתה ... פקבל אן יזף בהא, literally, 'he contracted a marriage for his daughter ... but before he delivered her to be wed.'

[19] See Goitein, *Med. Soc.* (see n. 15 above) II, pp. 399–400, 613, n. 19.

[20] On child brides in Islamic law, see S. D. Goitein, 'An Introduction to Muslim Law' in Goitein and A. Ben Shemesh, *Muslim Law in Israel* (Hebrew; Jerusalem, 1957), pp. 131–32 (note the Islamic equivalent of *me'un* discussed there).

[21] Goitein, *Med. Soc.* III (see n. 1 above), pp. 76–77. The classmark of the manuscript was inadvertently omitted in the note but T-S NS J218 was certainly intended.

[22] Bodleian MS Heb. e. 58 (2864), ed. B. M. Lewin, *Otzar ha-Geonim* VII (Jerusalem, 1936), pp. 219–220, no. 544. The manuscript is fragmentary and in many places effaced but most is correctly deciphered by Lewin; for a few emendations, see S. Abramson, *'Inyanot be-Sifrut ha-Ge'onim* (Jerusalem, 1974), p. 193, n. 3. See the illuminating discussion by Dinari, *'Me'un'* (see n. 9 above), pp. 324–26 (the responsum's distinction between a minor girl married by her father and an orphan is not adequately emphasized there, nor is the basis for the distinction that Dinari draws between *bogeret* and *gedola*). As Dinari has shown, R. Ḥananel's citation of a Gaon who opposed

A newly identified and complete responsum, whose seventy-three lines are preserved in three separate, contiguous fragments in different parts of the Taylor-Schechter Collection, tells a unique story. The ruling is written, in Judaeo-Arabic, by R. Judah Kohen b. Joseph, an Egyptian Jewish scholar in the latter half of the eleventh century, who, as Goitein has shown, was so revered that he was referred to simply as 'the Rabbi' (הרב). An indication of the veneration in which he was held is found on the *verso*, where the recipient, a *ḥaver*, or local judge, added in Arabic script after the Rabbi's demise: *hadhihi 'indī bi-khāṭṭihī raḥimahu 'llahu*, 'this is what I have in his handwriting, may God have mercy on him.' The question addressed to the Rabbi:

> concerns an orphan girl, who had not yet reached her majority, whose mother contracted a marriage for her, and her husband consummated the marriage. Some time later, she admitted of her own volition that a man had ensnared her and seduced her. Then the man who, she said, had fornicated with her was brought forward. He was questioned about what she had said and denied it. After being intimidated and threatened, he confessed that he had seduced her, that all that the girl had said was true, and that this was exactly what he had done.[23]

R. Sherira Gaon, perhaps joined by his son R. Hai, wrote a responsum (in Hebrew) to Fez, Morocco, concerning a minor girl who had been betrothed without her father's consent. In it, the writer mentions that earlier that year he had sent another responsum dealing with the same topic to Mesila, a town in central Algeria, the existence of whose Jewish community is uniquely documented by this statement.[24] A fragment of a copy of what is probably the original responsum (in Hebrew) to Mesila is found in the Taylor-Schechter Collection. The query begins as follows:

---

me'un was taken from this responsum, where in fact the Gaon voiced disapproval of marriages of child brides in general and objected adamantly to marriages of orphaned child brides, rather than *me'un* as such; Grossman, 'Child Marriage' (see n. 4 above), pp. 111, 116, is to be corrected accordingly. See also the discussion in *Yiḥuse* (see n. 8 above), pp. 216–17. For *makrūh* (or its equivalent) in Jewish legal sources, see M. A. Friedman, 'Two Maimonidean Letters' (Hebrew), *I. Twersky Memorial Volume* (in the press), n. 29, and the literature cited there.

[23] T-S 12.397 + AS 155.329 + G1.5a (I intend to edit the complete responsum elsewhere); the last fragment is mentioned by S. D. Goitein, '*Ha-Rav*', *Tarbiz* 45 (1975–76), p. 65, n. 5, but because it was not connected with the two other pieces, its contents were not accurately identified. The passage quoted here is found on the first two fragments, the postscript on the *verso* of the first. On R. Judah Kohen b. Joseph, see the literature cited in Friedman, *Polygyny* (see n. 7 above), p. 136, n. 1 (and index).

[24] S. Assaf, 'Responsa by R. Sherira (and R. Hai?) to the Residents of Fez', *Ginze Qedem* 5 (1933), pp. 113–15; B. M. Lewin, *Otzar ha-Geonim* IX (Jerusalem, 1939), pp. 120–22, no. 273. Mesila: see Assaf, 'Responsa', p. 110. H. Z. Hirschberg, *A History of the Jews in North Africa* (Hebrew; Jerusalem, l965), I, p. 352, n. 38, cites a Genizah document from 1034 that mentions the granddaughter of Ibn al-Jāsūs al-Masīlī (see Goitein, *Med. Soc.* II (see n. 15 above), pp. 202–3), but he does not refer to this responsum.

> A minor girl was betrothed by her mother and brother, without the knowledge of her father, who was abroad. (Upon returning,) her father did not voice his protest to them. He entered a partnership with his (new) son-in-law, saying to him 'You are my son', and he told whoever inquired about him, 'He is my son-in-law, my daughter's husband'. He spent about a year with him. Then they quarreled, and he said to him: 'You have no wife with me. My daughter is still a minor, and she is in my authority. I did not receive betrothal from you in accordance with the Sages' teaching: "Her father receives her betrothal, and her father receives her bill of divorce" '. He replied: 'But I have spent a year with you and you did not object to me...'[25]

A brief summary of the material is now in order. My preliminary discussion and Goitein's study on child brides in the Genizah documents explicitly dealt only with girls who were legal minors, not young teenagers.[26] Most of the cases found in the Genizah involve girls orphaned from their fathers (some may have been orphaned from their mothers, but this is not mentioned), one of them a girl whose father was abroad. The Geonim strongly censured any judge who officiated at the betrothal or wedding of a child bride who was an orphan, but some were still performed. These documents predominantly concern engagements or betrothals and not marriages proper, and this point, of obvious significance for understanding the social impact of the phenomenon, has not been adequately emphasized in earlier discussions. The weddings and consummation of the marriages were routinely postponed until the bride reached her majority. Only three Genizah documents that clearly testify to actual marriages of girls who had not reached their majority have so far been identified. All concern orphans for whom sexual relations proved a disaster: two found it impossible to engage in them and the third was seduced by another man. Another bizarre case involved the proposed substitution marriage of a ten-year-old whose married sisters had died, the last of whom presumably left small orphans who needed care. Having complemented and refined Goitein's observations, we are led by our review to confirm his conclusions. Marriages of child brides (still legal minors!) as reflected in the Genizah documents were indeed unusual occurrences.

Most of the cases in the sources adduced by Grossman from outside the Genizah similarly concern orphan girls and engagements or betrothals rather than marriages. The custom of the Jews of Damascus to marry off girls aged only eight or nine, as described in a query submitted to Maimonides, is certainly most exceptional. It was a local custom that does not reflect the general practice found in the Genizah documents. Moreover, a word of

---

[25] T-S Misc.28.186. 'Her father receives': see M. *Ketubbot* 4.4, BT, *Ketubbot* 46b. On the subject of the responsum, compare *Sha'are Ṣedeq* 3.3.1, p. 16b. Another responsum in the same manuscript deals with a man who informed the court that he had contracted his daughter's betrothal but later denied it, and there were no witnesses to the betrothal. For this responsum, see S. Assaf, *Teshuvot ha-Ge'onim* (*Mada'e Ha-Yahadut* II; Jerusalem 1927), pp. 58–59, no. 46; Lewin, *Otzar ha-Geonim* IX (see n. 24 above), pp. 153ff., no. 354.

[26] In his comments, Grossman, 'Child Marriage' (see n. 4 above), pp. 108–9, does not discuss Goitein's treatment, elsewhere in his book, of the frequent marriage of young girls of legal age and its consequences; see below.

caution is called for, since that responsum is preserved only in a Hebrew translation of the original Arabic, and the details in such translations are notoriously unreliable.[27]

Genizah documents suggest that brides often entered the wedding chamber shortly after they had reached their majority, or while they were still young teenagers.[28] A formula found in many marriage contracts mentioned that the bride had reached her majority. It was probably introduced because the bride was often not much older than the minimum age; otherwise it may be regarded as superfluous.[29] As already noted, the man who wrote to the judge Elijah wished to marry a girl in Alexandria as soon as she came of age.[30] A geonic responsum found in the Taylor-Schechter Collection concerns a *betrothed* girl 'who has reached her majority; she finished her thirteenth year and entered her fourteenth.'[31] In another query, we read of a girl 'who had reached her majority and had already passed the age of fifteen' and whose father had contracted a *betrothal* for her to which she objected, since she wanted to marry another man.[32] And an appeal for financial assistance in marrying off a daughter speaks of the religious merit of having a daughter married near the age of sexual maturity.[33]

For the time being, the data for estimating the average age of men at their marriage are sparse. The scribes did not find it necessary to note that the groom was of legal age, and I assume that this was usually evident to all those present at the wedding. A boy, described in a query from Qayrawan sent to a Babylonian Gaon as being 'in his father's jurisdiction' when a marriage was contracted for him, had, in all likelihood, already reached his majority, yet was still a young teenager; but such information is exceptional.[34] From the tenor of his letter, the groom who appealed to the judge Elijah was clearly not a young teenager.[35] Goitein concludes from a study of the economics of marriage that grooms were several years their brides' senior but considerably younger than in fourteenth-century Italy,

---

[27] R. Moses b. Maimon, *Responsa*, ed. J. Blau (Jerusalem 1960), p. 705, no. 427; see Grossman, 'Child Marriage' (see n. 4 above), p. 114. The responsum's style betrays it as a translation.

[28] See Goitein, *Med. Soc.* III (see n. 1 above), pp. 163, 186.

[29] See Friedman, 'Ethics' (see n. 2 above), p. 87; *JMP* I (see n. 7 above), pp. 109–10, 222–23; *Polygyny* (see n. 7 above), p. 105, n. 61; compare Goitein, *Med. Soc.* III (see n. 1 above), p. 102; Grossman, 'Child Marriage' (see n. 4 above), p. 111.

[30] Mosseri IV,3 (L7).

[31] T-S Ar.50.198.

[32] T-S G1.18. The query is addressed to '*Rosh Ha-Seder*' who could be any one of a number of scholars, including 'the Rav', Judah Kohen b. Joseph.

[33] ENA NS 21.11, apparently from the early thirteenth century (addressed to 'our master', perhaps Abraham Maimonides). For the phrase (l. 17) המשיא נשים סמוך לפרקן, see BT, *Yevamot* 62b and parallels; compare *Yebamoth*, ed. Liss (see n. 9 above) II, p. 404, n. 130; Schremer, 'Age' (see n. 6 above), p. 51, n. 21.

[34] T-S Ar.50.197, ed. Friedman, 'Qayrawan' (see n. 18 above), p. 225 (see also p. 216); compare Goitein, *Med. Soc.* III (see n. 1 above), pp. 92, 445, n. 82, where this and a somewhat similar case are discussed. For the case of a minor coming of age who wished to enter levirate marriage with his sister-in-law but was rejected by her, see Goitein in that volume, p. 471, n. 223. See also Schremer, 'Age' (see n. 6 above), p. 52, n. 23.

[35] Mosseri IV,3 (L7).

where there was a wide disparity in the ages of the spouses.[36] Moses Maimonides did not take a wife until he was close to thirty-five years old, and his son Abraham and other descendants encouraged their disciples to marry when they were about that age or older. Marriage at such an advanced age was a late, irregular phenomenon in Genizah society. It was advocated by the pietist movement and was intended to give a man ample opportunity to nurture his scholastic and spiritual growth before being encumbered by a wife and children. The reference to Moses Maimonides as 'Ark of the Covenant' in a letter of congratulations sent to him on the occasion of his marriage around the year 1170 reflects his stature at that time.[37]

In antiquity and the medieval period, people expected youth to assume adult responsibilities at an earlier age than is today thought appropriate. The young teenage bride may have been capable of reproducing but she was hardly mature emotionally. This phenomenon must have had significant social implications. These have already been touched upon in the scholarly literature, so we shall not dwell on them here.[38] The newlyweds frequently lived with the groom's family who looked forward to the opportunity of 'completing the education' of the bride, by which, of course, they did not mean sending her to high school or adult education courses.[39] The misery of many young brides – often referred to for years to come as 'babies' – in the homes of their husbands' families is a repeated theme in the Genizah documents.[40] Wives who were immature teenagers were, as suggested by Goitein and Grossman, more likely to be physically abused by their older husbands. Wife beating was not, in my opinion, a rare phenomenon in the Genizah

---

[36] See Goitein, *Med. Soc.* III (see n. 1 above), pp. 131, 141.

[37] JTSL Marshall Case MS. 8254.16 (ENA 2560), ed. Friedman, 'Maimonidean Letters' (see n. 22 above). The phrase 'Ark of our Covenant' in reference to a scholar is discussed in Appendix 2 of that article.

[38] In the light of the high infant mortality rate, Grossman ('Child Marriage' (see n. 4 above), p. 123) doubts whether the early age at which women began reproducing increased the number of children in the family; but presumably the more babies that were born, the more survived.

[39] See Goitein, *Med. Soc.* III (see n. 1 above), p. 163. In T-S 16.288, l. 11 (see Reif, *Published Material* (see n. 16 above), p. 258), a father urges his son to bring home his bride (a cousin), ונתם תרביתהא פי חוגרי, literally 'and I shall complete her education under my jurisdiction'; see S. D. Goitein, 'Chief Judge R. Hanan'el b. Samuel, In-Law of R. Moses Maimonides', (*Tarbiz* 50, 1981, p. 392, n. 84). The four-word Judaeo-Arabic quote is mistranslated by A. Ghosh, *In an Antique Land* (New York, 1993), p. 328: 'and [we shall] prepare a couple of rooms for her'; on this phrase, see further S. D. Goitein and M. A. Friedman, 'Abraham ben Yijū, a Jewish trader in India', *Te'uda* 15 (1999), p. 286, n. 102. Grossman (see n. 4 above), pp. 123–24, suggests that the young age of brides inhibited their (formal) education, but society provided little opportunity for this even before marriage; see S. D. Goitein, *Jewish Education in Muslim Countries based on Records from the Cairo Geniza* (Hebrew; Jerusalem, 1962), pp. 63ff.; and *Med. Soc.* II (see n. 15 above), pp. 183–85. The mother's immaturity must have had a detrimental effect on the upbringing of children.

[40] On this usage of 'babies', see Goitein, *Med. Soc.* III (see n. 1 above), pp. 160–63.

society, and was probably not restricted to the lower strata of society, although it is difficult to assess its true extent.[41]

I would now like to leave the child brides behind and briefly touch on the issue of extreme domestic violence, a blight from which even so-called enlightened societies still suffer in modern times. In a sub-section of his book entitled 'marriage and the authorities', Goitein cites a Genizah fragment that concerns a dispute over the estates of Sitt al-Bayt, 'Mistress of the House', and her daughter Sitt al-Ḥusn, 'Lady Beauty'. Both were killed at the same time in 'the famous murder case'. Goitein observed that he had not found a single instance of a Jewish murderer in the Genizah documents and suggested that the text referred to an outburst of marauding soldiers or bandits who murdered Sitt al-Bayt, Sitt al-Ḥusn and the latter's 'two husbands'. The daughter, already a widow, had contracted marriage to two men presumably as the result of a procedural mishap, since Jewish society does not sanction polyandry. The first must have been absent for years when she contracted a marriage with the second. Both men happened to be in the wrong place at the wrong time, and mention of their murder served no purpose in the court record.[42]

The Judaeo-Arabic text has some grammatical irregularities, not uncommon in these documents. 'The famous murder case', as I read it, constitutes a somewhat different set of circumstances. Sitt al-Ḥusn did not have two husbands simultaneously. Her first husband apparently died of natural causes. She was not fortunate in her choice of men, and her second marriage ended when she and her mother were murdered – not by marauding soldiers or bandits, but by her second husband. I translate the beginning of the operative portion of the document as follows:

> The Creator, may he be praised, decreed the death of Sitt al-Bayt the daughter of Mevorakh the cantor, may he rest in Eden, who is the daughter of the sister of the cantor Abū Manṣūr, may God have mercy on him, and the death of her daughter, Sitt al-Ḥusn, the daughter of our lord and master, Isaac the elder, may he rest in Eden, who had first been the wife of 'Ammār the banker, may he rest in Eden, in the famous murder case. The one who had married this Sitt al-Ḥusn killed both of them (namely, Sitt al-Ḥusn and her mother) together, simultaneously, as is well known.[43]

---

[41] See Goitein, *Med. Soc.* III (see n. 1 above), pp. 175, 186; compare Grossman, 'Child Marriage' (see n. 4 above), p. 124; Friedman, 'Review' (see n. 1 above), p. 130 (on the extent to which the data on wife beating are representative).

[42] T-S 8.111; see Goitein, *Med. Soc.* III (see n. 1 above), pp. 80–81, 443, n. 41. I fail to understand the import of Goitein's comment in that note to the effect that 'the very wording of the document supports my interpretation: "When the Creator decreed that [these women] should die." ' At the beginning of documents describing various acts, e.g., marriage or divorce, the court scribe who wrote this document, Ḥalfōn Halevi b. Manasseh (dated documents 1100–1138), frequently wrote a similar phrase, ascribing events to divine decree ('when the Creator facilitated ...'); see, e.g., Friedman, *Polygyny* (see n. 7 above), p. 90, n. 2.

[43] The key clause, T-S 8.111, lines 4–5, reads: וקתל אלתי כאן תזוג׳ סת אלחסן דא להמא ג׳מיעא פי וקת ואחד. Goitein, *Med. Soc.* III (see n. 1 above), p. 443, n. 41: 'The continuation *wa-quṭil allatī kān*(!) *tazawwaj* (!) [...] is clumsy.' Perhaps he understood the clause something like: They were murdered, together with the two to whom Sitt al-Ḥusn had been married, etc. But throughout this

The estate of the woman who had died first was inherited by the other woman before her own death. The uncertainty as to the order of the deaths led to conflicting, exclusive claims to the women's estate by Sitt al-Bayt's first cousins, two brothers who were also cantors, and Sitt al- Ḥusn's relatives, two brothers who were probably her first cousins on her father's side. If the mother died last, her cousins, the cantors, inherited all; if the daughter died last, her relatives had exclusive rights to the estate. As is clarified in a second fragment that deals with the same case, possibly from another copy of the same document, the two sets of relatives eventually reached a compromise to divide the estate equally. Now they had only to contend with the not so simple matter of having it released by the Office of Estates of the government ('may God increase its majesty') which, having been approached unsuccessfully several times, obviously saw itself as having a prior and exclusive claim backed by force. Such problems in cases where Jews died without first-degree heirs are mentioned in several Genizah documents.[44]

These fragments not only portray the marital history of a cantorial family and shed light on Jewish-Muslim relations concerning estate law but also tell a bizarre story of murder within the family. Our perception of the past tends, at times, to be somewhat idealized,

document, even where there is no possibility of reading the word a different way, the scribe Ḥalfōn writes *ḍammas* – the vowel *u* – and would have been expected to do so here had he intended *wa-quṭil*. I transcribe the first two words *wa-qaṭal allatī* (!)(the continuation as did Goitein, but without exclamation marks), and take the second word to be an irregular usage, attested elsewhere, of the masculine; see Blau, *Grammar* (see n. 18 above), p. 237, and compare Friedman, 'Review' (see n. 1 above), p. 131.

[44] The second fragment is T-S NS 31.9, ed. G. Weiss, 'Legal Documents written by the Court Clerk Halfon ben Manasse' (Ph.D. dissertation, University of Pennsylvania, 1970), no. 193. See l. 6 for the phrase 'the two murdered women mentioned above.' The cantor Abū Sa'īd, mentioned in l. 13, was one of Sitt al-Bayt's cousins named in T-S 8.111. A word of caution is in order for Genizah students. After examining the two fragments in microfilm, I assumed that they were parts of the same document, since they are in the same hand and both obviously refer to the same case. T-S 8.111 appeared to come from the top of the document, and T-S NS 31.9, which seemed to continue the text after a short break, from the lower right side. But a look at the originals demonstrated that they were from two separate documents, since the right margins are of different widths, as are the spaces between the lines. Since parts of two lines in T-S NS 31.9 are deleted, it may have been a draft. More likely, the two fragments come from identical copies, one intended for each pair of relatives; in this connection, see the *verso* of T-S 8.111 which has the notation: 'for the cantor Bū Sa'īd'. From text intact in the two fragments, I assume that the reason why there is no mention of the possibility that the murderer (or his heirs – his fate is unknown) might inherit from Sitt al-Ḥusn is because of the principle implied in 1 Kings 21:19 ('Would you murder and take possession?'), namely, that a murderer loses his right to inheritance. The latter principle in Jewish law is discussed by J. Rivlin, *Inheritance and Wills in Jewish Law* (Ramat Gan 1999), pp. 120–31. As for the Hebrew phrase in T-S 8.111, l. 9, 'the state, may God increase its majesty', this is used in other documents, e.g., T-S 13J2.25, lines 3–4, ed. Friedman, *Polygyny* (see n. 7 above). On the problems that medieval Egyptian Jewry had with the Office of Estates, when one died intestate, see M. A. Friedman, 'Responsa of Abraham Maimonides and his Contemporaries from the Cairo Geniza' (Hebrew), *Bar-Ilan* 26–27 (1995), p. 272, and the literature cited in n. 72; compare H. Rabie, *The Financial System of Egypt, A.H. 564–741/A.D. 1169–1341* (London, 1972), pp. 127–32.

and we have a predilection, when interpreting fragmentary historical data, for being influenced by our own moral values. Modern sociology has found that family violence is ubiquitous, and not restricted to the lower strata, as is often assumed. The same was probably true in Genizah society but we lack the data to demonstrate this since the Genizah documents emanate mainly from the middle and lower layers of society. In any event, if my analysis is correct, Genizah society was not inherently unlike modern society, even concerning murder of a wife and mother-in-law.[45] But the abundant Genizah sources at our disposal that make no mention of this phenomenon appear to testify to a significant difference in degree between the two. While other relevant documents may yet appear among the Genizah papers, we may conclude with a reasonably high degree of certainty that domestic violence escalating into murder was a most rare occurrence. The one instance here identified was consequently referred to as 'the famous murder case'.

It seems fitting to conclude in a more positive vein, namely on the subject of spousal mutuality as exhibited in the marriage contract formula. The traditional *ketubbah*, written according to the custom of the Babylonian academies, is a completely unilateral deed, issued by the groom to the bride, who remains a thoroughly passive participant in the pact. The contract includes his undertaking to 'serve, honour and support you, in the manner of Jewish men who honour and support their wives faithfully'. Contrariwise, the tenth- and eleventh-century marriage contracts written according to the custom of the Rabbanites of the Land of Israel (the 'Palestinian style'), and found among the Genizah fragments, contain elements of reciprocity. Primarily, the groom's undertaking is balanced by a separate clause listing the bride's obligations to him. This is also present in Genizah fragments of marriage contracts written according to the Karaite practice.[46]

These formulae are primarily of declarative, symbolic value and were hardly intended to constitute new obligations or convey a difference in legal status, although such interpretations may sometimes have been offered by jurisprudents. A symbolic proclamation of egalitarian tendencies is, however, significant in its own right, and the notion of a pre-nuptial contract whereby both bride and groom undertake to base their household on mutual respect and co-operation may even have substantial appeal on the contemporary scene. An examination of the evidence for the emergence of these formulae and their dissemination among different segments in the Jewish community is not without interest. Here we concern ourselves essentially with the relationship between the Palestinian and Karaite traditions, a question whose investigation may have broader consequences for the study of the contacts between the two communities and their legal systems.

There are many variations in the wording of the clause concerning the bride's obligations in Palestinian-style marriage contracts. A translation of the original Aramaic

---

[45] In our society, homicide within the family is hardly carried out exclusively by firearms, and Goitein's comment (*Med. Soc.* III (see n. 1 above), p. 80) that 'they had no revolvers in those days' fails to take this into account. Goitein alludes to his educational goals in Genizah research in his 'The Life of a Scholar,' in R. Attal, *A Bibliography of the Writings of Prof. Shelomo Dov Goitein* (Jerusalem, 1975), p. xxviii.

[46] See the discussion and sources in Friedman, *JMP* I (see n. 7 above), pp. 181–91.

in a typical text reads as follows: 'Similarly, this PN daughter of PN, accepted and undertook to esteem, honour, attend and serve her husband in purity, in the manner of virtuous women, the daughters of Israel, who esteem, honour, attend and serve their husbands in purity and cleanness. And she consented to become his wife and the mother of his children.'[47] Besides 'virtuous', כשירתה, we often find 'modest', צניעתה, and for the unique Aramaic בדכיו ובנקיו, 'in purity and cleanness', the Hebrew words בטהרה ובקדושה, 'in purity and sanctity', frequently appear.[48] The following is a translation of the clause from the Hebrew of a Karaite marriage contract written in Jerusalem in 1028: 'And this bride ... consented to be married to him and to be his wife and companion in purity, sanctity and reverence, to obey, honour, esteem and help him, to do in his home all that the virtuous daughters of Israel do in their husbands' homes, to conduct herself in love and compassion, and to be under his rule with her desire for him' etc.[49]

The Karaite formula is more elaborate than its Rabbanite Palestinian counterpart; it mentions love and compassion and has biblical references to both companionship and male dominance. In reference to the latter characteristics, Goitein compared this to the formula covering the obligations of the spouses in the Muslim marriage contract, that states, to cite a Genizah document edited by Geoffrey Khan: 'he must make companionship with her pleasant ... she has the same obligation towards him that he has towards her, but he is a rank higher.'[50] The latter phrase is a quote from the Qur'an (2:228). In Goitein's view, the similarities between the Muslim and Karaite marriage contracts reflect analogous social milieux, and the formulae were not fully developed in a parallel fashion in the Rabbanite documents due to the conservatism exhibited by that community in relation to these deeds.[51]

---

[47] CUL Or.1080 1.3, f. 1 *verso*, lines 1–10, ed. Friedman, *JMP* II (see n. 7 above), pp. 99 ff. The sentence 'she consented to become his wife' often precedes the obligations; see *JMP* I, pp. 179–81. The word 'consented' here translates שמעת. This verb appears as part of the bride's acceptance in seven Palestinian-style marriage contracts (*JMP* I, p. 180, notes 97–98), of which several contain no detectable Babylonian influence and only one is from Tyre. J. Olszowy-Schlanger, *Karaite Marriage Documents from the Cairo Geniza* (=*KMD*) (Leiden, 1998), p. 210 ('appears mainly in the *ketubbot* from Tyre, which were under Babylonian influence') is to be corrected accordingly.

[48] See Friedman, *JMP* I (see n. 7 above), pp. 186–87. Instead of 'modest', one might translate, following Goitein, *Med. Soc.* III (see n. 1 above), p. 166, 'chaste', 'unassuming', 'knowing her place', 'one who knows how to keep a secret'.

[49] CUL Add.3430; see Reif, *Published Material* (see n. 16 above), p. 414; Gil, *Palestine* II (see n. 18 above), no. 305, pp. 555–58; Olszowy-Schlanger, *KMD* (see n. 47 above), no. 339, pp. 388–94. On 'wife and companion' see Malachi 2:14 and Friedman, *JMP* I (see n. 7 above), p. 161; Olszowy-Schlanger, *KMD*, p. 207; on the phrase 'to be under his rule' etc., see Genesis 3:16, and Olszowy-Schlanger, *KMD*, p. 209.

[50] T-S 18J1.10, ed. G. Khan, *Arabic Legal and Administrative Documents in the Cambridge Genizah Collections* (Cambridge 1993), no. 32, pp. 193ff. Khan dates the contract between 1028 and 1036. Some time during the subsequent decades, the paper made its way into the Jewish community, was cut to a smaller size, and, in 1072, had a complete death-bed will written on its reverse side.

[51] Goitein, *Med. Soc.* III (see n. 1 above), pp. 50 ff.

But how are we to explain the obvious correspondence between the Rabbanite and Karaite formulae, both in content and in precise wording ('She consented to be married to him and to be his wife ... in purity and sanctity ... to honour and esteem and help him ... like the virtuous daughters of Israel'), found exclusively in these two traditions? The parallels are certainly too striking to be explained as mere coincidence. Given that the Karaite sect crystallized in the East, in Iraq and its environs, at a relatively late stage in Jewish history, that Karaites began immigrating to the Land of Israel in the late ninth century, and that the Genizah has preserved Palestinian-style Rabbanite marriage contracts that are earlier than Karaite ones, the simplest *a priori* explanation would be that the Karaites borrowed and adapted this formula from the Rabbanites of the Land of Israel.[52]

In her recent, detailed study, *Karaite Marriage Documents from the Cairo Geniza*, Judith Olszowy-Schlanger compared these manuscripts clause by clause to deeds in other traditions and demonstrated that in most cases the Karaite formulary resembles that of Babylonian Rabbanite documents. In the light of the geographical setting of nascent Karaism, it is not surprising to find confirmation that early Karaites wrote marriage contracts that resembled the local Rabbanite documents and brought their Eastern tradition with them when they immigrated to the Land of Israel. Olszowy-Schlanger, however, goes a step beyond this and concludes that the Karaite *ketubbah* 'received its final shape' in its entirety before the immigration to the Land of Israel and that no 'imprints of the local Palestinian tradition on such an important domain of legal doctrine as the marriage formula' are to be found.[53]

In her opinion, the Muslim contract is the likely source for mention of the bride's obligations by the Karaites. As to the source for the striking correspondence between the Karaite and Rabbanite Palestinian formulae, without parallel in the Muslim deed, she admits that 'it appears extremely difficult at present to specify which of the two traditions was the model for the other.' But 'the difficulty of this assessment acknowledged, it seems more plausible that the Karaites were the first to borrow the Arabic clause.'[54]

While it is true that the wide-ranging complexities in the evidence often frustrate scholarly attempts to establish influences or parallel developments between similar phenomena in different cultures, the difficulties in identifying the model in the relationship between the Palestinian and Karaite formulae appear to have been exaggerated by Olszowy-Schlanger. The earlier occurrence of the Palestinian formula need no longer be a matter of speculation. The *ketubbah* from Antinoopolis, Egypt, from 417 CE, published in 1986, parallels the Rabbanite Palestinian-style marriage contracts from the Genizah in much of its formulation. Though seriously damaged, this papyrus contains, I believe, incontrovertible evidence of the wife's obligations in Jewish marriage contracts in the

[52] See Friedman, *JMP* I (see n. 7 above), p. 191.

[53] Olszowy-Schlanger, *KMD* (see n. 47 above), pp. 270–71.

[54] Olszowy-Schlanger, *KMD* (see n. 47 above), p. 268. On p. 269, she admits: 'However, this important question clearly needs to be further researched, and its implications remain to be worked out.' Concerning the formula for the bride's acceptance, she writes (p. 210): 'Nevertheless, the common origin of this formula in Karaite and Palestinian documents seems evident', implying that here too the Palestinian Rabbanites borrowed it from the Karaites!

early fifth century. I say 'I believe' because I am hardly an impartial observer, since I previously suggested that the Karaite formula for this clause as well as for some other marriage clauses is borrowed from the Rabbanite one and I am also responsible for restoring the papyrus at this point and identifying the bride's undertaking there. I therefore present the evidence and invite other scholars to suggest alternative readings and interpretations.

Olszowy-Schlanger was of course familiar with the papyrus, but she asserts that the bride's obligations are absent there. ('This absence includes the *ketubbah* of Antinoopolis [417 A.D.], where such a clause has been proposed by the editors. However, the manuscript is seriously damaged in this particular place, and it is not possible to establish the existence of this clause.')[55] What *is* preserved in the disputed lines is a fragmentary clause that follows the groom's obligations to the bride and that includes an undertaking made to the groom to be performed 'in purity' – using the same unique Aramaic word בדכו as in the Genizah Palestinian *ketubbot* (there: בדכיו) – and in sanctity. The clause concludes with the words 'the modest (women) of Israel.' The phrase 'she undertook to honour him' is indeed seriously damaged but paleographers have, on the basis of the remnants of the letters that are intact and the spaces for missing letters, verified this reading. In the following text, letters preserved in their entirety (or almost so) are printed in large type, partially preserved letters in small type, and those completely missing in brackets.

בקושט[ה] ... קבלת למ[ה]וי מוק[רה י]תה
לשמואל ברת (!) בר סמפטי בדכו וב[קדו]שה וב[טהרה כהלכת בנת]
ישראל צניעתה

faithfully. ... she undertook to hon[our h]im [and to ...]
to Samuel son of Sampati, in purity and in [san]ctity and in [pureness, in the manner of the daughters of]
Israel, the modest.[56]

The two kinds of Egyptian fragments, that is, the Antinoopolis papyrus from the fifth century and the Genizah documents from the tenth and eleventh centuries are thus mutually illuminating. Were it not for the Genizah fragments, the relevant passage in the papyrus could hardly have been identified and deciphered.[57] Although some words are

---

[55] Olszowy-Schlanger, *KMD* (see n. 47 above), p. 210.

[56] See C. Sirat, P. Cauderlier, M. Dukan and M. A. Friedman, *La* Ketouba *de Cologne: Un contrat de mariage juif à Antinoopolis* (Opladen 1986), p. 22, lines 11–13. A photograph of the papyrus and a paleographical reconstruction by A. Yardeni appear as plates I and II.

[57] Olszowy-Schlanger, *KMD* (see n. 47 above), p. 210, n. 23: 'This reconstruction is not of course implausible, but it is important to stress that it was modelled upon later Palestinian-style marriage contracts from the Cairo Geniza.' The latter observation implies that the reconstruction may have been prejudiced. We are not, however, dealing exclusively with a reconstruction but with a text that has preserved elements of the clause, which, thanks to the Genizah documents, are clearly identifiable. Furthermore, a reconstruction modelled upon sources of the same genre is preferable to one based exclusively on intuition. Olszowy-Schlanger does not suggest any alternative

missing, the identification and decipherment of the intact portion are, in my opinion, beyond reasonable doubt. I maintain that the clause in the papyrus conclusively proves that the formula for the wife's obligations, previously known from the Genizah texts, dates back in the Jewish marriage contract to late antiquity, to the Byzantine period, centuries before the advent of Islam and the Karaite schism. This demonstrates that it was added to the essentially Babylonian formulation of the Karaite contracts after the Karaite immigration to the Land of Israel. The addition clearly bears the imprint of the Rabbanite Palestinian-style *ketubbot.*[58]

---

identification of the words that are intact, or any other reconstruction or source upon which to model one.

[58] Additional evidence of the imprint of the Palestinian-style *ketubbot* on the Karaite marriage formula will be re-examined elsewhere. [See now M. A. Friedman, 'On the Relationship of the Karaite and the Palestinian Rabbanite Marriage Contracts from the Geniza', *Te'uda* 15 (1999), pp. 145–57.] I am grateful to the Librarians and Directors of the Genizah collections from which materials have been cited for their cooperation and to the University Library and the Faculty of Oriental Studies at Cambridge for arranging the series of lectures in which this paper was delivered. I also wish to acknowledge the contribution of the Taylor-Schechter Genizah Research Unit at Cambridge, under its Director, Professor Stefan C. Reif, to Genizah research as a whole over the past quarter-century. The research for this paper was assisted by the Joseph and Ceil Mazer Chair in Jewish Culture in Muslim Lands and Cairo Geniza Studies, Tel Aviv University.

10

Women Speak for Themselves

JOEL L. KRAEMER

In memory of Agnes Lewis and Margaret Gibson

'In the Jewish books of the past, one learned about women from men. There was, however, one place where the female voice was heard directly and emphatically: in the papers of the Cairo Genizah. Here, Jewish women spoke for themselves.'[1]

As we celebrate the centenary of the official presentation of their Genizah Collection to the University of Cambridge by Solomon Schechter and Charles Taylor, we cannot overlook the vital contribution of two women, Agnes Lewis and Margaret Gibson, twin widowed sisters with scholarly and antiquarian interests.[2] Agnes Lewis tells how they reported their momentous find of an important text from the Cairo Genizah to Schechter.[3] There is a feminist touch to her narrative that we should not overlook. Mrs Lewis and her sister were amused and gratified that Ben Sira, 'a woman-hater,'[4] had suffered just retribution in that the original Hebrew text of his book, that had virtually disappeared for fifteen centuries, was brought to the attention of a European scholar 'of his own nation' by two women.

Women's letters in the Genizah

Agnes Lewis and Margaret Gibson would also have been delighted to know that, thanks to their initiative, numerous documents containing women's letters were found

---

[1] See S. D. Goitein, 'New Revelations from the Cairo Geniza: Jewish Women in the Middle Ages', *Hadassah Magazine* (October, 1973), p. 14.

[2] A. W. Price, *The Ladies of Castlebrae: A Story of Nineteenth-Century Travel and Research* (Gloucester, 1985).

[3] A. Lewis, *In the Shadow of Sinai (1895–1897)* (Cambridge, 1898), pp. 168–80. This was in May, 1896. Genizah papers had already been acquired by Cambridge University Library and by other institutions, but the Lewis-Gibson acquisition inspired Schechter's visit to Cairo and the transfer of the remaining Genizah papers to Cambridge; see S. C. Reif, *A Guide to the Taylor-Schechter Genizah Collection* (Cambridge, 1973), pp. 3–5.

[4] For instance, 'Better a man's wickedness than a woman's goodness' (Ben Sira 42:14). The remainder of the verse reads: 'but better a religious daughter than a shameless son.' Agnes Lewis might have cited other verses as well but, in fairness to Ben Sira, these sentiments were commonplace in his society and culture (second century BCE); see *The Wisdom of Ben Sira*, trans. P. W. Skehan (New York, 1987), pp. 7, 90–92. For a more negative assessment of Ben Sira's bias, see W. C. Trenchard, *Ben Sira's View of Women: A Literary Analysis* (Chico, California, 1982).

in the treasure that Schechter brought to Cambridge. These documents are rare and precious. Manuscripts containing women's letters are original documents, to be distinguished from letters reproduced in literary sources that have invariably undergone textual processing and stylization and may not even be authentic. The Genizah documents embody the words of the women, embedded in the actual paper and written with the very ink that they (or their scribes) used. This direct, unmediated writing is priceless for the cultural historian. The writing is often spontaneous and unaffected, abounding in colloquialisms, misspellings, slips of the pen and corrections. Socially inferior as they were, their mode of address is informal and unceremonious, and letters to them may also be in a lower speech register.

I came across women's letters in the course of examining the documentary portion of the Cairo Genizah, where I was looking for materials pertaining to elite figures such as Moses Maimonides. One letter to Maimonides was from his sister Miriam.[5] The writer demands that the recipient act in accordance with her requests. She complains that her son has abandoned and neglected her and does not write or send her anything, a rather typical complaint in women's letters, as we shall see. She presumes that Moses knows or can discover his whereabouts, and that he can influence the young man to contact his mother. The letter was taken down from her dictation by a scribe as we learn from a marginal notation, 'The writer of this letter....Jacob the cantor sends best greetings [to all of you].'

This letter led me to wonder if there was a feminine sociolect. I collected more letters, and found them fascinating and of great historical value and human appeal. I then proceeded to search systematically for documents and now have a corpus of some one hundred and eighty letters.[6] Goitein had already highlighted the value of women's letters for understanding the *mentalité* of Mediterranean people. He edited and translated numerous letters and cited others in his publications.[7] Jewish women have,

[5] T-S 10J18.1; see Goitein, 'An Autograph of Maimonides', *Tarbiz* 32 (1962–63), pp. 188–91; J. Mann, *The Jews in Egypt and in Palestine*, (2 vols; Oxford, 1920-22), vol. 2, p. 319 and Goitein's corrections in the reprint (New York, 1970), p. xxxv; Goitein, *A Mediterranean Society*, 6 vols including the index completed by P. Sanders (Berkeley, Los Angeles and London, 1967–93), vol. 1, p. 351; vol. 3, pp. 5 and 237; Reif, *Published Material from the Cambridge Genizah Collections*: *A Bibliography* (Cambridge, 1988), pp. 141–42. The letter is written in a clear Spanish style. The key word *ukhtuka* ('your sister') at the end of the first line, according to Goitein's reading, no longer appears in the actual document and evidently flaked off during the process of conservation in the 1960s (as Stefan Reif informed me). The word does appear in the microfilm of the document.

[6] I include women's appeals to authorities, as well as petitions, wills and last testaments. I intend to publish translations of these documents in a special volume.

[7] See, for example, Goitein, 'The Position of Women according to the Cairo Geniza Documents', *Fourth World Congress of Jewish Studies*, vol. 2 (Hebrew; Jerusalem, 1969), pp. 177–79 (English summary, p.192). My indebtedness to Goitein is clear throughout the notes. His command and thoroughness were such that, often, I found women's letters in the Genizah only to discover that Goitein had included some reference to the document in his *Mediterranean Society* (see n. 5 above).

in general, received much attention from historians.[8] Nothing, however, compares with documentary sources in providing firm ground for historical understanding. In the confines of this paper, I can offer only a tiny savour of the lavish feast that these letters provide.

Although *literary* sources cite personal correspondence by Muslim and Christian women from the medieval orient, the only treasure trove of *documentary* sources recovered to date is the one from the Cairo Genizah.[9] It is true that a number of women's letters written in Arabic on papyri have been preserved[10] but these, while of great interest, contain few signs of the kind of women's self-expression that is found in Genizah letters. Nevertheless, in form and style they are similar to the Genizah letters written much later, indicating a long epistolary tradition in Egypt. Many of these papyri letters concern business matters, as those written to Abū Hurayra by his mother. We have similar mother-son letters, with references to commercial affairs, in our Genizah documents.

Our letters, then, compensate appreciably for this relative dearth of primary source materials pertaining to medieval women in the Near East. While the women here represented belong to the Jewish community, they were akin to their sisters in neighbouring societies, and their letters therefore supplement our knowledge about the status of women in the Mediterranean basin. The women whose letters are preserved in the Genizah resided in the vicinity of non-Jews and had frequent contact with them.

[8] The works of Goitein and of M. A. Friedman are pioneering. For women in the Greco-Roman world, the writings of Ross Shepard Kraemer are illuminating; see, e.g., *Her Share of the Blessings* (Oxford, 1992). For women's status in rabbinic literature, see Judith Hauptman, *Rereading the Rabbis: a Woman's Voice* (Boulder, 1998), and Tal Ilan, *Jewish Women in Greco-Roman Palestine* (Tübingen, 1995). And for general introductions, see Elizabeth Koltun's *The Jewish Woman: New Perspectives* (New York, 1976); Judith R. Baskin's *Jewish Women in Historical Perspective* (Detroit, 1991); and especially the fine collection by Yael Azmon, *A View into the Lives of Women in Jewish Societies: Collected Essays* (Hebrew: Jerusalem, 1995). For a later period than that treated here, see Ruth Lamdan's *A separate People: Jewish Women in Palestine, Syria and Egypt in the 16th Century* (Tel Aviv, 1996).

[9] This is the family archive of a Jewish woman named Babata (or Babatha) the daughter of Simeon, found in a cave in Naḥal Ḥever (*ca.* 132 CE), where a commander of Bar Kochba's forces took refuge along with members of this family. Babata could not write herself, but she could sign her name.

[10] See Y. Rāghib, *Marchands d'étoffes du Fayyoum au IIIe/IXe siècle* (2 vols; Cairo, 1982–85), vol. 2, nos VIII, XIII–XV, XXIII, XXVII, XXVIII, XXXVI–XXXVIII, containing family and business letters to and from female members of a certain Abū Hurayra's family (ninth century). There are business letters from Abū Hurayra's mother to him, a phenomenon found also in the Genizah material. There are also mother to daughter letters on family and business matters, and there is a letter from Abū Hurayra's sister Anubis to him written in a hand very similar to his. The most personal is a letter from the wife of a Muḥammad b. Ḥamadiyya to the wife of Abū Hurayra expressing concern for her health. She had sent her some medicament. The address has only the names of the husbands, also a typical feature of women's letters from the Genizah.

They also lived under a legal system similar to that of Muslim women. Indeed, Jewish women often appealed to Muslim courts for the redress of grievances.

These letters give us a fine *aperçu* into the socio-economic and cultural status of women and into the entire family structure. Virtually all family ties are exemplified, giving us a representative segment of the female population. We have letters between wife and husband, brother and sister, sister and sister, mother and son, daughter and father, daughter and mother, aunt or uncle and niece. Women in all life's stages write letters: young daughters prior to marriage, recent brides, pregnant women, mothers, grandmothers, orphans and widows. Poor, abandoned and mistreated women present petitions and appeals to leaders and to the community. Women on their deathbed declare their bequests, expressing what they consider worth leaving as a material and spiritual legacy. Their wills are valuable documents for the historian; they are often precious résumés of their lives and contain valuable details about the clothing and property they owned.

The geographical distribution of the letters covers a wide vista. Many are from Old Cairo (Fustat) and are addressed to other parts of Egypt, especially the countryside, or sent from the provinces to Fustat. We also have letters to Cairo from distant places, such as Aden, Byzantium, India, Seleucia, Tiberias and Tunisia. And we find letters from Cairo to foreign cities like Aleppo and Tripoli (Libya). For example, a man sends a magnificent letter of consolation from Jerusalem to his sister in Toledo (in 1053), apparently copied on the way in Cairo.[11] The letters thus encompass the entire Mediterranean basin. The women are of North African, Spanish, Italian, Egyptian, Palestinian and Syrian descent. These documents compensate for the lack of literary production by Near Eastern Jewish women in the medieval period.

Whereas for medieval Christian women we lack such a lavish treasure of documentary sources, there are many Christian women's letters cited in literary sources, a rich tapestry of literary creativity, and abundant evidence of self-expression, despite their being disadvantaged vis-à-vis their male counterparts. The plaintive voice of European women is heard in literature, but there is also some documentary evidence of women's self-expression as, for example, in court testimonies. For instance, the self-understanding and world view of an illiterate peasant girl in Provence named Grazida Lizier (born 1297/8) are reported in interrogations into the Cathar heresy by the bishop of Pamiers, Jacques Fournier (later Pope Benedict XII).[12]

The best known female correspondence from medieval Europe is certainly that of Heloise (*ca.* 1100–1163), whose three surviving letters to Peter Abelard are a poignant

---

[11] T-S 13J9.4. See below, p. 205.

[12] P. Dronke, *Women Writers of the Middle Ages* (Cambridge, 1984), pp. 203ff. The testimony has been published by J. Duvernoy, *Le registre d'Inquisition de Jacques Fournier* (3 vols; Paris-La Haye, 1978). This kind of evidence (for Jewish women) has been studied by Renée Levine-Melammed in her Brandeis University doctorate (1983), 'Women in Spanish Crypto-Judaism, 1492–1520'. See also 'Sephardi Women in Post-1492 Spanish Crypto-Jewish Society' in Azmon (see n. 8 above), pp. 209–22, and see now her *Heretics or Daughters of Israel?: The Crypto-Jewish Women of Castille* (New York, 1999).

testament of tragic love.[13] Her self-expression is dramatic and lucid, revealing her innermost emotional and mental states. She expresses intense yearning and loneliness, and reproves Abelard for abandoning her. (These are ubiquitous themes in women's letters from the Genizah, as we shall see anon.) Heloise may have edited her correspondence over the years to leave a coherent and approbatory record of her association with Abelard, and it is possible that another hand collected the letters and made editorial changes to the letters of both.[14]

Hildegard of Bingen (1098–1179) is survived by a vast volume of literary works and an extensive Latin correspondence.[15] After she experienced prophetic visions, a monk was allegedly appointed to help her record them in writing, with some of her nuns also assisting her. She was taught to read and sing the Latin psalms, sufficient for the chanting of the Divine Office, but apparently never learned to write. Hadewijch of Antwerp (thirteenth century), a learned mystic visionary, wrote her *Letters* in the tradition of didactic epistolography and a *Book of Visions*, as well as *Poems in Stanzas and Poems in Couplets*.[16] The writings of Catherine of Siena (1347–80), Dominican tertiary and mystic, all of which were dictated, include about four hundred letters, prayers, and the four treatises of *Il libro della divina dottrina*, also known as the *Dialogo* or *Treatise on Divine Providence*.[17]

Marie de France (wrote *ca.* 1160–80), the first recognized French poetess, composed verse narratives on romantic *topoi* (lays) and authored Aesopic and other fables (called *Ysopets*). She was apparently a regular visitor in the sparkling court of troubadours and Gascon knights who assembled in the castles of Anjou and Guyenne around Henry II and Queen Eleanor. Her poems, in octosyllabic verses, recount the chivalrous deeds of Breton knights for the sake of their lady-loves.[18] Christine de Pisan (*ca.* 1364–*ca.* 1431), daughter of an astrologer to King Charles V, was reared and educated in the Parisian court in ancient languages and literatures. She married Étienne du Castel, who became court secretary. When her husband died, she took up writing in order to support herself and her three young children. Her earliest poems

---

[13] Dronke (see n. 12 above), ch. 5. Editions of the correspondence are noted by Dronke, p. 326.

[14] Dronke (see n. 12 above), p. 108.

[15] Dronke (see n. 12 above), ch. 6; F. Bowie and O. Davies (eds), *Mystical writings of Hildegard of Bingen* (New York, 1990); A. Führkötter (ed.), *Briefwechsel [von] Hildegard von Bingen* (Salzburg, 1965).

[16] B. McGinn, *The Flowering of Mysticism: Men and Women in the New Mysticism* (1200–1350) (New York, 1998), pp. 200ff. And see on Mechthild of Magdeburg (thirteenth century), authoress of *The Flowering Light of the Godhead*, on pp. 222ff., and on Marguerite Porete (fourteenth century), pp. 244ff.

[17] V. D. Scudder (ed. and trans.), *Saint Catherine of Siena as Seen in her Letters* (London, 1927); S. Noffke (ed. and trans.), *The letters of Catherine of Siena* (Binghamton, N.Y., 1988).

[18] R. Hanning and J. Ferrante (trans.), *The Lais of Marie de France* (New York, 1978); H. Spiegel (ed. and trans.), *Fables* (Toronto, 1987).

were ballads lamenting lost love in memory of her husband.[19] Her *Épistre du dieu d'amours* (1399) was a defence of women against the parody of Jean de Meun in the *Roman de la rose*. In *Le Livre de la cité des dames* (1405) she lauded women acclaimed for their valour and virtue. Her *Livre des trois vertus* (1406) was a collection of moralistic instructions for women in various social positions. Her autobiography, *La Vision de Christine* (1405), was a rejoinder to her critics.[20] There were also woman troubadours who wrote secular poetry, and there was a luxurious burgeoning of female poetry in the eleventh and twelfth centuries.[21] And then, if we move to East Asia, there was the tenth-century Japanese female author Murasaki Shikubu, who wrote the charming and profound *Tale of the Genji*,[22] still popular and read by Japanese school-children. The Genizah yields nothing of this kind.

The cultural and social context of the Genizah papers is Arab-Islamic civilization. The legal status of women in medieval Islamic societies was similar to the position of women in Jewish communities. Yet the learning and literary creativity of women in Islamic societies dramatically surpassed such accomplishments on the part of Jewish women. In the pre-Islamic and early Islamic period we find a number of female poets. In most cases, they wrote elegies (*marāthī*) commemorating brothers, fathers and husbands slain in battle. Al-Khansā' (born *ca.* 575, died after 634), who bridged the pre-Islamic and Islamic periods, was famous for her poetry, especially her elegies, which became models for their genre, and commemorated her two brothers killed in tribal skirmishes. Layla al-Akhyaliyya, in the Umayyad period (seventh century), wrote funereal elegies, some for her slain lover, Tawba b. Ḥumayyir. In her poetic diatribes, she also competed with the famous poet al-Nābigha al-Ja'dī.

In Andalus, where women were more autonomous than in the Eastern parts of the Islamic world, poetry written by women flourished.[23] Wallāda, daughter of the (Spanish) Umayyad caliph al-Mustakfi (reigned in 1025), exchanged poems with the famous Ibn Zaydūn, who desperately loved this proud and independent princess. She broke off with him in favour of rivals. Ḥafṣa Bint al-Ḥājj (d. 1190/91) of Granada, endowed with literary refinement and poetic talent, was inspired in most of her poetry by her love affair with the poet Abū Ja'far ibn Sa'īd. After his execution Ḥafṣa wrote poetic elegies, but then gave up poetry for the teaching and education of princesses in the royal court. On the more erotic side was the libertine poetess Nazhūn (twelfth century). It was in Spain that we have examples of female Jewish poetesses, the wife

[19] Other women turned to writing as consolation and therapy after the death of husbands. We think immediately of Glückel of Hameln, who wrote her *Memoirs* (1690–91) to drive away 'melancholy thoughts' after her husband's demise.

[20] E. J. Richards (trans.), Christine de Pizan, *The Book of the City of Ladies* (New York, 1982).

[21] See Dronke (see n. 12 above), ch. 4; M. Bogin, *The Woman Troubadors* (New York, 1976).

[22] See R. J. Bowring, *Murasaki Shikubu, The Tale of the Genji* (Cambridge, 1988).

[23] See M. J. Viguera, 'On the Social Status of Andalusī Women' in S. K. Jayyusi (ed.), *The Legacy of Muslim Spain* (2 vols; Leiden, 1994), pp. 709–11.

of Dunash ibn Labrat and a woman named Qasmūna, who wrote plaintive romantic verse.[24]

Arab women were also entertainers, singers, musicians and poetesses (*jāriya qayna*: 'female slave singer') in royal courts. Many of them could extemporize verse and even competed with male court poets. Thoroughly educated in poetry and prose, they wrote eulogies of prominent people, elegies, and poetry about wine and love. Some of them maintained literary salons, as did Faḍl al-Shā'ira (d. 871 or 874), a court entertainer, songstress and lute player, who had an illustrious literary salon in Baghdad. Women are prominent in Sufism, the best known being Rābi'a al-'Adawiyya.[25] Many women were transmitters of traditions (*ḥadīth*). Cultures work with models, and since 'Ā'isha, wife of Muḥammad, was a transmitter of tradition, this became a commended activity for women.

The intense involvement of women in Arab-Islamic culture is exemplified by the vast number included in Kaḥḥāla's collection of female biographies, *A'lām al-Nisā'*. There are about 3,400 entries in the five volumes. Many of the personalities listed are pious women, donors to religious institutions, and wives of famous men. But that still leaves numerous women who were poets, musicians, scholars, teachers and transmitters of tradition. None of this cultural activity entailed literacy. This was basically an oral culture, and it was possible to write poetry and to transmit *ḥadīth* without knowing how to read and write. Still, the cultural productivity of women in the Arabic cultural sphere is astounding.[26] Aside from the wife of Dunash b. Labraṭ and Qasmūna, there is no counterpart to this in Jewish communities of the time. In Arab societies, the courtly culture of rulers, dignitaries and notables provided a stimulating milieu for female artistic creativity.

Learning and literacy of Jewish women in the age of the Genizah

As 'Ā'isha, an expert in prophetic traditions, was an exemplar for Muslim women, so Beruriah, wife of the Tanna R. Meir, was a model for Jewish females. Renowned for her legal opinions and teaching, she allegedly came to a bad end, seduced by one of the young scholars.[27] Rabbinic disapproval of female learning is thus reflected in the

---

[24] On the wife of Dunash ibn Labraṭ (mid-tenth century), see E. Fleischer, 'On Dunash Ben Labraṭ, his Wife and his Son: New Light on the Beginnings of the Hebrew-Spanish School', *Jerusalem Studies in Hebrew Literature* 5 (Hebrew; 1984), pp. 189-202. On Qasmūna, see J. M. Nichols, 'The Arabic Verses of Qasmūna bint Ismā'īl ibn Bagdāla', *IJMES* 13 (1981), pp. 155–58 and J. A. Bellamy, 'Qasmūna the Poetess: Who Was She?', *JAOS* 103 (1983), pp. 423-34.

[25] M. Smith, *Rabi'a: The Life & Work of Rabi'a and Other Women Mystics in Islam* (Oxford, 1994).

[26] For a brief survey, see W. Walther, *Women in Islam from Medieval to Modern Times* (Princeton, 1993), pp. 143–53; and see Gavin R. G. Hambly, *Women in the Medieval Islamic World* (New York, 1998).

[27] Rashi quotes this anecdote in his comment on BT, *'Avodah Zarah* 18b. According to the talmudic account, R. Meir ordered a student to seduce Beruriah. She eventually succumbed and thereafter committed suicide, her husband fleeing to Babylonia in shame.

Beruriah legend. Legal precept, at least according to the majority view, excluded Jewish women from study of Torah. The view of the Tanna R. Eliezer is widely cited: 'Whoever teaches his daughter Torah, it is as though he teaches her lewdness.'[28] The general consensus that a woman was not obligated to study the Torah became a legal precept prohibiting women's study.[29] As a result, few women were learned. To be sure, there is always the anomalous case. The daughter of Samuel b. 'Āli, head of the Yeshivah in Baghdad (1161–93), was learned in Bible and Talmud, and taught these subjects to male pupils. She instructed them through a window so that she was hidden from their view.[30] We also know of female scribes, as it was natural for young women who assisted their fathers to continue independently in the same profession.[31]

Maimonides, whose legal opinions carried enormous weight in this environment, ruled that women (like slaves and minors) are exempt from studying Torah.[32] Nevertheless, a woman who studies Torah has a reward, though it is not equivalent to a man's reward, as she is not obliged to study.[33] The Sages, Maimonides says, commanded that a man refrain from teaching his daughter Torah, as the minds of most women are unfit for instruction, and they twist the words of Torah into nonsense. He takes the statement of R. Eliezer about teaching lewdness to refer to the Oral Torah, but decides that even the Written Torah should not be taught to a female, although if her father taught her, it is not as though he taught her lewdness.

These legal strictures presuppose that women lack the capacity to learn or to take studies seriously. The pessimistic opinion of women's cognitive abilities in rabbinic sources was certainly influenced by the low estimation of women current in late hellenistic antiquity, but it persisted into the Middle Ages. A vicious cycle is created, as low expectations and the neglect of female education create a female population lacking cultural ambitions.

On the legend, see the discussion in D. Boyarin, *Carnal Israel: Reading Sex in Talmudic Culture* (Berkeley, 1993), pp. 183–96, where rabbinic 'ambivalence' towards Beruriah is stressed. Boyarin sees the Babylonian Talmud's legend of Beruriah's erudition as reflecting a Palestinian reality, but there is no evidence of this, and Tal Ilan is probably right in saying that female learning did not exist either in Palestine or Babylonia. See her *Jewish Women* (see n. 8 above), pp. 27, 197–200.

28 Mishnah, *Soṭah* 3.4; BT, *Soṭah* 21a. Ben Azzai held the opposite view, namely, that a man must endow his daughter with knowledge of the Torah. See Hauptman, *Rereading the Rabbis* (see n. 8 above), pp. 22–23, 44.

29 *Siphre ad Deuteronomium*, § 46, ed. L. Finkelstein (Berlin, 1939), p. 104; T. Ilan, 'A Window into the Public Realm: Jewish Women in the Second Temple Period' in Azmon, *A View* (see n. 8 above), p. 48; *Jewish Women* (see n. 8 above), pp. 31, 191.

30 Petaḥiah of Regensburg, *Sibbuv*, ed. L. Grünhut (Jerusalem, 1905), pp. 9ff.; S. W. Baron, *A Social and Religious History of the Jews* (18 vols and index; New York^2, 1952–1993), vol. 5, p. 323, n. 89.

31 This was also true in the period of the Sages. A woman could write her own bill of divorce; see Mishnah, *Giṭṭin* 2. 5. Torah scrolls, *tefillin* and *mezuzot* written by women are invalid; BT, *Menaḥot* 42b. See Ilan, 'A Window' (see n. 29 above), pp. 50–51; *Jewish Women* (see n. 8 above), pp. 190–204.

32 *Hilkhot Talmud Torah*, 1.1.

33 *Hilkhot Talmud Torah*, 1.13; and see Ilan, *Jewish Women* (see n. 8 above), pp. 191–93.

There were also socio-economic obstacles to female literacy.[34] The traditional roles of women limited the time available for educational pursuits. There was no social pressure on women to acquire literacy skills; quite the opposite. Education cost money, and parents did not consider it profitable to invest in girls' education, unless its aim was the acquisition of domestic proficiency in techniques like embroidery. Daughters were destined for household labour and reproduction, not for social functions requiring literacy skills. Rosamand McKitterick has stressed the social function of literacy and the mental, emotional and other adjustments required to accommodate it.[35] Female literacy had, in fact, no appreciable function in Genizah society. If women developed reading and writing skills, they could only rarely be put to use. For writing letters, which is our main concern, literacy skills were not required. Where necessary, women dictated letters and had letters read to them.

Women learned the rudiments of reading for prayer and for ritual purposes. The Talmud enjoins that while women, slaves and minors are exempt from reading the *Shema*'[36] and from wearing phylacteries, they are not excused from prayer (*tefillah*),[37] from *mezuzah*[38] or from reciting the Grace after Meals.[39] Women attended synagogue services, though they sat in a separate area.

While women were discouraged from learning, their natural desire to acquire knowledge often overcame this prejudice, as is attested in our documents. For instance, in one of our letters, a dying woman urges her sister to provide the former's daughter with an education. She reminds her sister that their mother had been pious.[40] Piety, then, required some kind of literacy. We find another attestation that female education was not totally neglected in a responsum by Maimonides to a query concerning a group of girls who studied with a blind schoolteacher and who would not consent to study with anyone else.[41] Two interesting details in the query illuminate the

---

[34] On Jewish women's learning and literacy, see Goitein, *Jewish Education in Muslim Countries* (Hebrew; Jerusalem, 1962), pp. 63–74; *Mediterranean Society* (see n. 5 above), vol. 2, pp. 183–85; vol. 3, pp. 309, 321; and see Stefan Reif's contribution to Rosamond McKitterick's *The Uses of Literacy in Early Mediaeval Europe* (Cambridge, 1990), 'Aspects of Mediaeval Jewish Literacy', esp. pp. 153–54.

[35] See McKitterick in her introduction to *The Uses of Literacy* (see n. 34 above), p. 5.

[36] The recitation of Deuteronomy 6:4–9, 11:13–21; Numbers 15:37–41.

[37] That is, the *Shemoneh 'Esreh*, the rabbinic prayer *par excellence*.

[38] The encased parchment inscribed with two passages from the Bible (Deuteronomy 6:9, 11:20), affixed to the doorpost of the entrance to houses and rooms.

[39] Mishnah, *Berakhot* 3.3; BT, *Berakhot* 20a–b. See Hauptman, *Rereading the Rabbis* (see n. 8 above), pp. 231ff.

[40] MS ENA Misc. 6; trans. Goitein, *Jewish Education* (see n. 34 above), p. 66; ed. and trans. Goitein, 'Side Lights on Jewish Education from the Cairo Geniza', *Gratz College Anniversary Volume*, eds I. D. Passow and S. T. Lachs (Philadelphia, 1971), pp. 85–87, 100–1; *Mediterranean Society* (see n. 5 above), vol. 3, pp. 353–54; p. 506, n. 198; vol. 5, p. 226. See also Reif, 'Aspects' (see n. 34 above), pp. 154–55.

[41] J. Blau, *R. Moses b. Maimon: Responsa*, (4 vols; Jerusalem, 1957–61 and 1986), vol. 2, pp. 524–25, no. 276 [MS British Library 5519B]; vol. 4, p. 9; see M. A. Friedman, '*Qeṭa'im Ḥadashim shel She'elot u-Teshuvot ha-Rambam*' in *Studies in Geniza and*

situation of women. The questioners report that the girls refused to remove their veils before any other teacher. The girls also declined to have women teach them because women, they claimed, taught incorrectly (*ṭa'ut*).

Although women taught in elementary schools, this was discouraged because female teachers had to have social contact with fathers who came to fetch their children from school. When a woman, forced to teach because her husband kept deserting her, queried Maimonides about the legitimacy of her activity,[42] he responded that the husband must prevent his wife from giving either vocational instruction or from teaching Torah reading.[43] He advises that the recourse (*ḥīla*)[44] open to the woman, assuming she is really telling the truth, is for her to rebel (*timrod*)[45] and leave her husband, giving up her delayed payment.[46] In a separate responsum, which appears to be the husband's query in the same case, Maimonides replies that the husband may prevent his wife from teaching young children.[47] The court must censure her for this and restrain her. If she demands a divorce on grounds that her husband prevents her from teaching, she should not be granted one: 'doors should rather be shut and ways blocked, and her affairs should be placed in custody for a long time until she relents and agrees to behave properly toward her husband.'[48]

Although young girls were taught to read so that they could pray and follow the rudiments of rituals, this does not mean that they could write.[49] The two skills were not co-extensive. In fact, relatively few women could write, and their letters had to be dictated to scribes, relatives and acquaintances. But in these cases, female illiteracy was a blessing in disguise, at least for the historian and sociolinguist. For when an uneducated woman dictated a letter to a son, daughter, brother, husband, friend, or young child, her words underwent only minor text processing, and the document is close to natural speech. Dictation may thus be more authentic than writing, for a writer naturally strives for a speech register above that of ordinary language. In a fascinating husband-wife letter (sixteenth century), the man has departed for Mocha in South

---

Sephardi Heritage presented to Shelomo Dov Goitein, eds S. Morag, I. Ben-Ami and N. A. Stillman (Hebrew vol.; Jerusalem, 1981), pp. 119–20, for other versions; Goitein, *Mediterranean Society* (see n. 5 above), vol. 2, p. 183.

[42] J. Blau, *Responsa* (see n. 41 above), p. 49, no. 34.

[43] See Mishnah, *Qiddushin* 2.1; *Hilkhot Talmud Torah* 2.4; *Issurey Bi'ah*, 22.13.

[44] *Ḥīla* is a technical term in Islamic law, meaning a legal device or subterfuge; see *Encyclopedia of Islam* (Leiden², 1960–), vol. 3, col. 510b, s. v. *ḥiyal*. In the Genizah papers the term is often used for 'recourse,' 'refuge'.

[45] For *moredet*, or rebellious wife, see BT, *Ketubbot* 63a; *Hilkhot Ishut* 14. 8–9. See M. A. Friedman, *Jewish Polygyny in the Middle Ages* (Hebrew; Jerusalem, 1986), p. 29, n. 90; 'The Ransom-Divorce', *Israel Oriental Studies*, 6 (1976), pp. 288–307; 'Divorce upon the Wife's Demand', *Jewish Law Annual* 4 (1981), pp. 103–26.

[46] The *mu'akhkhar*, or later installment of the marriage gift, or bride price, was paid at the time of divorce or death of the husband.

[47] Blau, *Responsa* (see n. 41 above), vol. 1, p. 71, no. 45.

[48] See Mishnah, *Qiddushin* 4.13 ('a woman may not be a teacher of children'); *Hilkhot Talmud Torah*, 2. 4; *Issurey Bi'ah*, 22.13.

[49] See McKitterick's introduction to *The Uses of Literacy* (see n. 34 above), pp. 3–4.

Arabia, evidently on a business trip, and the daughter writes as her mother's scribe.[50] She is one of three sisters of the Perdonel family.[51] She and her mother had trouble pronouncing Arabic, and confused many consonants, also jumbling long and short vowels. The letter contains a generous sprinkling of colloquialisms.

When a learned scribe wrote for a woman, the required epistolary style ensured that the text took on more lofty and formal contours. An elegant letter from the wife of Ḥalfōn b. Manasseh Halevi to her brother ʻAlī b. Hillel b. ʻAlī, concerning business and news, is in the handwriting of Ḥalfōn b. Manasseh, a member of the Fustat rabbinical court in the second half of the twelfth century.[52] Women's letters addressed to communal officials tended to be direct and relaxed especially when dictated to professional scribes. A woman's petition to Maṣliaḥ Gaon (head of the Egyptian Jewish community in the years 1127–38), in which she complains that her husband abuses her (a not uncommon complaint as we shall see below), is written in the vernacular, possibly by a schoolboy.[53] Formal elements were sometimes introduced by professional scribes in superscriptions, preambles and salutations. And petitions and complaints often betray the hand of a court or communal bureaucrat. To be sure, not all dictated letters imply *illiteracy*, for women often engaged scribes even when they were capable of writing on their own, just as businessmen did.

Letters sent *to* women often reflect a similar lowering of speech register. They were sometimes delivered to a third party who would read the contents to the female recipient.[54] In general, letters were read aloud to more than one person, and were therefore less private than correspondence is today. But some letters were indeed personal and confidential and intended only for the eyes of the woman herself, as in a letter by a husband to his wife, the daughter of a judge, in which the writer openly professes deep love for his spouse and begs her to rejoin him.[55]

---

[50] T-S 13J24.22, see Reif, *Bibliography* (see n. 5 above), p. 172; Goitein, *Mediterranean Society* (see n. 5 above), vol. 5, p. 222; J. L. Kraemer, 'Spanish Ladies from the Cairo Geniza' in *Jews, Christians, and Muslims in the Mediterranean after 1492*, ed. A. M. Ginio (London, 1992), pp. 248–49.

[51] See Goitein, *Mediterranean Society* (see n. 5 above), vol. 5, p. 568, n. 17.

[52] T-S 13J20.22, see Reif, *Bibliography* (see n. 5 above), p. 169; Goitein, *Mediterranean Society* (see n. 5 above), vol. 5, p. 243.

[53] T-S 8J22.27. See Goitein's remarks and translation in *Mediterranean Society* (see n. 5 above), vol. 3, p. 186; vol. 5, p.189; Reif, *Bibliography* (see n. 5 above), p. 123.

[54] T-S 10J13.24 is a consolation letter from a man to his sister after the death of their mother, addressed to his maternal uncle but meant for her; see Goitein, *Mediterranean Society* (see n. 5 above), vol. 3, p. 242. T-S 13J28.16 is a letter from a man to his son but meant for his wife and flowing with bitter complaints; see Goitein, *Mediterranean Society* (see n. 5 above), vol. 1, p. 449; vol. 3, pp. 338, 468. There are instances of letters addressed to the famous judge Elijah b. Zechariah that are intended to be read out to women. On him, see Aryeh Motzkin's doctoral dissertation, *The Arabic Correspondence of the Judge Elijah and his Family* (University of Pennsylvania, 1965).

[55] CUL Or.1080 J23. See Goitein, *Mediterranean Society* (see n. 5 above), vol. 3, pp. 219–20 (translated); and for further references, see Reif, *Bibliography* (see n. 5 above), p. 404.

Language and style

The letters from the classical period of the Genizah (approximately from the tenth to the thirteenth century) are predominantly in Judaeo-Arabic, but a number are in Hebrew, the prestigious language of the community. Those in Hebrew were often written by (or for) learned women, or addressed to them. The few late letters of the fifteenth and sixteenth centuries are mostly in Hebrew, along with a number in Judaeo-Spanish, and several in Yiddish.[56] In what is presumably the earliest woman's letter preserved (on papyrus, dated to the eighth century), a sister writes to her brother in Aramaic. Arabic had apparently not yet replaced Aramaic as the *lingua franca* of the Near East.[57] Judaeo-Arabic, widely used by Jews in Arab countries in everyday speech and writing, predominantly written in Hebrew characters, is widely regarded as a dialect (version) of Middle Arabic containing an admixture of Hebrew (and Aramaic).[58]

Letters had a conventional structure and formal elements. They usually began with a superscription, such as 'In your name, O Merciful One.' (Letters of appeal continued with biblical verses.) Then came blessings and salutations showered upon the recipient. The writer would thereafter mention either the receipt or non-receipt of the correspondent's letter(s). This was usually followed by expressions of longing for the addressee. And subsequently came the main body of the letter, ending with greetings to family and friends.

Social reality versus legal norms

Women's letters from the Cairo Genizah show that legal prescripts and conventions restricting women's rights and freedom of action were often observed in the breach. A major thesis emergent from the Genizah material is that life and social reality often belied legal precepts. So, while women did internalize social norms they also managed to subvert them in other ways.

In this society, as in the surrounding Islamic environment, there was strict segregation of the sexes, with men assigned to the public domain and women to the private sphere. Another way of putting it is that in the nature-culture discourse, male society considered females to be closer to nature. Females are perceived as closer to the body and its natural and procreative functions, undisciplined of mind, tending towards inconclusive deliberation, bound to the domestic circle, the biological family and the world of children. Ruled by passions and the anarchical forces of nature, females are

---

[56] See E. Gutwirth,. 'A Judeo-Spanish Letter from the Genizah' in *Judeo-Romance Languages*, eds I. Benabu and J. Sermoneta (Jerusalem, 1985), pp. 127–38; 'The Family in Judeo-Spanish Genizah Letters of Cairo (XVIth-XVIIIth C.)' in *Vierteljahrschrift für Sozial-und Wirtschaftsgeschichte* 73 (1986), pp. 210–15; Kraemer, 'Spanish Ladies from the Cairo Geniza' (see n. 50 above); C. Turniansky, 'A Correspondence in Yiddish from Jerusalem Dating from the 1550s', *Shalem* 4 (1984), pp. 130–208.

[57] Bodleian MS Aram. e 1 (P) 2809; see Goitein, *Mediterranean Society* (see n. 5 above), vol. 3, p. 22.

[58] The authoritative analyses of Judaeo-Arabic are by Joshua Blau, *A Grammar of Mediaeval Judaeo-Arabic* (Hebrew; Jerusalem[2], 1980) and *The Emergence and Background of Judaeo-Arabic* (Jerusalem[2], 1981).

regarded as needing subjection by a culture that is figured as male, active and rational.[59] Males as patriarchs had custody of their wives and were the guardians and protectors of their virtue.[60] Women were perceived as having ardent sexual urges, uncontrolled by a mature deliberative capacity, and therefore having the potential for subverting the social order.[61] Maimonides gives a philosophical elucidation of the hierarchical subjugation of the female by the male. He represents matter as female as opposed to form, which is male. Matter is passive and receptive. It is multiple and changing as it takes on new forms, like a married harlot. Matter is associated with the imagination, while form is allied to intellect. Form has power, domination, rule and control over matter and subjugates it.[62]

Women were expected to be modest, pious and withdrawn from public view.[63] The sexual mores of the time in both the Islamic environment and in Jewish society required that wives be restrained from entering public space and from having any contact with men other than their husbands.[64] They were not legally permitted to testify in court. Women were thus segregated and confined to domestic activities. Maimonides rules, however, that a woman is entitled to visit her father's house, a house of mourning or a wedding feast,[65] 'for she is not in a prison where she cannot come and go.'[66] Still, it

[59] On public and private, see, e.g., S. B. Ortner, 'Is Female to Male as Nature Is to Culture?' in M. Z. Rosaldo and L. Lamphere, *Woman, Culture, and Society* (Stanford, 1974), pp. 67–87; P. R. Sanday, 'Female Status in the Public Domain' in the same volume, pp. 189–205; and see the comments by Lila Abu-Lughod in *Veiled Sentiments: Honor and Poetry in a Bedouin Society* (Berkeley, 1986), especially chs 3 and 4. On nature/culture, see also *Nature, Culture, and Gender*, eds C. P. MacCormack and M. Strathern (Cambridge, 1980); J. Butler, *Gender Trouble: Feminism and the Subversion of Identity* (New York, 1990), p. 37; for Europe, see C. Thomasset, 'The Nature of Women' in Klapisch-Zuber, *A History of Women II* (Cambridge, Mass., 1992), pp. 43–44.

[60] The patriarchal bargain is similar to the *dhimmī* bargain in that protection was given in exchange for submissiveness and proper conduct; see D. Kandiyoti, 'Islam and Patriarchy: A Comparative Perspective' in N. R. Keddie and B. Baron, *Women in Middle Eastern History* (New Haven, 1991), p. 36.

[61] L. Rosen, *Bargaining for Reality: The Construction of Social Relations in a Muslim Community* (Chicago, 1984), p. 37.

[62] *Guide of the Perplexed*, trans. S. Pines, [Introduction to First Part], p. 13; I, 17 (p. 43); I, 28 (p. 61); III, 8 (pp. 430–32); S. E. Shapiro, in 'A Matter of Discipline: Reading for Gender in Jewish Philosophy' in *Judaism Since Gender*, eds M. Peskowitz and L. Levitt (New York and London, 1997), pp. 158–73 gives a sound reading of the texts.

[63] The usual word for modesty, *ṣeni'ut*, has the semantic range of Arabic *ḥasham* as used for the modesty code of women in dress and conduct that entailed restraint and tact, lowering the eyes before superior authority and power, and the concomitant masking of passions and true feelings; see Abu-Lughod, *Veiled Sentiments* (see n. 59 above), pp. 105–8, 112–17, 154–56 *et passim*.

[64] *Siphre ad Deuteronomium* (see n. 29 above), §190 (ed. Finkelstein, p. 230). Cf. Tosefta, *Sanhedrin* 5. 2, and see BT, *Ketubbot* 74b; Ilan, 'A Window' (see n. 29 above), p. 48; *Jewish Women* (see n. 8 above), p. 163.

[65] Maimonides, *Hilkhot Ishut*, 13. 11. Rabbinic pronouncement permits a husband to prevent his wife by force from going out to the market place; see *Bereshit Rabbah*, 8. 12

is unseemly for a woman to be constantly going out abroad and into the streets, and the husband should prevent his wife from leaving the house except once or twice a month as the need may arise. Rather, it is proper for a woman to sit in the corner of her house, for it is written, 'The honour of the king's daughter is within' (Psalms 45:14).

Women here, as in other androcentric societies, become defined by social norms of a hierarchical male hegemony. They become subjects and assume personal identities, undergoing 'subjectivation' (*assujetissement*), that is, subjection and subordination.[67] The social norms of subordination are internalized and limits to freedom become self-imposed. Subjection denotes both the process of subjection and becoming a subject with a personal and social identity. By assuming a subordinate role, constraints, and limitations, the female secures male respect, which gives her self-assurance and worth.[68] This does not mean that women did not also oppose their husbands verbally, ignore their strictures and disobey their orders. Women gathered in the home and at the public bath and talked about men derisively and subversively.

Social reality does not march in step with legal precept. We learn from our letters that women did appear in court, owned property, engaged in business, and worked outside the home (often to the chagrin of their husbands). Women were mobile and independent beyond what legal norms prescribed. Wives often wanted to escape the stifling surroundings of the household and its myriad chores, from nagging children and insensitive husbands. This aspiration for freedom caused tension and was a blow to male self-esteem. The employment options for women were limited but they gave some scope for a degree of autonomy. Women became elementary school teachers, seamstresses, embroiderers, or weavers working outside the home. Some managed to earn better incomes than their husbands. A number eventually left home altogether. Their role as teachers was an extension of their domestic function as educators of young children, which they undertook until children reached the age of nine. They seem to have been responsible for their daughters' education even beyond that.

It is hard to estimate the number of female business women, but there were some, particularly among unmarried women. Widows were more independent than other women and able to engage in real estate investment and commerce.[69] They might have inheritances from their husbands and the remainder of their dowries at their disposal.

(ed. Theodor-Albeck, p. 66); see Ilan, 'A Window' (see n. 29 above), p. 47; *Jewish Women* (see n. 8 above), p. 128.

[66] Goitein, *Mediterranean Society* (see n. 5 above), vol. 3, p. 153, plausibly suggests that the remark may allude to Muḥammad's Farewell Sermon, in which he said, 'Your wives are like prisoners of war; they have no free disposition over themselves.'

[67] On this phenomenon, see J. Butler, *The Psychic Life of Power: Theories in Subjection* (Stanford, 1997), p. 83.

[68] See, for example, on acceding to the veil and segregation, U. Wikan, *Behind the Veil in Arabia: Women in Oman* (Chicago, 1982), p. 184; and Kandiyoti, 'Islam and Patriarchy' (see n. 60 above), p. 34.

[69] See Kraemer, 'Spanish Ladies' (see n. 50 above), p. 253; M. Rozen, *The Jewish Community of Jerusalem in the Seventeenth Century* (Hebrew; Tel Aviv, 1984), pp. 239–59.

Upper-class and wealthy women were not forced to be totally powerless and submissive. Property bestows power.

The successful business woman Karīma (='noble lady') bint (='daughter of') 'Ammār, also called Wuḥsha, appears in our documents as a determined and resourceful female.[70] She succeeded her father in the banking business. Wuḥsha had a lover, named Ḥassūn, who came to Cairo from Ashkelon. (He may have left a wife back home whose marriage contract stipulated that he could not take a second wife; polygyny was, of course, permitted in that society.) Wuḥsha's relations with Ḥassūn combined business and pleasure, for the Ascalonian owed her eighty dinars. She had a son by him, and was consequently not admitted to the Synagogue of the Iraqis on the Day of Atonement on account of her 'improper conduct'. But she bore them no grudge, and bequeathed money to the same synagogue in her will. She willed nothing to Ḥassūn, who apparently remained indebted to her to the end, whereas she provided handsomely for her son. All told, she left a large estate of 689 dinars. Typically, she set aside a lavish sum for her own sumptuous funeral. Women favoured elegant attire and ornate adornment for their worldly exit, perhaps more as a respectable adieu to this world than as decorous provision for the next. Though unusual, Wuḥsha's case was not unparallelled. Other resolute and vigorous women appear in our documents. Of course, many women who appear in our letters were simple, poor, elderly, sick, or widowed.

Mobility, travel, and separation

In this period, travel was both precarious and incessant. The mobility and travels of merchants, scholars, poets and others are typical of medieval Near Eastern societies in general and Jewish communities in particular. Businessmen and traders journeyed far and wide, from remote India in the East to distant Morocco in the West, and from Europe in the North to Yemen in the South. Some of them were itinerant merchants, commuting on a regular basis from Egypt to Sicily and Tunisia or the Maghreb (including Spain), or to Greater Syria (including Palestine). There was also substantial local travel. Men travelled on their own without wife and children. A husband's absence from his family could drag on for years. For both husband and wife, separation entailed an intense emotional wrench, deep yearning and severe feelings of abandonment. Many poignant letters express the ensuing human tragedy. The motif of yearning, recurrent in our documents, goes to the deepest roots of cultural sensibility in the Islamic environment. It is predominant in elegiac and erotic poetry and especially in the amatory preludes to odes. The frequency of absence and longing covers the era with a pallor of melancholy.

---

[70] On Wuḥsha, see especially T-S Ar.4.5. See S. D. Goitein, 'A Jewish Business Woman of the Eleventh Century' in *The Seventy-Fifth Anniversary Volume of the Jewish Quarterly Review*, eds A. A. Neuman and S. Zeitlin (Philadelphia, 1967), and *Mediterranean Society* (see n. 5 above), vol. 1, pp. 230, 259; vol. 2, pp. 110–11; vol. 3, pp. 348–50 (her will); p. 505, n. 175; vol. 4, pp. 189, 210, 215; vol. 5, pp. 163, 186. And see Reif, *Bibliography* (see n. 5 above), p. 184.

Occasionally, when husbands moved to a new domicile, wives refused to accompany them. Some women refused to move from the countryside to the city, while others preferred an urban environment to the provinces. Marriage contracts might stipulate that the wife was obliged to follow her husband if he moved to a new location, or include a condition releasing her from this obligation.

The distant husband

As in Islamic societies, the conjugal tie was not particularly close. There were many reasons for the loose bond between husband and wife – early and arranged marriage, easy divorce, polygyny, and the threat of abandonment. Still, a substantial number of letters express love and yearning for absent spouses. A common cause of female grief was the absence of her husband. He may have absconded or may genuinely have been detained.[71] These women were dependent upon their husbands, so that being deserted was profoundly traumatic. Women often write in desperation to husbands who have forsaken them with no means of sustenance. To be sure, husbands sometimes sent letters or funds and gifts that never reached their destination, but there were many cases of real neglect. These women had to remain married without adequate financial support. The deserted wives were occasionally unaware that their husbands had found other women to marry or to keep as concubines.[72]

Husbands occasionally absented themselves for incredibly long periods of time. In a bizarre case, a mother-in-law (named Sa'd) writes to her son-in-law living in Seleucia, Anatolia (*ca.* tenth to eleventh century).[73] The mother writes in the name of her daughter. The letter is actually addressed to a religious authority named Aaron *he-ḥaver* (= 'member of the academy'), a prominent figure in the community, who will deliver the letter to the husband. Aaron's active intervention is obviously anticipated and desired by the sender. The letter was apparently written by a learned scribe, as is attested by the use of Aramaic phrases. The formal writer in this case is the scribe, and the formal recipient is Aaron *he-ḥaver*, the style of the letter conforming to the discourse level of the erudite scribe and the educated addressee. The actual partners in this dialogue are, nevertheless, the husband and the wife. The husband had been absent for twenty-three years! 'I wish to inform you that your wife (namely, the

---

[71] On the absent husband in general, see Goitein, *Mediterranean Society* (see n. 5 above), vol. 1, pp. 47–59; vol. 3, pp. 189–205.

[72] See Y. Assis, 'Sexual Behaviour in Mediaeval Hispano-Jewish Society' in *Jewish History: Essays in Honour of Chimen Abramsky*, eds A. Rapaport and S. J. Zipperstein (London, 1988), p. 34, and see pp. 36ff. on concubines and sex with women of other religions (miscegenation). That evidence is for Spain. Goitein states that he often wondered what these absent husbands did about sex during extended periods of separation from their wives, as he had found no evidence of taking other wives or concubines; see 'The Sexual Mores of the Common People' in *Society and the Sexes in Medieval Islam*, ed. A. L. al-Sayyid-Marsot (Malibu: Undena, 1979), p. 57.

[73] T-S 12.179, published by Goitein, *Palestinian Jewry in Early Islamic and Crusader Times in the Light of the Geniza Documents*, ed. J. Hacker (Hebrew; Jerusalem, 1980), pp. 277–78; Reif, *Bibliography* (see n. 5 above), p. 231.

writer's daughter) is in great trouble with your children. You left her for these twenty-three years and did not yearn to see them. Why should you do such a thing to your wife and children?' This is the longest period of absence attested in our documents. The biblical verse at the beginning sets the tone for the writer's admonition: 'Those who love Your teaching enjoy well-being; they encounter no adversity.'[74] The hint is that one who does not follow the divine teaching of the Law will not prosper but rather suffer adversity. The mother-in-law begins with a typical expression of longing to see the recipient. She had recently heard that the delinquent husband was still living, inquires about his well-being and offers any help needed. She then gets to the main point, the tone mounting in severity. He has been away for twenty-three years and is oblivious to the harm he has caused his wife and children. He had sent word that he was ill. This was the sign of life that elicited our letter. The writer wishes him good health. The tenor is one of constrained admonition, and expresses more concern than anger.

Absenteeism was frequently generated by family tensions. Husbands absconded, fleeing from responsibilities. Husband and wife often sparred in a grievance contest. 'Don't tell me about your troubles; mine are worse' – meaning, in effect, 'Don't ask me for help; you help me.' The solicitation of help or compassion was usually prefaced by a stream of complaints often in the form of 'Don't ask what I've been through' or 'I don't wish to burden you with my troubles', thus conveying misery by circumlocution. This was not simply emotional bartering. It was an effort at 'negotiating reality', by which different actors, having distinct views of what is true, assess responsibility or guilt and innocence, attempting to make their own definition of the situation prevail, arriving at a reality by a process of negotiation.[75] At the same time, each party tries to establish a social identity that will be acceptable to the public.

In a letter from a merchant to his wife, the husband says that he cannot describe for her in a letter his infirmities and ravaging illnesses because he does not want to disturb her and increase her anxiety, adding to her weakness and inability to bear up under burdens.[76] 'I am only obliged to mention (my poor health),' he says, 'so that my letter may substitute for my actual presence.'[77] He has to tell her everything, even to the point of upsetting her, so that his letter may represent his true state of being. Then he alludes to a letter which she wrote to him: 'You speak of your longing, loneliness, isolation and infirmity of body and soul...'

Another woman writes to her husband, away on a journey, recounting difficulties she has experienced during his absence. [78] First, she had a dreadful trip home,

---

[74] Psalms 119:165.

[75] T. J. Scheff, 'Negotiating Reality: Notes on Power in the Assessment of Responsibility' *Social Problems* 16 (1968), pp. 3–17; Rosen, *Bargaining* (see n. 61 above), pp. 42–43.

[76] T-S 16.278, translated by Goitein, *Mediterranean Society* (see n. 5 above), vol. 3, pp. 221–23; see also vol. 5, p. 229 and Reif, *Bibliography* (see n. 5 above), p. 257.

[77] The letter as a substitute for actual presence is a topos, part of the formal ritual of epistolary style.

[78] T-S 10J15.9. The document is mentioned by Goitein, in *Mediterranean Society* (see n. 5 above), vol. 3, p. 261; vol. 5, p. 559, n. 15.

evidently after having accompanied her husband to his destination. She endured much abuse from her mother-in-law: 'Don't ask what I suffered from your father's wife!' [79] This was rather a common situation. In general, however, the husband's family had been supportive. The woman's brother-in-law urged her to divorce her husband, promising that *he* would provide for her! She may have sent this shocking news so as to expedite her husband's return. We are left in suspense as to the outcome.

A husband, separated from his wife, Sitt al-Faḍl, because of a marital crisis over dowry payments by the wife's family, appealed to the court of the Nagid. [80] While the answer was pending, a daughter was born, a first child, whom the husband did not come to see. This was not because the newborn was a girl, as Sitt al-Faḍl surmised. (Her suspicion shows how female births were viewed by fathers.) He celebrates the birth of a girl as an auspicious omen for them. He refrained from visiting because of his wife's antagonism towards him:

> I am pleased with my child. If the first born is a girl, shall I reject her? God forbid! I rather say that God has blessed me with good fortune, and that it is an *auspicious omen*[81] for both of us. Moreover, it may get you to stop hating me. Had a very lovely son been born instead of her, still I would not have come to see him. This is not because I have contempt for a child of mine but as result of your hatred for me. I entreat God, the blessed and exalted, that He replace the animosity between us with goodwill.

The husband seeks reconciliation, but he will not come home until financial matters are settled so that the couple can live in contentment. He ends his letter in a marginal note: 'And do not think I remain away any longer than necessary. I am only waiting for a reply to the letter I sent to our lord, the Head [of the Jews].[82] There is no sense in our being reunited only to go on fighting all the time. No less than these twenty dinars will improve your life and mine.'[83]

The absent wife

It was not uncommon for wives, especially mature or elderly women, to travel and extend their absence from home. Visiting a son or daughter living elsewhere, they

---

[79] This implies that her mother-in-law was not her husband's mother. The 'don't ask' motif is rather frequent in our letters. The effective meaning is 'don't ask because I can't tell you, but I'm going to tell you anyway because I want you to know that I am suffering more than you are.'

[80] T-S 10J15.23, mentioned and partially translated by Goitein, *Mediterranean Society* (see n. 5 above), vol. 3, p. 228; and see vol. 5, pp. 218–19.

[81] A female is an auspicious omen because she deflects the evil eye that accompanies the birth of a boy and also because sons, it was believed, will follow; see BT, *Baba Batra* 141a; Goitein, *Mediterranean Society* (see n. 5 above), vol. 3, pp. 228–29.

[82] *Sayyidunā al-rayyis* may be Rabbenu Abraham, son of Moses Maimonides.

[83] Apparently the balance of the dowry that the wife was supposed to bring to the marriage.

might find the accommodation congenial and prolong their stay. Mothers were routinely summoned to be at the side of a pregnant daughter, and delayed their return.

One woman left Alexandria for Fustat in order to give her seven-year-old son a better education.[84] The woman, named Milāḥ,[85] appeals to the Nagid Rabbenu Abraham, claiming that her husband wishes to marry a second wife, and she fears that he will then take her son away from her. She states that she will not concede her delayed payment and requests that the Nagid instruct the judge of Alexandria not to let her husband marry until he convey it to her. She evidently dictated the letter.[86] The *verso* has an anonymous appeal, written mostly in Hebrew, adding a request urging the Nagid to help the woman.

Husbands occasionally wrote frantic letters to their wives summoning them home. In a desperate plea, a man writes a letter to his son that is actually intended for the ears of the boy's mother.[87] The husband had written previously. He is gravely ill and fears that he may die before seeing his wife and son. This, he says, will then be on their conscience. The husband is extremely importunate, almost frenzied, and he, or the scribe, as the case may be, repeats the urgent message in the postscript. He switches his mode of address from second person plural (the son and wife) to singular masculine (the son), or feminine (the wife). The shift in persons is rhetorically fascinating. The 'writer' is both the husband and the scribe, and the 'recipient' is both the son and the wife. Emotional and physical dependence of male upon female can hardly be more vividly drawn even if we allow room for exaggeration.

Women occasionally refused to follow their husbands when they relocated. This was either because they wished to remain close to their own extended families or simply because they were attached to their environment and homes. A woman living in a provincial town writes a brief letter to her husband, a man named Khalaf, who has left for the capital, the big city.[88] She complains that he has stayed away too long and has not written a letter 'as normal people do.' She refuses to travel to the capital to join him. Also, he should give up the idea that she will eventually come. Her ensuing dissatisfaction would assuredly bring unhappiness to both. Distance, she says, is preferable to discord. We thus have a tug-of-war between the conjugal pair. A woman could afford to take such an independent stand if she could rely on her own resources or family protection.

---

[84] T-S 8J22.22; see Friedman, *Jewish Polygyny* (see n. 45 above), pp. 225ff.; Goitein, *Jewish Education* (see n. 34 above), p. 71; *Mediterranean Society* (see n. 5 above), vol. 5, p. 490; Reif, *Bibliography* (see n. 5 above), p.123.

[85] The name Milāḥ (= 'Beauty') is short for Sitt al-Milāḥ; Goitein, *Mediterranean Society* (see n. 5 above), vol. 3, p. 318; Friedman, *Jewish Polygyny* (see n. 45 above), p. 225, n. 2.

[86] Friedman, *Jewish Polygyny* (see n. 45 above), p. 226.

[87] Bodleian MS d 76.65; cited by Goitein, *Mediterranean Society* (see n. 5 above), vol. 3, p. 339.

[88] T-S 6J3.22. The letter is mentioned by Goitein, *Mediterranean Society* (see n. 5 above), vol. 3, p. 178; see also Reif, *Bibliography* (see n. 5 above), p. 109.

A man married to the daughter of the judge of al-Maḥalla, a town in the Nile Delta, writes to his wife, Umm Thanā, from Fustat.[89] The letter is personal and explicit in its profession of love, suggesting that the wife was literate, since such an outspoken letter was normally intended for private reading. The husband had gone to Fustat, ostensibly to pursue his career as a judge. His wife did not wish to accompany him, preferring to be near her own natal family. Her marriage contract may have stipulated that the couple would live in al-Maḥalla unless the wife agreed to a change.[90] The writer opens with typical expressions of yearning, in this case beyond merely formal trappings. His yearning, he says, is unendurable and he begs her to return to him without delay. He knows that she is virtuous and valiant, but he too has merit. He is pious and loves her, and so she should not neglect him. He exhorts her to answer his letter in full and not cause him worry.

Having dealt first with emotional aspects, the husband goes on to report his situation. He reports that all the people of the two synagogues[91] have turned out for his lecture, which was successful and brought him renown. It was a pity that she had not been there to share in the glory. The husband ends with a fairly common threat. If she comes, fine. But if she does not, he will leave the country and go elsewhere. He ends his letter on this desperate note: 'In brief, there remains no one who loves me, O Umm Thanā, except you. Come, then, or else I shall forsake this country and vanish.' The emotional dependence of the man cries out here. The threat carries weight, for many husbands not only left town but country as well.

Elsewhere a husband puts pressure on his wife to leave Fustat and accompany him to a provincial town, but she refuses, apparently fearing that the atmosphere would be stifling.[92] The wife's uncle, who, it seems, had been involved in arranging the marriage, warns her that if she does not comply, the husband will either leave the country or marry a second wife. Her uncle cautions her that she has no one to rely on except her husband. The writer ends with practical advice:

> Take the small copies of the Bible and the quires and place them in a pouch and sew them up. And take the articles that you wish to, and whatever is heavy for you put in custody with the judge and get a receipt (*ruq'a*) for them. The wine (*nabīdh*) should be sold and a silver bracelet purchased for your wrist. Get in touch with Abū al-Ḥajjāj b. al-Ṭabīb, may God the exalted have mercy upon him. He will undertake its sale and

[89] See Or.1080 J23, mentioned above (see n. 55).

[90] The letter is translated in Goitein, *Mediterranean Society* (see n. 5 above), vol. 2, p. 219. Goitein (Goitein Laboratory in the Institute of Microfilmed Hebrew Manuscripts at the Jewish National & University Library in Jerusalem) identifies the handwriting as that of Peraḥya b. Joseph Yijū of Mazara in Sicily, who was originally from al-Mahdiyya in Tunisia. He appears as a judge in al-Maḥalla in 1187. If the identification is correct, his wife won the dispute and he returned to al-Maḥalla.

[91] The synagogue of the Palestinians and the synagogue of the Iraqis in Fustat.

[92] T-S 13J28.19; Goitein, *Mediterranean Society* (see n. 5 above), vol. 3, pp. 167–68, 177–79.

> will purchase the bracelet for you. And whatever you have with you put in custody with the judge as I told you.

The language of nostalgia

Our letters show that husbands away from home frequently expressed yearning for their wives. The equivalent of 'I've missed you,' regularly stated close to the beginning of a letter became a conventional epistolary motif. Husbands poured out their hearts about their loneliness, but etiquette restricted explicit language about sexual yearning. At most, a husband could allude to pining for sexual intimacy by circumlocution. He might say that he missed giving his wife her conjugal rights on Friday nights and holidays. For instance, a merchant we have met writes to his wife that 'the most difficult thing for me is every Friday night when I light the candle and put it on whatever table that God provides, and then think about you. God only knows what comes over me.'[93] Friday night was the traditional time for a scholar (*talmid ḥakham*) to be intimate with his wife.[94] The combination here of the sacred (sabbath, candles, divine provision) with amorous desire is moving. The merchant's wife had written to him bemoaning his prolonged absence and neglect. He informs her that he is healthy after having recovered from diverse maladies that he cannot describe because he does not wish to aggravate her own afflictions by raising her anxieties. But he does so all the same. The husband exonerates himself by appealing to a conventional motif – the letter as surrogate for actual presence. He claims that he mentions his poor health only so that the letter might represent him as he really is. Absent husbands stressed their ailments and misery in an effort to countervail their wives' grievances and desperate pleas for their return.

The merchant had received letters from his wife after a long and disturbing hiatus. He describes precisely his shifting reactions and mood swings as he contemplates her letter. His first reaction was joy at receiving it. That joy was immediately followed by anxiety at the possibility of hearing bad news. Then he was relieved to read that his wife was in good health, although he suspected that she might have been sparing him anguish. Having gone from joy through apprehension and on to relief, he eventually becomes disquieted by things she has written. She had spoken of her longing and solitude and 'sickness of the heart that produces sickness of the body.' The husband is annoyed that his wife has harped on her misery to arouse his pity and guilt. He counters by amplifying details he had not previously mentioned, lingering over his anxiety, loneliness and business problems. He wants to dispatch his business and return sooner for her sake and so that they do not die while apart.

At this point in the letter he dramatizes his plight, as though her carping and complaining had opened the floodgates in this grievance contest. The poor man is not

---

93 T-S 16.278 (mentioned above, n. 76). The letter is translated by Goitein in *Mediterranean Society* (see n. 5 above), vol. 3, pp. 221–23.

94 See Maimonides, *Hilkhot Shabbat*, 30. 14; *Ishut*, 14.4; cf. PT, *Ketubbot* 5, 30b. And see *Hilkhot De'ot*, 4. 19; 5. 4. The husband may light the sabbath candles in his wife's absence.

eating or sleeping well. He cannot prepare proper meals; he is too exhausted, worried and lonely. He is unable to sleep, lies awake most of the night. During his long vigils, if he is not overly fatigued, he recites religious prayers and poetry, hoping for the light of morning. Occasionally, when his mind is tormented by loneliness, he goes to stay overnight with his wife's son Abū Isḥāq in the dyehouse. This diverts him for a while. Sensing that he is overdoing his complaints (having criticized her for the same thing), he explains his need to cry on her shoulder and feel her consoling presence. We witness here the husband's emotional dependence on the wife for comfort and support. He harangues her with his misery because he does not want her to think that he is lolling around merrily leading a *dolce vita*, carrying on with business, oblivious to her (as she, to be sure, suspected). Even if he were enjoying himself, totally involved in his commercial activities, he says, he would not stop thinking of her. He cannot be called happy when he is apart from her, particularly when his situation is so difficult.

Having depicted his own state of being, he returns to her complaint. A Muslim acquaintance had told him that she came to his shop (accompanied by a man) and wept there, presumably when her husband was mentioned. The husband reiterates that his wife's misery depresses him. He implores her to control her emotions and not be upset on his account. She should rather pray to God to help him and bring them together soon. Perhaps when he returns and is reunited with her, she will regret pressuring him and realize that he might have remained away even longer. In any case, God has meanwhile helped him with his affairs and he plans to return home soon, although he cannot say when. God's salvation is 'like the twinkling of an eye.' If he could come home one day, he would not stay until the next. He refuses to be blamed for anything he has said because he writes under duress, with the messenger standing over him as he finishes the letter. He sends greetings to various people and concludes by saying that he was deeply moved when he read over the letter that he had just completed.

This is a long and poignant letter. We learn about the wife's feelings only from what the husband tells us. She clearly loved and missed him, and her emotional state undermined her health. She had accused him of combining business with pleasure, neglecting her, staying away for longer than necessary. She bursts out crying in the shop of a Muslim acquaintance of her husband. The husband's reactions are formalized in the letter in a less than sincere tone. He does not mind being absent quite as much as he claims. His purpose is to defend his absence, control her emotions and buoy up her hopes while not committing himself to a time of return. This depends on God. But never mind, divine salvation may be sooner than we think.

Letters had a strong emotional impact, since the written word was then more powerfully charged than today. A letter was commonly said to substitute for the beloved, to evoke his or her presence. Separation devastated loved ones, and people living apart frequently exhibited depressive tendencies. Wives often write that they are fasting and mourning until the husband's return. Husbands sometimes expressed themselves in similar fashion, but fasting was more common among women.[95]

---

[95] Cf. also C. W. Bynum, *Holy Feast and Holy Fast: The Religious Significance of Food to Medieval Women* (Berkeley, 1987), p. 192. She notes that in ancient Judaism fasting is

Husbands and wives separated for long periods of time took on tokens of mourning and melancholy. To be sure, such expressions were often an epistolary topos, a *façon de parler*. Occasionally, we sense that fasting was used as a weapon to coerce a wayward husband to return, a kind of 'fasting to destrain,'[96] projecting guilt onto the other person as responsible for the abstinence and martyrdom. We hear of one husband unwilling to submit to this emotional extortion. His wife writes to him, describing him as a man of flawless character and high social position.[97] The husband, we learn, was enraged that he had to live in the house of his wife's family and pay rent. He stayed away, returning home only for the sabbath, when it was his wife's legal right to be with him. She assures him that the rent he paid could be refunded, and she is ready to accompany him to another place, having learned from the example of her sisters (who apparently had the same problem). She went on a (daytime) hunger strike until the matter would be settled, informing him of this after he had stayed away even on the sabbath. The *verso* of the letter has his definitive answer: 'I greet his sublime honour,[98] and apologize for being away on the day of the sabbath...You[99] have taken an oath not to break your fast. If so, I shall not come to the house on the day of the sabbath nor on any other day.' The husband deprives his wife of a potent weapon in refusing to be coerced by her 'fasting.'

Husbands also took vows of abstinence pending reunion. A husband writes poignantly:[100]

> I have sworn an oath not to wash the clothes I wear until I return to you, nor cut my hair, drink wine or enter a bath until I come home. People know how I am constantly weeping, crying out and sobbing. By the Torah of Moses, peace upon him, I have not forgotten you, nor have I ever replaced you with someone else, or forgotten your piety and love; may God not let me die out of desire for you. I entreat you not to forget me in your prayers ... I wish to treat you with kindness, may God fulfill my hopes in this regard. I ask that I should be able to bedeck you with jewels beyond every woman in Sicily.

Note that whereas the woman gave up food, the man surrendered hygiene. Our letters reflect polar reactions to absence: 'Out of sight; out of mind' was one. 'Absence makes the heart grow fonder' was another.

---

virtually the only religious performance for which women (e.g. Sarah, the mothers of Samuel and Samson, Esther, Judith) are the main models of piety.

[96] Bynum, *Holy Feast* (see n. 95 above), p. 192

[97] Westminster College Ar. II.51; mentioned by Goitein, *Mediterranean Society* (see n. 5 above), vol. 3, pp. 168, 195–96.

[98] The sentence begins by addressing the wife (second person singular feminine), and then goes on to address 'his sublime honour', presumably his father-in-law.

[99] Here he is addressing his wife.

[100] MS Mosseri VII,162.3 (L 230); Goitein, *Mediterranean Society* (see n. 5 above), vol. 3, p. 193.

Love between husband and wife

It is said by the talmudic sages that a man without a wife lives without joy, blessing, and good, and that a man should love his wife as himself and respect her more than himself.[101] Husbands and wives often expressed deep adoration for one another and for their children.

A cantor who pines for his wife asks her to take care of their little son as an act of love for him.[102] The letter is from the itinerant scribe and cantor, Isaac b. Barukh, to his wife. It was sent from Sammanūd to Fustat and addressed to his father-in-law, the well-known cantor Abū al-Bayān, to whom greetings are also conveyed in the text of the letter. The letter is written in Hebrew, either because the writer hailed from a Christian country — the form of address seems to be that of a foreigner — or because the cantor's father-in-law, and perhaps his daughter, were educated, and it was fitting to use Hebrew. Cantors, as composers of liturgical poetry, usually had an excellent command of Hebrew.

The cantor is on the road, performing in various towns, and he describes his misery and tears quite vividly: 'Though I am assured of your well-being, my own situation is bitter because I am apart from you and from the eyes of the lad – my darling, beloved and precious son. I weep, sigh and wail night and day, and gaze in all four directions, but there is no one who pities me save the Holy One, blessed be He.' He tells his wife not to worry about him: 'Do not worry about me at all. Were I able to ride on a swift cloud in all my travels, I would do so without delay. If God wills, I shall finish my job and return soon, with Heaven's help, with a full purse and a gay heart.'[103]

Intense professions of love are, however, rare, because letters were often read out to women. They survive in cases where the recipients were literate and able to read on their own[104] or when the letter was never sent because of its frank and personal language. An exception is a letter in which Bū al-Faraj writes to Umm Joseph, a relative of his, via the Judge Elijah b. Zechariah.[105] 'May R. Elijah be so kind as to read this note[106] to Umm Joseph, the mother-in-law of al-Shaykh al-Bayān al-Bakhtāj,

---

[101] See BT, *Yevamot* 62b; Maimonides, *Hilkhot Ishut*, 15.19–20: 'The Sages have likewise ordained that a man should honour his wife more than his own self, and love her as himself; ...and that his discourse with her should be gentle' (trans. Isaac Klein, *The Code of Maimonides*, Book Four, *The Book of Women* (New Haven, 1972), p. 98).

[102] T-S 13J20.9. The text of the letter was published by Mann, *Jews* (see n. 5 above), vol. 2, pp. 307–8; see corrections by Goitein (see n. 5 above), p. xxxv. The letter is translated in Goitein, *Mediterranean Society* (see n. 5 above), vol. 3, pp. 220–21. See also Reif, 'Aspects' (see n. 34 above), p. 153 and Reif, *Bibliography* (see n. 5 above), p. 168.

[103] The expression is in Aramaic. Goitein read *kisa la malya* ('an empty purse'), but the *lamed* is actually crossed out in the manuscript, and so the reading is *kisa malya*, meaning 'a full purse', which makes more sense here. The normal desire of a traveller on business is to return home with a happy heart and a full purse; *Mediterranean Society* (see n. 5 above), vol. 3, p. 472, n. 248.

[104] See, for instance, CUL Or.1080 J23 (see n. 55).

[105] T-S 8J17.3; Goitein, *Mediterranean Society* (see n. 5 above), vol. 2, p. 144; Reif, *Bibliography* (see n. 5 above), p. 120.

[106] The word is *biṭaqa*, from the Greek *pittakion*.

and not delay it for a moment, for I heard about her illness.' The writer describes his love as distress (*shidda*)[107] and says that it struck him from the day the two met in the synagogue and previously. 'From the one who loves you and is grateful for your affection, Bū al-Faraj, who informs Umm Joseph[108] that I have been tormented by this distress I have been in from the day you met me in the synagogue and previously.[109] My heart has not been void of thinking about you and those with you.' In a marginal comment he adds: 'If I could, I would be there instead of the note (*ruq'a*) but the situation is not hidden from you.' Again, the letter is a substitute for presence.

Brother and sister

The natural bond between brother and sister was close. Women were keenly aware of their precarious status. As they got older, they could be divorced or replaced by another wife. Under such conditions, a brother, like a son, was a permanent and steady prop and mainstay. A brother's absence was especially painful.

A widowed sister in Mahdiyya, Tunisia, writes to her brother in Egypt at the time of the Norman invasion there: [110]

> O my dear brother, you know that I have no one but God and you, may the Creator not hinder me from seeing your face. All year, my brother, I anticipated that I would receive a letter from you, so that I would know how you were. The mail carriers (*al-fuyūj*) arrived, but we did not see a letter to me when I went out and made inquiries. They said to me that you were weak, and I went out of my mind and swore that I would not have breakfast during the day or change my clothes or enter a bath, neither I nor my daughter until a letter comes from you so that we know how you are.

She says that she anxiously awaits a letter from him. She is mired in abysmal debt and is starving. Her letter is a desperate cry for help: 'Now, my brother, consider me a captive woman. I come to you to release me. Look at me, O brother, and do everything you can to help me in this debt.' The frenetic cry for help contains two recurrent motifs. 'I have no one but God and you', a conventional expression of dependency, is reiterated in the letter. Then there is the theme of self-denial to achieve some objective or even to coerce the recipient to comply.

---

[107] The word comes form a root meaning 'to be(come) hard, vehement, intense' and occurs very often in the Genizah papers in the sense of 'stress' and 'distress'.

[108] 'Umm Joseph' is also written by a different hand superlinearly.

[109] Goitein, *Mediterranean Society* (see n. 5 above), vol. 2, pp. 144–45, has 'when I last met you in the synagogue.' He contends that this can refer only to the lane or the court fronting the building, noting that the synagogue included the whole compound surrounding the house of worship.

[110] T-S 10J14.20. Another version of the same letter is preserved in T-S 10J19.20; see Goitein, *Mediterranean Society* (see n. 5 above), vol. 3, pp. 21–22; and the many entries in *Mediterranean Society* (see n. 5 above), vol. 6, *Cumulative Indices*, p. 169; Reif, *Bibliography* (see n. 5 above), p. 139.

Another woman writes to her brother, the great merchant Ismāʿīl b. Barhūn, of the famous Tāhertī family, that she did not receive letters from him but is compelled to write again:[111]

> Your letter reached us mentioning your well-being, thank God, after we had undergone anxiety and tension. I had been fasting and praying that God extend His kindness in accordance with his everlasting generosity. I entreat God to prolong your life. May He make me your ransom from evil and protect me by your life. May He reunite us as I greatly desire, for my heart is firmly set on this. I entreat God to give you and all who are with you good fortune, and may He help you realize your plans ...What is more, I relish writing to you because I can then envisage that I am actually speaking to you.

Again we find self-sacrifice as the price the person pays to attain some desire, along with the notion of substitute suffering contained in the idea of being someone's ransom from harm, that is, offering one's life for the other.

While women frequently turned to brothers for support, brothers occasionally solicited help from sisters. For instance, a man writes a letter to the Judge Elijah b. Zechariah (and for his eyes only), requesting that it be read aloud to his sister.[112] He needs her assistance. The writer is suffering great stress. He had been arrested, and he depicts in gory detail the torture he underwent at the hand of government authorities.

In a letter from the fifteenth or sixteenth century a brother in Tripoli (Lebanon) writes a letter to his sister in Cairo begging for her help in a tone of great urgency and desperation.[113] The letter is lengthy and repetitive. Addressing her as 'my sister, my darling, my faultless dove',[114] he tells her of a calamity he suffered while he was in Alexandria. Police had arrested him, and he was apparently detained for two months. For this and other reasons he became impoverished. He had borrowed money for rent and food. 'I therefore entreat you[115] to forgive me for the love of God, for He knows how distressed I was at my separation from you. Perhaps God will give me the opportunity for the sake of his mercy to return to you, for the desire is engraved in my heart.' Towards the end of the letter there is a reference to his mother, who was living with his sister, or nearby. 'I kiss the hands and feet of my lady, my mother and entreat her to pray to God for me and so that I see your faces.' After sending greetings once more to 'my sister, my darling', he begs her: 'for the sake of God, do not neglect the matter, speak with Solomon to send the money with the first traveller.' If he has spent

---

[111] T-S 12.262. See Goitein, *Jewish Education* (see n. 34 above), p. 25. The letter is partly translated in Goitein, 'New Revelations' (see n. 1 above), pp. 38–39; see *Mediterranean Society* (see n. 5 above), vol. 6, *Cumulative Indices*, p. 196; Reif, *Bibliography* (see n. 5 above), p. 262.

[112] T-S 10J7.4; see Goitein, *Mediterranean Society* (see n. 5 above), vol. 3, p. 373; vol. 2, p. 609; vol. 3, p. 43; Reif, *Bibliography* (see n. 5 above), p. 135.

[113] T-S 16.265; Kraemer, 'Spanish Ladies' (see n. 50 above), pp. 255–57.

[114] Song of Songs 5:2.

[115] This is in the plural, out of respect.

the money, she should send 20 *bunduqī* (Venetian sequins). The brother's frantic need is accompanied by guilt for leaving his sister and mother.

Not all brother-sister letters are cries for help. In a moving letter of consolation, a man named Barakāt wrote to his sister Rayyisa who was extremely despondent after her mother's death.[116] Rayyisa was obviously educated. He advises her to study Ecclesiastes and Proverbs for solace, and also a classic in Arabic consolation literature, *al-Faraj ba'd al-shidda* (*Relief after Distress*).[117] Pondering these books will save her from sinking into irreparable despair and self-annihilation. She will learn that others who lost relatives bravely endured God's judgement. Religious themes abound and afford insights into popular religious culture. The merit of the deceased, it is believed, supports people during their lifetime and sustains them after their death. The mother died because of their sins. Again we find the motif of self-sacrifice and substitute suffering. Themes from consolation literature prevail. Death is universal, and all of creation partakes of this cup of sorrow. Those who survive have been deprived, not the one who died. 'Do not weep for the dead and do not lament for him; weep rather for those who are leaving.'[118] The letter stresses God's unalterable decree and caring providence.

Barakāt has heard that Rayyisa weeps inconsolably and is in wretched despair over the death of her mother to whom she was deeply devoted.[119] Worried that Rayyisa will perish from the torment of her despondency and grief, the brother preaches self-control and emotional restraint. Weeping is futile and unavailing, and will only debilitate and destroy. She must be patient with God, resigned and submissive, and she will be recompensed. Whoever leaves behind someone like Rayyisa, says her brother, has not really died, thereby consoling Rayyisa with the idea that the deceased is present in the personality of the living.[120]

---

[116] T-S 10J9.1. See Goitein, 'New Revelations' (see n. 1 above), pp. 14–15, 38–39. The letter is translated in Goitein, *Mediterranean Society* (see n. 5 above), vol. 5, pp.180–81; and see Reif, *Bibliography* (see n. 5 above), p. 136.

[117] The reference is to the famous Arabic work, *al-Faraj ba'd al-Shidda* by Abū 'Alī al-Tanūkhī (d. 994). There was a Hebrew version, *Ḥibbur Yafeh me-ha-Yeshu'ah*, by R. Nissim b. Jacob ibn Shahin of Qayrawan (*ca.* 990–1062) ; see W. M. Brinner (trans.), *An Elegant Composition concerning Relief after Adversity* (New Haven, 1977), introduction, especially pp. xxiv–xxvii; and Goitein's note there (pp. xxvii–xxxiii) on 'Genizah Correspondence on *al-Faraj ba'd al-Shidda*' where there is a reference to our letter, erroneously given as 1059, f. 1, for 10J9.1.

[118] Jer. 22:10. The writer altered the singular 'he who leaves' of the verse to the plural. Goitein, *Mediterranean Society* (see n. 5 above), vol. 5, p. 557, n. 298, notes that Hebrew 'going away' (*halakh*) means 'perishing' in Arabic (*halaka*). The writer uses the verse to refer to weeping for him who destroys himself by immoderate mourning.

[119] See Goitein, *Mediterranean Society* (see n. 5 above), vol. 5, p. 180.

[120] See Goitein, *Mediterranean Society* (see n. 5 above), vol. 5, p. 557, n. 297, who observes that this is an Arabic adaptation of an Aramaic phrase: 'He who has gone away, but left behind someone like himself, has not gone away', used, for example, by Samuel ha-Nagid of Granada in a letter of condolence to R. Ḥananel of Qayrawan on the death of his father Ḥushiel.

While imploring his sister not to grieve and mourn excessively, Barakāt confesses that he is writing after refreshing his eyes with tears, overwhelmed by the loss of his mother's love. He expresses guilt over having been apart from her and takes pains to justify this and to register how intense the strain of his separation from her was for him. Now he is separated from his sister. She was with their mother when she died. Nor can Barakāt come and console her personally. He has removed his protection from her, and hopes that her son will stand by her. Barakāt prays that God will keep her company. Twice he uses the word *'iṣma*, a term meaning the protective care that a male gives female members of his family. The mother was evidently a widow, and the sister Rayyisa is either a widow or divorced. Several expressions intimate widowhood. Barakāt, detained by his own family and business concerns, did not remain physically close to either of them, and he expresses appropriate remorse.

In one of the most calligraphically exquisite letters in the entire Genizah, a man in Jerusalem, Simeon son of Saul, writes a very personal letter to his sister Ballūṭa in Toledo, Spain, in the autumn of 1053, during the period when the city was still under Muslim rule.[121] Simeon and his elderly father Saul had migrated from Spain to Jerusalem some years previously. The letter is actually sent by both the father and brother, but only Simeon speaks. He explains to his sister how he takes care of their elderly father in the course of his illness. The letter's tone implies that Ballūṭa (like Rayyisa) was educated. She is a mature woman with married children. Names in the letter are in Arabic, Hebrew and Romanesque. The letter is a copy written by a scribe. As it was found in the Cairo Genizah, it was evidently copied before the letter was forwarded to Toledo. The document contains fascinating information about Karaites in Ramla and Jerusalem.

Mother and son

Relations and correspondence between mother and son were complex and emotionally charged. Many letters of this genre preserved in the Cairo Genizah were written by mothers to sons who were far away. Again, we encounter the leitmotif of loneliness, nostalgia and resentment. Mothers constantly urged sons to return home or at least to give a sign of life, lamenting their absence and neglect, often with great bitterness. Their protests might be accompanied by requests for gifts, mainly of clothing. They occasionally give 'fatherly' advice to their sons on how to behave, as in a letter from a mother in Aden to her son in Old Cairo in which she exhorts him, 'Be a man, my son'! (see below). Mothers did not hesitate to take their sons on a 'guilt trip'.

---

[121] T-S 13J9.4; ed. E. Ashtor in S. Assaf, *Texts and Studies in Jewish History* (Hebrew; Jerusalem, 1946), pp. 108–13; re-edited with Spanish translation by Ashtor, 'Documentos Españoles de la Genizah', *Sefarad* 24 (1964), pp. 47–59 and *The Jews of Moslem Spain*, trans. A. Klein and J. M. Klein (2 vols; Philadelphia, 1973–79), vol. 2, pp. 226–27; M. Gil, *Palestine during the First Muslim Period (634–1099)* (3 vols; Hebrew; Tel Aviv, 1983), vol. 3, no. 457, p. 89; Goitein, *Mediterranean Society* (see n. 5 above), vol. 3, p. 229. A partial translation is given by Goitein in *Mediterranean Society* (see n. 5 above), vol. 3, p. 241.

An aristocratic elderly mother writes (*ca.* 1050) from the town of Raqqa on the Euphrates River (Syria) to her son Abū Manṣūr Dosa b. Joshua in Fustat.[122] She is disappointed that she has not heard from him, and repeatedly expresses her longing. If she could only glance at him for a moment, she would not mind 'being extinguished like a candle'.

The Dosas were an old and established family, who first settled in Jerusalem and then in Lādhiqiyya (Latakia) (Syria).[123] For some reason, the Lādhiqiyya Dosas scattered, the father going in one direction and two sons relocating in Cairo, a dreadful situation that could only gladden their enemies' hearts, says the mother. After the father's death, three years before this letter was written, the sons decided that their mother should move in with a married daughter living in Raqqa. She hated the arrangement. 'How long can a person live in other people's houses?' The cry of distress is surprising, as her son-in-law, Sahl b. Ḥātim, with whom she was staying, sent the letter. To be sure, he too may have been at his wits' end and eager to be rid of her, or perhaps he was not expected to read it. The letter was apparently dictated by the mother to someone else. A pupil of the recipient, Sulaym, sends regards and may have been the copyist of the letter. The writer barely mentions her own daughter with whom she lives. The letter was written *ca.* 1050, at any rate before 1070, as references to Jerusalem indicate.[124]

> I have become weary writing to you, my son, without receiving a response. I do not even know how to get greetings from you.[125]
>
> I get letters from your brother, may God preserve him, but don't find any from you among them, although you are both living in the same place. You seem unaware that when I receive a letter from you it is a substitute for (seeing) your face. And you don't realize that my life[126] depends upon news about you.[127] Nothing less than a letter from you will cheer my spirits. Do not kill me before my time!
>
> I only want you to write a letter every once in a while so that I know that you are in good health. I looked forward to the summer when letters might come from you.[128] But the summer passed, and I didn't get to read a single letter of yours. I wanted you to let me know how long you are going to stay in Fustat so as to cheer my spirits before I die. I wish that you were close to us in Jerusalem or in this country. I entreat God to be good to you. I fast and pray for you night and day.

---

[122] T-S 13J23.5. See Goitein, *Mediterranean Society* (see n. 5 above), vol. 3, p. 227; and vol. 5, p. 224 (long summary). The sender (and presumably writer) is the woman's son-in-law, Sahl b. Ḥātim. See Reif, *Bibliography* (see n. 5 above), p. 171.

[123] For the Dosa family, see Mann, *Jews* (see n. 5 above), vol. 2, p. 270.

[124] See *Mediterranean Society* (see n. 5 above), vol. 3, p. 227, and the long summary in *Mediterranean Society*, vol. 5, p. 224.

[125] The translation is uncertain.

[126] Lit. 'my heart'.

[127] 'You' here is plural.

[128] The delivery of mail was easier in the summer than during the winter.

> I would like you to send me, my son, twenty dirhams of pure antimony and five dirhams of zinc oxide.[129] By God, you must send me your worn and dirty shirts to restore my spirit.[130] Do not withhold your letters. By God, you must be careful that nothing untoward happens to you. Watch the roads and your coming and going. When you were still with me I was anxious about your safety.

This letter is filled with projections of guilt. The son's neglect will kill her, the mother avows. She fasts and prays for him night and day. The self-affliction casts guilt on the son and is aimed at coercion. The mother then deals with some business affairs. This is fairly typical of mother-son letters. Mothers often attended to the son's affairs while he was in absentia. She asks for some token of his presence, his soiled shirts that will remind her of his body. And she ends by conveying her anxiety for his safety, a more subtle projection of guilt.

Sons, racked by mother-induced guilt, often wrote to their mothers apologizing for not visiting or else urging their mothers to visit them. The mother's status in Islamic societies was precarious.[131] She risked rejection and abandonment by divorce, replacement by a younger second wife or widowhood. Encumbered by so much anguish, a woman naturally transferred her deepest affections to her children.

In the Muslim environment of the time, where gender antagonism is high and female status low, women tend to find their deepest emotional satisfaction in the mother-son relationship. The son is a mother's sole guarantee of security and stability. Sons represent insurance in sickness and old age and a surety against fate in the case of repudiation by the husband. Every mother dreams of becoming a venerated and protecting mother-in-law, reigning over her sons' wives, her daughters-in-law. Her subordination to the husband was balanced by control over her daughters-in-law. It was in her interest to assure that the conjugal bond between her sons and their wives was subsidiary.[132] Women wanted as many children as possible to insure protection. Upbringing in Muslim societies was authoritarian and emasculating, and the mother became the only haven for sons threatened by the father. Mother and son combined forces to delimit patriarchal power. They relished outwitting the father in a bond of complicity, both of them harbouring enormous resentment. The mother protects the son from the severity of the father. The son consequently lives in a state of eternal gratitude to his mother.

A complex of emotions similar to that described by Bouhdiba existed in Jewish society and is expressed in our letters. A son's absence or neglect was a hard blow for a mother and evoked anxiety and bitterness. The obligation imposed on a son was

---

[129] Zinc oxide was used for making collyrium.

[130] Goitein sees a connection with the story of Joseph and his father Jacob who was revived by contact with his son's shirt; Qur'ān 12:93 (Genesis. 45:27); *Mediterranean Society* (see n. 5 above), vol. 3, pp. 227, 474, n. 24.

[131] See A. Bouhdiba, *Sexuality in Islam* (London, 1985), ch. 13 ('In the Kingdom of the Mothers').

[132] See Kandiyoti, 'Islam and Patriarchy'(see n. 60 above), p. 33.

often too much to tolerate. His responsibility to his mother created overbearing stress. And the subversive complicity of son and mother against the father generated guilt and shame. It is no wonder that sons, like husbands, absconded and took themselves to places far distant from home and from an overly dependent mother.

A mother writes to her son, Abū al-Ḥasan, who is away from Fustat with his family.[133] His children are mentioned, and we may gather that his wife was also with him. According to epistolary etiquette and the sexual mores of the time, one did not mention a man's wife explicitly but referred to her only indirectly. In our letter greetings are sent at the end to whoever is surrounded by the recipient's care. The son had neither answered letters nor had he come to visit, and the mother harps on her private disappointment and also his sister's yearning for him. The mother announces the engagement and impending marriage of his niece (his sister's daughter), and consequently urges him to return along with his own children and with her sister, the bride's aunt (and his as well) who lived near him. She was not married at the time. The mother also orders a new cloak and imported chest. These are not to be gifts. She wants to know the cost so that she can reimburse her son. Here is the entire letter:

> In the name of the merciful one.
>
> From the mother of Abū al-Ḥasan.
>
> My letter is to my son, the dearest person to me – may God prolong his life and perpetuate his honour and favour, and always bestow good fortune upon you. Apart from this, do not ask how much we yearn for you. We sent you a number of letters but have not received your response. You said that you and the little ones were coming to me for the holiday, but you did not come, so that our hearts were very despondent. Your sister misses you greatly, and she keeps watching the door, longing for you.
>
> I should like to let you know[134] that the little one[135] has become betrothed,[136] and she will marry on the twenty-fifth [day of the month]. So come in a hurry, and by all means bring your little ones with you.[137] We would like you to ask her aunt[138] to come with you. And be kind to her, for she has only God and you.

---

[133] T-S 10J7.5; see Goitein, *Mediterranean Society* (see n. 5 above), vol. 3, pp. 115, 236; see Reif, *Bibliography* (see n. 5 above), p. 135.

[134] Lit. 'What you would like to know is'.

[135] *Al-ṣaghīra*, that is, the sister's daughter, the recipient's niece.

[136] See Friedman, *Jewish Polygyny* (see n. 45 above), pp. 232–33; Goitein, *Mediterranean Society* (see n. 5 above), vol. 3, pp. 69, 95, on the terms *milāk*, *imlāk* ('betrothal', 'engagement').

[137] Invitations extended to celebrations and holidays always included children; Goitein, *Mediterranean Society* (see n. 5 above), vol. 3, p. 236.

[138] The word is *khāla*, meaning maternal aunt.

> We would like you to buy me a new outer garment[139] that costs three dinars or less and a Rūmī chest[140] costing a dinar or less. Do not neglect this. And let us know how much you pay for them, so that we can reimburse you.
> I send greetings to you and whoever is surrounded by your care.

A widowed mother called Umm al-Sadīd, living in Aden in Southern Arabia, writes (some time between 1226 and 1228) to her son Moses in Fustat, reprimanding him for travelling so far from home and chiding him for sending her a ridiculous dress.[141] She rants and raves about her son's absence and neglect. He had complained that she wrote little, but she had written nine letters without receiving an answer. She protests that another son has also left. Amidst all this, she gives much maternal advice, bidding him 'to be a man'.

The letter contains information about the situation of Yemenite Jews some time after 1218. They were forbidden to drink wine (as prohibited by Islam) in public, and were severely punished for breaking the law. The letter was dictated to a scribe, but the mother's speech is clearly conveyed. The mother's grief at her son's remoteness is intensified by the incident of the risible dress and by her having to bear responsibility for her son's debts. The segment on business is characteristic of mother-son letters.

> [Your mother] informs (you) that your noble writ has arrived and that she has pondered its contents. You complain to me about my infrequent writing, but I have written nine letters and have not received a reply. I hope that you are well occupied.
> Don't ask how I weep on account of your absence day and night. You wrote that you sent me a dress. Aren't you ashamed to send me attire that everyone laughs at? Better had you not sent it at all. If you wish to do something nice, then send me a dress for the Day of Atonement.[142] The only benefit I have from you others enjoy.[143] I actually have no assistance from you[144] but only harm, while your help goes to someone else. They exacted from me the poll tax you owed.[145] So I had to mortgage the house for thirty dinars until you pay yours and your brother's tax.

---

[139] The word is *malḥafa*. It was a night-time cloak that served as an outer garment in day time, a wrap; see Goitein, *Mediterranean Society* (see n. 5 above), vol. 6, Cumulative Indices, p. 24 (esp. vol. 4, p. 116).

[140] 'Rūm' refers specifically to the Byzantine empire, and also in general to Western Europe, often Italy, whence furniture was imported to Egypt; Goitein, *Mediterranean Society* (see n. 5 above), vol. 4, pp. 106, 303, 377.

[141] Bodleian MS Heb. d 66.21 (2878.21). The letter was published and translated into Hebrew by Goitein, in *Yemenites: History, Communal Organization, Spiritual Life*, ed. M. Ben-Sasson (Hebrew; Jerusalem, 1983), pp. 48–52; see also Goitein, *Mediterranean Society* (see n. 5 above), vol. 3, p. 246; vol. 5, p. 222 (with partial translation).

[142] This was the day when it was customary to wear fresh new clothes, according to rabbinic tradition; Goitein, *Yemenites* (see n. 141 above), p. 49, n. 20.

[143] Did she give the dress away?

[144] 'You' is plural in this sentence, that is, the two brothers.

[145] The government authorities forced her to defray the *jizya* (poll tax) that her son owed.

> Know, my son, that roaming over countries and seas gives no blessing. Far better for you to stay put in your own hometown.
>
> Jacob b. Abraham b. Peraḥ received his letters, one of them being a letter from you, but I did not receive along with them either a letter or a garment. This distressed me greatly—I wish you health.[146] I sent you seven *rubāʿiyya* of aromatic betelnut[147] with the friend of Jacob b. Abraham b. Peraḥ the Aleppan. If he delivers it to you, well and good. If not, do not let him go until you get it.
>
> And you my son, be a man,[148] and be clever and watch over the merchandise of Abraham b. Bundār.[149]

Mother and daughter

The mother-daughter affinity was also intense, fortified by a shared common gender inferiority and sense of solidarity. A daughter writes to her mother in Fustat about her feelings of isolation and longing.[150] She had been married in al-Maḥalla, Egypt, to a man from Aleppo and had moved with her husband to the village of ʿIbbilīn in the Western Galilee. She complains of her turbulent life from the time of her departure. Her husband wanted her to remove herself further by going with him to his home in Aleppo. But she was languishing with longing for her mother. 'My yearning and loneliness caused by our separation is something that I cannot describe,' she writes.

The plight of women: virilocal marriage

Women married early, often at the age of thirteen or so. As marriage was virilocal (woman moving in with the husband's family), the young bride had to adjust to a situation in which her husband's mother was in control of the household. The wife was called the little one (*ṣaghīra*), and other epithets signifying her immature, virtually infantile status, such as 'baby' (*ṭifla*) and 'girl' (*ṣabiyya*), as opposed to her mother-in-law, the grand one (*kabīra*), or dowager.[151] She had to pay proper respect to the mother-in-law, who lorded it over her daughters-in-law, and also to her sisters-in-law, and she was frequently mistreated.

A woman named Umm Sitt al-Nās writes to her uncle, her mother's brother, who had apparently taken her under his protection and brought her up as her mother had

---

[146] Having expressed anger, the mother immediately adds a wish for his good health.

[147] The word is *fofal*. Betelnut is the seed of the Indian date (Areca catechou), which is made along with the Indian betel plant and some lime into a gum resin that is chewed for its narcotic effect even today. It is also used for medicine and cosmetics. See Goitein, *Yemenites* (see n. 141 above), p. 49, n. 22; p. 95, n. 8. A *rubā*ʿ*iyya* is a Sicilian quarter dinar.

[148] MS *rajul,* occasionally, as here, in the sense of a real man.

[149] He was related to the Nagid of Yemen. The name Bundār is Persian; see Goitein, *Yemenites* (see n. 141 above), p. 50, n. 23, and pp. 78–82.

[150] T-S 10J12.18; *Mediterranean Society* (see n. 5 above), vol. 3, p. 177; and see other references in Reif, *Bibliography* (see n. 5 above), p. 138.

[151] Goitein, *Mediterranean Society* (see n. 5 above), vol. 3, p. 162.

acquired a bad reputation after her father died.[152] The writer was married to her cousin, who was a son of her mother's sister. First cousin marriage was preferred in Genizah society, as in the Near East in general. And this letter reflects the complex family situations that ensue. The uncle of Umm Sitt al-Nās is the brother of these two sisters, who are the writer's mother and her mother-in-law.

She complains to her uncle that he does not protect her sufficiently. Her mother-in-law (the addressee's own sister) had caused her to leave Dammūh (a town opposite Fustat on the West Bank of the Nile), not of her own accord. Her husband treats her miserably and is egged on by his mother. We learn that the mother-in-law's enmity is fueled by her hatred of her sister, the writer's mother. Umm Sitt al-Nās is suspected by her father-in-law (a cousin of her uncle, the addressee) of misconduct with her elder cousin. The writer was forced to leave her house with nothing, and is staying with a widow who is infirm. Now she needs money to be able to travel to her uncle so that he can take care of her. She depicts a situation of extreme abuse by her husband and his mother.

> I have not left Dammūh by my own preference but rather by the lovely choice of your sister.[153] But I myself had nothing to do with this ... And do not ask what (my husband) does to me. Let us rather ask God to requite him.
>
> We had all moved into a single house. Then shortly thereafter my mother-in-law (*'ammati*)[154] began to act against me and to alienate people from me by implanting enmity to me in her son. The least of what she said was, 'Go and be like your infamous mother.' You know the lovely character of your cousin.[155] He suspected me with my elder cousin. You yourself know how all reacted in the case of Baqā, your sister.[156]
>
> I cannot describe to you the (miserable) state I am in until God brings us together, so that I can inform you of what your sister has inflicted upon me this year, both she and her son. You know that I have no one save God and you.

---

[152] T-S 10J9.13. See Goitein, *Mediterranean Society* (see n. 5 above), vol. 3, pp. 175–76, for a partial translation; Reif, *Bibliography* (see n. 5 above), p. 136. Prof. Moshe Gil kindly helped me decipher the margin of this document.

[153] The sister of the recipient is the mother-in-law of the writer. The reader must bear in mind that she married her cousin.

[154] This is the same person referred to above and below as the recipient's sister. The style in Genizah letters was to relate a person first to the recipient of the letter and then to the writer if need be; see Goitein, *Mediterranean Society* (see n. 5 above), vol. 3, p. 464, n. 79; and see also *Mediterranean Society*, vol. 2, pp. 236–37.

[155] He was apparently her father-in-law.

[156] She is probably the writer's own mother; see Goitein, *Mediterranean Society* (see n. 5 above), vol. 3, p. 464, n. 80.

We have already met the woman who remonstrated with her absent husband with a long list of complaints, including the reproach, 'Don't ask what I suffered from your father's wife!'[157]

As in Muslim society, mother-in-law and wife may also enjoy a bond of amicable collaboration. The mature woman gives the young wife advice and support, and the young woman is a mainstay to lean upon. Such a warm attachment is evident in a beautiful letter (from the thirteenth century), in which a mother-in-law, whose son Abū al-Khayr has died, and who is alone, invites her daughter-in-law, Sitt al-Nās bint Moses b. Josiah, to come and live with her and take the place of her deceased son.[158] She tells her daughter-in-law: 'You shall be like a child to me.' In trying to lure her daughter-in-law to join her, she gives, *en passant*, valuable information about Damascus which, she says, is a city famous for its prosperity, where Jews live 'like Arabs and upper class people.' The mail address clarifies the relationships between the writer and the recipient of this letter. Two brothers, sons of Josiah, are mentioned. The writer was the daughter of one of them, Joseph, and the recipient was the daughter of another, Moses. Thus, they were cousins. And this may, in fact, help explain the personal warmth of the letter. The mother-in-law's eagerness to have her daughter-in-law join her is amplified by her concern for own fate.

> And now accept from me what I tell you and sincerely advise you. Pick up and leave, and may God give you success. I put the clothing that I still have at your disposal. I have no relative aside from you, and you will be like a child to me. So do not delay. I have no idea what fate[159] has in store for me. When you arrive, God willing, my heart will be at ease. I shall be delighted to have you nearby. I shall recuperate by setting eyes on you and be revived by your presence. I pray to God to sustain my life by you.

Appeals and petitions

A large number of petitions to communal leaders and appeals to the congregation preserve touching descriptions of female anguish and distress. We obviously have no basis for deciding what proportion of women turned for help. Despite their low status and subjugation, the mass of women must have found life tolerable enough not to appeal to the authorities for redress of grievances or, if it was intolerable, they were too inured and desperate. Nevertheless, a woman's voice could be heard in public.

Women's petitions to communal leaders tended to be in an informal speech register. Females were insistent and resolute in making their requests. When a woman petitions a communal leader, she often avoids lofty titles, but comes straight to the point and speaks directly and naturally. Perhaps they were unable to hire professional scribes adept in these formalities. Or perhaps their own social status being low, they were free

---

[157] T-S 10J15.9. See above, n. 78.

[158] T-S 18J3.4. The letter is mentioned by Goitein, *Mediterranean Society* (see n. 5 above), vol. 3, pp. 26, 30, 433, 434. He gives a table of the family genealogy on p. 433, n. 7.

[159] The word is *zamān*, meaning 'time', often used in Arabic poetry for fate.

from employing conventional decorum. In an unusual petition by a woman to the Nagid David,[160] she demands that he retrieve her husband from a Sufi convent. She reminds the Nagid that he is quite capable of doing this: 'Our lord, may God prolong his life, governs an entire region (*iqlīm*) and his high endeavour is not inadequate to prevent the aforementioned (husband of mine) from going up to the mountain and getting him to attend the synagogue and undertaking the maintenance of his family.' She then adds a personal request, typical in this kind of letter: 'Our lord has promised the little one some remedy for his ear,[161] for he is complaining of an earache. No harm is done by experimenting, for even the barber is treating him without his having any experience, God have mercy.' The tone is direct, the language register is vernacular, and the letter is laced with Hebrew phrases, a trait of women's letters.

A common accusation was neglect and mistreatment by husbands, who were either indigent or indisposed to support their wives. In one case, a woman complains to a judge that her husband, a pauper, mistreated her. The rest of his family lent a hand. His sister beat her with a shoe; his father cursed her; they all besmirched her name.[162]

Physical abuse of women by husbands cannot have been rare.[163] We have seen that husbands were permitted to use force to prevent their wives from going out.[164] Violence against women was an extension of the husband's custodial role. An anonymous (and unique) geonic ruling permits wife beating: 'Even if he beats her, she should be silent as modest women are.'[165] Avraham Grossman suggests that this precept should be contextualized within the Islamic environment. Physical violence against women is sanctioned in the Qur'ān (4:34): 'As those you fear may be rebellious admonish; banish them to their couches, and beat them' [trans. A. J. Arberry]. And he suggests that both Islamic influence and the geonic precedent may account for Maimonides's severe ruling, 'A wife who refuses to perform any kind of work that she is obligated to do may be compelled to perform it, even by scourging her with a rod.'[166] But this strict measure may also have been due to Maimonides's own stern

---

[160] He is most likely David II Maimonides, head of the Jewish community in Egypt as of 1355; T-S 8J26.19; Goitein, 'A Jewish Addict to Sufism in the Time of the Nagid David II Maimonides', *Jewish Quarterly Review* 44 (1953–54), pp. 37–49; *Jewish Education* (see n. 34 above), pp. 72–74; *Mediterranean Society* (see n. 5 above), vol. 5, pp. 471–74 (long summary and translation); Reif, *Bibliography* (see n. 5 above), p. 124.

[161] She uses the colloquial *widne* instead of standard *udhn*.

[162] This petition to a judge against her husband and his family was written for her by a scribe or assistant; see MS ENA NS 16.30; and see the references in Goitein, *Mediterranean Society* (see n. 5 above), vol. 3, pp. 175, 189.

[163] See Goitein, *Mediterranean Society* (see n. 5 above), vol. 3, pp. 184–89.

[164] See above, n. 65.

[165] This is cited by A. Grossman, 'Violence against Women in Medieval Mediterranean Jewish Society' in Azmon, *A View* (see n. 8 above), pp. 187–88. The ruling is assigned to R. Yehudai Gaon (eighth century), but Grossman rejects this ascription.

[166] *Hilkhot Ishut*, 21:10. A man who injures his wife is, however, obliged to pay her; see *Hilkhot Ḥovel u-Meziq*, 4.16. Maimonides's opinion on the use of force was contested by R. Abraham b. David of Posquières, but it was accepted by Naḥmanides and Solomon b. Adret; see Grossman, 'Violence against Women' (see n. 165 above), pp. 192–95.

Maghrebi standards and his dismay at the loose morals of Fatimid Egypt.[167] There is no evidence that wife-beating was more rampant in the Islamic environment than it was in Europe,[168] although European rabbinic authorities were more strict in prohibiting wife-beating.

Appeals by women to the community were customarily made in the synagogue when the Torah scroll was removed from the ark. Their appeals were read out by a representative or by the scribe who wrote down the text. The woman would come to the front of the women's gallery while her complaint was being read out to the congregation below.

Arranged marriages, which were fairly common, created outrageous *mésalliances*. Women were married off to men who were not of their choice, sometimes much older. Orphans, in particular, were prey to these mismarriages. A prominent source of female anxiety was polygyny. Biblical and talmudic law permitted a man to marry more than one wife. (This was outlawed for European Jews by the edict of R. Gershom Me'or Ha-Golah [*ca.* 960-1028].) Polygyny was, of course, practiced in the Islamic environment. One way for a wife to avert this threat was by a stipulation in her marriage contract that her husband could not take another wife or hire a female servant without her permission.[169]

Many appeals to the community were brought by abandoned wives. In one such appeal, a woman claimed that her husband Maʿānī absconded to Alexandria, leaving her 'a widow in life' burdened with a three year old infant girl, bemoaning that 'we are starving, naked, and helpless'.[170] She describes herself as 'a weak-sighted woman who cannot distinguish between night and day or be guided along the right way.' If not for God and a certain elder Abū ʿAlī, she says, they would not have survived at all. The appeal begins, as most do, with three or four biblical verses. A marginal note says that she is the wife of Maʿānī who ran away.

In a petition to the head of the Jerusalem congregation in Fustat, Eli b. Amram, a woman named Ḥayfa bint Sulaymān of Acre describes her horrifying plight.[171] She depicts herself as 'a poor[172] foreign woman'. 'I have no one to complain to about my situation,' she says, 'except the Holy One, blessed be He, and his honour, my lord the *ḥaver*, may God exalt him.' She was abandoned by her husband and his family when she was pregnant, then he returned and stayed until she conceived again when he

---

[167] See Goitein, *Mediterranean Society* (see n. 5 above), vol. 3, p. 185.

[168] An exception may be Spain, where wife-beating among Jews was widespread; see Assis, 'Sexual Behaviour' (see n. 72 above), p. 34. Assis considers this as part of a general violent tendency in Hispano-Jewish society; see also Assis, 'Crime and Violence among the Jews of Spain (13th–14th centuries)', *Zion Jubilee Volume* 50 (1986), pp. 221–40.

[169] See Friedman, *Jewish Polygyny* (see n. 45 above), pp. 55ff.

[170] T-S 13J18.18. The document is mentioned by Goitein, in *Mediterranean Society* (see n. 5 above), vol. 2, pp. 324, 595, 598; vol. 3, p. 472; see Reif, *Bibliography* (see n. 5 above), p. 166.

[171] T-S 13J8.19. See Goitein, *Mediterranean Society* (see n. 5 above), vol. 3, pp. 196–97 (partial translation), and vol. 5, p. 569, n. 37.

[172] The word is *ḍaʿīf* meaning 'weak' but here having the sense of 'impoverished' etc.

vanished once more.[173] He returned another time only to abandon her again in Jaffa, a foreign city for her. Necessity forced her to return to her own family, who reproached her with cruel words, presumably for marrying such a scoundrel. She finally arrived at Fustat by begging along the way. 'I left on my own and travelled, humiliating myself,[174] until I reached Fustat.'

Many appeals for help are preserved by indigent women, and by those who were foreign, elderly, weak or too ill to care for themselves, and without family support.[175] These pathetic souls often claim that they have never before had to beg for help, or uncover their face (*kashafa al-wajh*). This may have been literally true in some cases, but it seems to have become a stock phrase meaning, 'I am not really like this.' There is a moving appeal to the community by an elderly woman whose mantle (*ridā'*) had been stolen while she was washing it in the Nile.[176] She begs the population to contribute toward a large shawl (*izār*) for her. When she was healthy she never asked for support. The text was obviously written for her, taken down from her description. 'Know my lords, judges — may the Merciful One preserve them — and community, may they be blessed, that I am a feeble elderly (*hālika*) woman. I had a mantle with which I covered myself at all times. Now I had to go the [Nile] river to wash it. When I was not looking, (the mantle) was stolen, so that nothing remains for me to wear. I have an eye ailment. Only God, the exalted, knows the state I am in. Do not neglect me!'[177]

The frailty of women could be turned into a source of strength. When they failed to obtain satisfaction from Jewish tribunals, they often threatened to turn to Gentile, that is, Muslim, courts. There, they might receive better treatment, as Islamic law was at times more lenient than Jewish legislation in matters of marriage and inheritance. Needless to say, such cases were treated with urgency by the Jewish authorities.

A woman married to a senile paternal cousin (presumably an arranged marriage) writes to the lord, 'head of the assembly' (*ra's al-kull = rosh kalla*) Sahlān b. Abraham complaining that her husband taxes her with all kinds of errands and does not even sleep at home.[178] She presumably noted this grievance because it constituted neglect of his conjugal duties and thus reinforced her case. She tells Sahlān b. Abraham 'to give

---

[173] The case is similar to that of the woman whose husband would go away, come home and impregnate her and then go away again; see above, n. 42.

[174] Lit. 'uncovering my face' (*wa-kashaftu wajhī*), that is, by begging for charity.

[175] The word *munqaṭi'a* occurs often in the sense of 'abandoned', without family or means of sustenance.

[176] CUL Or.1081 J8. The document is mentioned by Goitein, *Mediterranean Society* (see n. 5 above), vol. 2, pp. 500, 555; see Reif, *Bibliography* (see n. 5 above), p. 410.

[177] The woman uses the same word (*ghafala*) that she had previously used to describe her unmindfulness of the mantle as if to say, 'Do not neglect me as I neglected my mantle.'

[178] T-S 18J3.2. See Goitein, *Mediterranean Society* (see n. 5 above), vol. 3, pp. 217–18 (full translation). And see additional references in Reif, *Bibliography* (see n. 5 above), p. 181.

me my rights; for if not, I shall go to the Gentiles'.[179] Two female orphans petitioned against two older married sisters who may have been from a different mother, threatening to take their case to a Muslim court (*dine goyim*).[180] They add, 'We have no one to assist us except the Lord of Worlds and Israel and their judges.' Their appeal was expeditiously acted upon by the court.

In female wills, we find carefully drawn lists of clothing, even costly garments, to be worn in the funeral bier. In her will, Sitt al-Ḥusn, wife of Judge Nathan b. Samuel, a friend of the famous poet Judah Halevi, sells her share in the ownership of a house behind the mosque, which she possessed in partnership with the government, 'may God support it', for income to be spent for her shroud, coffin, cantors, tomb, pall bearers, and all other burial expenses.[181] If this is insufficient, then an ornamented tiara, that was in her husband's hands, should be sold. These were proud women who, when the time came to leave this world, wanted to depart in style. We are fortunate that, thanks to the Genizah documents, their voices are not silent.[182]

---

[179] *Ummot ha-'olam* (lit. 'nations of the world'. The usual term for Gentile courts in our documents is *dine goyim*.

[180] MS ENA 2348.1; Goitein, *Mediterranean Society* (see n. 5 above), vol. 2, p. 324 (translation); and see vol. 5, p. 227.

[181] T-S 13J22.2; ed. Goitein, 'Wills and Deathbed Declarations from the Cairo Geniza', *Sefunot* 8 (1964), pp. 111–13; and *Mediterranean Society* (see n. 5 above), vol. 5, pp. 146–47 (translation).

[182] I wish to thank Prof. Stefan Reif and his staff for their generous help during various stays in Cambridge, when I copied most of the documents cited above. I am also indebted to the staff of the Bodleian Library at Oxford and to Prof. Meir Rabinowitz and the personnel of the rare books and manuscript room at the library of the Jewish Theological Seminary of America in New York. And I am always appreciative of the constant co-operation of Dr Abraham David of the Institute of Microfilmed Hebrew Manuscripts at the Jewish National & University Library in Jerusalem. A number of documents were read and deciphered along with Mordechai A. Friedman, whose contribution to my understanding is gratefully acknowledged. My thanks also go to the Women's Board of the University of Chicago and to Dean Clark Gilpin of the Divinity School for their support, and to Aviva Kraemer for her valuable assistance and encouragement.

INDEXES

INDEXES

INDEX OF NAMES, PLACES AND INSTITUTIONS

INDEX OF SUBJECTS AND SOURCES

INDEX OF MANUSCRIPTS CITED

PLATES

Plate 1: T–S B17.36: *Hafṭarot* for *Sedarim* in Deuteronomy, according to the Palestinian triennial cycle; *see* p. 2

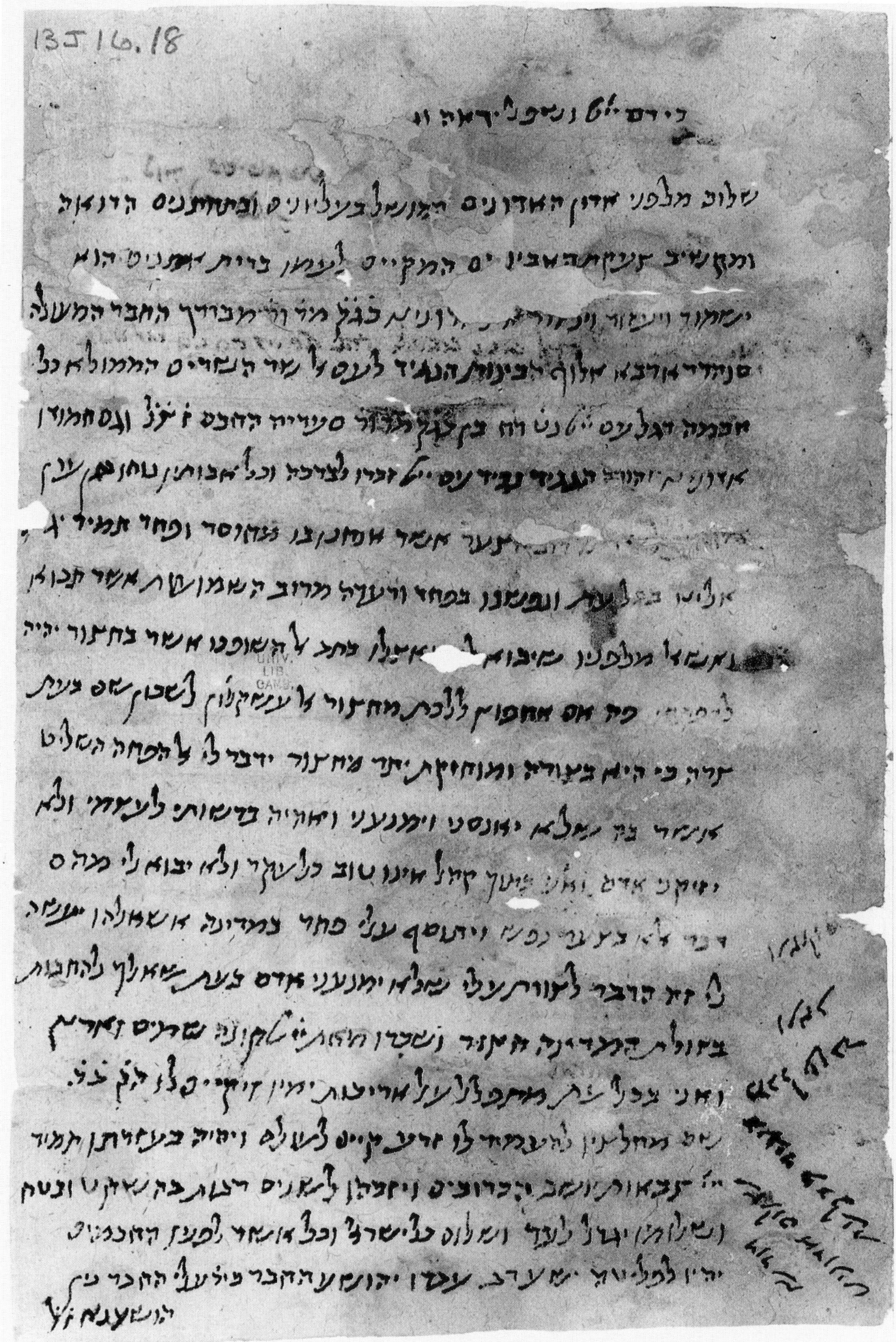

13J16.18

Plate 2: T–S 13J16.18: R. Joshua writes to the Nagid Mevorakh requesting a visa for resettlement in Ashkelon in view of the Crusader invasion; *see* pp. 16–17

Plate 3: Or.1102: Hebrew text of Ben Sira; *see* p. 37

Plates 4 and 5: T–S AS 213.4, *verso*: and T–S 12.727, *verso*:
Leaves from MS C of Ben Sira; *see* pp. 36–46

Plate 6: Or.1080 B18.1: Palestinian Targum readings for special sabbaths and festivals; *see* p. 54

Plates 7 and 8: T–S B13.4 and T–S NS 218.61:
Palestinian Targum readings for special sabbaths and festivals; *see* p. 54

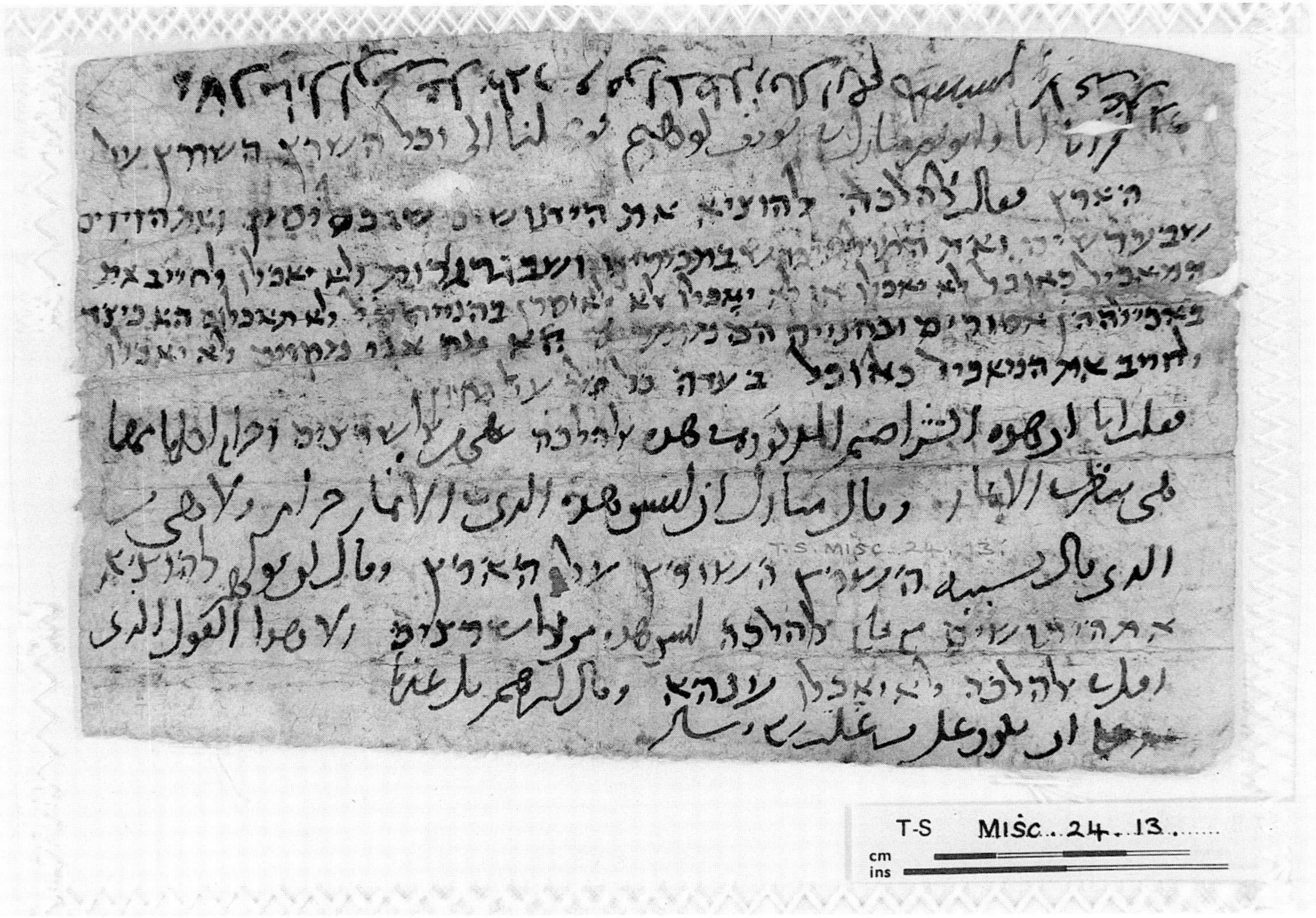

Plate 9: T–S Misc.24.13, *recto*: Judaeo-Arabic commentary of Yeshu‘ah b. Judah to Leviticus, citing a section of *Sifra*; *see* pp. 59–73

Plate 10: T–S Misc.24.1 (3 long thin strips sewn together):
A ninth-century liturgical handbook; *see* pp. 74–122

Plate 11: T–S Misc.35.64, *recto*: Folio from the classical *diwān* of Judah Halevi, praising his host in Alexandria; *see* pp. 123–35

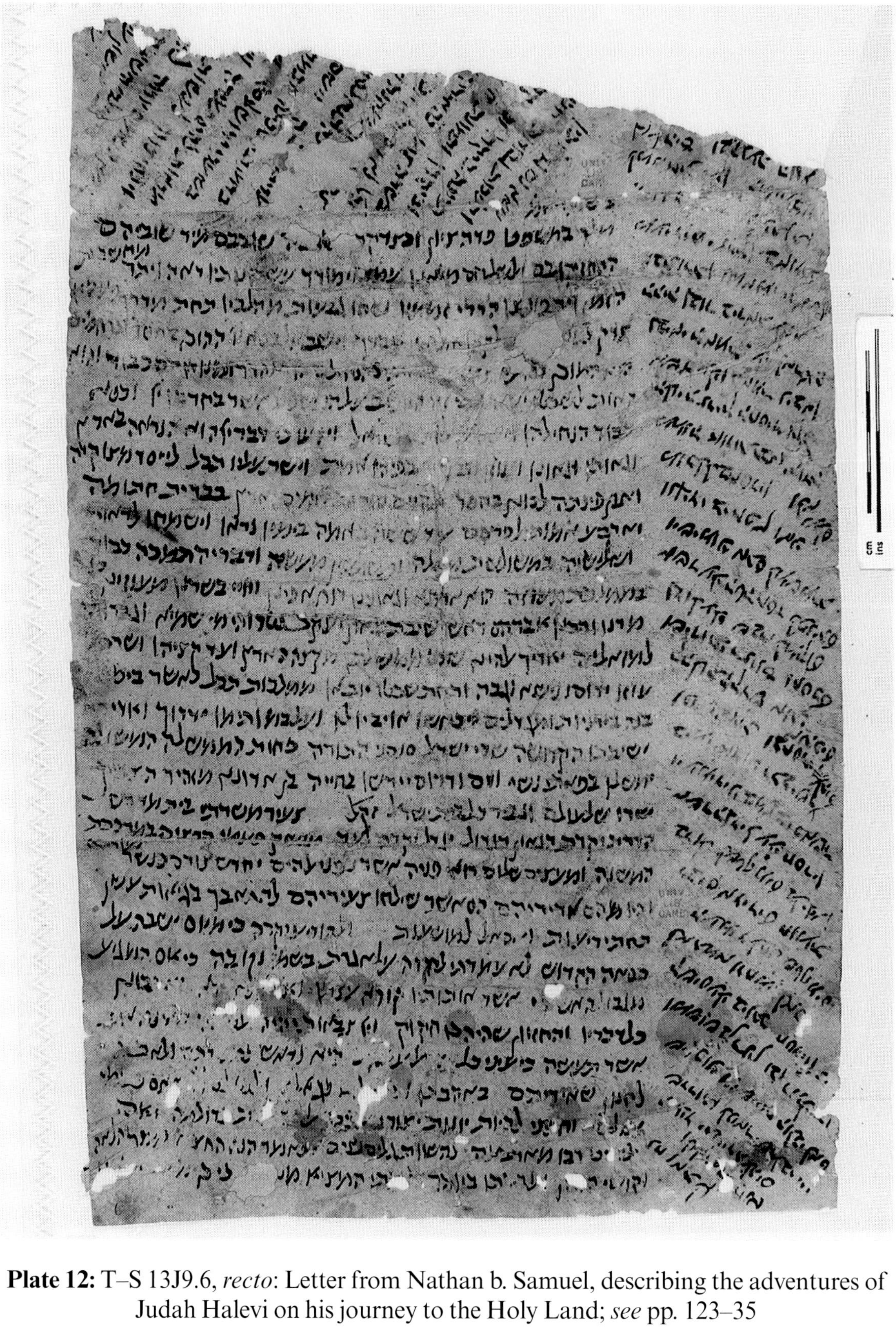

Plate 12: T–S 13J9.6, *recto*: Letter from Nathan b. Samuel, describing the adventures of Judah Halevi on his journey to the Holy Land; *see* pp. 123–35

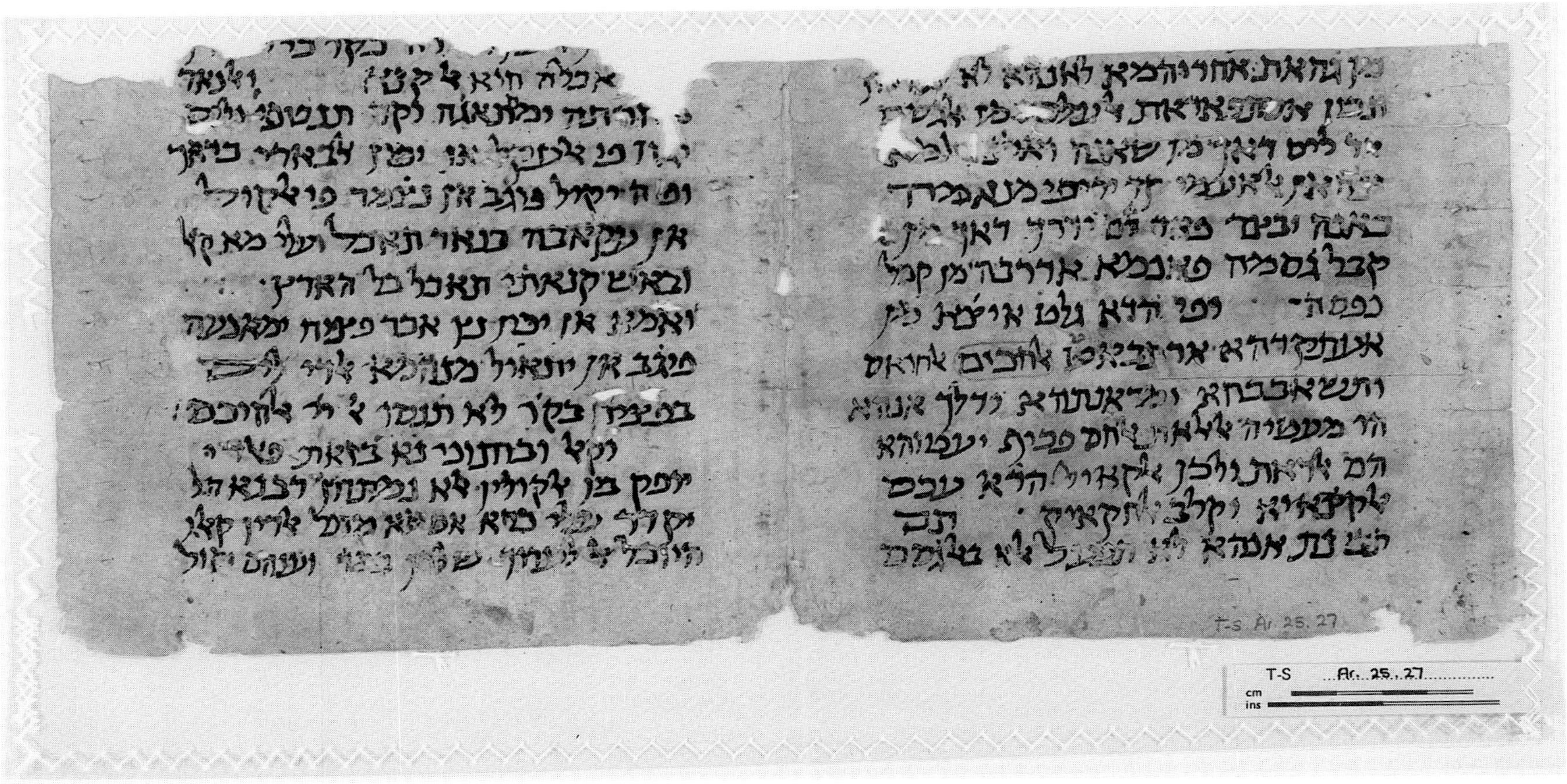

Plate 13: T–S Ar.25.27: Bifolium from Saadya's *Book of Beliefs and Convictions*, *Kitāb al-Amānāt*; *see* p. 146

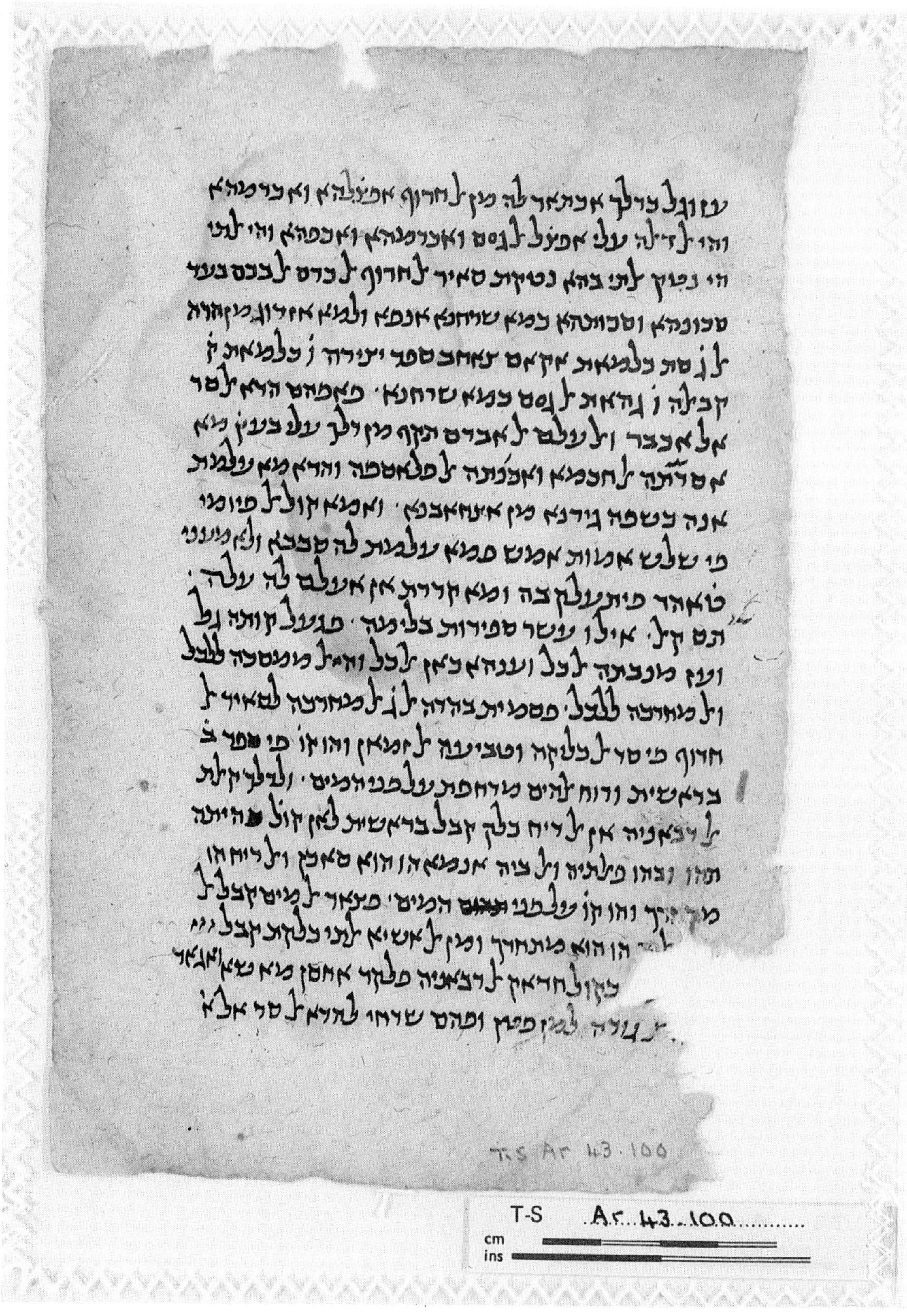

Plate 14: T–S Ar.43.100: Fragment of the original Arabic text of the commentary on *Sefer Yeṣirah* by Dunash b. Tamim; *see* pp. 136–51

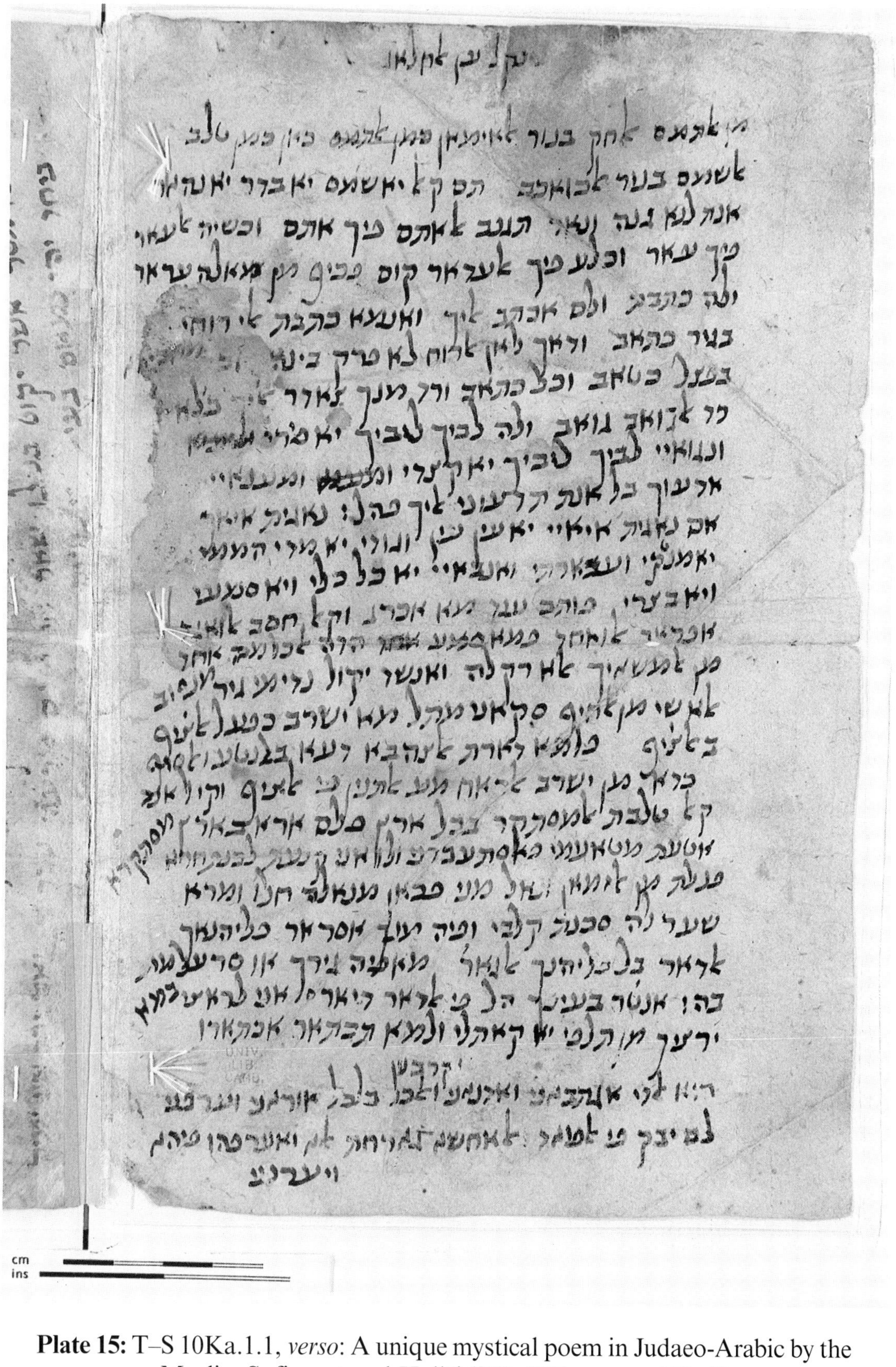

Plate 15: T–S 10Ka.1.1, *verso*: A unique mystical poem in Judaeo-Arabic by the Muslim Sufi martyr al-Hallāj (858–922); *see* pp. 152–59

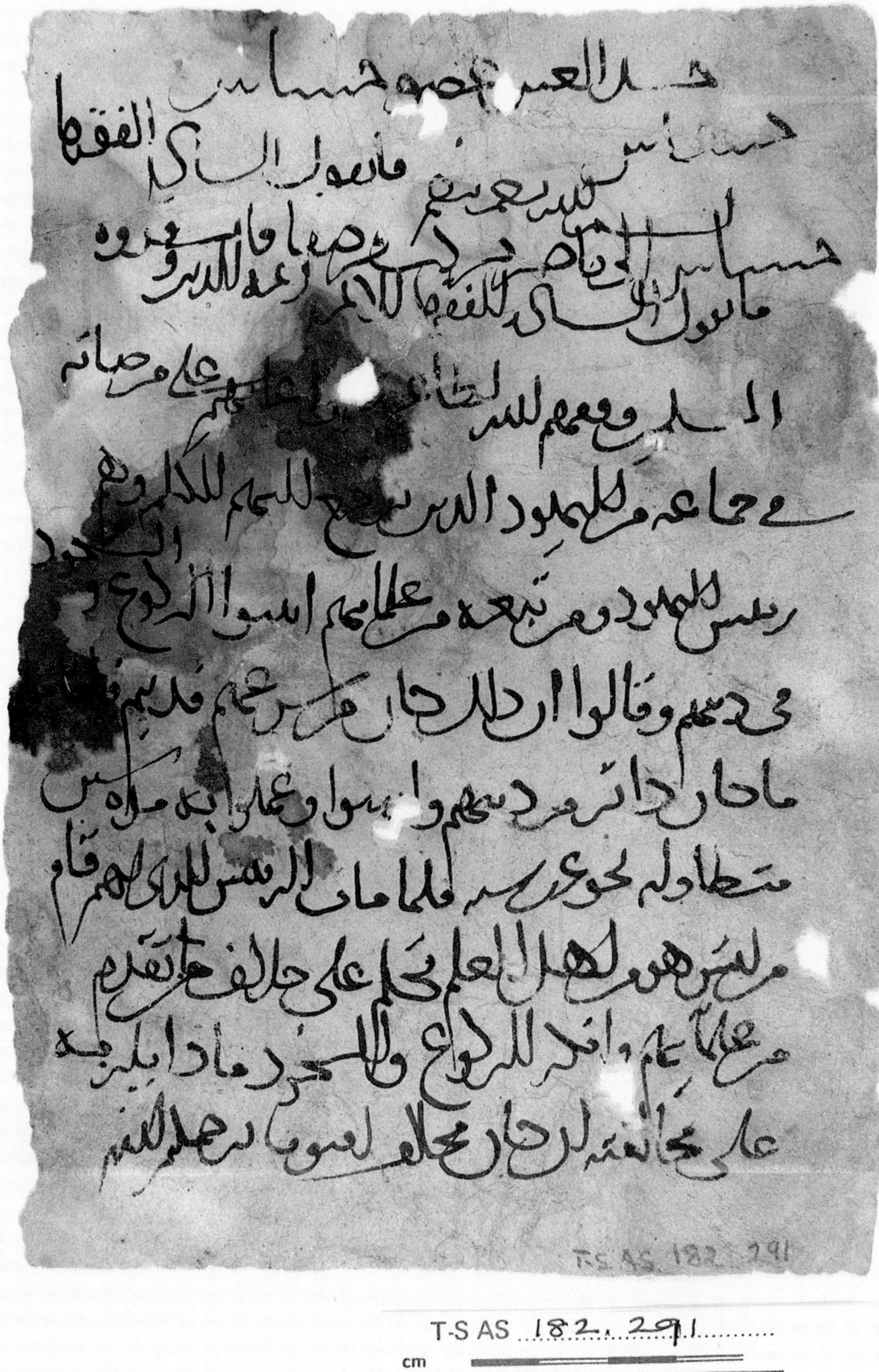

Plate 16: T–S AS 182.291, *recto*: A Jewish enquiry addressed to a Muslim court on the matter of a liturgical dispute; *see* p. 159

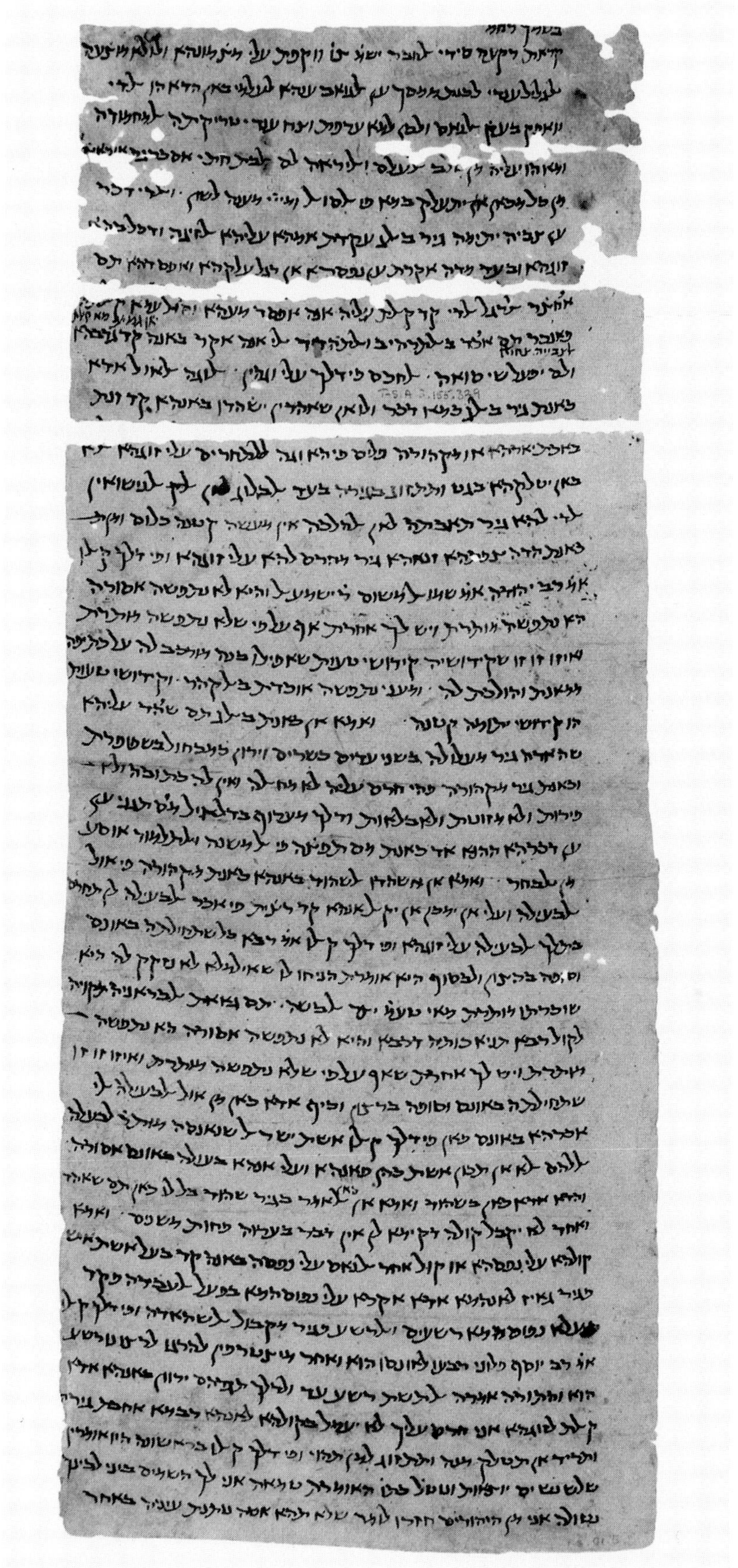

Plate 17: T–S 12.397, AS 155.329 and G1.5a, *recto*: Responsum in Judaeo-Arabic by R. Judah Kohen b. Joseph about the seduction of an orphan girl; *see* p. 167

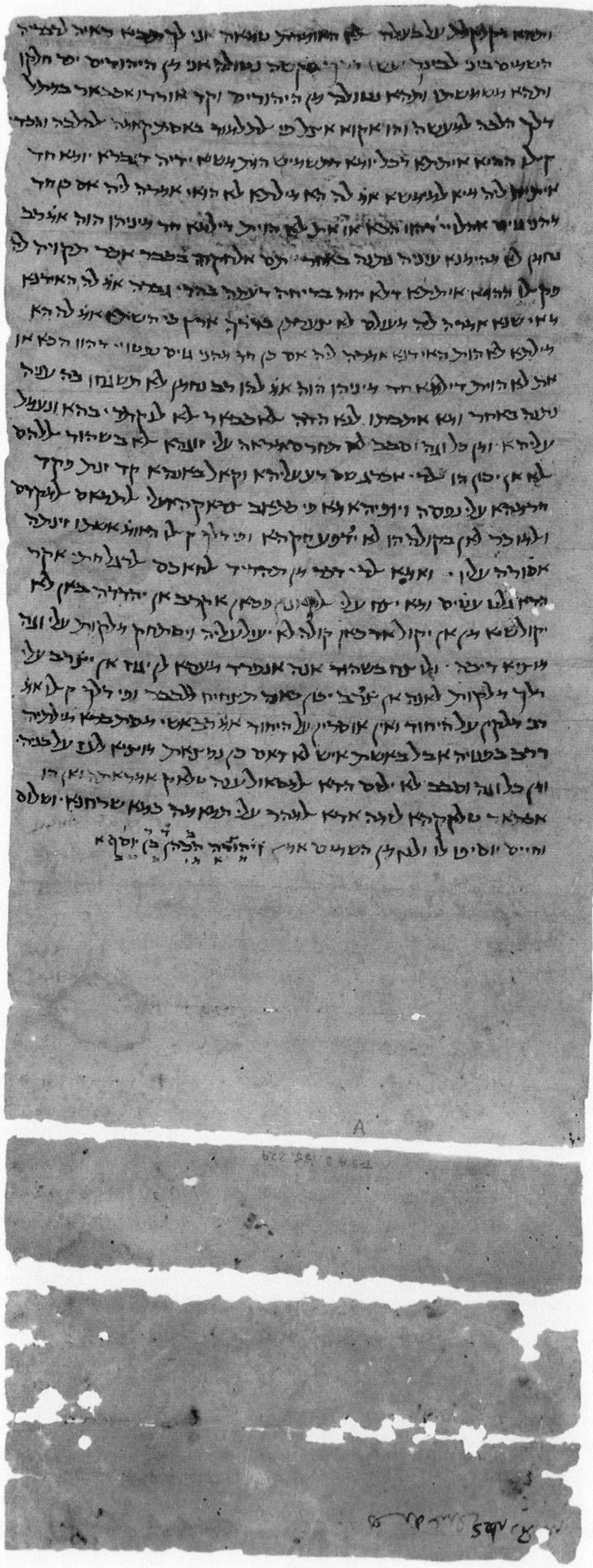

Plate 18: T–S 12.397, AS 155.329 and G1.5a, *verso*: Continuation of responsum by R. Judah Kohen b. Joseph; *see* p. 167

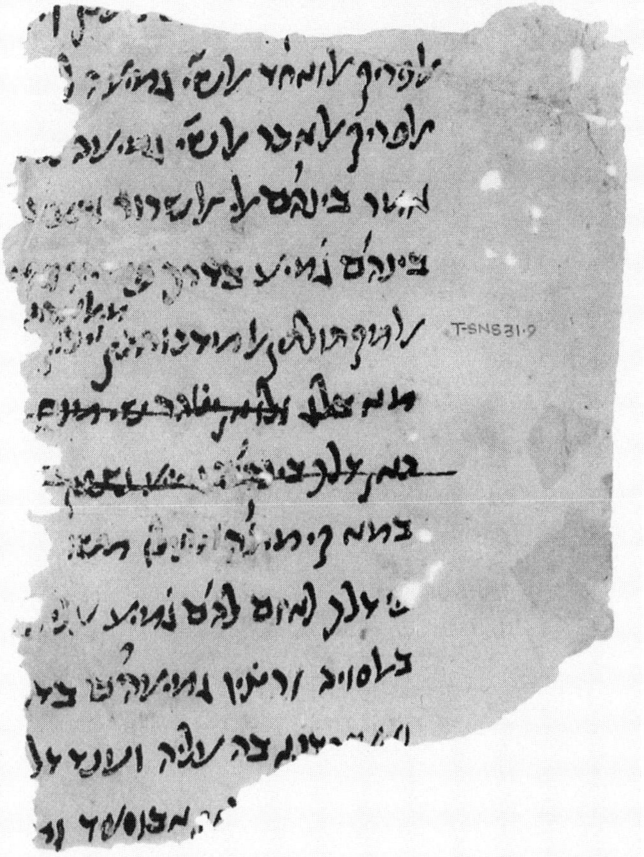

Plates 19 and 20: T–S 8.111, *recto*: and T–S NS 31.9, *recto*:
Document relating to a dispute over the estates of a woman and her daughter, both murdered at the same time; *see* pp. 23, 171–72

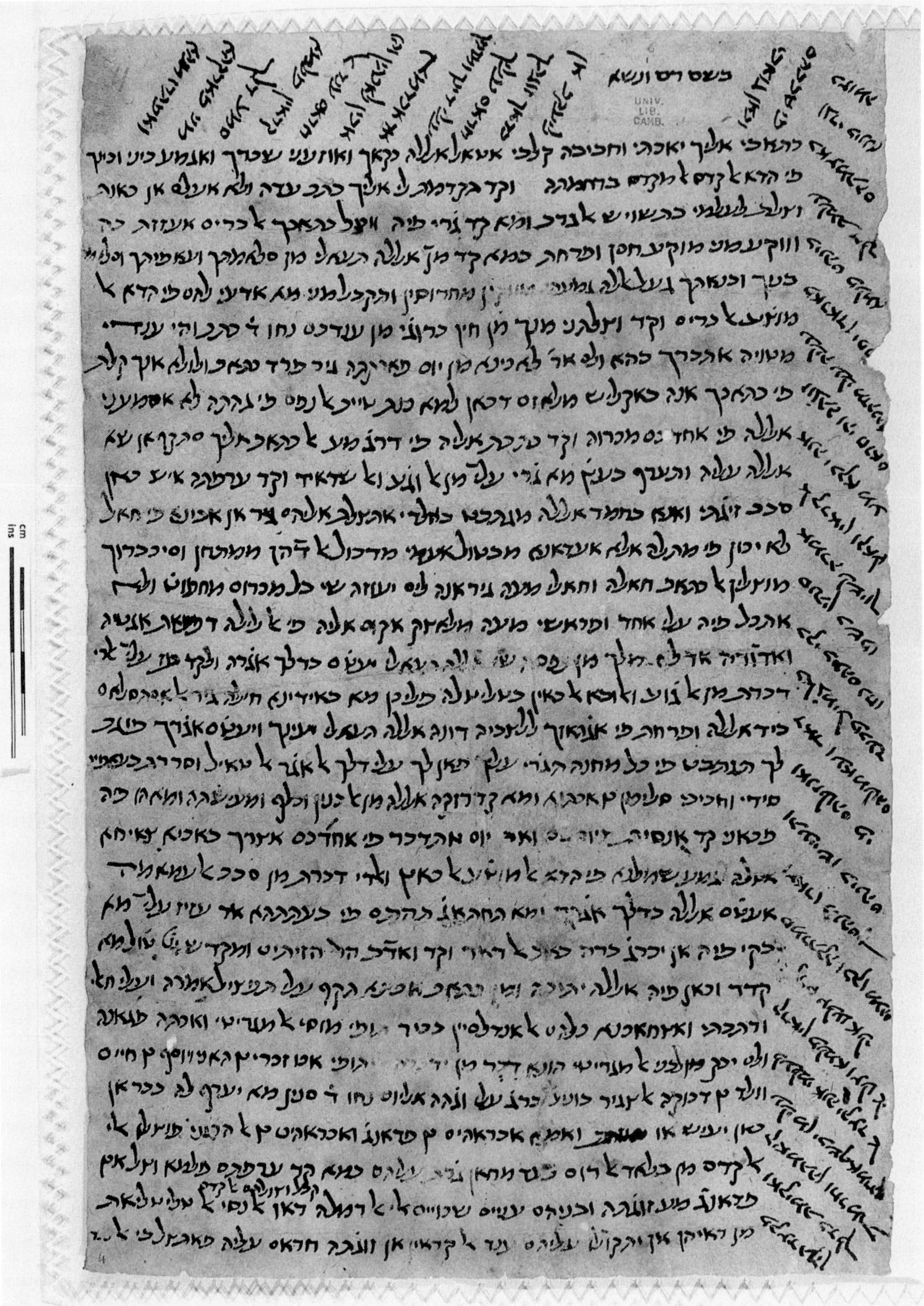

Plate 21: T–S 13J9.4, *recto*: Letter of consolation from a man in Jerusalem to his sister in Toledo in 1053; *see* pp. 181, 205

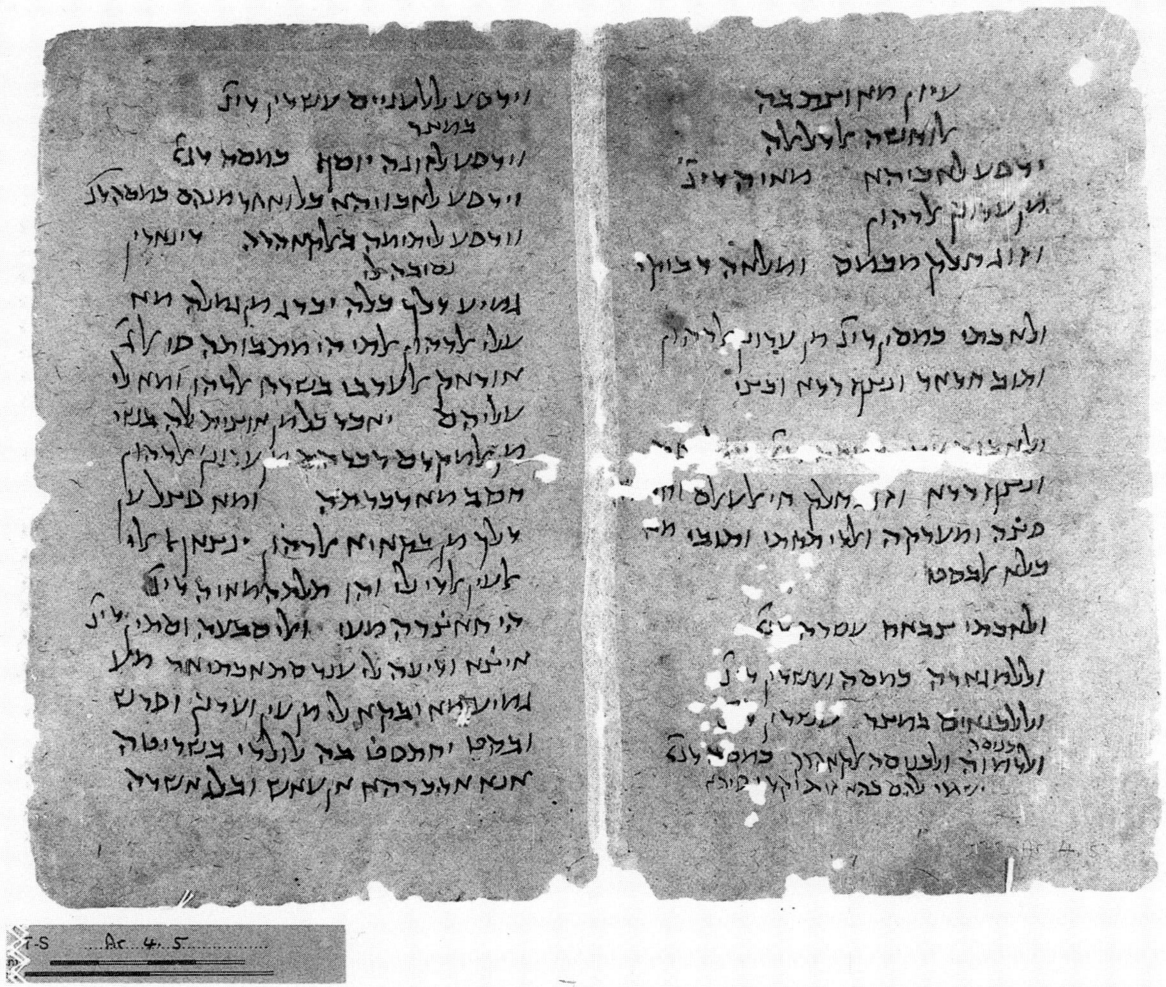

Plate 22: T–S Ar.4.5, *verso* of bifolium: Document relating to Wuhsha, a successful twelfth-century business woman; *see* pp. 23, 192